WEBBER

A CRITICAL BIOGRAPHY BY

MICHAEL WALSH

CONTENTS

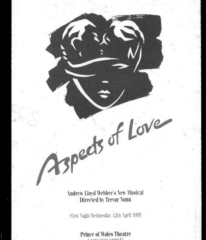

VIKING

Published by the Penguin Group

27 Wrights Lane, London W8 5TZ, England

Viking Penguin Inc., 40 West 23rd Street, New York, New York 10010, USA

Penguin Books Australia Ltd, Ringwood, Victoria, Australia

Penguin Books Canada Ltd, 2801 John Street, Markham, Ontario, Canada L3R 1B4

Penguin Books (NZ) Ltd, 182–190 Wairau Road, Auckland 10, New Zealand

Penguin Books Ltd, Registered Offices: Harmondsworth, Middlesex, England

First published in the USA by Harry N. Abrams, Inc., New York, 1989

First published in Great Britain by Viking 1989

10 9 8 7 6 5 4 3 2 1

Editor: Charles Miers

Designer: Bob McKee

Photo Editor: John K. Crowley

Photo and Text Research: Kate Walsh

Printed and bound in Italy

A CIP catalogue record for this book is available from the British Library

ISBN 0-670-83041-0

PREFACE

Writing a critical biography of a man who is still alive may seem at first a quixotic endeavor. Still, in the case of Andrew Lloyd Webber, the obligation to end in medias res should not negate the attempt. By accident, design, and some lucky combination of both, Lloyd Webber has become the dominant figure of the postwar musical theater. He has earned more money from his music than any theater composer who ever lived. His musical empire stretches around the world, from London to Tokyo. For anyone concerned with opera, operetta, music drama, *Gesamtkunstwerk* or plain old Broadway musicals, it is imperative to understand how and why this unlikely, unprepossessing Englishman has become an international force.

While reasonable men may disagree over the worth of Lloyd Webber's shows, no one can deny that his is today the biggest name in a field whose glories at first glance seem to belong more to the past than to the present. Broadway has been the Fabulous Invalid for decades, but its health has never been more despaired of. The primal spring of American talent that has fed it since George M. Cohan appears to have dried up, and the great line of German- and Russian-Jewish composers that dominated Broadway since Irving Berlin seems to be played out: George Gershwin, Jerome Kern, Lerner and Loewe, Lorenz Hart, Rodgers and Hammerstein, Jule Styne, Arthur Schwartz, Jerry Herman, Leonard Bernstein, Cy Coleman, Marvin Hamlisch. Not only are there no Gershwins or Rodgerses roaming greater New York, there are not even any Frank Loessers. Only Stephen Sondheim, whose career began as a lyricist, in collaboration with Styne and Bernstein, remains a potent force in the American musical theater.

Many theories for Broadway's decline have been advanced. Chief among them is the economic argument: it costs a fortune to mount a new show these days, and it takes months, if not years, to recoup, even with a hit. A corollary to this is the putative power of *The New York Times*, whose drama critic is said to be able to close a show at the blink of a cursor. Investing in a Broadway show has never been riskier.

Such showbiz Marxism, however, fails to explain the dearth of contemporary American creative talent. Instead, the answer may be found in the changing nature of the medium. For the truth is that Broadway—the Broadway of Moss Hart and Sardi's and book musicals and "Climb Every Mountain"—is dead, as dead as *The New York Herald,* and the other newspapers that once chronicled its exploits. Every attempt to revive it, whether by composers or critics, is only rouging the corpse. Yet, like some religious cult gathered around a dead body, convinced that the deceased will rise and walk at any minute, many theater professionals in America still obdurately await the resurrection.

Into this vacuum has stepped Lloyd Webber. It is not the first time the English have arrived to give a jolt to a quintessentially American art form. When the first wave of rockers, such as Elvis Presley and Jerry Lee Lewis, showed signs of exhaustion around 1964, along came the Beatles, the Rolling Stones, The Who, and the Kinks to kick out the jams. Lloyd Webber's contribution has been to recognize that the Rodgers and Hammerstein musicals he grew up with are as closely aligned to their time and place as Mozart's operas or Wagner's music dramas to theirs, and that the circumstances that gave rise to them are irrevocably changed.

In his music, Lloyd Webber has not arbitrarily stopped the clock at 1962; in the theater, he has recognized the unhappy fact that a new generation of audiences has been weaned on Hollywood and records and that, when the curtain goes up, they expect to see and hear something that vaguely approximates both. For many listeners today, music is something that comes out of a loudspeaker, not something emitted directly from a human being, and Lloyd Webber accordingly has employed a battery of microphones, speakers, sound boards, and synthesizers to put his songs across.

One can bemoan either of these factors but one cannot gainsay them. It is ridiculous to argue, as many theater critics do, that pop music has no place in the theater: it has since the eighteenth century. As for technology, once developed, it inevitably will be used. I hold little brief for amplification—it is especially superfluous in Lloyd Webber's most recent show, *Aspects of Love*,—but at this point it can only be controlled, not banished.

Indeed, a subtext of this book is the inability of theater critics to come to grips with the nature of modern musical theater. As a music critic I may be accused of special pleading, but it has long seemed to me the height of folly to have critics with manifestly inadequate musical knowledge and training covering the musical theater. It is a shame of journalism and a gross disservice to the art form. Just because straight plays and musicals share the same turf in the West End or mid-Manhattan is no reason to confuse what are, after all, two entirely different undertakings. A play, when reduced to secondary form, is a text; a musical is a score. Very few people will pay money to hear a play recited on disc; millions, however, will buy an original cast album of a musical. Yet the lazy venue-determines-coverage attitude of newspapers and magazines continues unabated.

The idea of writing a book about Lloyd Webber first occurred to me in January 1987, just after I had seen the West End version of *The Phantom of the Opera*. Before I left London, a package arrived for me at my hotel: a demo tape of the original cast recording, followed a few days later by one of the first copies of the double album. My bags were packed, so I carried the record under my arm. The hotel doorman asked me where I had gotten it. So did the taxi driver on the way to Heathrow. So did several travelers in the airport, one of whom rushed up to me and demanded to know where he could buy it. Obviously, the show had touched a chord in the general public, too, and I wanted to know why.

I had written about Andrew before, in a 1984 cover story for the international edition of *Time* magazine, on the occasion of the London opening of *Starlight Express*. We got on well, mostly because we had several things in common, including our professions, our generation (Andrew is a year and a half older), our colleges (the Royal College of Music in London and the Eastman School of Music in Rochester, N.Y., are sister schools), and several friends and acquaintances. A second *Time* cover story, this one for the larger U.S. edition, followed in January 1988, as *Phantom* prepared to open on Broadway with a record sixteen million dollars in advance sales.

I had first become aware of Lloyd Webber's music while traveling through Europe during the summer of 1970. A Dutch girlfriend kept singing a musical phrase over and over: "Je-sus Christ/Su-per Star . . . . " When I asked her what it was, she told me it was a new song by someone named Andrew Lloyd Webber. By February of the following year, I couldn't escape *Superstar* and nor could anyone else, for the double album (the show's first incarnation) had landed at number one on the American charts and had become an international sensation.

Eight years passed before I noticed Lloyd Webber again. In the summer of 1979, during the California tryouts of the Broadway *Evita*, I covered the show in my professional capacity as music critic of *The San Francisco Examiner*. *Evita* was a revelation. The boldness of the subject (widely misinterpreted then—as now—as an implicit endorsement of Eva Perón), the daring accomplishment of the music, and the brilliance of Hal Prince's staging told me that here was something that deserved being taken seriously. I resolved to watch Lloyd Webber's career more closely. Subsequent encounters with the Broadway production of *Joseph and the Amazing Technicolor Dreamcoat*; the recordings of *Tell Me on a Sunday* and the *Variations*, and their London stage embodiment as *Song and Dance; Cats* in London, New York, and Hamburg; *Starlight Express* in London and New York; the *Requiem* in Manhattan; *The Phantom of the Opera* on both sides of the Atlantic and in Tokyo; and *Aspects of Love* both at its first performance at the 1988 Sydmonton Festival and its April 17, 1989, London premiere further served to convince me Lloyd Webber is an important figure in contemporary musical theater.

Americans, for whom Lloyd Webber is either that clever man behind *Cats* or the carpetbagger who is ruining Broadway—but who would not recognize him on the street—may be surprised to discover that in Britain he is a celebrity of the first order. His every move is charted, and his wealth is the subject of widespread speculation. The paparazzi dog him and his wife, Sarah Brightman, while the talk shows pursue him relentlessly. His round moon face and cat's eyes are staples of caricaturists and editorial cartoonists. The fact that he is also Prince Edward's employer only boosts the public's appetite for more stories about him. Information—and misinformation—about Lloyd Webber fill the pages of the British press every day.

This book, however, is offered as the first serious treatment of Lloyd Webber as man and musician. The only previous biography was Gerald McKnight's 1984 *Andrew Lloyd Webber: A Biography* (St. Martin's Press), a journalistic hagiography that is almost entirely unreliable. My text has been written with Lloyd Webber's cooperation, but it is by no means an authorized biography. Neither the composer nor anyone from the Really Useful Group, the production company that administers the rights to his works from *Cats* onward, has had the right of manuscript review or quote approval. While there are many opinions expressed about Lloyd Webber and his works in this book, the prevailing one is my own.

Many people assisted in the creation of this book. Lloyd Webber himself generously gave of his time and his personal artifacts and patiently sat for hours of questioning and requestioning in New York, London, and at his Hampshire estate, Sydmonton Court. Jean Lloyd Webber, the composer's mother, proved an invaluable font of information about her son's early life, and Julian, his brother, also contributed some crucial reminiscences.

A book about the shows of Lloyd Webber would be unthinkable without the contribution of Tim Rice, the coauthor of *Joseph, Superstar,* and *Evita,* whose life is still inextricably bound up with that of his former partner. In many, if not most, respects, Andrew's story is Tim's story too, and this book could not have been written without Rice's gracious cooperation and assistance. In interviews at his Oxfordshire estate and on the telephone, Rice was unfailingly helpful and generous; warmest thanks indeed to him.

Special thanks also to Robert Stigwood, who kindly provided access to his files on *Joseph and the Amazing Technicolor Dreamcoat, Jesus Christ Superstar,* and *Evita.*

In England, I would also like to thank Sarah Brightman, Elaine Paige, Trevor Nunn, Anthony Bowles, David and Lisa Crewe-Read, John and Penny Gummer, Don and Shirley Black, Charlotte Gray, James Woodhouse, Nick Allott, Mrs. Patricia Vowden of the Colet Court School, Angela Clayton, Liz Buck, Tina Morris from "The South Bank Show," Louise Martin, Catherine Ashmore, Rosalind Poole of Dewynters, Mark Grosvenor at Gilchrest Studios, and the household staff at Sydmonton Court. Sue Knight, Juliet Simpkins, Katherine Bendel, Ben Hilliard, Martin Levan, Marion O'Hara, Nobby Clark, Donald Cooper, and Clive Barda were also very helpful.

Special thanks also to Jane Rice for her good offices and to Jane Fann, Lloyd Webber's personal assistant, on whom the brunt of my requests fell. Thanks also to Biddy Hayward of the Really Useful Group, who helped smooth the way in so many areas, and to David Robinson for his expert handling of the lyrics permissions.

In New York, thanks to Harold Prince, Bernie Jacobs, Fred Nathan, Merle Frimark, R. Tyler Gatchell, Jr., Thomas Z. Shepard and Irene Clark Shepard, Dina Oswald, James Daley, and Music Theater International, which provided musical scores. Peter Brown's formidable knowledge of pop-music history—derived from his own involvement with both the Beatles and Lloyd Webber—was often called on.

Thanks also to our landlords in Munich, Hans and Lisa Prugger, for providing a most congenial place to work, and to their son, our downstairs neighbor, Florian, whose computer printer pinch-hit while mine was temporarily hors de combat.

Regretfully, Sarah Norris, Lloyd Webber's first wife, decided she could not speak to me. Although disappointed, I respect her decision, for sometimes it can be harder and more painful to speak at all of the living than to speak ill of the dead. Which, of course, makes the living harder to write about as well.

Thanks also to Charles Miers, my editor at Harry N. Abrams, Inc., who read the manuscript carefully and thoughtfully and made many excellent suggestions; to John Crowley and Bob McKee of Abrams; to my agent, Don Congdon; to Paul Gottlieb, Abrams' president and publisher, and to Peter Carson, publishing director of Viking Penguin in Britain.

There is, however, another person without whom this book could not have been written. She is my wife, Kathleen, who conducted many of the interviews and who functioned as the project's researcher and fact checker. Without her professional-caliber musical ear and her dogged patience in collecting reliable data and appealing photographs on an elusive subject, this book would still be in the planning stages. Therefore, in deepest gratitude and with much love, it is dedicated to her.

Munich
May 1989

Introduction: THE OPERA GHOST

"I could make deaf stockbrokers read my two pages on music," wrote George Bernard Shaw, who forsook the rough-and-tumble of London music journalism for the more enriching purlieus of the theater, "the alleged joke being that I knew nothing about it. The real joke was that I knew all about it." Andrew Lloyd Webber might well agree. Rarely does musical history offer such a disparity between a composer's popular reputation and his critical estimation. Despite his indisputable box-office prestige—deaf stockbrokers, among others, lap him up—Lloyd Webber repeatedly has seen his works critically disdained (indeed, savaged), especially in the United States. Their plots are scorned, their musical content derided as the meretricious parroting of Lloyd Webber's Broadway betters and higher-toned operatic antecedents. There is even one school of thought that considers Lloyd Webber fundamentally derivative—nearly a plagiarist—who preys on his audience's ignorance and childish love of spectacle.

In the U.S., a class distinction habitually is made between high art (opera) and low culture (musicals). This is partly a result of the natural American inferiority complex that asserts itself whenever "real" art is under discussion. Americans, however, are unique in the world in not considering their greatest contribution to music theater, the Broadway show, "real" art. In Britain, the history of popular music theater extends at least as far back as the early eighteenth century, when John Gay and Johann Pepusch's *The Beggar's Opera* drove Handel's Italian operas from the stage. Pepusch's arrangements of folk songs from the British Isles (and a cheeky steal of the march from Handel's *Rinaldo*), set to Gay's sardonic political allegory, established freewheeling eclecticism as the norm. Today, no one in England considers *The Beggar's Opera* low culture; on the contrary, it has been revived and arranged repeatedly by some of the kingdom's most eminent musicians and staged by its finest directors.

During the nineteenth century W. S. Gilbert and Sir Arthur Sullivan essentially invented the form of the British operetta, welding the techniques of opera—often deliberately parodying Verdi or the earlier bel canto composers such as Donizetti and Bellini—to a broader-based entertainment. In the first half of the twentieth century Ralph Vaughan Williams and Gustav Holst expanded on the folk influences in operas such as *Hugh the Drover* and *The Wandering Scholar,* adding to them elements of the church-music choral tradition to produce that distinctive sound we think of as particularly "English." Opera, opera parody, folk music, and church music: it is precisely from this tradition that Lloyd Webber emerges. Whatever else one might accuse him of, to accuse him of being a mere pastiche artist or plagiarist is purely an expression of historical ignorance.

A few words about opera, a much misunderstood term with unfortunate connotations of high-mindedness. Considering *Joseph and the Amazing Technicolor Dreamcoat* in 1981, one American critic, in noting that the show had been expanded for Broadway, wrote: "It has become a full-blown musical in the Rice–Webber tradition, which is to say it is operatic in form. In other words, no dialogue." Well, not exactly. In other words, no. There is plenty of spoken dialogue in Mozart's *The Abduction from the Seraglio* and *The Magic Flute,* and no one has ever said they weren't real operas. And even in opera that is entirely sung—*The Marriage of Figaro,* to take another Mozart example— the dialogue is conveyed through a device called recitative, a kind of speech-song. Dialogue, or lack of it, has nothing to do with whether a work is an opera.

Throughout its history, opera has always drawn on contemporary musical and cultural influences (see Mozart, Verdi, Puccini, even Berg), but many still persist in thinking of it as an "exotic and irrational entertainment" (to quote Dr. Johnson), sung in a foreign language to an audience of uncomprehending, but rapturous, initiates. Operaphiles themselves have done little to disabuse others of this notion; opera today has become synonymous with the mummified artifacts on exhibit at the Metropolitan Opera, the Royal Opera, and elsewhere—and not the far greater range of musical theater. The venue has come to delimit the form.

Yet a case can be made that, along with Philip Glass's *Einstein on the Beach,* the finest operas of the seventies were Lloyd Webber's *Evita* and Stephen Sondheim's sanguinary fable, *Sweeney Todd.* Indeed, Sondheim already has breached traditionally operatic battlements: *Sweeney Todd* has been produced at the New York City Opera, and *Pacific Overtures* opened an English National Opera season in London. Despite radical differences in their musical idioms, Lloyd Webber, Sondheim, and Glass, as well as the American John Adams, are the most important opera composers of the day. Lloyd Webber may be no Mozart, but neither is he Jerry Herman, or Pee Wee Herman, for that matter.

What, precisely, do his detractors object to? The indictments are contradictory: (a) his music all sounds the same, and (b) it all derives from elsewhere—even though that elsewhere is only rarely specified, and when it is, it is usually wrong. "It's not so much that Lloyd Webber lacks an ear for melody as that he has too much of a one for other people's melodies," wrote John Simon in *New York* magazine of the Broadway *Phantom of the Opera.* Or, in his review of *Cats*: "Never have I had such a yen to hire a private tune detective to track down the provenance of these songs . . . ." But even the sophisticated Simon can do little more than round up the usual suspects. Still, the charge has become the stuff of conventional wisdom, parroted by others who would dazzle their readers by collaring innocents such as Richard Strauss and Offenbach and charging them with influence in the first degree.

Of course, the critical reception is not always consistent, even in the writings of the same critic. Simon could praise the 1982 revival of *Joseph* at the Entermedia Theater in Manhattan as "the best work Webber and Rice have done so far [it was their first], as it wildly runs the gamut from country and western through French ballad to calypso while retelling—anachronistically, absurdly, chirpily—the story of Joseph and his brethren in a way to amuse even Thomas Mann, let alone any other man, woman, or child." One has to admire a critic who can press-gang Mann's most unread major work into a discussion of a children's show, even if he, like his colleagues, cannot seem to find a stable aesthetic by which to judge the musical stage.

It is true that Lloyd Webber writes with a remarkable, and, to some, suspicious facility; the Rossini of his day, he can whip up a song, or dive into his drawer to retrieve one, in practically no time. Whatever else one can say about him, no one can dispute his wide knowledge of his field. Although a middling pianist, Lloyd Webber can sit down at the keyboard and play obscure songs from forgotten disasters like Irving Berlin's *Mr. President,* singing all the words. He has the musical theater's vast repertoire at his fingertips.

The question is: too much so? The resemblance of some of Lloyd Webber's tunes to earlier Broadway and classical melodies is an implicit accusation that has dogged him throughout his career. There is some merit in it. As early as *Superstar,* there is a whiff of (of all things) the Grieg Piano Concerto, and in Lloyd Webber's *Variations* a motif from the slow movement of Dmitri Shostakovich's Symphony No. 15 shows up. While Lloyd Webber freely acknowledges his melodic debt to Puccini—and even parodies it in the "Growltiger's Last Stand" number of the American version of *Cats*—the match between a phrase from *The Phantom of the Opera* (it is heard at the words, "Yet in his eyes/all the sadness/of the world . . .") and Liu's suicide music from the third act of Puccini's opera *Turandot* is obvious. Similarly, the snarling chromatic scale that depicts the Phantom has a nearly exact cognate—right down to its orchestration—in a theme from Vaughan Williams's *London Symphony,* while the rising fifth that distinguishes *Phantom*'s title song figures prominently in "The Battle on the Ice" from Serge Prokofiev's cantata *Alexander Nevsky.*

Another melodic coincidence involves the first few notes of the Phantom's lullaby, "The Music of the Night," and the opening of "Come to Me, Bend to Me" from *Brigadoon* by Lerner and Loewe. The first theme of the revised version of *Joseph* seems to come from Hammerstein and Kern's 1927 musical, *Show Boat* (it is the piano piece that Magnolia is practicing on board the *Cotton Blossom*), while the "Rolling Stock" number from *Starlight Express* bears an amazing likeness to the *Show Boat* number called "It's Getting Hotter in the North," itself paraphrased from Magnolia's little offstage instrumental.

What does all this add up to?

For all the evidence, not much. Musical history abounds in uncanny resemblances, some intentional, some not. It would have been difficult, for example, for Lloyd Webber to have appropriated "It's Getting Hotter in the North," since it was cut in previews before *Show Boat* opened on Broadway in December 1927, not rediscovered until 1978, and first heard only in 1983 at the show's Houston Grand Opera revival. As musicians know, the important thing is not whether the notes line up exactly in sequence, but whether they feel the same when sounded. There may be a fine line between homage and horse thievery, but so far, at least, Lloyd Webber has not crossed it. In the instance of "Come to Me, Bend to Me" and "The Music of the Night," the Loewe and Lloyd Webber tunes diverge almost immediately, and the songs themselves are completely different in mood, scope, function, and ambition. True, the unfortunate similarity extends not only to melodic intervals, but also to rhythm and tempo. And no doubt Lloyd Webber knows *Brigadoon* very well. But every composer soaks up music into his subconscious; a particular series of notes may sound "right" to him as he doodles at the keyboard, because he has heard them before, without remembering quite where. When George Harrison was sued over the close parallels between his song "My Sweet Lord" and the Chiffons' 1963 hit, "He's So Fine," the former Beatle explained: "Because of my lack of formal training, I think of myself as a jungle musician." Lloyd Webber is no jungle musician, but, with the equivalent of an American high-school education (albeit at an expensive private school), his formal training on paper is not very much greater than Harrison's. As far as the classical influences go, Lloyd Webber does not seek to hide them. He makes no bones of his admiration for Puccini and Prokofiev, for example, and while he denies that the Liu quote in *Phantom* was intentional, its provenance is unmistakable.

Those who seek the real source of Lloyd Webber's melodies need look no farther than Lloyd Webber himself. Like many composers, the man is a musical pack rat, salting away useful tunes in the knowledge that some day they will come in handy. Like several of the songs in *The Phantom of the Opera*, "The Music of the Night" originally was conceived for *Aspects of Love* during that show's first incarnation in 1983. At that time, the song was called "Married Man"—not to be confused with the song of the same name in "Tell Me on a Sunday"—and was written for female voice (Sarah Brightman's), not for a tenor. Brightman even recorded it with David Caddick, Lloyd Webber's latter-day musical director, conducting the London Philharmonic Orchestra. But that was at the height of her affair with the composer and the breakup of his marriage to his first wife, Sarah Tudor Hugill. Lloyd Webber was advised not to release the suddenly·inappropriately named song. So into the drawer it went; when it came time for the Phantom's big number a few years later, Lloyd Webber dove into the bureau and came out brandishing the song. Et voila! "The Music of the Night."

The campy "King Herod's Song" from *Superstar* originally was written for a never-produced musical with Rice called *Come Back Richard, Your Country Needs You*. The hit love song from *Superstar* was a pop number Lloyd Webber and Rice had written earlier and sold to a publisher; its rights were bought back by David Land, then Lloyd Webber and Rice's manager, and it got a new set of lyrics. Thus the pedestrian "Kansas Morning" became the soaring "I Don't Know How to Love Him." A number that was cut from the ill-starred *Jeeves* wound up as the big tune in *Variations*; outfitted with words, it was then inserted into the "Song" part of *Song and Dance* where it was first called "When You Want to Fall in Love" and later, "Unexpected Song." The short piéce d'occasion, *Cricket,* for which Lloyd Webber and Rice reunited briefly in 1986 for Queen Elizabeth's sixtieth birthday, was ransacked for the principal themes of *Aspects of Love*. And, of course, the original *Aspects* score turned—*poof!*—into *Phantom*. Still, there is no law against stealing from yourself, and whenever Lloyd Webber reuses a tune he generally improves it. Like the best Broadway composers, he has the showman's knack for putting the right song in the right place in the right form.

Lloyd Webber himself attributes the hostility of his sternest critics to simple jealousy, and he may be partly correct. In less than twenty years, he has gone in critical estimation from being the exciting, and penniless, young firebrand who was bringing a fresh new voice to a tired genre to the millionaire hack whose overwrought works are emblematic of what ails Broadway. And all this before he turned forty. Such are the pleasures and pitfalls of celebrity in a media-besotted, Warholian age: lauded today, vilified tomorrow. Additionally, as perhaps the only critic-proof composer in the world, he has no need to fuel the egos of drama critics by running their blurbs in his ads. To a very great extent, Lloyd Webber exists independent of the theatrical world.

Whatever the reasons, there is no question that Lloyd Webber inspires considerable media hostility even as the public has taken him to its breast. He knows it. Lloyd Webber's habitually stiff, defensive body language—the shoulders drawn up protectively, as if he were about to ward off a blow from an unseen hand—bespeaks a man still not entirely comfortable confronting the world. As photographs of the young Andrew attest, it is a pose that has not changed since childhood.

That child was father to the man.

Chapter One: A SCANDAL IN BOHEMIA

South Kensington is not London's most elegant neighborhood, nor its most important, nor its most renowned, merely its most congenial. On the Cromwell Road, its northern boundary which leads west out of the city to the combustive congestion of the M4 motorway, the Victoria and Albert Museum and the Natural History Museum serve as elegant reminders of England's imperial past. Along the Old Brompton Road, its heart, the middle-class brick row houses, all gables and crooks, frown over newly fashionable restaurants and shops, while further south lie the statelier whitewashed mansions and pleasing green square of Onslow Gardens. South Ken today is a district whose sweeping crescents and short streets are more cartographical punctuation marks than thoroughfares, whose resolute humanity of scale creates a cozy, homey feel. Kensington and neighboring Chelsea may lack the glamour of Belgravia, the ambience of Mayfair, or the nightlife of Soho, but to those who know London, its charms are no less great.

It was here that Andrew Lloyd Webber came squalling into the world on March 22, 1948, the first of the two sons of William ("Bill") Southcombe Lloyd Webber and Jean Hermione Johnstone. Both the aristocratic resonance and the Welsh echoes of the double surname are deceiving. Originally, it had been just Webber; Bill's father, William Charles Henry Webber, was a plumber, as his father had been before him, plying his trade in the Royal Borough of Kensington and Chelsea. Bill was born on March 11, 1914. Until he was a seventeen-year-old organ student at the Royal College of Music, he was called simply Bill, or Billy, Webber. However, at the college there was another organist named W. G. Webber, so Bill hit upon the idea of using his third Christian name as a second surname to distinguish himself: thus W. S. L. Webber became William S. Lloyd Webber. Bill liked the sound of it so much that he had both Andrew and his brother, Julian, baptized "Lloyd Webber."

The patrimony was resolutely English, the Webbers commingling with the Gittinses (Andrew's paternal grandmother). There was musical talent. William Charles Henry Webber's father had played the violin, and William Charles himself was a singer, an alto soloist in his youth and, in manhood, a fine tenor who sang with the George Mitchell Choir and the Black and White Minstrels, as well as in the choir of All Saints, Margaret Street (the leading Anglo-Catholic, or "High" Anglican, church in Britain) and at Winchester Cathedral. Young Bill grew up with the sound of church music in his ears. A prodigy who was giving organ concerts around London at the age of ten, he went on to hold positions first at All Saints and then at Central Hall, Westminster, a leading Methodist church.

Bill Lloyd Webber was a splendid practical musician as well. He could sight-read anything, and once he heard a score it was in his ears and fingers forever. Bill's real desire, though, was to be a composer. The period between the wars was an exciting time to be a classical musician in England. At the turn of the century, Sir Edward Elgar had written *fine* to the long drought of native English composition that had obtained since Handel had arrived from Germany in the eighteenth century. After the Great War, Frederick Delius, Ralph Vaughan Williams, and Gustav Holst had made their mark, and a younger generation that included Benjamin Britten, William Walton, and Arnold Bax was on its way. There were great British concert performers as well, among them Adrian Boult, the conductor, and Eva Turner, the Wagnerian soprano. English music was undergoing a renaissance, and Bill Lloyd Webber wanted desperately to be a part of it.

He never quite made it. Not that Bill was a failure; far from it. By any measure he had a solid professional career: a top student at the Royal College of Music, music director at two prestigious churches, longtime professor of composition and harmony at the Royal College of Music — just a few blocks up the Exhibition Road from the family home — and, finally, director of the London College of Music. In 1980 he was made a Commander of the British Empire. But it was not enough. The success he craved was that of a composer. Not a church-music composer, either, but a real composer.

Bill Lloyd Webber's career as a concert composer had been sidetracked first by the war and later by his own diffidence. As a youth, he played the organ in the silent-movie houses, improvising full scores from the barest cue sheets. His father's background in minstrelsy came in handy, and Bill quickly became adept in both the classical and pop idioms; as an adult he retained a taste for both. During the war years, he worked long hours in the Royal Army Pay Corps in Chelsea, this in addition to his regular duties as the organist and choirmaster at All Saints. It was hard enough for him to write in a calm environment conducive to contemplation, but working two jobs under the stress of the Blitz made creative work nearly impossible. So he gave it up, to concentrate on earning a living.

Bill Lloyd Webber was bitter about this decision for the rest of his life. He had done his bit for the war effort, derailed his compositional career — and for what? The case of Benjamin Britten, who had sat out the war safely in America, particularly rankled. By 1945, Britten had already composed his first operatic masterpiece, *Peter Grimes,* while Bill was still doling out pay packets. Bill became so bitter, in fact, that he actively discouraged his sons from careers in music, telling them what a terrible profession it was and what a difficult life it made for. Enter music as a last resort, only if there is absolutely nothing else you can do, he said — not, please note, if your talent simply won't permit you to do anything else. Strange advice from a lifelong professional music educator.

What Bill's emotions were on seeing his son Andrew succeed in the very field that had been closed to him, therefore, are not hard to fathom. In his desperate moments he would become maudlin and self-pitying, cursing the fate that had denied him his dream. He had offered the boy very little guidance and precious little acknowledgment: "If you ever write a song as good as 'Some Enchanted Evening,' I'll tell you," he said to Andrew. He never did.

Was Bill Lloyd Webber's desire to become a famous composer just a fantasy? Or did he have talent? Most of Bill's output was sacred songs and church music, but by taste and temperament he was a high romantic and an admirer of the operas of Giacomo Puccini, a composer then very much out of fashion in Britain. Once Bill was offered the chance to do a film score but turned it down; too much trouble, he said. More likely, it wasn't serious enough. He very likely would have been good at it.

W. S. Lloyd Webber's only major orchestral work is *Aurora,* an unpublished ten-minute tone poem for symphony orchestra written sometime between 1948 and 1951, when it was broadcast by the BBC. The composer wrote of the work:

> Arriving from the East in a chariot of winged horses, dispelling night and dispersing the dews of the morning, Aurora was the Roman goddess of the dawn. This short tone poem attempts to portray in reasonably respectable sonata first movement form, the inherent sensuality of her nature.
>
> Consecutive 6/4 chords introduce a bit of night music soon to be dispelled by the dawn theme, announced by the flute. Aurora's theme forms the second subject and (it is hoped) is of a suitably lyrical nature, as befits such a beautiful goddess. Her amorous adventures can possibly be imagined in the development section, and in the recapitulation her theme occurs twice — the first time with a light textured orchestration, and then with all the instruments that were available at the time of writing the piece.
>
> At the moment of climax, the night music returns again and Aurora has to leave us. However the final cadence has a hint of her theme, and there is always the promise of a new day.

This little document is more remarkable than the piece. First, there is the characteristically English self-deprecation: "attempts to portray," "reasonably respectable sonata first movement form," and the shy modesty of the parenthetical remark. Some of this is simple middle-class propriety and academic circumlocution, but surely so many apologies in such a short exegesis indicate how Lloyd Webber saw himself as a composer. Second, there is its frank eroticism. The "inherent sensuality" of the "beautiful goddess" whose "amorous adventures can possibly be imagined" leads to a "moment of climax" — pretty strong stuff for a church organist.

Bill was very proud of *Aurora* and would often listen to it on 78s, air-checks that were made during the performance.* If the music never quite measures up to its complex program, it is pleasant to listen to, well crafted, handsomely scored, and entirely representative of

---

Aurora received its first formal recording only in 1986, at Julian's instigation, as a filler for the cello-and-orchestra version of Andrew's *Variations,* for which Julian was the cello soloist.

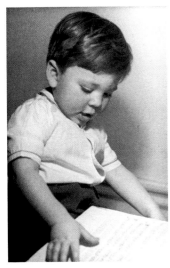

The composer in his studio: at home in Harrington Court, Andrew Lloyd Webber, twenty months old, examines one of his father's musical scores.

On one of their early London walkabouts, Andrew (left), age eight, and his brother, Julian, age five, feed the pigeons in Trafalgar Square.

*W*illiam S. ("Bill") Lloyd Webber in 1960.

A family outing the same year: (from left) Julian, Bill, Andrew, and John Lill.

The toy theater in which Andrew staged eight youthful musicals.

Viola Johnstone Crosby, Andrew's aunt. The actress's influence was decisive on Lloyd Webber's early development.

Andrew as a young teenager with his favorite cat, Perseus.

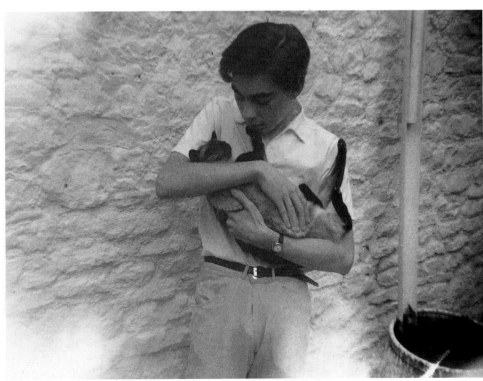

The assembly hall at the old Colet Court school in Hammersmith, where the premiere of Joseph and the Amazing Technicolor Dreamcoat took place in 1968.

Andrew and Tim Rice strike a Beatles-style pose during the early days of their partnership.

Opposite:

Andrew and Tim Rice in the summer of 1973, at Lloyd Webber's home in Brompton Square.

*S*ydmonton Court *during the 1988 Sydmonton Festival at which* Aspects of Love *was first presented. The oldest section of the manor house dates from the sixteenth century, although there are considerable Georgian and Victorian accretions. Inside, over the grand staircase, is Millais's painting* Design for a Gothic Window, *the only surviving piece of Pre-Raphaelite architectural design.*

Right:

*T*he chapel located on the grounds of Sydmonton Court, in which Lloyd Webber has tried out all his works since *Evita in 1976.*

Opposite, top left:

*L*loyd Webber with his mother, Jean, at the New York premiere of *The Phantom of the Opera.*

Opposite, top right:

*T*he composer with *Phantom director Hal Prince and choreographer Gillian Lynne.*

Opposite, bottom:

*L*loyd Webber in rehearsal for *Cats.*

Andrew and Sarah in front of the Paris Opera House during a 1987 photo shoot for Vanity Fair.

The Lloyd Webbers at home. Sarah created the role of Christine Daaé in Phantom *and also sang the soprano part in the premiere of the* Requiem.

mainstream twentieth-century British composition. The piece is cast in a Delian mold—English Impressionism. *Aurora's* soaring theme, reminiscent though it may be of the slow movement of the Debussy String Quartet, is suitably seductive; though the piece is slight, it leaves a gentle, poignant impression, like the close of day.

Whatever history's final verdict on William Lloyd Webber, his musical activities had one happy outcome: he met his wife. In 1938 Bill had been named organist at All Saints, Margaret Street, in Marylebone. In addition to his church duties he was also composing small musicals on the side for the junior department of the Royal College of Music. There, he was first seen by a fourteen-year-old violinist in the junior orchestra. Three years later, when Bill's church choir was evacuated to the countryside during the Battle of Britain, he brought in students from the Royal College to sing, and the young woman, who had by now developed a crush on him, contrived to make the trip to All Saints to sing in his ad hoc choral group. In short order, they met.

Her name was Jean Johnstone. The youngest of three children, she was born on March 30, 1922, to a Scottish military man, Charles Campbell Johnstone, and his half-Scottish wife, Molly Hemans, in Eastbourne, Sussex. (Like many British musicians, including some of the kingdom's finest composers—the Irish Sir Arthur Sullivan, for example, or the Welsh Ralph Vaughan Williams—Andrew has a healthy dollop of Celtic blood.) Jean's parents' arranged marriage was not a happy one. Molly was against it from the start; indeed, on her wedding night she threw her ring down the loo. Johnstone, a major in the Argyll and Sutherland Highlanders, was wild, irresponsible, and impossible. Somehow, Molly tolerated him for ten years and three children, but she divorced him when Jean was two. The other children were a daughter, Viola, who was eight years older than Jean, and a boy, Alastair, five years older. When Jean was five, the family moved to Harrow-on-the-Hill in Middlesex, and Alastair attended the famous school as a day boy.

Alastair was a neurasthenic lad, sensitive, artistic, and mystic, preparing to go to Cambridge with his abilities as a writer and naturalist already manifest. He even had a job lined up upon graduation at the *News-Chronicle* (then an important national newspaper, now defunct). He loved the countryside and would visit it often, bringing back with him such fauna as snakes, fantail pigeons, guinea pigs, hedgehogs, rabbits, crows, even a barn owl named Job, which the family would keep as pets.

The summer before he was to head up to university—he was eighteen—Alastair went bird-watching in Dorset with a friend. Although he was not a strong swimmer, he and another boy decided to take a small sailboat out on the ocean. About a hundred yards off the coast, the boat capsized. The friend, who had remained onshore, swam out at once, and the other boy in the boat managed to swim in. But it was too late for Alastair: the strong tides washed him out to sea, and his body was never found. In grief, Molly Johnstone sold the house and moved to London, where she took a flat at Number 10, Harrington Court on Harrington Road, hard by the South Kensington Underground Station.

Jean was devastated. In Alastair she had more than a brother, she had a soul mate. Viola and she were quite different—the vivacious, outgoing Vi was already on her way to a successful career in the theater as an actress, occasionally performing with the likes of John Gielgud and Raymond Massey, most often in the provinces but sometimes in the West End as well. Jean, shier and more introspective, was naturally drawn toward her like-minded brother, and it took her many years to recover from his tragic death. In many ways, she never did.

After dating for three years, Bill Lloyd Webber and Jean were married at All Saints on October 3, 1942. He was twenty-eight, she was twenty; the groom took a forty-eight-hour leave, and the honeymoon was spent in a small country inn outside London. The couple set up house in Mrs. Johnstone's top-floor flat in Harrington Court. Due to the war, they decided to postpone having children, contenting themselves with cats.

For a time, Bill and Jean also kept a monkey, a female macaque tiny enough to fit in one's pocket, which had been named Mimi after the heroine of Puccini's *La Bohème*. Bill got her in 1947 from a Polish sailor who had smuggled the creature into England; a companion male, inevitably named Rodolfo, had jumped overboard during the voyage. The Lloyd Webbers loved their little monkey. Every day, they would wash her, comb her hair, and dress her in a little jersey. Bill said Mimi held hands better than any girl he had ever met. One day, inexplicably, Mimi flew at Jean in a jealous rage and had to be given away. Soon after, Jean discovered she was two months' pregnant.

Physically and emotionally the firstborn son largely took after his father. Bill Lloyd Webber was a bespectacled, somewhat heavyset man with thin lips and dark, bushy eyebrows. His most remarkable physical feature was his dark eyes—exotic and enigmatic, like a cat's—and he passed them, together with his receding hairline and tendency to put on weight, on to his son. Andrew was a difficult child. From the time he was born, he yelled, screamed, and wailed so loudly that the neighbors complained. At night, he refused to sleep. About the only thing that would calm him was music—not the symphonies of Mozart or the operas of Verdi but, of all things, the rumbas of bandleader Edmundo Ros. In the middle of the night, when Andrew's cries shattered the building's repose, Jean or Bill would stagger to their feet, crank up the gramophone, and soothe the little boy's savage breast with "The Wedding Samba" ("Olé, Olé/the wedding samba/will bring a timid senorita to . . .").

The newest Lloyd Webber was, on the whole, a healthy child, but when he was three he came down with appendicitis and had to be rushed to University College Hospital. Although the doctors were not certain the boy's condition was appendicitis, they finally decided to operate and found that the appendix had indeed burst, causing great pain. Given the boy's temperament, it was out of the question that he would stay in the hospital overnight by himself: for the next three days, Andrew and his mother were forced to move from room to room and wing to wing as his screams got them evicted time and again. At four, he contracted a mild case of polio from another child who later developed the full-blown disease, then one of childhood's scourges. No paralysis developed, and Andrew recovered fully.

Hyperactive seems to be the best word to describe the juvenile Lloyd Webber. He simply could not sit still; forever rushing around the flat, crashing into this, knocking over that. In response, his father dubbed him "Bumper"—an inelegant nickname, perhaps, but better than, say, "Bunny" or "Stinky." Despite his predilection for noise making, young Andrew could hardly tolerate the sounds made by others. When, at age three, he went off to his first school, Wetherby (a private elementary school, then located in South Kensington, where his mother had just started teaching music), he would stand for hours with his hands over his ears, shutting out the noise of his fellow pupils. Even then, the sounds he preferred to hear were his own.

His brother, Julian, was born on April 14, 1951. There was little sibling rivalry between the two. In any case, Julian was physically and temperamentally the opposite—his mother's son, in the same way that Andrew was his father's. Where Andrew was of medium height, Julian was tall; where Andrew was round of face, Julian was narrow; where Andrew was explosive, Julian was calm. There were some crossover traits, though: from their father, Julian got his florid coloring; from their mother, Andrew got his steel.

As a boy, Julian engaged in all the normal pursuits that Andrew eschewed: taking objects apart, boring holes through walls, inserting sharp implements into electrical sockets, that sort of thing. Julian loved sports, which Andrew hated, and wasn't afraid to stand and fight with another child if honor or circumstances demanded it, whereas Andrew preferred the better part of valor.

It was about this time that Jean's life took a decisive turn. Jean had left the Royal College in 1942 and had gone immediately into teaching. The family needed the money to augment Bill's meager earnings as an academic, doubly so after the boys arrived. Jean usually worked from eight o'clock in the morning, when she arrived at Wetherby, until ten o'clock at night, when she finished with the last of her private piano students. She became obsessed with helping others, as concerned with the lives of her pupils, especially the best and the brightest of them, as she was with the lives of her own sons. In particular, she devoted herself to a group of wartime refugees from Gibraltar, to the annoyance of Bill, who was jealous of her obvious affection for a tenor named Louis.

Jean came by her social activism naturally. Her mother, Molly, was, by nature, mildly socialistic and highly sympathetic to the idealistic tenets of Sir Richard Acland, who in 1947 had founded the short-lived Common Wealth party, and to the nonconformist Christian writings of Dr. Leslie Weatherhead. Still, Molly was no marching suffragette, and stories of her running socialist soup kitchens in Reading are apocryphal. She was poor—there was, of course, no alimony from her husband—and she spent her life struggling to earn a living as a secretary and, later, as a doctor's receptionist. The doctor was named George Crosby and Molly, still a handsome woman, may have been attracted to him. As luck would have it, though, Crosby met Molly's daughter Viola and married her. After Julian was born, Molly retired, to stay home and help raise the boys.

The Lloyd Webbers believed in letting their children guide their own development, never discouraging their enthusiasms; on the contrary, Jean and Bill positively indulged them. Just after his third birthday, Andrew was given a violin and, soon after, a horn. Unlike his brother, who displayed instrumental dexterity early on, Andrew, it was soon apparent, was never going to be a virtuoso; even his piano technique was mediocre. Still, it was abundantly clear that the boy had talent. In his piano lessons he balked at learning the repertory pieces that torture all children. Instead, he made up and performed his own music.

Even without its resident simian, chez Lloyd Webber is best described as bohemian. Its location over the rumble of an underground line was perhaps its least unusual property. There was the father, Bill, a remote and solitary figure tucked away in his study and lost in his dreams. There was the mother, Jean, a resolute Mrs. Jellyby, concerned with the welfare of London's disadvantaged youth at the expense of her own. There was Andrew, hammering away at one of the household's several pianos, desperately pumping out notes on the horn, or sawing madly on the violin. There was Julian, practicing the cello or, more noisily, the trumpet. There was also Molly Johnstone, who later moved into a smaller flat next door when it became available. This in addition to an odd assortment of cats—the favorite, Perseus, as well as Dmitri (Shostakovich), Serge (Prokofiev), and others more or less domesticated—and a steady stream of musicians who came calling on Bill or Jean. From time to time the family would even visit the zoo to which Mimi had been banished; Jean would call to her erstwhile pet, and Mimi would dutifully hop over to eat out of Jean's hand.

In his 1986 memoir, *Travels with My Cello,* Julian has provided a good description of the chaos. "Life at Harrington Court—the large, run-down, late Victorian, red brick block of flats just by the South Kensington tube—was chiefly memorable for the astonishing, ear-blowing volume of musical decibels which seemed to burst forth from every room most of the day and night. My father's electric organ, mother's piano, grandmother's deafening (she was deaf) television, elder brother's astounding piano and French Horn and my own scrapings on the cello and blowings on the trumpet by themselves would have made the cannon and mortar effects of the *1812 Overture* seem a bit like the aural equivalent of a wet Sunday morning on Hackney Marshes. . . ." Very little of the music emanating from Number 10 was recorded, for Bill's record collection consisted of only a handful of 78s. (The long-suffering neighbor below, Carleton Hobbs, famous in Britain for his radio portrayal of Sherlock Holmes, complained on only two occasions during the twenty years the Lloyd Webbers lived above him—once when Julian emptied a bag of bricks on the floor and once when Andrew's pianistic pedal stomping finally shattered the peace of his ceiling.)

For all its togetherness, the family unit was not close. Indeed, to outsiders it often seemed that the Lloyd Webber household was made up of complete strangers; one could hardly imagine them, for example, all sitting down at the same dinner table and having a chat about the day's events. Different as they were, Lloyd Webber père and mère both subscribed to the laissez-faire school of child rearing, a philosophy, at least in Jean's case, only partly necessitated by the demands of two careers. (Molly did most of the actual day-to-day supervision.) There was little of the conventional parental pressure to do well in school; when Julian brought home a poor school report one time, Jean read it aloud to gales of laughter. *MOTHER*

One indulgence in particular affected the whole family. At age seven, Andrew declared that he wanted to be chief inspector of ancient monuments in Britain when he grew up. To that end, Lloyd Webber summer family holidays became devoted to traipsing around Britain, scrutinizing the old piles of stones that had been castles or abbeys in the days before Henry VIII dissolved the monasteries. In London, Andrew would roam the streets, tracking down the important Victorian churches and buildings with a guidebook in hand, furiously annotating it with his own observations.

Andrew's interest in historic architecture was far more than a passing youthful fancy. He wrote several monographs on the subject, the scope of which is astoundingly sophisticated for one so young. "ANCIENT MONUMENTS in THE HOME COUNTIES, by Andrew Lloyd-Webber," runs the title page of one. (This period of his life seems to have been the only time Andrew ever used the hyphen. Even then, it was arbitrary; some of the monument studies employ it, others don't). "First edition; November, 1959, and Second edition, (revised) February, 1960. Also Author of Ancient Monuments in England and Wales, and, Our Monastic Heritage, not yet in print, 8 volumes." The eight volumes of monasticism never seem to have seen daylight, but there were also treatises on "Roman Remains in England and Wales" and "The Welsh Border Castles: Their origins, histories and purposes," among several others. Showing his business acumen at an early age, Andrew even put prices on some of them.

The flavor of these neatly typed and illustrated (with postcards and black-and-white pictures clipped from magazines) volumes may be gleaned from the introduction to "Ancient Monuments in the Home Counties":

```
             THE INTRODUCTION TO THE FIRST EDITION.
              by the author, November, 1959.


       How many times have you said to yourself, " I wish I knew of some more
   ancient ruins at London, I could easily visit in my spare time?" Many times?
   It is a question that I have asked many people who are in the least way
   interested in ancient monuments, and who live in London.  They all say, " I
   know of Berkhampstead, - but there is little now left there, Windsor, but
   everybody knows it so well that it is hardly worth a visit, Waltham Abbey,
   but that too has almost vanished," and so they go on.
       There is little, unfortunately, left of note in the vicinity of London.
   The city, itself, having extended to an unearthly boundary, has swallowed
   up many of the smaller remnants that remained in a comparatively good state
   of preservation, and it looks as if it is going to continue to do so.  But
   despite all of this, you would be surprised what you can find.
       In this volume I have tried to write down the monuments I have come
   across in my own travels, and I hope that I will show to you a great number
   of the remnants of our past near the city, and I hope you will be able to
   visit them easily.

              Andrew Lloyd-Webber,
                 November, 1959.
```

There follows a detailed listing of ruins near London. However much of the information was gleaned from the encyclopedia or from Dugdale's (the foremost reference work on monasteries, a copy of which was the first thing Andrew bought with his first professional royalties), the project reveals a formidable and determined young mind at work. So great was the young Lloyd Webber's interest in monuments that in 1961 he wrote a letter to the Ministry of Works:

10. Harrington Court,
S.W.7.

August 20th.

Dear Sir,

I am very concerned about the state of ancient monuments which are not under the care of the Ministry of Works.

I have been making a tour of the castle buildings on the Welsh border, and in the course of this two or three horrible examples of decaying buildings were visited. The first was Usk Castle. This is covered with ivy and plants to the extent that one can hardly make out the periods of construction. An old lady who appears to own the site told me that it was almost impossible to consolidate the remains owing to lack of finance.

An even worse example can be seen at Clun. The castle here is owned by the parish council and it is in a terrible state. The keep, which is somewhat unique in that it uses one side of the motte as a wall, stands almost to its full height but a huge split has appeared from top to bottom. It is completely overgrown and no attempt is being made to excavate or, more important, to consolidate remains. It seems that excavations would be rewarded, but nothing seems to be done.

The last is at Whittington in Shropshire, which, I understand, has been offered to you for preservation, but due to lack of finance you are hesitating to accept. This is the most terrible state of affairs and surely something can be done about it.

Yours sincerely,

Andrew Lloyd-Webber.
(Aged 13.)

Everyone was sure Andrew was going to be a historian. At the same time, though, his fascination with music—and in particular musical theater—was growing rapidly. Under the influence of his glamorous Aunt Vi, a frequent visitor to Harrington Court, Andrew had discovered the world of the theater, and soon he was taking himself to the cinema to see films such as *Gigi* and *South Pacific,* which he saw twelve times, and to the West End, where he caught most of the hit musicals, starting with *My Fair Lady.**

The effect on Andrew was electric. Here, at last, was something that combined both his passions in one joyful noise. Did he love architecture? The theater offered realistic sets and splendid costumes—as many as the imagination could wish. Did he love music? The entire enterprise was supported on glorious wings of song. With Aunt Vi's encouragement, the eleven-year-old Andrew built a toy theater in which to give rein to his already fecund imagination. This enterprising structure was no childish toy, but a fully functional house built out of bricks and boards, with a proscenium arch, wings, flys, even a revolving stage made out of a gramophone turntable. The productions were on a vast scale. Andrew populated his showplace with toy soldiers—the pit orchestra was a military band—and animals; Julian would manipulate the characters while his brother sat at the piano, playing the show tunes. Like Elgar copying out the Mozart Symphony No. 40, but substituting his own themes in order to see how Mozart had done it, Andrew would stage works such as Rodgers and Hammerstein's *Flower Drum Song* to study their stagecraft. Later, he transformed the theater into a mock television studio.†

With the toy theater came a burst of musical imagination as well. Andrew had sketched out his first original composition when he was seven and had been diligently composing on the piano ever since. In 1959 the British magazine *Music Teacher* published excerpts from Andrew's op. 1, *The Toy Theatre,* a suite of six short pieces. "I have been rather amused at the efforts of my own boy, Andrew, to find his own harmonies

---

*When Dr. Crosby retired from practice in 1962, Vi and he moved to Ventimiglia, in Italy, where Andrew would visit them in the summers. Viola had long since given up the stage, but she was active as a prolific author of cookbooks. The Crosbys lived in Italy until 1973, when they returned to England and settled in a house in Bristol purchased by their now rich and famous nephew. Viola by this time was mortally ill and died soon after.

†The fate of this remarkable dollhouse is unclear. It was apparently trucked to Sydmonton and disposed of during a wholesale housecleaning.

for the tunes he composes on his play-room piano," wrote Bill. "He makes up various 'incidental music' for plays, which he 'produces' in his play-room theatre: it is all quite spontaneous, and this branch of his music-making is deliberately left 'self-taught' at the moment. In the six pieces he has composed, the tunes and the harmonies are all his own: and all I have done is to do the slight editing which is obviously necessary to make them acceptable to players." The magazine added: "*Music Teacher* believes that the pieces, which are clearly the product of a gifted child of one of our most distinguished musicians, will be enjoyed because of their natural and spontaneous qualities."*

In 1956 Andrew had left Wetherby for the Westminster Underschool for boys aged eight through thirteen, then located in Eccleston Square not far from Victoria Station. The family had no money, of course, but Molly had come into a small inheritance, with which she set up a small trust fund to pay for the boys' tuition. Musically, Andrew was already displaying an eclectic mind, dragging home the latest records by Elvis, the Everly Brothers, Bill Haley and the Comets, and Bobby Vee in addition to his burgeoning collection of show tunes. Scholastically, his reviews were mixed. He was an in-and-out student, bright and engaged one day and bored and uninterested the next. Presaging the reaction of his critics in later years, some of his teachers thought him genuinely gifted, others merely facile.

From the underschool, Andrew entered Westminster proper in the fall of 1961 and was assigned to Rigaud's House, where the day boys went. Again he proved a dilatory student, his only academic distinction coming in history. Of far greater importance to his development were his musical activities. At Christmas 1961 Andrew made his debut with a Rigaud's school show called *Cinderella Up the Beanstalk (and most everywhere else!)* — a title nearly as provocative as Bill Lloyd Webber's program notes for *Aurora*. The "pantomime" was a new activity at Rigaud's, having begun the year before; the lyrics were by an older boy, Robin St. Clare Barrow, who also starred in the play. Lloyd Webber's maiden voyage was followed the next year by something called *Utter Chaos or No Jeans for Venus*. This piece, a spoof of Greek mythology in which everyone from Zeus to James Bond makes an appearance, was also known as *Socrates Swings or Lovers and Friends*.

Utter Chaos included such songs as "I guess that we're better apart," "Laughter is better than tears," "I came in time to say goodbye," and "Nothing left to break." A program note says, "They are all Barrow–Webber compositions so you may have heard them before under different titles"—a criticism, or at least a prescient comment, that would be much heard in the future.

The best students at Westminster, though, were not day boys, they were Queen's Scholars, boarders who had won their places through a special examination. In 1962, shortly before his fourteenth birthday—the age limit—Andrew applied for the coveted Challenge Scholarship, good for roughly half the school fees, then four hundred pounds a year. The examination consisted of two math papers and essays in history, French, English, Greek, and Latin. Somewhat to everyone's surprise, he won it, largely on the strength of an iconoclastic paper on Victorian architecture that caught the eye of the history master, Charles Keeley. Andrew had learned from his father the value of standing out in a crowd—"Ah, here's one with the slightest hint of an original theme!" Bill would cry while grading composition papers—even if he was deficient in the other subjects. Characteristically, it was Aunt Vi who suggested celebrating Andrew's triumph, which they did at the then-chic Porto Fino restaurant in Camden Passage, Islington; neither Bill nor Jean had thought to do so. At fourteen, Andrew Lloyd Webber left home.

And John Lill moved in. Jean Lloyd Webber's missionary work had been leading up to something like this, but with Lill, then eighteen, it reached its apogee. Jean had met Lill two years before, through Julian, who had gotten to know him during the Saturday morning classes at the junior department of the Royal College of Music. Lill was the junior department's star pupil, a promising pianist who possessed a brilliant piano technique. Everyone predicted great things for him: at the time Jean found him he was well on his way to becoming the Great British Pianistic Hope. At first Lill, who came from an impoverished family in Leyton, in London's East End, stayed in South Kensington one night a week, but after Andrew departed, Jean invited—commanded is more like it—Lill to move in. Which he did.

There was plenty of room. Number 10 was huge, big enough to accommodate three pianos and Bill's electric organ; Andrew and Julian even had their own sitting room. Next door in Number 2A, reached from the main flat through the French windows of the living room and a short balcony, Mrs. Johnstone had three bedrooms (one of which soon harbored Lill's grand piano). Space was hardly the problem. Still, no one, aside from Jean, was happy with the arrangement. To Andrew and Julian, John Lill was both a big brother and an interloper; Andrew in particular must have felt a little like Alex in Anthony Burgess's novel *A Clockwork Orange*, who comes home from prison only to find that another young man has usurped his place in the affections of mum and dad. When the family went out, John came along; when the family went on holiday, John came too. Andrew and Julian liked John well enough, but, understandably, they wished that, just once, they could have an outing without him—a real family holiday.

To Mrs. Lill, who was working three jobs to free the family of the debts run up by her husband, John's departure was dangerously near an insult. Here was this do-gooding socialist in a cloth coat from South Ken slumming on a weekly trip to the East End to commandeer her son

---

*Thirty years later, one of these tunes, a little descending scale, became the "Chanson d'Enfance," the Pyreneean "folk song" of Lloyd Webber's 1989 show, *Aspects of Love*.

for her own good! What Bill felt is not recorded; from the safety of his study, nothing Jean did could surprise him. Besides, there was no use protesting: the force of Jean's will carried the day against all objections.

This extraordinary episode fairly cries out for explanation. Jean's socially liberal upbringing was obviously one impulse: she was a woman who not only enjoyed doing good, she *had* to do good, and there was simply no doing anything about it. Further, with her high hopes for Bill's classical music career dashed, she saw in John Lill a vetting of her talent-scouting ability—just as, a few years later, she would see Julian also win considerable success. Finally, there was her own natural emotional reserve, which may have blinded her to the effect her actions were having on her family. Whatever the case, there is little question that Jean's pronounced concern for Lill and her Gibraltar boys was the central formative emotional experience of Andrew Lloyd Webber's life and goes a long way to explaining some of his own aloofness and insecurity.

At school, among the forty Queen's Scholars at College House, Andrew was progressing slowly. A solitary, shy boy, physically unprepossessing, he was far from the hale-fellow-well-met beau ideal of the British public-school tradition—a poor mixer, terrible at sports, and, it almost goes without saying, utterly inept in the quasi-military environment of the compulsory cadet corps. (In all this, he was backed by his mother; in no uncertain terms, she had informed one of his housemasters that Andrew needn't waste his time with sports when it was perfectly obvious to everyone that he was no good at them, would never need them later in life, and could spend his time far more profitably on his music.) Just as he had been at the Underschool, Andrew was a hit-or-miss scholar at Westminster: not the best student, not the worst. Perhaps his most notable characteristic was his emotional volatility, seemingly undiminished from childhood; Jean and Andrew, aggrievedly descending on some hapless house tutor, must have been a terrifying sight.

Aside from history, there was only one other subject that interested him. That, of course, was music. College House was not a strictly controlled environment; the boys were expected to be mature young men and their comings and goings were relatively unfettered. During his years as a boarder, from 1962 to 1965, Andrew haunted the concert halls of London, arguing the relative merits of Prokofiev and Puccini far into the night with John Lill and Julian. (By this time, Lill's own concert career was taking off; in 1963 he made his debut at the Royal Festival Hall playing the Beethoven *Emperor* Concerto; in 1970, his career would reach its zenith when he won the Tchaikovsky International Competition in Moscow. Jean's musical judgment had been resoundingly validated.)

Andrew's third and last show at Westminster, *Play the Fool,* hit the boards on June 30, 1964. The variety show was something of a coming-out party for Lloyd Webber not only as a composer but as a writer and producer as well. Westminster, after all, was the school that gave Britain and the world John Gielgud, Peter Ustinov, the comedy team of Swann and Flanders and, latterly, the pop singing duo of Peter and Gordon. Pop music was in the air; the remarkable flowering of British rock was underway from Liverpool to London. "[Westminster] now feels strong enough to present an entire show of its own," ran a notice in *The Daily Sketch.* The revue featured a number of homegrown pop groups, including the Hi-Five, the Witnesses, and the Trekkers, whose lead singer, Twinkle, had a hit at number four on the charts later that year with a song called "Terry."

But Andrew was the center of attention. Even then people were predicting great success for him. A "Note on the Producer" ran:

> Ever since Andrew Lloyd-Webber came to the school, it was obvious that here was someone with no ordinary genius for music and the theatre. . . . But Andrew's real interests lie outside the school. Not only is he making quite a stir as a composer and writer, but as an entertainer in his own right.
>
> "I expect I'll give up writing 'pop' soon [said Andrew]. Then I'll devote myself to composing for the musical theatre."

Among the thirteen of his songs were such titles as "Play the Fool," "Run Wild," "Regrets," and "Make Believe Love." Andrew's musical language was already attracting attention. At fourteen, Andrew had signed with the Noel Gay Organisation (Gay, by that time deceased, had written the music for *Me and My Girl*), most likely through a contact with Harold Fielding, a leading impresario. Already fiercely self-promotional, Andrew had sent an idea and some songs for a musical—a kind of Ruritanian fantasy—to Fielding (the lyrics were by a friend of his Aunt Vi's, an actress named Joan Colmore); Fielding had turned it down but was spreading the word that here was a bold young talent who might be worth investigating. A short time later, someone from Gay called.

Andrew's contract with Gay was short-lived, but in late 1963, through a record producer named Charles Blackwell, he wrote and recorded his song "Make Believe Love," although it was never released. Again, one must admire the lad's audacity. Andrew had sent a demo tape of the song to Decca Records, who passed it along to Blackwell. The song was even published, which led to an exclusive contract with Southern Music, under Bob Kingston. Blackwell, as it turned out, was a client of Desmond Elliott's, the publisher of Arlington Books, and a prominent literary agent who was struck by the possibilities young Lloyd Webber seemed to represent. Taking a flyer on a musician, Elliott signed Andrew up. (If it seems unusual that a teenager would have an agent, remember that British pop music at this time was, literally, child's play. The

Beatles had been teenagers when they first clicked, and the other English singers and groups were all young too: Cilla Black, Gerry and the Pacemakers, the Dave Clark Five, The Who, the Kinks, and the Rolling Stones.)

On June 10, 1964, Andrew played the piano at Elliott's invitation for the Midnight Cabaret, an entertainment that took place at the Author's Ball during the World Book Fair in London. First there was dinner ("Robert Carrier's Summer Soup," fisherman's pie, trio of spring lamb chops, and pineapple pride), with a fine selection of wines, such as a Château Léoville Poyferre 1955. Then came the show, which consisted of several pastiche songs to popular tunes with words by Desmond Elliott, Michael Turner, and Desmond Briggs and with "Andrew Lloyd-Webber" at the piano. One of them, "Where There's a Will," was a parody of Shakespeare and Bacon; another, "Ever So Romantic," jibed at Barbara Cartland.

What did Lloyd Webber's music sound like? A juvenile admixture of half-digested classical references, half-assimilated musical comedies, and half-heard rock idioms, it was at heart unabashedly romantic; here, again, the son of the father was showing his hand. Perhaps unconsciously, Andrew was seeking a middle ground between the lavish melodies of Richard Rodgers that he so admired and the more acerbic rock idiom that was then ferrying across Britain from the Mersey. To the professors, it was too pop-oriented, while to his fellow students, Andrew's aural evocations of *The Sound of Music* were square, even eccentric.

Still, a little eccentricity is a much-appreciated commodity in England, and the reputation of the lad did not particularly suffer. Not that he was particularly popular. On the contrary, Andrew tended to be a loner, rightwardly inclined politically at a time when left was best. His closest friend was a boy named Gray Watson, whose Wildean flamboyance was looked at askance by his classmates and privately led to speculation about the real nature of his relationship with Andrew. That relationship appears to have been purely platonic. (Transient homosexuality is hardly unknown in the British public-school system, but Lloyd Webber's life-style has always been committedly heterosexual.) Andrew and Gray enjoyed guying Molly Johnstone by adopting the most outrageous right-wing positions they could think of.

At school, Andrew was muddling through, but without distinction. The whole school, therefore, was shocked when in December 1964 he applied for, and won, an Exhibition scholarship to Magdalen College, Oxford. He had applied for an internal scholarship to the ancient university, this one to Christchurch College, and was turned down. But, once again, on the strength of a paper on Victorian architecture, he won the open award.

In heading up to Oxford, Lloyd Webber had a hidden agenda. He didn't want to be a historian, he wanted to be a songwriter. Lloyd Webber had heard Oxford was home to the country's most promising lyricists, a hotbed of artistic ferment that he badly needed. Westminster may not have taught him much, but one thing it had taught him was the importance of a good lyricist. Barrow's lyrics had been sentimental schoolboy affairs—"I Continually Reflect on My Present State of Mind" ran a song from *Cinderella*—and after Barrow had left there had been nobody. Surely at Oxford he would meet someone witty, someone clever, someone imaginative. Someone, in other words, very like Tim Rice.

Rice, however, was not at Oxford. He was in London, laboring as a dogsbody in a solicitors' office and dreaming of the days when he, too, would be a big pop star. Timothy Miles Bindon Rice had been born on November 13, 1944, in Amersham, Buckinghamshire, about twenty-five miles from London, and had grown up near Hatfield and St. Albans, in Hertfordshire. The oldest of three boys, he attended religious primary schools—one of them in Tokyo, where the family lived for a year—and Lancing College, a secondary school in Sussex near Brighton (like Andrew, he was a public-school boy); later, he briefly studied at the Sorbonne in Paris. If Andrew secretly harbored the desire to be the next Richard Rodgers, then Tim in his heart wanted to be the next Elvis. Or at least the next Cliff Richard.

Rice's first calling, though, was less glamorous—he spent the summer of 1963 as a petrol-pump attendant. In September he joined the London law firm of Pettit and Westlake as an intern, where he stuck it out until May 1966. By then, it was manifestly apparent that Tim's future was not to be argued out in a court of law, so he turned instead to the court of public opinion. Through his father, an executive with De Havilland Aviation, he wangled a place at EMI, Ltd., one of Britain's foremost record companies, and soon found himself working for Norrie Paramor, a well-known bandleader, orchestrator, arranger, and record producer—the Mitch Miller of Great Britain.

Tim was mad for pop music, and his knowledge of it was encyclopedic. Three years older than Andrew, Rice was old enough to remember vividly the impact Elvis had when he first burst on the scene in the mid-fifties, and was practically an eyewitness to the ascent of the Beatles. Tim had the whole rock repertoire at his fingertips—not just song titles and artists, but what year the song was released, how high it went on the charts, which label had released it. Far more than Andrew, he knew the power, both emotional and remunerative, of rock—the evidence was right under his nose every day—and he wanted to be a part of it. At twenty, Tim Rice had set his cap for fortune and fame.

The problem was how to achieve it? EMI had a flourishing rock business, but to a gofer like him it was tantalizingly near yet frustratingly far away. As a law student, he had managed to sell a couple of songs; one of them, "That's My Story" (words and music by T. Rice) had even been recorded as an "A" side by a group called the Night Shift, and though it wasn't a hit, it was an encouragement.

Perhaps, then, a literary tack. For some time, he had had an idea for a book on pop songs, a kind of *Guinness Book of Hit Singles* (a concept that finally bore fruit years later). Fate brought Tim and his notion to Desmond Elliott. Elliott wasn't interested in the book but he was interested in Tim's ambitions as a lyricist. Here was a bright young lad who obviously knew his way around the English language. Why not hook him up with Andrew Lloyd Webber? Elliott suggested that Rice get in touch with Lloyd Webber and see what he was all about. Who knew, maybe something would come of it.

11 Gunter Grove

LONDON, S.W.10.

April 21 1965

Dear Andrew,

   I have been given your address by Desmond Elliott of Arlington Books, who I believe has also told you of my existence. Mr. Elliott told me that you "were looking for a 'with-it' writer" of lyrics for your songs, and as I have been writing pop songs for a short while now and particularly enjoy writing the lyrics I wondered if you consider it worth your while meeting me. I may fall far short of your requirements, but anyway it would be interesting to meet up - I hope! Would you be able to get in touch with me shortly, either at FLA 1822 in the evenings, or at WEL 2261 in the daytime (Pettit and Westlake, solicitors are the owners of the latter number).

     Hoping to hear from you,

         Yours,

         Tim Rice

         Tim Rice.

A few days later, Tim popped round to the Lloyd Webber flat at Harrington Court and introduced himself. And that was that. No "You have been in Afghanistan, I perceive," or "Doctor Livingstone, I presume?" Just a shy hello.

It was apparent from the beginning that the two young men were, in almost every way, polar opposites. Rice was tall, blond, blue-eyed, affable, gregarious, and good-looking, tremendously successful with women. He had swagger, he had style: put a flowered shirt or a tweed cap on him and he looked great. Andrew, by contrast, was smaller, darker, and less handsome, introspective but sentimental. He wanted to have style, but he just couldn't seem to manage it: put a flowered shirt on him and he just looked affected.

Further, their objectives were quite different. Tim had never even seen a musical. He wanted to write "Twist and Shout"; Andrew wanted to write "Climb Every Mountain." It took six months of negotiation before they actually wrote anything together. Still, Andrew realized almost at once that in Rice he had found the lyricist he was looking for. Well, almost at once. There was this little matter of the scholarship to Magdalen College. In the fall of 1965 Andrew dutifully trudged up to Oxford, ready to read history.

He lasted a single term and hated every minute of it. His impression of Oxford had been mistaken: there were no promising lyricists there, at least none as promising as Tim Rice. (Robin Barrow was there, but he didn't seem to matter much anymore.) At Elliott's suggestion, he and Tim had finally hit upon something they thought would make a good subject for a musical comedy: a show about Dr. Barnardo, the famous Victorian philanthropist and founder of children's homes, to be called *The Likes of Us*. Far better he should go back to London and work with Tim than waste his time at Oxford. Agonized telephone calls began to fly back and forth between Andrew and his parents, with the upshot that at Christmas 1965 Andrew announced he was dropping out of Oxford—the fig leaf being that he was going on leave for two terms—to pursue a career as a professional musician.

In the end, neither Bill nor Jean raised much of a fuss. Most middle-class folks would have been appalled at the prospect of their eldest son voluntarily withdrawing from one of the world's most prestigious universities, especially in light of the expensive education it took to get him there. But not the Lloyd Webbers. Both Jean and Bill made sure Andrew knew what he was doing, and when he told them he knew, they gave him their blessings.

This beneficent and enlightened aspect of Lloyd Webber's upbringing was, in retrospect, crucial to his development and, later, to his success. If Jean and Bill could sometimes seem distressingly nonjudgmental—Lloyd Webber's habitual characterization of them was "perfectly liberal parents"—they also had enough faith in their boys to let them make their own decisions. Bill's reasoning was clear enough. Circumstances had denied him the chance to be a professional composer: why should he deny it to his son?

Jean's case was more complicated. She hated the idea of Andrew's leaving university—so did her mother—but there wasn't much she could do about it. Part of this stemmed from Jean's own natural fatalism. In the past, she had consoled herself over the fate of her brother Alastair with the thought that the fragile lad would have been physically and emotionally incapable of dealing with the war, and perhaps it was a blessing that God had taken him when he did. Jean had pushed Julian hard on the cello because she could hear that he was good at it; by the same token, she had not insisted that Andrew pursue his piano lessons because it was just as clear that he was not interested. She had hoped Andrew would become the historian of childhood's wish; as he developed his passion for the theater, Jean found herself increasingly out of her depth. It was time to let him go, to let him find whatever lot the gods had in store for him.

Most children have to leave their families to find themselves. Andrew Lloyd Webber came home. His daring decision demonstrated a firm knowledge of his own mind and a high degree of self-confidence. True, he was not exactly down and out; he had a home to go back to and parents who would take care of him. But the courage and self-possession his choice bespoke should not be underestimated.

Back at Number 10, then, this time with Tim in tow. Granny had an extra room: why not rent it—at three pounds a week—to Rice? For three quid a week Tim would live with anybody, and into the menagerie he came. So now it was Bill and Jean and Molly and Andrew and Julian and John and Tim. Soon enough, there would be Joseph, too.

Chapter Two: GO, GO, GO JOSEPH

The years between 1966, when Andrew dropped out of Oxford for good, and 1968, when he and Tim first saw their work performed in public, might appear to have been uneventful: there was no big overnight success to cement the partnership of Rice and Lloyd Webber, no single to suddenly soar to the Top of the Pops and announce to the world that here was a formidable new entry in the British musical sweepstakes. Things were colorful enough, all right: with the noise pouring out of Number 10* in unending abundance, John Lill—and, around Christmas 1966, Tim Rice— cheek to jowl with Grandma in Number 2A, and Andrew hustling his and Rice's songs all over town, life could not have been dull.

But productive? Naturally, the answer is yes. Lloyd Webber could no more sit still than speak Chinese, and Rice's ambitions fired him to an almost equal degree. Ill-matched as they were in so many ways, each offered the other something he lacked. To Andrew, Tim Rice was older, more sophisticated, and, perhaps most important, already working in the pop business. He was also the best lyricist Andrew could hope for, and Lloyd Webber knew that if something didn't happen fairly soon he would lose Tim to another, more successful, composer. If Tim had been worth chucking Oxford for, he was certainly worth scrambling for.

Strangely, Rice felt much the same way about the younger man. To Rice, a properly brought-up child of the upper middle class, life with the Lloyd Webber family was a bracing, even liberating experience. Tim had, for example, never heard parents use four-letter words in front of their children before, nor was he used to the parade of London musical personalities that periodically marched on Number 10. Andrew—by turns saturnine and sanguine—was relentless, a quality the more diffident Rice admired. Tim may have had an in with Norrie Paramor, but Andrew had already had contracts with real live agents and publishers. Further, Tim trusted Andrew's musical judgment; if he said some unknown actor up at Oxford whom he had gotten to know was perfect for their first show—"the Olivier of his generation," as Andrew called David Marks, the proposed lead—then Tim believed him. Andrew knew best; in fact, Andrew was very nearly always right.

And so they embarked on *The Likes of Us,* a musical based on the life of Dr. Barnardo. The dialogue and story line—the "book," in theater parlance—was by Leslie Thomas, the best-selling author of *The Virgin Soldiers* and *Orange Wednesday,* who was also one of Desmond Elliott's clients. Having found their subject, Lloyd Webber and Rice worked quickly. The first lyric that Rice wrote went, "Here I have a lovely parrot,/sound of wind and limb./I can guarantee that/there's nothing wrong with him."

---

*Sadly, today's gutted and modernized Harrington Court—a block of impersonal service flats owned by Arabs—is but a pale shadow of its former bohemian self. The Lloyd Webbers were forced out in 1973, relocating to the remarkably similar Sussex Mansions on the Old Brompton Road, nearby.

Initially, the idea was to produce the show at Oxford, since Andrew was still technically enrolled there, and so, although he was on "sabbatical," Andrew trooped regularly up to Oxfordshire to plan the production; he and Tim had gone so far as to engage production and lighting designers. On January 26, 1966, *The Daily Express* announced:

After Rodgers and Hammerstein, Lloyd Webber and Rice? A long-distance forecast which could be right.

Andrew Lloyd Webber, 17-year-old Oxford undergraduate son of Dr. William Lloyd Webber, 51, director of the London College of Music, has collaborated on a full-scale musical show with his friend Timothy Rice, 21.

Andrew has been given time off by his college, Magdalen, to complete the 14 songs for the show, which is set in the nineteenth century.

Rather quickly, though, it became apparent that Oxford was not the ideal venue for *The Likes of Us.* The show, a kind of *Oliver!* knockoff complete with orphans and street urchins, needed a large cast and a sizable complement of child actors. Besides, Elliott had his eye on a bigger prize: the West End. He persuaded Tim and Andrew they should forget about Oxford and go for the real money—fifty thousand pounds in Britain alone if the show was a hit. "Andrew has written some very colourful tunes," Elliott told the press. "I've every confidence that we can get this on to the West End in the autumn."

His confidence turned out to be misplaced. Indeed, one wonders why Elliott ever thought he could produce a full-scale musical by two unknowns, the younger of whom was not even eighteen yet. Elliott may have known his way around London's literary and publishing circles, but he was inexperienced in the ways of the West End; although Elliott enlisted the assistance of another friend in publishing, the formidable Ernest Hecht, he still found it impossible to raise the necessary money to produce the show. He and Hecht bravely announced a Dublin premiere for the fall of 1968, but nothing ever came of it. In the end, only a demo record was produced for Southern Music; the score was not published, and *The Likes of Us* slunk back into obscurity.

In retrospect, it is easy to see why *The Likes of Us* never made it. For one thing, Britain didn't really need a Lionel Bart homage, honored as Bart may have been at the time for reviving the flagging fortunes of the British musical in 1960. One Bart was enough. For another, Lloyd Webber's music simply wasn't very good: the surviving demo is a ragamuffin's chorus based on a simple, undistinguished sequential idea—a patter song that, mercifully, Lloyd Webber never reused. Other tunes, however, were banked for future employment: twelve years later, one in particular would resurface as the centerpiece of the *Variations* for solo cello and rock band.

Lloyd Webber learned a number of lessons from the failure of *The Likes of Us.* The first and most important was: any performance is better than none. Far better that Dr. Barnardo should have tried to save his souls at Oxford, far better that Andrew and Tim have a chance to see and hear how their ideas played on an amateur stage than that they wind up with nothing to show for their efforts. Juvenilia aside, Andrew had never heard his music performed; having dropped out of university, he had denied himself the opportunity that every student composer has to try out his works on his fellow students, to hear his music come to life and not just have it sit mutely on score paper.

It is interesting to speculate how the Lloyd Webber–Rice career might have fared had they had the opportunity to try out *The Likes of Us,* for it set a pattern they were to follow almost as long as they worked together—and is the source of much criticism that has followed them ever since. Both *Jesus Christ Superstar* and *Evita* were developed in the recording studio, not in the theater: to get them on stage, they had to be wrung into performing shape by directors with strong ideas of their own. *Jeeves,* which Lloyd Webber wrote with Alan Ayckbourn, was the first Lloyd Webber show expressly written for the theater, and it was a disaster.

Of even more consequence, as far as Andrew's personal finances were concerned, was some advice he got from Bob Kingston of Southern Music. When Andrew and Tim were about halfway through the show's composition, Kingston called Lloyd Webber into his office. "Listen," he said, "under the contract you have with us, we're entitled to 50 percent of anything you earn. But we cannot morally, as publishers, take it out of the theatre royalties. That's something different, and it's called a grand right." A grand right is what a composer earns from theatrical presentations of his music, as distinct from publishing royalties. This was the first time Andrew heard the two magic words that became firmly etched in his mind, to his great enrichment.

Undaunted by the failure of *The Likes of Us,* Tim and Andrew soldiered on. In April 1967 they had a pair of songs recorded on EMI by a singer named Ross Hannaman, a blond who had been named by the readers of *The Evening Standard* as Girl of the Year. Hannaman had come Tim's way in his capacity as a management trainee, and he was supervising her debut. Released a few months later, the disc was called "Down Through Summer," backed with "I'll Give All My Love to Southend." On the "A" side, Hannaman sang: "I don't care if I live or die/days go on drifting by." Later that same year, they wrote two more songs for Hannaman, "1969" and "Probably on Thursday," released, like the first disc, on EMI's Columbia label. (Only in Britain is the Columbia name owned by EMI; in the United States and elsewhere, the brand name belongs to CBS.)

These records, which were not hits, are nonetheless valuable documents for what they reveal about Andrew and Tim. The melody for "1969," for example, is a direct note-for-note appropriation of Beethoven's *Für Elise,* the little study that every beginning pianist encounters, slightly souped up with a pretentious harpsichord arrangement. The ballad "Probably on Thursday" owes its patrimony to the luminous slow movement of Dvorak's *New World* Symphony. Stealing from dead classical composers is an old and honorable pop tradition, not a capital offense: a group called the Toys had done it with a keyboard piece by Bach, which they had released two years earlier as "A Lover's Concerto," while Dvorak's luminescent melody had already been a hit for the jazz trombonist and singer Jack Teagarden under the title, "Goin' Home." But nowhere on "1969" is there any indication that the song is anything other than an original work by Andrew Lloyd Webber. (As we shall see, tunes from "Down Through Summer" and "Probably on Thursday"* later found their way prominently into two of Lloyd Webber's theater scores.)

Equally revealing are the lyrics. Those for "1969" give a hint of the gloomier, more pessimistic core that even then lurked beneath Tim's sunny exterior:

> *And then I heard the songs they sung*
> *A hundred tongues*
> *Began to shout*
> *And then a panic in the hall*
> *I heard them call*
> *We can't get out*
> *The world had died*
> *They meant it to*
> *And no-one cried*
> *For no-one knew*
> *I took a photo of the night*
> *In black and white*
> *In colours too*
> *Hey I hate the picture 1969*
> *Lord I hate the picture 1969*

If anything, the lyrics to "Probably on Thursday" are even gloomier: "You never listen/You want to hurt me/You'll be unfaithful/Possibly on Wednesday/Probably on Thursday." This was a side of Tim that only a few knew about. Andrew may have seemed the moody one, but in fact his humors were like passing storms: a brief, intense eruption of rage and then sunny skies. Tim, on the other hand, was slower to boil and slower to cool; unlike Lloyd Webber, Rice was capable of harboring a grudge and carrying it for years. The impermanence of relationships, the inevitability of betrayal—these are themes that recur in Rice's lyrics, reaching their apogee of alienation two decades later in his masterpiece, *Chess.*

At this point, neither Rice nor Lloyd Webber had a clear idea of what they were about. Andrew wanted to write shows, and Tim wanted to write pop songs; they had tried each path, so far with little success. With the future of the partnership in doubt, Andrew decided to further his formal musical education, in the hopes of improving his technique and becoming a better composer. Shortly after leaving Oxford, he had taken a course in orchestration at the Guildhall School of Music, where Bill had recommended a teacher named Barclay Wilson. Now, for the 1967–1968 school year, he enrolled in the Royal College of Music for further orchestration study.

One of the hoariest anecdotes in the Lloyd Webber canon concerns his father's remark that Andrew ought not to spend too much time at the Royal College for fear that the conservatory would educate away his natural melodic gifts. This may tax the credulity of non-musicians, but Bill was right. In the mid-sixties, conservatories in both America and Europe were in the grip of twelve-tone fever, the academics having succumbed to the relentless proselytizing of the modernists. A young composer who wandered into their clutches writing like Dvorak would, a year later, wander out writing like Webern. (Imagine what a Webernist "Probably on Thursday" would sound like.) Progressivism was the

---

*More than twenty years later, Lloyd Webber maintained that the melody of "Probably on Thursday" had been altered by the arranger to more closely approximate the Dvorak tune. In 1989 he recorded a demo tape in Paris of the original version of the song with his wife, Sarah Brightman. Tim Rice even wrote some new lyrics, a portion of which was used.

death of melody, deemed a hackneyed and useless relic of a discredited romantic past. Bill, an insider whose infatuation with romanticism was undiminished, knew this perfectly well. By crippling Andrew's technique he very likely saved his soul.

In the midst of this floundering, relief came from an unexpected quarter. Andrew and Tim had been so dazzled by the lights of the West End that they were blindsided when Alan Doggett, the choir director at Colet Court,* wrote to them requesting a cantata for the school's annual spring concert. Doggett, a discreet homosexual, was enthusiastic about music but only modestly gifted. He had been at Westminster Underschool as a history teacher, but he had also led the school choir. One of his choirboys was Julian; thus he made the acquaintance of the Lloyd Webber family, and from time to time he would help out Andrew with the niceties of notation, making sure, among other things, that the number of beats in the bar equaled the key signature.

Doggett's offer was simple: to write a short piece—fifteen minutes or so—suitable for an end-of-term concert. There was no suggestion of subject matter, although it was understood that the work would have some quasi-religious significance. The year before, Doggett had had success with a piece by composer Herbert Chappell called *The Daniel Jazz,* and had even recorded it. Religious pop was in the air: Novello (Bill's publisher) had also brought out a piece called *Jonah Man Jazz* by Michael Hurd. Something along the same line, then, would be most welcome.

Colet Court was in Hammersmith, at the time in a fine old red-brick pile in Hammersmith Road built in 1890. In early 1968 both Colet Court and Saint Paul's were preparing to take possession of their new premises just across the river. The piece by Lloyd Webber and Rice, to be premiered on March 1, would be the last event in the old Assembly Hall, a three-sided room that also functioned, inconveniently, as a passageway. It was hardly the most auspicious of venues, but any dream would do.

Andrew and Tim talked it over. What did they have to lose? They wanted to write songs, and if the Bible had to be their text, well, what of it? At least there would be an audience, even if it consisted solely of bored parents dragged there by their importunate offspring. It certainly was a challenge, writing a dramatic work for a chorus of prepubescent boys. And so they took the job, receiving a one-hundred-guinea advance from Novello. From the beginning they knew that, unlike *The Daniel Jazz,* there would be soloists in their piece. They also knew that it would be musically simple, suitable for the small-scale kind of entertainment it was to be. There would be no orchestra, of course, just a piano. But it was a start.

Working mostly at nights and on weekends (Tim, after all, was gainfully employed, and Andrew was studying at the Royal College), they finished the piece in about two months. Some of the arrangements were done on a visit to Aunt Vi in Ventimiglia. In collaborating, first they talked out the plot, then Andrew wrote his melodies, after which Tim would fit his lyrics to them. It was a pattern they would follow throughout their partnership.

As his source, Tim nominally raided Genesis, but in reality his inspiration was *The Wonder Book of Bible Stories.* Unlike *The Likes of Us,* there was to be no dialogue; the action would be told entirely through song. "We realized," Andrew said later, "that it was possible to put together something continuous without a narrative line, without that ghastly moment when the violins are lifted and the dialogue stops. Without realizing it at first, we found that you could switch styles crazily throughout the whole thing, mixing up musical comedy numbers with calypso, country and western and Elvis Presley. And the basic story is such a good plot." Without meaning to, they had stumbled across the form, if not yet the content, of opera.

The story was the tale of Joseph and his brethren, one of the Bible's great epics of upward mobility, and one of Tim's favorites. Joseph, the favorite of Jacob's twelve sons, is resented by his brothers, both for his dreams (which predict that he will one day lord over them all), and his splendid coat of many colors. One day, the brothers set upon him, rend his coat, and sell him into slavery in Egypt. The predictive power of Joseph's dreams, though, eventually brings him to the attention of the pharaoh. The young man forecasts the seven years of plenty and the seven years of famine, whereupon he is made Egypt's economic minister and guides the land through the years of crisis. His father and brothers, refugees from Canaan, come to beg for food and, at the end, all are joyfully reunited.

What to call the show? *How to Succeed in Egypt Without Really Trying,* suggested Tim, characteristically. Or how about *Pal Joseph*? Finally, they settled on *Joseph and the Amazing Technicolor Dreamcoat,* and so *Joseph* was born—a bright, innocent child of its time, the go-go British sixties, brought into the world by a church organist's son and a wry agnostic who hadn't been to church for a decade.

Joseph was premiered with Doggett conducting, doggedly. The several hundred or so parents in the audience applauded politely and went home. No agents called; the West End and Broadway were mum; in the far distance, Hollywood was silent. But one man liked it very much, and that man was Bill Lloyd Webber. He was unwilling to see *Joseph* die so quickly; after all that effort, he was not about to let his elder son get

*Started in 1881, Colet Court is the preparatory school for Saint Paul's School, which was founded in 1509 by John Colet, dean of the cathedral.

discouraged and quit music before he knew whether he could really do it or not. "He'd be fed up all his life," said Bill, who knew something about being fed up. Dr. Lloyd Webber organized a second performance, this time at his church, Central Hall, Westminster. That performance—revised, expanded, and reorchestrated to include a rock group—took place on May 12, 1968, at eight o'clock in the evening. It changed everyone's life:

POP GOES JOSEPH

> *'Give us food' the brothers said.*
> *'Dieting is for the birds.'*
> *Joseph gave them all they wanted*
> *Second helpings, even thirds . . .*

Even on paper the happy bounce of lyrics like these comes through. They are exactly right for singing by several hundred boys' voices. With two organs, guitars, drums and a large orchestra the effect is irresistible.

The quicksilver vitality of *Joseph and His Amazing Technicolor Dreamcoat,* the new pop oratorio heard at Central Hall, Westminster, last Sunday, is attractive indeed. On this evidence the pop idiom—beat rhythms and Bacharachian melodies—is most enjoyably capable of being used in extended form.

Musically, "Joseph" is not all gold. It needs more light and shade. A very beautiful melody, "Close Every Door To Me," is one of the few points when the hectic pace slows down. The snap and crackle of the rest of the work tends to be too insistent, masking the impact of the words which, unlike many in pop, are important.

But such reservations seem pedantic when matched against "Joseph's" infectious overall character. Throughout its twenty-minute duration it bristles with wonderfully singable tunes. It entertains. It communicates instantly, as all good pop should. And it is a considerable piece of barrier-breaking by its creators, two men in their early twenties—Tim Rice, the lyricist, and Andrew Lloyd Webber, who wrote the music.

The performers last Sunday were the choir, school and orchestra of Colet Court, the St. Paul's junior school, with three solo singers and a pop group called The Mixed Bag. It was an adventurous experiment for a school, yet Alan Doggett, who conducted, produced a crisp, exciting and undraggy performance which emphasized the rich expansiveness of pop rather than the limitations of its frontiers.

Thus Derek Jewell, the jazz and pop critic, in *The Sunday Times* of May 19, 1968. Jewell had not come to the concert in his professional capacity; his presence was serendipitous, occasioned by the fact that his son Nicholas was in the chorus. Jewell was not in the habit of attending, much less reviewing, school concerts, but he finally relented to his son's pestering and went along.

Joseph was very short, so to round out the evening, the concert was turned into a Lloyd Webber family affair: Bill played the organ, Julian played the Saint-Saens *Cello Concerto,* and John Lill played piano pieces by Haydn, Prokofiev, and Chopin. Admission was two shillings sixpence (about thirty cents in American currency at the time), and the proceeds went to the Westminster International Centre's drug addiction section.

As luck would have it, Jewell was not the only journalist present among the crowd of more than two thousand. Meirion Bowen of *The Times Educational Supplement* was also there, as were officials from the BBC. "Overlong" and "poorly planned" was the verdict; Bowen called Bill's solos "indifferently played" and said Bill spoiled Julian's concerto with his "tepid piano accompaniment," although there were kind words both for Julian and John Lill. Of *Joseph,* Bowen wrote that it "leaves a curious impression of indiscriminately mixed media . . . it has no real dramatic structure . . . what it eventually boils down to is a series of pop-tunes of the crusading type featured by Cliff Richard, strung together in various ways. None of the tunes is exceptional. . . . In spite of these strictures, it offered abundant evidence of the composer's talent. Contact with the wider world may deepen his vision, but he certainly has the skill and talent to become a successful composer/arranger."

The word had been passed: *Joseph* was on its way. Novello announced that it would bring out the work, and Norrie Paramor, Tim's boss, said he would record it for Decca (having left EMI in February to form his own company and taken Tim along with him). Another performance followed on November 9, 1968, this one at Saint Paul's Cathedral at the invitation of the dean, the Very Reverend Martin Gloster Sullivan; still growing, the changeling *Joseph* now lasted thirty-five minutes. Andrew, resplendent in his velvet frock coats with the upturned collars—a mod Mozart manqué—and Tim, of the long, flowing blond locks, were fast becoming catnip to London's enthusiastic press corps, and reporters fell hungrily on Tim's quotable witticisms. "Look up Chapter Thirty-Nine, it's hysterical," Rice challenged *The Sunday Times* just before the concert. "Potiphar's wife rips off Joseph's clothes, then doesn't want him. The mind boggles as to why." The reviews were glowing.

In response to Bowen's criticism, Tim and Andrew added several new songs to *Joseph*, including the vaudeville two-step, "Potiphar," which contained the memorable lyric:

> *Potiphar had very few cares,*
> *He was one of Egypt's millionaires.*
> *Having made a fortune buying shares in pyramids.*
> *Potiphar had made a huge pile,*
> *Owned a large percentage of the Nile,*
> *Meant that he could really live in style and he did.*

In writing the new material, Rice and Lloyd Webber had their eyes on the November concert—and, beyond that, to a Central Hall encore scheduled for January 28, 1969—but already the recording was taking on a life of its own and even superseding the idea of a live performance. When the Decca album was released at the beginning of 1969 (the single, issued simultaneously, was "Close Every Door" and "The Coat of Many Colors"), it created something of a splash. Decca plugged it with a large advertisement in *Record Mirror,* in which the name of the ad hoc performing group, The Joseph Consortium (consisting of a rock group called the Mixed Bag, whose lead singer David Daltrey was a distant cousin of The Who's Roger Daltrey; Bill on the Hammond organ; and Tim Rice singing the role of Pharaoh) was given greater prominence than the work's title—and the names of the composers were nowhere to be found. Another ad, in *Record Retailer,* quoted Jewell's review, among others, and shouted: "1969's most astounding album is here already. . . ."

The January 1969 release of *Joseph* received wide coverage—improbably wide, by American standards, for it was reviewed in every major newspaper and numerous record journals as well. Not bad for a couple of unknowns. But Rice and Lloyd Webber were benefiting from their Little England environment: living in a comparatively small country, with only one city of any importance in the entertainment world and a hotly competitive media center at that, they were practically assured recognition and a certain implicit support, at least initially. Besides, Paramor was behind the project, and everyone respected his talent and taste. Not to mention his marketing muscle: the album sold three thousand copies in the first month.

Again, the reviews were glowing: "This is going to anger a few, niggle a few more—and astound and delight a lot, many, many more," said one; "Ways are now open for a real pop opera," said another. In an attempt to capitalize on the album's press, Daltrey and the Mixed Bag released "Potiphar" on January 31, also on Decca: "some excellent lyrics and melodies and really all absolutely splendid" said *Record Mirror.* (Daltrey was never able to duplicate his famous relative's success, though, and he and the Bag faded away.)

So, so, so: *Joseph.* From unlikely beginnings, it evolved into a charming show with a complicated performing history. Essentially, there were five versions of *Joseph and the Amazing Technicolor Dreamcoat.** First came the original Colet Court performance in March 1968. Version Two was the slightly longer arrangement heard twice at Central Hall, once at Saint Paul's, and recorded. The third version was presented at the Edinburgh Festival in September 1972 in an imaginative production by director Frank Dunlop of the Young Vic and starring Gary Bond; it soon thereafter found its way to the Young Vic and then to the Roundhouse. Version Four was an even further expanded *Joseph,* created when the Dunlop production moved to the Albery Theatre in February 1973; it was recorded that fall, and four years later the Albery version was presented at the Brooklyn Academy of Music in New York City. The last edition was seen at the Entermedia Theater in lower Manhattan in 1981, was transferred uptown to the Royale Theatre in January 1982, and was recorded the same year. In 1973 there was talk of a film version, but nothing ever came of it. Keeping track of *Joseph* is not quite as complicated as tracing the various editions of *Boris Godunov,* perhaps, but it is tricky just the same.

Although *Joseph* underwent a number of transformations as it wended its way from Hammersmith to Broadway over a span of fourteen years, its core remained remarkably stable. Whenever Lloyd Webber and Rice revised it, they simply added to it, in the style to which audiences had become accustomed. Inevitably, there is the aura of the soufflé about *Joseph:* puncture the two-act, ninety-minute Broadway version and it quickly collapses almost to its original size. But what remains is still tasty.

In setting the tale, Lloyd Webber adopted a straightforward, diatonic approach. The keys are basic and, aside from a few 7/8 bars, so are the time signatures; on the page, *Joseph* is disarmingly simple. This naïveté, of course, was partly dictated by the original venue and partly by Andrew's own inexperience. Yet *Joseph* is not to be lightly regarded. Even then, Lloyd Webber's music had a way of looking ordinary and sounding extraordinary, a trait the best composers share. From first note to last, *Joseph and the Amazing Technicolor Dreamcoat* is a bold debut.

---

*The American orthography was the result of legal action by Technicolor, which insisted that Rice and Lloyd Webber also use the trademark ® sign in the title. When Andrew replied that they would change the word to "Eastmancolor," or even "Color-by-Deluxe," the demand was dropped.

The basic *Joseph* begins with a chorus, "Jacob and Sons," a cheerful up-tempo E-major shout in 4/4 that relays the story's background with simple joy:

Way way back many centuries ago,   Jacob, Jacob and sons,
not long after the Bible began,   depended on farming to earn their keep,
Jacob lived in the land of Canaan,   Jacob, Jacob and sons,
a fine example of a family man.   spent all of their days in the fields with sheep.

In the Dunlop production, when *Joseph* finally made it to the stage, this number was preceded by an overture that, in true Broadway style, teased the audience with a number of themes to come: the coat song, the country-and-western parody "One More Angel in Heaven," and Joseph's final number, "Any Dream Will Do," in which he comes on stage and sings: "May I return/to the beginning/the light is dimming/and the dream is too," thus turning the show into a flashback. By this time, too, the character of the Narrator had entered the picture, a dispassionate observer who relates the events of the story and provides a framework for the drama.

On Broadway, the Narrator's role was further expanded to include a new prologue called "You Are What You Feel," a beautiful song that gives *Joseph* something of the feel of Carl Orff's exquisite folk opera, *Der Mond* (which also uses a narrator). Its melody, heard again at the beginning of the second act in "Pharaoh's Story," is a gentle variation of the trumpet fanfare that will open "Jacob and Sons"; instead of launching headlong into the action, it leads the listener in reflectively.

The opening chorus turns into an ode to Joseph's splendid coat and hints at the boy's narcissism. No wonder the brothers don't like him:

I look handsome, I look smart
I am a walking work of art
Such a dazzling coat of many colours
How I love my coat of many colours.

The coat was "red and yellow and green and brown and scarlet and black and ochre and peach and ruby and olive and violet and fawn and lilac and gold and chocolate and mauve and cream and crimson and silver and rose and azure and lemon and russet and grey and purple and white and pink and orange and blue."

"Joseph's Dreams" follows, a rocking F-major lullaby in 6/8 in which Joseph relates his night visions of his brothers' sheaves of corn bowing to his sheaves and of the sun, moon, and eleven stars bowing down before his star; at its end, the song turns into a jaunty syncopated chorus in B-flat in which the brothers sing: "The accuracy of the dreams we brothers do not know/But one thing we are sure about, the dreamer has to go." (One of the principal differences between the early forms of *Joseph* and its stage incarnation is a slight emendation of the words to make the characters active participants. Thus, the original form of the lyric above read: "The accuracy of the dreams the brothers did not know/But one thing they were sure about, the dreamer had to go.")

After "Poor, Poor Joseph," a short recitative for the Narrator and chorus recounting Joseph's enslavement, comes "One More Angel in Heaven," the first of the score's overt pastiches. This song and the later numbers "Those Canaan Days" and "Benjamin Calypso" were added for the Dunlop production at the Albery. They contribute little, except to give the brothers more to do. "One More Angel," an ersatz country ditty—one of the worst songs Lloyd Webber ever wrote—is followed by a reprise of "Poor, Poor Joseph." Reviewing the show at the Albery in February 1973, Michael Billington of *The Guardian* compared the expanded West End manifestation unfavorably with its Edinburgh Festival form. "We now get witless jokes like a pearl-dripping Sphinx and a drag Queen Victoria appearing to Joseph as he is led into Egypt. And new tunes have been added including a sublimely irrelevant Western number to be sung round Jacob's old homestead, now apparently shifted to Arizona: this is not so much painting the lily as pulling its petals apart one by one." The "once charming" *Joseph,* said Billington, "has been sacrificed on the altar of the great god, Showbiz."

Dunlop's high camp production, though, had many happy elements as well, and overall the reviews were quite favorable. There was a soft-shoe number by the brothers clad only in bath towels and gold lamé boaters (indeed, the cast was nearly naked throughout the show). "Song of the King," Rice and Lloyd Webber's homage to their idol Elvis Presley, was done up in true white-suited, pelvis-wriggling style. The cast included Bond as Joseph, Peter Reeves as the Narrator, Joan Heal as Potiphar's Wife, and an actor billed simply as Gordon was Pharaoh; Anthony Bowles conducted.

JOSEPH AND THE AMAZING TECHNICOLOR DREAMCOAT

Bill Hutton, star of the 1982 Broadway version of Joseph, *displays his coat of many colors.*

Two scenes from the 1982 Broadway production of Joseph. *Above: Not recognizing their long-lost sibling, Joseph's brethren plead for Benjamin's life near the end of the show. Left: Jacob gives Joseph his amazing technicolor dreamcoat.*

Two scenes from the Broadway Joseph, *the show's fifth incarnation, which opened at the Entermedia in New York's East Village before moving uptown. Right: Tom Carder's Pharaoh was a homage to Rice and Lloyd Webber's fondness for Elvis Presley.*

T*wo scenes from the high-camp Frank Dunlop production of* Joseph, *first seen at the Edinburgh Festival and brought in 1974 to the West End. Gary Bond played Joseph.*

The controversial 1971 Tom O'Horgan staging of Jesus Christ Superstar at the Mark Hellinger Theatre in New York. The cast included Jeff Fenholt as Jesus, Yvonne Elliman as Mary Magdalene (left and top), and Ben Vereen as Judas (above).

O'Horgan's elaborate Broadway production of Superstar *was the subject of protests from Christians and Jews alike. The American Jewish Committee issued a seven-page report denouncing the show. Some blacks even objected to the casting of Vereen as Judas. Still, the show ran for almost two years.*

Above, right, and opposite, top:

O'Horgan's 1972 restaging of Superstar *at the new Universal Amphitheater in Los Angeles. In the dramatic open-air setting, the show was a sensation.*

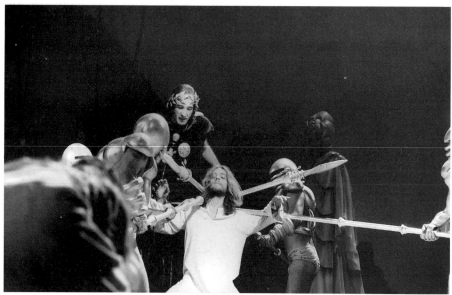

Left:

○*ne of the many stadium concert performances of* Superstar *during the summer of 1971.*

Superstar *around the world. Right: Elliman sings "I Don't Know How to Love Him," one of the show's hit songs. Below: The Los Angeles production of* Superstar. *Opposite: Scenes from the Shiki production: done Kabuki-style in Tokyo in 1973 (top), and the Jerusalem Shiki production in 1989 (bottom).*

Right:

Christ on the Cross, *as staged by Jim Sharman for the 1972* Superstar *London production, which went on to become the longest-running musical in British history. Paul Nicholas played Jesus.*

The original British album cover.

Right:

The Palace Theatre, where Superstar *played for eight years. In 1983 Lloyd Webber bought the theater.*

Scenes from the Sharman production.

David Hemmings as Bertie Wooster in Lloyd Webber's only flop, the ill-starred Jeeves. *Lloyd Webber wrote the show with the popular playwright Alan Ayckbourn, but burdened by a cumbersome, talky libretto, the show closed after little more than a month.*

When it was first seen in Edinburgh (where it was conducted by Alan Doggett) and later at the Roundhouse in London, the Dunlop *Joseph* was still only a single forty-minute act, on a double bill with excerpts from the medieval Wakefield miracle plays. For the Albery, it was decided that the show needed a hipper, more commercial first act, so Andrew and Tim set out to compose some new material. Andrew dutifully beetled away, but Tim, more susceptible to the comings and goings of the Muse, found himself unable to come up with much of anything. In the end, they only managed a few songs, among them something called "Seven Years," a narrative for Jacob, and "I Don't Think I'm Wanted Back at Home." In desperation, two television situation-comedy writers, Ray Galton and Alan Simpson, were commissioned to provide dialogue; based loosely on the miracle-play model, the new singspiel was dubbed *Jacob's Journey* and starred Paul Brooke as God.

At first bow, nearly everyone hated *Jacob's Journey*. "Instantly expendable," said Billington. "I suggest arriving at interval time," offered B. A. Young of *The Financial Times*. Only Irving Wardle of *The Times* had some kind words for the first half, although he managed to misname it *Joseph's Journey*. "Still," said Wardle, "the dialogue is out of tune with what surrounds it: it is too knowing, too close to show business to fit in with the work of Webber and Rice whose basic strength is that they think these stories worth telling without anachronistic sophistications or joke characters." Well before the end of the seven-month run, *Jacob's Journey* was dropped (Simpson mounted his own production, sans Jacob prologue, in Dublin in 1974), and *Joseph* was fleshed out by the simple expedient of reprising several of the show's songs at the end, during the course of which the Narrator thanks Joseph: "It's been great to narrate for you/I hope I can do it again." Clearly, it was a provisional, not a satisfactory, solution.

When the show came to Brooklyn, where it opened on December 30, 1976, with Cleavon Little (of *Blazing Saddles* fame) as the Narrator and David-James Carroll (who twelve years later would star in Rice's *Chess* on Broadway) as Joseph, the American critics were divided. Clive Barnes, then unaccountably riding a wave of Britcrit chic as the theater critic of *The New York Times*, called it "peculiarly dated . . . [the music] has no originality . . . the cast was pretty good." Martin Gottfried of *The New York Post* noted that Joseph's brethren "are so young, pretty, jeaned, and bare-chested that they seemed less likely to be cruising down the Nile than down 42nd Street. The few women in the show are costumed as grotesques—gold lamé and cantilevered bras. I wouldn't call this production obsessively straight."

After the longueurs of "One More Angel," the show's next number, "Potiphar," is one of its strongest, boasting one of Rice's wittiest lyrics and Lloyd Webber's deftest parodies. Joseph is falsely accused by Potiphar's wife of trying to rape her and is cast into prison; there, he sings the ballad "Close Every Door," a mournful waltz in F minor in which Joseph laments his cruel fate. For the first time, Andrew's gift for soaring melody is apparent.

The first act finale is "Go, Go, Go Joseph." In durance vile, Joseph interprets the dreams of his fellow prisoners:

> *Both men were servants of Pharaoh the King*
> *Both in the doghouse for doing their thing.*
> *One was his baker, a cook in his prime,*
> *One was his butler, the Jeeves of his time.*

The chorus cheers him on with shouts of "Go, go, go Joseph/You know what they say/Go, go, go Joseph/You'll make it someday," and the act ends in a G-major burst of glory.

"Pharaoh's Song" opens Act Two. The Narrator introduces the monarch to the strains of the prologue: "No one had right or a vote but the king./In short, you could say he was fairly right wing." The chorus mocks him, evoking the earlier "Poor, Poor Joseph"—"Poor, poor Pharaoh, what cha gonna do/Dreams are haunting you, what cha gonna do?" Then Pharaoh himself appears and launches into the "Song of the King."

This has emerged as the show's most popular number. Both Tim and Andrew were crazy about Elvis, and they affectionately send him up, replete with a Presleyan chorus of *bap shu wa du wa bop bap shu wa du wa*. "Don't be cruel, Joseph," sings the king. "Help me, I beg of you." Joseph forecasts the future in "Pharaoh's Dreams Explained"—"All these things you saw in your pyjamas/Are a long-range forecast for your farmers"—and Pharaoh hires him on the spot in "Stone the Crows." (This couplet is alternately praised by those who think Rice a clever lyricist and condemned by those who think his work meretricious—the Lloyd Webber–Rice critical reception in microcosm.)

At this point, the mock–Jacques Brel chanson, "Those Canaan Days," was interpolated, a tiresome bit of comic business for the brothers. They journey to Egypt ("The Brothers Come to Egypt") and throw themselves on the mercy of Pharaoh's minister ("Grovel, Grovel"), whom they do not recognize. Joseph seizes the opportunity to have a little vengeful fun and plants a golden cup in Benjamin's sack ("Who's the Thief?"). There follows the best of the pastiche songs, "Benjamin Calypso," in which the sons protest the lad's innocence: "Oh no/Not he/How you can accuse him is a mystery/Save him/take me/Benjamin is straighter than the tall palm tree." Joseph, of course, relents and reveals his identity ("Joseph All the Time") and embraces his father ("Jacob in Egypt").

The finale is "Any Dream Will Do," a radiant anthem in C major with a darker undercurrent in the text:

May I return to the beginning.   *Give me my colored coat, my amazing colored coat.*
The light is dimming and the dream is too.   *Give me my colored coat, my amazing colored coat.*
The world and I, we are still waiting.
Still hesitating. Any dream will do.

(In a recycling practice that would become habitual, the melody to which the final two lines of the show are sung had been used by Andrew before, as a minor phrase in the 1967 Ross Hannaman song "Probably On Thursday.")

Practically from the start, *Joseph* found a home in schools and colleges across Britain and, soon enough, in the United States. (Later, it played in English-speaking lands around the world, finding favor from South Africa to Australia.) In its primary form, *Joseph* was easily staged in an academic environment (or not staged at all, simply performed as an oratorio). It first came to America in May 1970, in a production at the College of the Immaculate Conception in Douglaston, Queens, New York City. One of its many amateur productions occurred in Philadelphia on May 1, 1974; the local critics were not enchanted, but *Variety* was. "The music sells the show," noted the showbiz bible. "*Dreamcoat* is proof enough that Webber and Rice are no flash-in-the-pan team." The cast of eighteen was augmented by the Philadelphia Archdiocesan Boys Choir. But the days of *Joseph* as a show performed for and by children were numbered.

"*Dreamcoat* is dream come true for producer, 25," ran the headline in the January 10, 1982, edition of the *Baltimore Sun.* The young impresario was Susan R. Rose, who with her colleague Gail Berman had acquired performing rights three years earlier from the Robert Stigwood Organisation, which by this time owned them, to mount *Joseph* professionally. With twenty-seven investors backing the show, *Joseph* ran for seven months at Ford's Theatre in Washington. There it attracted the attention of Broadway producer Zev Bufman, the man who had put Elizabeth Taylor in *The Little Foxes.* Bufman offered to coproduce it in New York City. Both Lloyd Webber and Rice, by this time in the last stages of their partnership, were hesitant in light of the critical thumping the Dunlop *Joseph* had received in Brooklyn. Eventually, though, they agreed, and the show opened on November 18, 1981, at the Entermedia Theater, a former Yiddish theater on Second Avenue (once known as the Jewish Rialto) in the East Village, with Bill Hutton, a blond beachboy, in the title role.

There were several important changes. The score was reorchestrated (by Martin Silvestri and Jeremy Stone), new sets were designed by Karl Eigsti, and the show was directed by Tony Tanner with verve and panache. The tradition of having a black male Narrator was broken: the Broadway *Joseph*'s great discovery was Laurie Beechman, whose previous credits had included minor roles in *Annie* and the swing understudy in *The Pirates of Penzance.* Outfitted in a red fez and flaring harem pants, Beechman's big, liquid brown eyes flashed, and her arresting, emotional contralto boomed. Far more involved in the action than previous Narrators (another Tanner innovation), Beechman gave the show a sturdier, more substantial feel. The choir boys, however, were gone: unlike in Britain, where boys' choruses grow on trees, choirs were scarce in America, and no producer was about to engage half a hundred or so Equity choristers for what by now had become a minor element. Out they went, their function made redundant by the eleven brothers and a few women.

This time, New York was conquered. Even the curmudgeonly John Simon of *New York* magazine was won over: "Tony Tanner has directed and choreographed it as a bright, impudent child might have done." Mel Gussow of *The New York Times* called Lloyd Webber, "one of the most inventive artists in contemporary musical theater." Only Clive Barnes, his cachet somewhat reduced by his demotion to the tabloid *New York Post,* remained resistant to *Joseph*'s charms. The production was so successful downtown that, on January 27, 1982, it moved up Broadway to the Royale Theatre (after being announced first for the Plymouth, where Trevor Nunn's day-long, one-hundred-dollars-a-ticket production of *Nicholas Nickleby* was holding forth); the cast album was made just before the move, in December. The top ticket price was twenty-five dollars, the lowest on Broadway—the last time an Andrew Lloyd Webber musical could make that claim.

Why the success this time? Part of it was quality, of course, but part was simple zeitgeist. *Joseph* was only one of many shows with religious themes to appear on and off Broadway that season. Always in motion, the pendulum of American culture had swung away from faux-Nietzschean, God-is-dead pessimism toward a renewed interest in religious subjects. Even when organized religion was savaged, as Catholicism was in Christopher Durang's vicious black comedy *Sister Mary Ignatius Explains It All for You,* its power was acknowledged. Inoffensive, even a little bland, *Joseph* capitalized on the feel-good spirit of the times; why, you could even take Sister Mary Ignatius to it.

But who had made smooth the path of the Lord?

"Next Venture" ran the short notice in *The Daily Mail,* just after the first *Joseph* album came out in 1969:

The musical *Hair* shows the new trend towards pop in musical shows: George Harrison is planning a musical written around life
at the Apple office, while Tim Rice and Andrew Lloyd Webber themselves have more ambitious plans in mind.
Their next venture is a pop musical based on the life of Christ.
John the Baptist will appear as a "superb Maharishi character" and Pontius Pilate as one of the all-time misunderstood men.
"But the musical won't be at all disrespectful," says Tim Rice. "One just presumes that Christ had a sense of humour."

The juxtaposition with the Beatles is interesting, indicative of the respect that Rice and Lloyd Webber already had won. Nothing ever came
of the George Harrison musical, nor did John the Baptist ever turn up in the next Lloyd Webber–Rice show, whether as a superb Maharishi
(then the Beatles' well-publicized spiritual and, as it turned out, distinctly fleshly minded guru) or anything else. Still, something was in the
works. It had to be. After an initial sales burst, the *Joseph* album had tailed off and not much was happening under Desmond Elliott's
management. Despite Andrew's exhortations to exclude the grand rights from *Joseph*, Elliott had allowed Novello, the publisher, to keep them,
infuriating the young composer. ("Why do you want to exclude the grand rights to something which is a concert piece?" Elliott asked him. "It's
never going to be done in the theatre.") His importuning sent Elliott back to Novello, where he managed to retrieve 80 percent of the grand
rights, but Andrew had so annoyed Elliott that the agent wrote a letter to Bill, telling him his son was a pest and that he wanted nothing
further do with him.

Now Tim and Andrew were on their own. What to do? Working with Paramor, Tim had access to some of the most important pop stars of
the day, including Cliff Richard, and it seemed likely to Andrew that unless something happened fairly soon the Lloyd Webber–Rice
partnership would last precisely as long as it took Tim to find someone else to write with. Accordingly, Andrew hit upon the rather screwy
notion of starting a museum of pop memorabilia in Carnaby Street—Tim was an expert in pop trivia—in which would be enshrined
everything from Elvis's guitar and John Lennon's dark glasses to P.J. Proby's split pants. In the spring of 1969 Andrew sent a letter to a man
named Sefton Myers, proposing the museum idea; with the note was included a copy of the *Joseph* album.

Myers, 42, had made a fortune in real estate, but like many tycoons, he yearned for something more glamorous. To that end, he had become
involved in the entertainment business; to assist him, he had brought in David Land as his show-business adviser. Land was a fixture in
Wardour Street, an old-fashioned, small-time British producer. He was well liked, but regarded by many in the industry as a figure of fun—a
man who incessantly talked big deals and money but who managed girl pipers and like acts.

Myers had discovered a number of quotidian pop singers and at the time was busy trying to make a star out of David Ballantyne, the brother
of Julian Lloyd Webber's girlfriend (later, wife) Celia. It was proving to be an impossible task, and he needed a new act. So when he received
Andrew's letter, Myers wrote back immediately. Forget the pop museum, he said; instead, he would like to meet both Andrew and Tim and put
them under contract as songwriters. The terms were relatively generous: two thousand pounds in the first year, twenty-five hundred the
second, and three thousand in the third, as advance against royalties, with options that would extend the agreement to ten years. Myers's
management commission would be a flat 25 percent of earnings—very high at a time when agents usually took 10 percent—but without much
hesitation, and no leverage, Rice and Lloyd Webber took the offer. On May 7, 1969, *Record Retailer* noted that Rice had left Paramor "to form
his own company with his writing partner, Andrew Lloyd Webber." The company would be called New Ventures Theatrical Management, Ltd.:

Tim Rice and Andrew Lloyd Webber, who are both being sponsored by property tycoon Sefton Myers, will launch their own firm,
which will be based at 1 Charles Street, London W1. Rice will continue to produce the Mixed Bag and David Daltrey for Norrie
Paramor and both Rice and Lloyd Webber will continue to have their material published by Norrie Paramor Music.

Shortly thereafter, the magazine announced: "Tim Rice and Andrew Lloyd Webber planning followup to *Joseph* album based on Richard the
Lionheart called *Come Back Richard, Your Country Needs You.*"
So Christ was not, after all, to be their next subject; the Crusades was. Or was it? *Come Back Richard* was intended as a sendup of the
peace movement, then approaching its height in the United States.* Tim and Andrew wrote a forty-minute show and put it on at the City of
London School, where Alan Doggett was now teaching. They also worked on the album in the studio, but all that ever resulted, at least as far
as Andrew was concerned, was a title single released by RCA on November 7, 1969. The "B" side, not from *Richard*, was called "Roll on Over

---

*For Tim, in a rare instance of a lyricist's being able to recycle an idea, *Come Back Richard* turned out to be the prototype of his 1983 musical, *Blondel,* written with
composer Stephen Oliver.

the Atlantic," and the performers were Tim Rice and the Webber Group.

Notices were mixed. "Lively little ditty with a join-in chorus and amusing lyrics. Has a gay and danceable rocksteady rhythm," ran one; "A novelty-type record which might just make it . . ." said another. "A rather amusing little ditty that could make it, if given enough playing," said a third. "It cannot be put into any particular slot of modern music, the nearest section being 'bubblegum,' but this has something in it which makes it far better than this form of pop music. Have a listen and see."

Few did. By the time "Richard" was released, however, Rice and Lloyd Webber had other, bigger fish to fry. Flushed by the success of *Joseph* at Saint Paul's, Dean Sullivan had offered the cathedral as the venue for their next biblical treatment and they had already written and recorded a song with the working title "I Only Want to Know."

After *Joseph*, many people had suggested the New Testament be their next subject. The dean, for one, had been especially insistent. At first, Rice wanted to call it simply *Jesus Christ*, but he was afraid that might give offense. So he tacked on an extra word, one that had been recently coined by Andy Warhol. He called the new piece *Jesus Christ Superstar*.

Tim Rice's eventual choice of the name *Jesus Christ Superstar* for his and Andrew's next project was simply good business. Neither Rice nor Lloyd Webber had any particular emotions about the holy name of Jesus: at first, Tim joked, they were thinking of calling the show just plain old *Christ!* — sort of like *Oliver!*, with a twist. No matter how irreverent they may have felt, though, both men knew that to jibe at Jesus without at least a fig leaf of respectability would be fatal, especially in America.

Just three years earlier, John Lennon had started on his downward path into the right's demonology when he made the controversial assertion, "We're more popular than Jesus now." To many teenagers, that puckish observation was nothing more than a slight exaggeration of the Beatles' lofty pop-cultural status, not an assault on the foundations of Christianity. To their less liberal-minded elders, already reeling from the tide of long hair, short skirts, premarital sex, pot smoking, and God, Jesus, or the Holy Ghost only knew what else, it was tantamount to blasphemy.

In Britain, Lennon's nose-thumbing drew the obligatory letters of protest to *The Times* and dark mutterings about the decline of the empire and the end of the world. But in the land of the free, where private morality had been a pressing matter of public concern since the Salem witch trials, the reaction was far more visceral. Parents were horrified and preachers outraged; in August 1966 the Beatles' records were thrown onto bonfires, and there were calls from the pulpit for Lennon's condemnation. Almost overnight, the Beatles had gone from those nice furry lads from Liverpool who only wanted to hold your (or your daughter's) hand to being agents of Satan, who threatened to suborn the youth of a nation.

So *Christ!* was definitely out. The American market, that vast money-making engine of pop culture, was simply too big and too important to risk offending. (The Beatles had been just another Mersey band until they released "I Want To Hold Your Hand" in the United States and appeared on "The Ed Sullivan Show" in 1964; only then had they really triggered international Beatlemania and brought on the big bucks.) What about *Jesus Christ*, then? Nobody had complained about either the subject matter or the treatment of *Joseph and His Amazing Technicolor Dreamcoat* — in fact, "with-it" prelates like the Very Reverend Martin Sullivan had positively endorsed the show.

Father Sullivan's trendiness was something of a national joke in Britain. In 1968 he had shocked fellow men of the cloth when he made a grand entrance by descending from the interior dome of Saint Paul's by parachute. *Joseph* had been part of something he had organized called the Festival of Youth, a rock bash in Christopher Wren's masterpiece during which the noise grew so loud that the dean's hearing was affected. Sullivan confessed later that he prayed for the Lord to "drop the dome on 'em" as he fled outside to the relative quiet of the cathedral steps.

The dean, however, was simply a man of his time. This was the age of pop religion, even in the Church of England, newly liberated across the sectarian divide by a burst of hip, post-Vatican II renewal. Far more than Anglicanism, though, Roman Catholicism was altered almost beyond recognition. The Latin liturgy that had united a global church for centuries was thrown out and replaced by hundreds of local vernaculars, and the great Masses of European composers discarded in favor of African chants and Appalachian folk services. Many Catholics were devastated, but the church officials tried to put the best face on things. Had the soul-satisfying certainties of the Latin Mass disappeared? Very well, then, bishops, priests, and nuns would find relevance, and some measure of solace, in the adolescent angst of Simon and Garfunkel. On high-school religious retreats across America, parochial students dissected the lyrics of "The Sounds of Silence" and other songs of the sixties, searching for hidden Christian significance. No wonder John thought the Beatles were more popular than Jesus. The clergy did, too.

Even so, maybe not *Jesus Christ.* During the summer of 1969, Tim and Andrew had written the title track of what they hoped would be their new album. To avoid controversy, it was called, inoffensively, "Superstar," with a "B" side of "John 19:41," an instrumental elegy. "We were going to call the single 'Jesus Christ,' but we knew we were bound to offend some people," Rice explained. "So we thought we'd reduce their sense of outrage by changing the title. After all, Jesus was a superstar of his day." To be on the safe side, Tim and Andrew enlisted Father Sullivan to provide an imprimatur. The trendy dean was only too happy to oblige:

> There are people who may be shocked by this record. I ask them to listen to it and think again. It is a desperate cry. Who are you Jesus Christ? is the urgent enquiry, and a very proper one at that. The record probes some answers and makes some comparisons. The onus is on the listener to come up with his replies. If he is a Christian let him answer for Christ. The singer says, "Don't get me wrong. I only want to know." He is entitled to some response.

Sullivan's blessing was crucial to the success of "Superstar"—not just the single but the album and, in the hazy distance, any possible stage presentation as well, whether at Saint Paul's in the spring of 1970 or somewhere else. For Tim and Andrew, the "Superstar" single was to be a test, to see if they could get away with it. If the song about Christ was a hit, then it would be on with the show. If, on the other hand, the establishment guardians of public morality—the C. of E., the BBC, et al.—came down on them hard, they would scrap the idea and get on with something else. Tim and Andrew had bandied about the notion of a musical about the Cuban Missile Crisis and, in any event, there was always *Come Back Richard.*

Having covered their High Church bases with Father Sullivan's blandishments (reproduced on the single's dust jacket), Rice and Lloyd Webber set about producing a pop record that would sell. To sing "Superstar," they engaged Murray Head, a twenty-three-year-old Scot from Wick. Head had been in the pop business since his teens. Over the previous three months, he had won a small measure of fame as a cast member of *Hair,* the "tribal love-rock musical" by Galt MacDermott that announced the dawning of the Age of Aquarius. Head's casting was Tim's idea. They had worked together during Tim's EMI days; in 1967 Tim had produced a Head single called "Someday Soon," which had gone nowhere. But Rice believed in Murray and thought his raw urgency was just the quality they were looking for to sell the new song.

Head had a raucous voice, a full crown of regulation, Beatles-issue hair, and dreamy good looks that would ensure attention for the disc. The fact that he had taken his clothes off briefly in *Hair* could not fail to help, either; "Mr. Head's current claim to fame is that he is one of the cast of the nudie musical *Hair,*" leered one newspaper, totally misrepresenting both the spirit and the substance of MacDermott's show. The first "Superstar" publicity photos of Head depicted him wearing a crosslike pendant around his neck. These were hastily retouched by MCA-UK, the newly formed British subsidiary of the Music Corporation of America, which was releasing the single; no sense provoking the public more than necessary.

Flying nearly blind, with only his textbook learning to draw on, Andrew needed six weeks to complete the orchestrations and arrangement for solo singer, backup vocals, rock band, symphony orchestra, and chorus. With Rice and Lloyd Webber acting as their own producers, "Superstar" was recorded, in stereo, in September and released on November 21, 1969. (Ever since his experience with "Probably on Thursday," Andrew insisted on being his own producer; Tim, of course, had produced many records while working for Norrie Paramor.)

Production values were high. Singing the part of a questioning Everyman—his character had not yet evolved into Judas—Head was supported by fifty-six orchestral players, including thirty-five strings, some of them drawn from the London Philharmonic, and by rock musicians from such groups as Joe Cocker's Grease Band, Juicy Lucy, and Wynder K. Frogg. Backup vocals were by the Trinidad Singers, a fourteen-member, all-female black choral group from the West Indies chosen with an eye toward stage presentation. "They not only sing well," said Tim, "but move well." Two other session singers were Sue and Sonny, a well-known U.K. backup vocal duo.

Then Rice and Lloyd Webber sat back to await developments. "I suppose the record will produce some controversy," Andrew told the press ingenuously. "But it is a completely serious attempt to stimulate discussion about Jesus Christ among record buyers." More honestly, it was a completely serious attempt to have a hit record, and if a little notoriety would help, so much the better.

Tim, as usual, was better at fanning these particular flames. "This is in no way intended to be a sensational disc," he said, disingenuously. "We feel that there are certain questions which it is fair to ask about Christ and the basic theme of the record is quite simply, 'What's it all about?'" To another interviewer, Tim allowed that "neither of us is religious: We just want to put on a good show. We're not trying to make any particular religious point. If people want to read into it that Christ was God or not, then they can." To a third, Rice said of his and Andrew's as-yet nonexistent show: "It is a rock musical but it is nothing like [*Hair*]. The only thing that you could say is that it will be more like *Hair* than *Oklahoma!* There will be no justification in the story for any actors to appear without any clothes on. It is not that I have any objection to anybody running around starkers, it's just that it did not happen that way."

With or without nudity, "Superstar" looked to be the right song at the right time, selling three thousand five hundred copies in Britain in a single day shortly after its release. Religious pop was in the air: the Edwin Hawkins Singers had had a hit with the mantralike gospel song "Oh Happy Day," and Norman Greenbaum had struck it rich with "Spirit in the Sky." The ubiquitous Simon and Garfunkel had contributed "Bridge over Troubled Water." Even the Beatles had hopped aboard the Jesus express; on "Let It Be," one of their last songs, Paul McCartney had sung, "When I find myself in times of trouble, Mother Mary comes to me, speaking words of wisdom, let it be." And in country and western, of course, God had never died: "If God is dead, who's that living in my soul?" sang Nat Stuckey and Connie Smith.

A few days before the official release date, Head et al. sang "Superstar" on David Frost's popular television show in Britain. As Frost knew it would, the program provoked angry telephone calls from reflexively offended viewers, who jammed the ITV switchboard for an hour in protest. "This phenomenal performance was depicted by a series of extraordinarily agonising gesticulations and neurotic sounds emanating from a very distressed young man, supported by a bevy of quite charming young ladies who provided a repetitive vocal background," wrote *The Daily Mail*. "I can hardly wait for the promised repeat of this production at Saint Paul's Cathedral." An angry Ulsterman, Mr. Arnold Corrigan of Derry, wrote, "Frost's Jesus Christ, the superstar, is the ultimate degradation and proves conclusively that in 1969 the one true God is— money."

"Superstar" was Andrew's best song to date, a three-chord rocker that evolves into a more complicated contest between the familiar Superstar chorus, symbolizing (or at least implying) Christ's eventual triumph, and the darker verse for Everyman/Judas. But, just as with *Joseph,* most of the attention was focused on Rice's lyrics. Rice's words were bold, they were frank and, in the context of the times, revolutionary:

> *Every time I look at you I don't understand*
> *Why you let the things you did get so out of hand.*
> *You'd have managed better if you'd had it planned*
> *Why'd you choose such a backward time and such a strange land?*
> *If you'd come today you would have reached a whole nation.*
> *Israel in 4 B.C. had no mass communication*
> *Don't get me wrong*
> *I only want to know*
> *Jesus Christ, Jesus Christ. Who are you? What have you sacrificed?*
> *Jesus Christ Superstar. Do you think you're what they say you are?*
>
> *Tell me what you think about your friends at the top.*
> *Who d'you think besides yourself's the pick of the crop?*
> *Buddha was he where it's at, is he where you are?*
> *Could Mahomet move a mountain or was that just PR?*
> *Did you mean to die like that? Was that a mistake or*
> *Did you know your messy death would be a record-breaker?*
> *Don't get me wrong.*
> *I only want to know.*
> *Jesus Christ, Jesus Christ. Who are you? What have you sacrificed?*
> *Jesus Christ Superstar. Do you think you're what they say you are?*

At once, the debate was joined. Everybody agreed on the quality of the disc; "one of the finest productions to come out of British studios this year," the Little England reviewers cheered. But it was the content, not the presentation, that drew the most attention. Tim's original impulse was to take Judas's point of view. "We'd like to give a fairer hearing to people like Pontius Pilate and Judas Iscariot, who get cursed every day in the Creed and never seem to have a fair hearing at all," he said. Father Sullivan's offer to stage the piece at Saint Paul's also provoked discussion. "People are bound to say that it is another gimmick, but when you are fifty-nine, one is a little old in the tooth for the gimmicks," said the dean, mixing his second and third persons. "I'm interested in young people, and I believe that they have every right to put their questionings in contemporary language. It seems to me that if you can't talk about Christ in pop terms, then you've got the wrong image of him."

Still, there was one potential obstacle to Saint Paul's being the site of *Jesus Christ*'s premiere: church approval. In late November all that the dean, or anybody else, had seen of the show was the single and a plot outline. "That's as far as it has gone," said the reverend. "I am not a corporation solely able to act on my own. When I have the script and a full recording I shall consult my colleagues in the chapter [the residentiary canons]. If they say 'No,' well that will be that."

Just as the dean was mulling it over, along came an extraordinary episode that finished any chance *Jesus Christ* ever had of being presented in Saint Paul's. The headlines, as they say, screamed:

BEATLE JOHN ASKED TO PLAY CHRIST

LENNON ASKED TO PLAY CHRIST

BEATLE CHRIST?

All the stories, which appeared in the newspapers on December 4, 1969, were substantially the same:

John Lennon has been asked to play Christ in a musical to be staged in Saint Paul's Cathedral—but he is still considering the offer, a spokesman for the Beatles' record company said last night.
"It all depends on whether it fits into his schedule," said a spokesman. "It is an idea which interests him."
The pop-influenced musical deals with the last six days of Christ's life.

Another paper embellished the tale a little:

Beatle John Lennon has been asked to play Jesus Christ in a musical planned for presentation in Saint Paul's Cathedral.
And he wants his wife, Yoko Ono, to play Mary Magdalene.

This was a sure prescription for disaster. Lennon's "We're more popular than Jesus" crack still rankled, and the very notion of putting Yoko Ono, widely regarded as the talentless, twice-divorced Japanese dragon lady who had seduced the tough Liverpool-Irish street kid and made a chump out of him—well, it was simply beyond the pale. One can imagine what the chapter thought of that.

Still, there was considerable reason to be suspicious of the Lennon story. Note the use of the passive voice: "has been asked." Who had done the asking? And was it a serious offer? And what clout did Rice and Lloyd Webber have with rock's greatest eminence, anyway?

The next day, the papers were full of retractions:

BEATLE JOHN WON'T PLAY CHRIST

CHRIST ROLE FOR BEATLE LENNON DENIED

LENNON NOT TO BE CHRIST

John Lennon will not play the part of Jesus Christ in a pop opera which may be staged in Saint Paul's Cathedral.
The MCA-UK record company said yesterday that the writers of the opera, Tim Rice and Andrew Lloyd Webber, prefer an unknown to play the role. "Someone like Lennon would imprint his personality to such an extent that people would read the star's character into the character of the part," the company said.

The Belfast Telegram, one of many British papers to cover the story, took its report a little further:

> There is an added complication. The opera has been specially written for [MCA-UK] and will be issued as an album. There could be contract difficulties if star names were used in the live production planned for Saint Paul's.
>   The company says that they considered the idea of Lennon as Christ and preliminary contact was made "as a politeness since they felt quite honoured that a Beatle should consider being involved in their work."

The Lennon trial balloon had collapsed almost as soon as it was floated. Still, that didn't stop the indefatigable letter writers from venting their spleen. A Mr. Tony Wilding of Hessle wrote to *The Daily Mail:* "I thought that your readers would be interested to know that on hearing that John Lennon may be playing Jesus Christ in a pop-influenced musical in Saint Paul's Cathedral, I immediately volunteered my services to the play's producers for the role of Pontius Pilate." One wit wrote a poem:

LITANY TO JOHN LENNON AS CHRIST

From "News of the World" gables
the Herald Angels (by permission of the
Grade Organisation) hailed Christ the King,
born in the city of David Jacobs
as agents watched their charts by night.
Tempted in all things as we are,
he passed through the Cilla Black
night of the soul to minister
unto us from the Mount of
Cocktail Olives or from a Yellow Submarine
in the Sea of Galilee. Delivered up
to judgment by scribes and Black Paper
seers, betrayed for thirty pieces of
Nems Enterprise, crucified by Rolling Stones
disc jockeys, he descended into
Tin Pan Alley, rose again in the
Sunday Times and ascended into Saint Paul's,
where he lies naked on the right hand
of Yoko Ono.

What had really happened was a classic tempest in a teapot, brewed by *The Daily Express* and served up for public consumption. Neither Lloyd Webber nor Rice had asked Lennon to play the part; nor had the Beatle expressed any interest in doing so. The whole thing was a figment of *The Daily Express*'s competitive imagination. "They called us and asked if we would like John Lennon to play Christ, and we said sure, why not, and then they called him and asked if he wanted to and he said he might be interested and that was all there was to it," Andrew told Jonathan Demme, who was then sharing an entertainment column in a London magazine with fellow film publicist Larry Kaplan.* That was the end of Lennon's putative participation, and also of Saint Paul's. The excuse made later was that the reverberation time in the cathedral was too long for the music to be heard adequately. More likely is that the church canons took one look at their morning newspapers on December 4 and just called the whole thing off.

Even without Lennon, though, *Jesus Christ* had a future. One who firmly believed in it was Brian Brolly, the head of MCA-UK. Brolly was an Irishman, but as far from the stereotype of the volatile Celt as could be imagined. Courtly, gentle, low-key, possessed of a keen business sense, he had been very impressed with the "Superstar" single and had taken an option on the complete album. Looking to make a splash as the chief of a new company, Brolly welcomed the controversy over the single and decided to exploit it. In mid-February 1970 MCA-UK ballyhooed a "search for Christ," a casting call for "unknowns" to audition for the roles of Christ, Mary Magdalene, and the Apostles, and sent the boys out to meet the press:

> Andrew says: "What we are trying to do is to bring Christ home to people; to make Him more real, and bring Him down from the stained glass windows.
>   "We've based the story on what is known of the last six days of His life; each track of the record will represent one day. We haven't altered the evidence, but we've interpreted it in our own way.
>   "The six days are shown through Judas's eyes. It's an attempt to explain what Judas did, and also why Christ went so meekly to his death.
>   "In the opera He's fallible, human, never sure of himself, whether or not He is God. He decides that He must die to attract more attention to His movement, which has gone as far as it can."

Christ's death, in other words, was a good career move.

---

*Demme later became a film director, the auteur of such witty, idiosyncratic movies as *Melvin and Howard, Something Wild,* and *Married to the Mob.*

This view of Christ was hardly original. In his 1955 novel, *The Last Temptation of Christ* (translated into English in 1960), Greek novelist Nikos Kazantzakis had depicted a questioning Christ, unsure of his divinity and manipulated by his followers; in 1964 the Italian Marxist film director Pier Paolo Pasolini offered a similar endorsement of Jesus' humanity in the film *The Gospel According to Saint Matthew.* The whiff of heresy, or at least of revaluation, was in the air. Rice's contribution to the argument was to put the questions in contemporary slang; while less high-minded than either Kazantzakis or Pasolini, his approach was more visceral than either.

Nowhere would the reaction be greater than in the United States, where Christians—liberal in the East and Far West, conservative in the Midwest and the South—could be expected to choose up sides on any furiously debated religious issue, and the vocal minority of Jews would also have a say through the American Jewish Committee and the Anti-Defamation League of B'nai B'rith. A week after the single was issued in Britain, MCA announced the forthcoming release of "Superstar" on its American Decca label (not to be confused with Decca in England, which was called London in the United States): "Interest in the record among MCA representatives points to it becoming one of the biggest single sellers internationally of all times."

From the moment the record hit American shores on December 1, 1969, controversy attended it. Some radio stations refused to play the song, although the ones who did (among them, WNEW-FM in New York City and KMET-FM in Los Angeles) reported a 75-percent approval rating among their listeners. Before airing the single, many stations preceded it by reading Sullivan's benediction. Station WQAM in Miami organized an entire show around the record, bringing on a panel of religious leaders and teenagers to discuss the moral implications of "Superstar" and inviting listeners to call in with their opinions. In Cleveland, station WAKR presented a half-hour show on December 7 with commentary by a minister and a Catholic priest; another Cleveland station, WWGO-FM, followed playings with taped commentary from local divines. In New Jersey, a Catholic priest requested permission to use the lyrics as the basis for a Sunday sermon. "This is where it's at," said the padre. "This song is exactly what the youth are asking for today."

Everyone expected "Superstar" to do well. *Record World* selected it as one of its "Sleeper Picks of the Week," observing: "The name of the artist is Murray Head. The name of the song is 'Superstar' (Leeds, ASCAP). First-rate lyric, first-rate production." On December 20, Decca took out a full-page ad in the trades reproducing Dean Sullivan's by now well-worn comments and promising that "Superstar" was "from the Rock Opera *Jesus Christ* now in preparation."

And yet . . . by January 24, 1970, "Superstar" had climbed only to number eighty-nine on the Cashbox charts, just ahead of Nina Simone's "To Be Young, Gifted and Black." (A group that really was young, gifted, and black, the Jackson 5, was riding high at number one with "I Want You Back.") The highest "Superstar" climbed was the mid-fifties. In England, it never got higher than number thirty-nine. Could it be that after all the fuss and the publicity, "Superstar" was a dud?

Just as it had with *Joseph,* help came from the unlikeliest quarter: the homosexual community. This time, Lloyd Webber's benefactor was an openly gay bar in Amsterdam, the most liberated city in Europe, whose patrons had seized on "Superstar" and played it over and over. Word soon filtered out to the liberal Dutch advertising men that here was a hip record worth promoting. By January 17, 1970, the single had risen to the top of the Dutch charts, leaping ahead of Santana's "Jingo" (number four), Elvis Presley's "Rubberneckin'" (five), and Led Zeppelin's "Whole Lotta Love" (eight). Then it caught on in Belgium, in Brazil, in New Zealand. Even the Vatican radio station played it. "Superstar" was finally on its way.

The album's composition took place between October 1969 and March 1970; by the end of June, the cast was set. Murray Head was to sing Judas, of course, even though he was busy filming *Sunday, Bloody Sunday* with director John Schlesinger, then trading on the success of *Darling* and *Midnight Cowboy.* From the British rock group Deep Purple, which had made a splash with some classical crossover work with the Royal Philharmonic Orchestra, came lead singer Ian Gillan as Jesus. Another rocker, Mike d'Abo, formerly with Manfred Mann, was cast as Herod, while Barry Dennen, an American-born actor in West End musicals, signed on as Pilate.

The real discovery, unearthed singing for five pounds a night in a Chelsea nightspot, was Yvonne Elliman. Born in Hawaii of a Japanese mother and a Wisconsin haole father, Elliman was seventeen years old when she landed in London with her guitar and her dreams; her gig at the Pheasantry Club was her first professional engagement. After she had finished her set one night, an intense, rather strange-looking long-haired young man had come up to her and muttered, "I've found my Mary Magdalene." Elliman had no idea who, or what, he meant, but she soon found out. The next night, Lloyd Webber returned with Rice, and they gave her Mary's two songs, "Everything's Alright" and "I Don't Know How to Love Him."* With a week of study, Elliman passed her audition, and *Jesus Christ,* as the album was still being called, was ready for the recording studio.

---

*The latter song was another Lloyd Webber recycling job. "I Don't Know How to Love Him" had started life several years before as a song called "Kansas Morning" ("I love the Kansas morning/Kansas mist at my window") and had been sold to Southern Music; Land bought it back for fifty pounds, and Tim outfitted it with a new lyric.

It had been a near thing. Armed with more than fourteen thousand pounds of MCA's money, Brolly had convinced Rice and Lloyd Webber that *Jesus Christ* had a future, but for it to have a future it also needed a present. As late as the fall of 1969, *Jesus Christ* simply did not exist except in broad outline. The week before Christmas, Andrew and Tim packed themselves off to a hotel in Herefordshire to break the back of the full score. In times of trouble, Paul McCartney may have turned to Mother Mary, but Andrew Lloyd Webber turned both to his talent and to his drawer: "Kansas Morning" was reborn, and from *Come Back Richard* came a campy buck-and-wing called "Those Saladin Days" that would turn into "King Herod's Song."* The Grieg Piano Concerto provided an instrumental theme symbolizing Judas's betrayal, a lick from Carl Orff's *Carmina Burana* made a fleeting appearance in the Gethsemane scene, and the ominous trudge of Prokofiev's "Battle on the Ice" from *Alexander Nevsky* materialized as well. There was original music sketched out in Herefordshire, too: Mary Magdalene's comforting "Everything's Alright," the Agony in the Garden scene, and the joyous shout for Simon Zealotes. The pieces of the "rock opera" were coming together.

For his musical idiom, Andrew once again adopted the style he knew best—indeed, the only style he knew: a semiconscious agglutination of rock, show music, and classical influences. The experience with *Joseph*, in which the performers had to contend with unusual (albeit infrequent) irruptions of 5/4 and 7/8 bars in the music, emboldened him to repeat those time signatures in *Superstar*. "Maybe in this way pop and other music idioms are being drawn together," he told an interviewer. "Look at Pink Floyd and the Beatles using electronic effects—why even Prokofiev veers towards the pop idiom. Eventually there may be a fusion of all these elements. At the moment one wonders about some of the music being written in the name of serious art—some of these people basically aren't very talented. There is a lack of melody—and melody in some form is vital."

And so was a catchy title. In the early summer of 1970, the British papers were announcing the forthcoming release of *Jesus Christ . . . Superstar*, the new "popera" by Tim Rice and Andrew Lloyd Webber, "followed by a stage version if the necessary backers materialise." It was a strange admixture of talent that had gathered for *Superstar*. There were the rockers like Head, Gillan, and d'Abo; there was Elliman, the Hawaiian folkie; there was John Lill, playing an uncredited piano. In a touching display of loyalty to a man whom events had already passed by, there was even Alan Doggett, gamely conducting the orchestra and a children's choir. It was an act of charity more than a musical decision, for Doggett's work was not up to professional standards, as Lloyd Webber and Rice soon realized.† Later, when it came time to film *Superstar*, André Previn was engaged as the conductor.

Andrew and Tim spent from March to July 1970‡ in the recording studio, painstakingly putting together the ninety-minute double album. Informed by Tim's experience with EMI and Paramor and recorded on sixteen-track tape at several different sound studios around London, the production was spectacular. The rock rhythm tracks were laid down first, separately. Then came the singers' voices, a process that allowed the soloists considerable latitude in their interpretations. Finally came the orchestrations, tailored to fit and superimposed over the voice-rhythm mix. There was much trial-and-error: a scene in which Jesus curses the fig tree ("I hope your leaves turn brown/May a vandal chop you down") had to be cut. But backed by Brolly, Lloyd Webber and Rice were finally getting what they had wanted—a shot at the pop big time.

Superstar dares much—so much that its real title should be *Judas Iscariot Superstar*. Although the subject is Christ's Passion, the perspective is Judas's. This is made clear right from the Overture, whose themes will be heard later in the opera in the Trial by Pilate scene. The last notes of the prelude will be the last notes of the opera: the theme of the Betrayal, followed by the soft major chords that will cheer and mock Judas and, finally, give Christ some measure of peace after his death.

Judas is given the first number, "Heaven on Their Minds," a hard-driving rocker in D minor with a middle section that abruptly switches from 4/4 to 7/8:

I remember when this whole thing began　　　　　*But every word you say today*
No talk of God then—we called you a man　　　　*Gets twisted round some other way*
And believe me—my admiration for you hasn't died　*And they'll hurt you if they think you've lied.*

---

*"Those Saladin Days" itself was a recycling of a Lloyd Webber–Rice song called "Try It and See," which was entered in the 1969 Eurovision song contest. It was not a winner. In 1983 Rice reappropriated the "Saladin" title, although not the lyric, for a song in *Blondel*.

†This was the end for Doggett. Having been let go at Colet Court, with rumors of his homosexual predilections swirling about him, he had caught on at another London school and then abruptly left to lead a choir called the London Boy Singers, for whom he composed a choral piece along the lines of *Joseph and the Amazing Technicolor Dreamcoat*. When one of the boys accused Doggett of molestation—apparently the accusation was false—the conductor was arrested and, as a condition of his bail, was forbidden to have any contact with his chorus. Depressed over the loss of his choir and the chance to lead his piece, Doggett traveled in February 1978 to his birthplace of Iver, in Buckinghamshire, lay down on a railroad track and was killed. A few days later, his handwritten suicide notes were delivered by post to his friends. At a memorial in the Royal Albert Hall, Doggett's choral piece was performed in tribute.

‡In May 1970 they interrupted the recording of *Jesus Christ Superstar* to make their first trip to America at the invitation of the College of the Immaculate Conception in Douglaston, Queens, where Father Christopher Huntington was staging *Joseph*. It was an all-expenses-paid trip; Tim and Andrew spent their first few nights in America at the Harvard Club on West Forty-fourth Street in Manhattan, and Tim even stayed a few extra days, visiting a girl in Boston and flying home from Logan Airport.

"What's the Buzz?" a jaunty rap for the Apostles follows, a transition piece constructed from unresolved seventh chords that leads into "Strange Thing, Mystifying," a dispute between Judas and Jesus over the propriety of Mary Magdalene's presence among the disciples, in which Judas's music is in G major while Christ's is in C minor. Right from the start, the two are speaking a different language.

The show's first hit song is Mary's bouncy lullaby, "Everything's Alright," sung as she ministers to Jesus. The melody is one of Lloyd Webber's happiest inspirations, a bright carefree tune in E major that is given irresistible topspin by its 5/4 time signature:

Try not to get worried, try not to turn on to
Problems that upset you, Oh—don't you know
Everything's alright yes everything's fine

And we want you to sleep well tonight
Let the world turn without you tonight
If we try we'll get by so forget all about us tonight.

Unimpressed, Judas angrily reproaches her in the parallel minor:

Woman, your fine ointment, brand new and expensive
Could have been saved for the poor.
Why has it been wasted? We could have raised maybe
Three hundred silver pieces or more.

People who are hungry, people who are starving
Matter more than your feet and hair.

In the council chamber in Jerusalem, the priests gather to discuss what to do about Christ in the ominous "This Jesus Must Die"; their gloomy tune, in F minor, recapitulates the first notes of the Overture. In the distance, the crowd is singing the "Superstar" tune, while Caiaphas intones, "We need a more permanent solution to our problem. . . ." The next song, "Hosanna," is the celebration of Palm Sunday. The crowd hails the Savior with a slangy, "Hosanna, heysanna, sanna sanna ho." Here, Lloyd Webber and Rice made a serious dramatic error by having Jesus join in the chorus, instead of simply being the object of the adoration—not for any scriptural reasons, but because Christ then appears uncharacteristically cynical and manipulative.

Although the score was widely criticized as not being rocky enough for the rockers and not operatic enough for opera-goers, the next number, "Simon Zealotes/Poor Jerusalem," is a fine, energetic soul shout. In "Pilate's Dream," the Roman governor sings a dark reverie in B-flat minor to a tune we have previously heard Jesus sing—establishing a fateful, psychic connection between the two powerful men. "The Temple," in which Jesus routs the money changers, is a relentless rhythmic ostinato in 7/8, broken up by Jesus' angry interjection; "My temple should be a house of prayer/but you have made it a den of thieves./Get out! Get out!" With the crowd quieted, Christ muses to a sad little tune of resignation in E minor that, at the opera's close, will turn into his elegy:

My time is almost through,
Little left to do,
After all I've tried for three years, seems like thirty,
Seems like thirty.

The members of the crowd then renew their shouting, this time threateningly begging Jesus to heal them, until he flees: "There's too—too many of you./Don't push me /Oh, there's too little of me/don't crowd me./Heal yourselves!"

Mary reappears to sing her second song, "I Don't Know How to Love Him," a folksy ballad in D major in which the former whore muses on her sacred and her profane feelings for Jesus. The twelfth scene, "Damned for All Time/Blood Money," switches back to Judas, seen bargaining with the high priests. Philosophically, it is the opera's central number, expressing Judas's terrible existential dilemma. As the instrument of Christ's martyrdom, he is damned if he does betray the Lord—and just as surely damned if he doesn't.

I came because I had to—I'm the one who saw
Jesus can't control it like he did before
And furthermore I know that Jesus thinks so too
Jesus wouldn't mind that I was here with you

I have no thought at all about my own reward
I really didn't come here of my own accord
Just don't say I'm
Damned for all time

As the act ends, and Judas takes the thirty pieces of silver to betray Christ, the chorus softly intones, "Well done Judas. Good old Judas."

Act Two opens with "The Last Supper," a complicated, well-constructed scene. The Apostles, who are depicted throughout the opera as silly, venal little men motivated solely by enlightened self-interest, sing a boozy song in G major: "Always hoped that I'd be an apostle/Knew that I would make it if I tried./Then when we retire we can write the Gospels/So they'll still talk about us when we've died." The key switches to the parallel minor as Jesus consecrates his body and blood, and the music moves into 5/4 when, to the rhythm of "Everything's Alright," Jesus predicts that his followers will deny him and betray him. Judas challenges him: "You want me to do it!/What if I just stayed here/and ruined your ambition?/Christ, you deserve it!"

Oblivious to this outburst, the Apostles continue their simple song, this time in F major; a quick modulation to F-sharp minor brings the first, brief statement of Judas's tune that will later figure prominently in the song "Superstar." Judas sings: "Every time I look at you I don't understand/Why you let the things you did get so out of hand/You'd have managed better if you'd had it planned. . . ." Back in G major (symbolically, a key remote from F-sharp minor), the Apostles continue their drunken ditty, and the scene ends with Christ pleading for one of them to stay awake with him during the agony to come.

"Gethsemane" begins with a poignant soliloquy in B-flat minor for Jesus, sung to the theme of resignation first heard in the temple scene:

> I only want to say
> If there is a way
> Take this cup away from me for I don't want to taste its poison
> Feel it burn me, I have changed, I'm not as sure
> As when we started

> Then I was inspired
> Now I'm sad and tired
> Listen surely I've exceeded expectations
> Tried for three years seems like thirty
> Could you ask as much from any other man?

A more spirited middle section ("I'd wanna know I'd wanna know my God . . . If I die what will be my reward?") leads again to the resignation theme ("God, Thy will is hard") and thence to Judas's arrival and the beginning of "The Arrest."

This scene opens with a reprise of "What's the Buzz?" as the Apostles awake and briefly struggle with the soldiers. As Christ is led away, he is mocked by the crowd ("Do you feel that you've had the breaks?/What would you say were your big mistakes?") to the same tune and rhythm that the halt and the lame had employed to plead for healing. As Christ forecast, Peter denies him, and Mary bitterly reproaches the future Pope for his cowardice. But Peter, too, is only acting according to God's plan; if he is caught and killed, there can be no Church.

"Pilate and Christ" displays the composer's debt to Prokofiev in its relentless tread of G-minor and F-sharp–minor chords. (Andrew had inherited a love of contemporary Russian music from his father, and Prokofiev's unique combination of crashing polytonal discord and seductive, sinuous melody appealed to him especially.) Pilate consigns Jesus to Herod: "You're Herod's race," he shouts at him, "You're Herod's case!" Outside, the mob ironically invokes the "Hosanna" motif.

"King Herod's Song" is the show's show-stopper. The tune that had originated with the Eurovision song contest and stopped off briefly at the Crusades here emerges as an infectious ragtime two-step with a nasty bite to its lyric:

> So you are the Christ, you're the great Jesus Christ
> Prove to me that you're no fool—walk across my swimming pool.
> If you do that for me then I'll let you go free
> C'mon, King of the Jews.

The only difference between the original double album and the staged version comes with the addition of the next song, Mary's frightened "Could We Start Again Please?," a D-major plea, in which Peter later joins. Meanwhile, Judas has regretted his bargain. In "Judas's Death," he curses Annas for leading him into temptation and then, to melodic reprises of "Blood Money" and "I Don't Know How to Love Him," he hangs himself: "God! I'll never know why you chose me for your crime, for your foul bloody crime. You have murdered me!" The chorus, ever watchful, intones "So long Judas, Poor old Judas," just as it had earlier sung "Well done, Judas."

"Trial Before Pilate" recapitulates the material of the Overture, and Christ receives the thirty-nine lashes to the rhythmic riff that underpinned "Heaven on Their Mind." As the crowd howls for Jesus' blood, Pilate becomes incensed with Christ's refusal to defend himself. "You're a fool, Jesus Christ," he shouts, "How can I help you?"

> Don't let me stop your great self-destruction
> Die if you want to, you misguided martyr.
> I wash my hands of your demolition.
> Die if you want to, you innocent puppet!

In the score's most chilling and dramatically apposite moment, the orchestra thunders out the "Superstar" motif, *maestoso*, in the radiant key of E major.

The original hard-rock single is now heard, with Judas returning from the dead and reincarnated as Everyman, mouthing the questions that Father Sullivan found so challenging. The musical language changes abruptly in "Crucifixion," an abstract, atonal setting of the Seven Last Words. Clearly, Lloyd Webber had been listening to Ligeti's eerie *Atmospheres* (used by Stanley Kubrick to depict the cold void of outer space in his film *2001: A Space Odyssey*) and to Penderecki's brutal choral work *The Passion According to Saint Luke*, both sensations of the late-sixties' avant-garde. Christ's last words are, "Father, into your hands I commend my spirit."

The mournful postlude, "John 19:41," which had been the "B" side of the "Superstar" single, is an instrumental meditation on the Resignation theme, closing quietly with the theme of Judas's Betrayal and the "Good old Judas" chords, played *pianissimo* and *pianississimo*. The bitonal clash—Judas's tortured D minor against the balm of the B-flat major chords—brings the work to an end on an uncertain note, the musical equivalent of ending with a question mark. Was Christ God? Or did he just think he was?

Jesus Christ Superstar became such a media event, so hotly debated on grounds irrelevant to its musical and dramatic content, that any consideration of its quality was immediately buried under an avalanche of ancillary issues. The score is not a masterpiece, but it is more cleverly constructed than most realized at the time. If its grasp ultimately falls short, it is only because its reach is so great: the melodic material is uneven, and there is too much reliance on thematic repetition without sufficient variation to give the tunes deeper meaning or added poignancy. Rice's libretto, too, is spotty—the occupational hazard of retelling the Bible's most solemn story in contemporary slang.

Yet, in conception and construction, *Superstar* is a daring, sophisticated, and well-calculated piece. Its slick evocation of a variety of musical styles had wide appeal, and its subject meshed perfectly with the spirit of the times. Rice's hip language was both exciting and shocking at a time when society was still not yet so jaded that nothing could excite or shock, while Lloyd Webber's music announced the arrival of a new talent with a bright future. In light of the authors' ages at the time, *Jesus Christ Superstar* was an impressive accomplishment. It deserves reassessment and revival.

Whether Lloyd Webber had any inkling of the fame and fortune that *Jesus Christ Superstar* would shortly bring his way is moot, but the subject of finances had always interested him. Even in mid-1970, before he had earned much of anything composing, he felt the urge to sound off to *The Evening Standard*. The missive, phoned in to the *Standard*'s "dictate-a-letter" service, was ostensibly in reaction to the call for military conscription then being raised in Britain. But the real subject was money:

A DUBIOUS KIND OF THERAPY . . .

I wonder if all the Evening Standard readers who are apparently in favour of conscription realise how much money Britain has made as well as saved by abolishing call up.

It is no coincidence that in the '60s Britain has held the lead in most areas where young people are involved in making money. This is because of the huge advantage British young people have over foreign rivals whose careers are held up by stretches in the forces. One shudders to think of Britain's current economic position had we not benefited from the billions of dollars earned abroad by young British fashions, music and films. All this was made possible by a healthy climate in which enterprising young people could get on with their careers without worry about call up. Besides, to throw a whole lot of inexperienced young people into the highly professional forces would be regrettable militarily. It also seems a highly dubious therapy for skin-heads.

Andrew Lloyd Webber
1 Charles Street, W.1.

In all, a good reflection of Lloyd Webber's state of mind. The bit about the skinheads—roving bands of youths in black leather jackets and "bovver boots" whose shaved heads were vivid tonsorial rebukes to the long hair of the hippies—is a nice touch. No *Clockwork Orange* for Andrew; at the age of twenty-two he was ready to get on with the serious business of making money.

He didn't have long to wait. *Jesus Christ—Superstar* (the ellipses had briefly become a dash) was released in October 1970 in Britain and later that month in the United States as *Jesus Christ Superstar*. In Britain, as before, the public reaction to the subject matter was a big yawn; nobody, aside from a few old ladies and a few old deans, got particularly excited about religion. Dramatically and musically, on the other hand, there was widespread praise, and not just of the "great-day-for-England" variety.

"Tim Rice's libretto is extremely clever, full of intelligent ideas, skillful in its incorporation of imagery and speeches from the Gospels, often poetic in the lyrics, absolutely consistent in the style of diction," said William S. Mann in the pages of *The Gramophone*. During the course of a long, thoughtful, and scholarly review, he wrote of the composer's contribution:

> Andrew Lloyd Webber comes of a family of musicians and he knows how to write straight music as well as numerous varieties of pop and rock. The Overture would not sound out of place in a sophisticated American musical; the Conclusion, describing the Entombment, might be called Grandson of Barber's *Adagio*. Several numbers use quintuple or septuple metres—rather self-consciously thumped out by the performers. Pilate's theme is a respectable pastiche of Prokofiev, while the sinister choral calls of "Well done, Judas" recall the Borough's off-stage shouts for "Grimes!" in Britten's first opera.* Just before this, when Gethsemane is mentioned, and at Judas's death and the Crucifixion scene, there are eerie sounds that tell you Lloyd Webber has studied his Penderecki and Ligeti.
>
> At first hearing I was inclined to mock at *Jesus Christ—Superstar* as a commercial confidence trick. ("Jesus was a hippie, so you too can come to church"). Then I sat down late at night, using stereo headphones and making copious notes; this time I had to admire the musical detail and the brilliant mixing and balancing. . . . It improves on acquaintance, as a whole, though the unconvincing bits become increasingly tiresome. This time I thought of it as a stage production and I believe it would make a positive effect, given a really strong cast, as here, and most of the enormous orchestral and choral forces employed.

In the life of every popular artist or entertainer, there comes a moment when the individual vision and the popular consciousness merge: the Big Bang theory of success. Such a moment came in the lives of Rice and Lloyd Webber when the complete *Superstar* hit the American market on October 27, 1970. The very thing that made the record, like the "Superstar" single before it, so objectionable to fundamentalist Christians—its content—also ensured that the album would be given widespread attention by churchmen. In Britain, Dean Sullivan stood out, a slightly dotty man of the cloth in furious pursuit of the fountain of youth. In America, where the Vatican II reforms had been gleefully embraced by Catholics and welcomed by Protestants, there were a million Father Sullivans, Brother Sullivans, and Sister Mary Ignatius Sullivans, eager to explain it all for you. Far from seeing *Jesus Christ Superstar* as offensive, they viewed it as the perfect teaching tool.†

Critical reception of *Jesus Christ Superstar* in America was largely positive. In *Time* magazine, the voice of upper middle-class America, music critic William Bender compared the work to Bach's *Saint John* and *Saint Matthew* passions: "With an appealing variegated score by Andrew Lloyd Webber and words by Tim Rice, *Superstar* builds to considerable impact and evocativeness, in part because it manages to wear its underlying seriousness lightly. What Rice and Webber have created is a modern-day passion play that may enrage the devout but ought to intrigue and perhaps inspire the agnostic young."

But *Superstar* didn't need critical encomiums to be a hit. As the album began a rapid, relentless climb to the top of the American charts, Rice and Lloyd Webber found their lives changed almost overnight. Despite the fact that the album was copyrighted material, spontaneous live performances of *Jesus Christ Superstar* began to flower across America, in part fueled by a nationwide publicity campaign on which Tim and Andrew embarked. For Sefton Myers and David Land, things were getting out of hand; from their base in London, they did not have the clout or the financial wherewithal to combat the pirates. In the words of *Variety*, *Jesus Christ Superstar* was on its way to becoming "the biggest multimedia parlay in show business history," and Myers and Land needed help.

Already, wolves were sniffing around the door, among them Britain's Lord Delfont, a prominent impresario looking for rights to produce the album on the stage. But the quickest wolf in the west was Robert Stigwood, an Australian who had landed nearly penniless in London in 1957. The son of an electrical engineer, Stigwood had parlayed his Aussie cheek and sass—and his keen business sense—into a formidable showbiz empire, hooking up with Brian Epstein's NEMS Enterprises for six months in 1967 at the height of Beatlemania and, after Epstein's death in August of that year, forming his own company, the Robert Stigwood Group. Ruddy complexioned, of medium height and a little thickset, with red hair falling nearly to his shoulders, Stigwood was a quick study with a nose for what would sell. Expressly denied the management of the Beatles and Cilla Black, Epstein's two biggest attractions, Stigwood was well aware of the money-making possibilities in rock. After being let go by NEMS when Brian died, he went out and signed up the Bee Gees and Cream for his fledgling company.

---

*Careful readers will note a small error. *Peter Grimes* was not Benjamin Britten's first opera; that honor goes to *Paul Bunyan*—unlikely as it seems, originally conceived for Broadway but never staged there.

†Some Americans took umbrage at the use of the New Testament as the basis for a "rock opera," but such an objection bespoke ignorance of mainstream English and Continental musical tradition. Certainly, the Passion was a big subject, but not one so big that British composers didn't regularly treat it and other sacred texts in their music. Elgar wrote three major religious oratorios—*The Dream of Gerontius, The Kingdom,* and *The Apostles;* Holst had written *The Hymn of Jesu;* John Stainer wrote *The Crucifixion;* Handel, an adopted Briton, had composed *Messiah,* among many other religious oratorios (that were, effectively, operas in disguise). The seven last words of Christ (both Haydn and Pergolesi had written works on *that* subject) were hardly terra incognita. Bill Lloyd Webber, too, had written big works on religious themes, including *The Saviour* and *Divine Compassion.*

The Bee Gees were fellow Australians, and Stigwood initially marketed them as the second coming of the Beatles. Cream, on the other hand, was the first rock supergroup: Eric Clapton, the greatest living rock guitarist; Jack Bruce, the ace bassist; and Ginger Baker, the wild drummer. Both bands went straight to the top; indeed, the Bee Gees stayed there for years, molting like some exotic antipodean bird and eventually transforming themselves from a Beatles clone into the blue-eyed soul brothers of *Saturday Night Fever.* His fortune made, Stigwood acquired Associated London Scripts, where his clients included Rita Tushingham and the script writers Galton and Simpson (of later, Stigwood-inspired *Jacob's Journey* infamy). With his foot in the theatrical door, it was but a short step to active production: Stigwood staged *Hair* and *The Dirtiest Show in Town* in London and coproduced *Oh, Calcutta!* By October 1970, when his company went public with a stock offering, Robert Stigwood was the Dino de Laurentiis of recordings and the theater, happily and profitably purveying popular entertainment to the masses.

Tim and Andrew had met Stigwood before. As luck would have it, Stigwood had lived in a building next door to Ross Hannaman's flat in Adam's Mews, Mayfair, and Tim would return from dates with Ross marveling at the proximity, for Stigwood was a major force in British show business. In 1968, when planning the "Superstar" single, Lloyd Webber and Rice had gone, with considerable trepidation, to see Stigwood, hoping to secure Jack Bruce's services as the bass player on the record. Stigwood had given the two unknowns about twenty minutes before showing them the door. After "Superstar," they went to see Stigwood again, to enlist his aid in getting the projected show on the stage; the Australian told them to finish the album first and send him a test pressing when it was ready. Then he would tell them just how stageworthy it was.

By the time Rice and Lloyd Webber encountered Stigwood again, at the end of October 1970, they had just flown in from London on a visit to New York; Andrew and Tim were in Manhattan to meet with MCA executives just before *Superstar* was released in the United States. Stigwood didn't want to talk about the album; he had something bigger in mind. He sent a limousine to pick up Lloyd Webber and Rice at the Drake Hotel and to bring them round to his rented townhouse at 120 East Seventy-eighth Street for a little chat.

He had received the test pressing, Stigwood told them, and he loved it. It was clear to him that the record was going to be an enormous hit; already, the buzz was beginning, and the record was jumping off the stepdowns. Stigwood realized that Lloyd Webber and Rice were in for a repeat of the "Superstar" single controversy, this time on a much larger scale, and he smelled a business opportunity. He wanted to put *Superstar* on stage. What would they say to his becoming their manager?*

It was the dream come true. Suddenly, Colet Court and Central Hall seemed very far away and long ago indeed; the bright lights of Broadway were dancing in their eyes. Tim's excitement was enhanced that evening at Stigwood's apartment when he recognized a slim, handsome fellow Englishman. "Do you know who that is?" he whispered to Andrew. "That's the famous Peter Brown." Andrew had no idea who Brown was, but Tim, the pop-music expert, knew exactly who he was: Peter Brown, Brian Epstein's right-hand man at NEMS; Brown, the head of the Beatles' company, Apple Corps; Brown, the best man at John and Yoko's wedding—why he was even mentioned in the song "The Ballad of John and Yoko." *That* Peter Brown, and here he was, dressing up the meeting. Tim was impressed.

There was some irony in Brown's presence. Back in 1966, it had been Brown who persuaded the mortally ill Epstein that Stigwood was just the man to come in and help run the company; it had been Brown, as administrative director of NEMS in 1967, who had been entrusted by Epstein to manage his beloved Beatles and Cilla Black, not Stigwood; and it had been Brown who had fired Stigwood from NEMS after Epstein's death. Now Brown was in Stigwood's living room; within three months, he would head Stigwood's operations in America, with direct responsibility for Tim and Andrew.

The one obstacle to Stigwood's getting *Superstar* on stage was Lloyd Webber and Rice's contract with Myers and Land. Stigwood had a simple solution: other promoters may have been seeking to buy the rights to *Superstar,* but he simply bought the company. In November 1970 Stigwood purchased Myers's 50.2 percent of New Ventures Theatrical Management, Ltd., for one hundred and fifty thousand newly issued shares in the Robert Stigwood Group, as well as ten thousand pounds in cash. (At the initial offering of RSG, the City had not been impressed; shares were selling for about sixteen shillings.) In May 1971 Stigwood bought out Land's 49.8 percent for one hundred thousand shares plus forty thousand pounds in cash; two months later, he paid an additional one hundred fifty-two thousand three hundred eighty shares, worth at the time about eighty thousand pounds. Lloyd Webber and Rice had come cheap.

Stigwood's purchase made a lot of sense. Myers had been diagnosed with terminal cancer and had only a couple of months more to live; shares in the publicly quoted Stigwood Group would be easy to value for estate purposes upon Myers's death. For his part, Land was wise enough to realize that he lacked the expertise and worldwide connections that Stigwood could offer. As far as Tim and Andrew were

---

*This, at least, is Stigwood's recollection of the meeting; neither Lloyd Webber nor Rice remember sending Stigwood a copy of the record. Another version is that the disc came to Stigwood's attention through a lawyer named Nat Weiss, who had done some work for the Beatles; after Stigwood bought out Land, Weiss was furious at Stigwood for years for not crediting him with the *Superstar* discovery.

concerned, provisions of the contract remained the same: Stigwood's cut would be 25 percent of earnings. Land was retained as their manager, at a salary and a percentage, but the name of the company was changed to Superstar Ventures, Ltd.

Stigwood moved quickly. There was nothing he could do about *Superstar*'s publishing rights and record royalties, for those belonged to MCA and its publishing division, Leeds Music (except, of course, for "King Herod's Song," which, in its first Eurovision incarnation, was still owned by Norrie Paramor Music). But he put the screws to MCA for what he viewed as a shamefully low royalty for Andrew and Tim, getting it doubled from 2.5 percent to 5 percent almost immediately.

The second—and more pressing—bit of business was to go after the numerous unlicensed productions of *Superstar* in the United States and Canada. This battle, which would be waged across North America for the better part of 1971, was enormously important. As part of his deal with Myers and Land, Stigwood had acquired the grand rights to *Jesus Christ Superstar,* and more than anyone he understood how valuable they were. From the performing rights to individual songs from the album, licensed through ASCAP (the American Society of Composers, Authors, and Publishers) Andrew and Tim each could expect to make about fifty thousand dollars in 1971; the grand rights, on the other hand, were worth millions. The lesson that Andrew had learned from Bob Kingston about grand rights a couple of years before was now about to be driven home dramatically.

Why were the grand rights so important? Stigwood and his phalanx of more than fifty lawyers (headed by John Eastman, Paul McCartney's brother-in-law, and Robert Osterberg of the law firm Abeles and Clark) took the position that to perform *Jesus Christ Superstar* in its entirety was, de facto, a theatrical performance—whether or not the performers had bought performance rights to each one of the songs individually from ASCAP. Legally, this was a gray area. The notion that a rock album could be viewed as a single entity, not a collection of disparate and unrelated tracks, was fairly novel. The Beatles had blazed that trail in 1967 with *Sergeant Pepper's Lonely Hearts Club Band* and The Who had followed with *Tommy,* which (unlike *Sergeant Pepper*) was frankly billed as a rock opera. Although Stigwood ended up spending well over a million dollars in legal fees, it was well worth the effort, for the grand rights to *Superstar* turned out to be worth many times that amount.

Besides the legal struggle, there was a public-relations battle to be fought, and in this Stigwood was not always successful. It was one thing to close down opportunistic professional productions like those of the National Rock Opera Company, the National Touring Company, the American Rock Opera Company (despite its name, a Canadian group), and the Canadian Rock Theater; it was another to go after nuns in Australia, as Stigwood did, and bust them too. But principle was principle; besides, the Loretto nuns in Sydney were charging twelve dollars a ticket and Stigwood already had plans for his own stage production there. "These nuns believe Jesus Christ is theirs," remarked an Australian impresario. "What they are forgetting is that there is such a thing as copyright." The nuns were put out of business.*

The pirate productions varied from one group to another, but generally they offered most of the music on the *Jesus Christ Superstar* album, with various addenda or omissions. To obscure the music's provenance, it would be performed under a different title, usually simply *Superstar;* to skirt the issue of grand rights, the numbers would sometimes be performed out of sequence, arranged by another hand, or combined with numbers from another show, such as Stephen Schwartz's *Godspell.* The National Rock Opera Company, based in Columbus, Ohio, even tacked on the Resurrection to its version, thus settling the issue for its Midwestern audience of whether Christ was God.

Just how persistent the problem was may be gleaned from the evidence of a single month. On August 6, 1971, Stigwood announced the successful halting of the sixteenth unauthorized *Superstar* productions, this one by the Canadian Rock Theater at the Hilton International Hotel in Las Vegas, Nevada. "It is patently clear that a small group of people have set out to mislead and deceive the public," he declared. "We intend, in every case, to pursue vigorously anyone who attempts to infringe on our copyrights." Productions had also been halted in such major cities as Washington, D.C., Baltimore, Richmond, Louisville, Cincinnati, New Orleans, Memphis, Philadelphia, Cleveland, St. Louis, Los Angeles, and San Francisco.

On August 11, 1971 (by which time, MCA announced, more than two million *Superstar* double albums and tapes had been sold at ten dollars apiece), Judge Lawrence Pierce of the U.S. District Court, Southern District of New York, in Manhattan, upheld a temporary restraining order halting all unauthorized productions of *Superstar* anywhere in the United States by a group calling itself the Original American Touring Company; on August 26 Stigwood got a fresh injunction against the group. Stigwood was not always victorious; sometimes the pirates won limited performance rights, as in Los Angeles, where a judge ruled that the Canadian Rock Theater could perform individual selections from the album as long as no more than twelve of the album's twenty-two songs were used and no more than three performed in succession. The pirates were indefatigable; every time one was slain, it seemed, two more popped up. "How come bank robbers keep robbing

---

*During rehearsals for *Jesus Christ Superstar* on Broadway, Stigwood was called into the lobby of the Mark Hellinger Theatre, where he encountered a nun with an Irish-Australian brogue. The good sister upbraided the producer furiously. "How dare you do this to us?" she shouted. "We owned Jesus first." Stigwood was growing more uncomfortable and embarrassed with every passing moment until he heard Rice, Lloyd Webber, and the cast laughing behind him. The "nun" was one of the cast.

banks although the guy next door just got caught last week?" wondered Stigwood's press spokesman, Sheldon Roskin. "They're out for a fast buck."

By then, however, Stigwood had mounted his counterattack. On July 12 he opened the first official touring version of *Superstar*—with twenty singers (including Elliman as Mary Magdalene, Carl Anderson as Judas, and Jeff Fenholt as Jesus), a thirty-two piece orchestra, and a rock band—at the Civic Arena in Pittsburgh, Pennsylvania, before an audience of more than thirteen thousand people. In the first four weeks, as it trekked through nineteen cities, the traveling show grossed one million three hundred thousand dollars. In Boston, one performance attracted an audience of more than fifteen thousand; in Chicago, eighteen thousand came on a single evening; in Los Angeles, two sold-out performances at the Hollywood Bowl in September 1971 (with a top ticket of nearly ten dollars) grossed more than two hundred thousand dollars. Stigwood estimated that in its first year, this company alone would gross more than twelve million dollars; in fact, it proved so successful that on September 17, in Providence, Rhode Island, Stigwood unleashed a second touring company and, later, a college touring company.

Although the "official" tours were often critically panned ("Ten dollars for a box seat? Incredible!"), they, too, minted cash. Further, Stigwood estimated, the merchandising royalties and radio-performance rights would bring in another one and three-quarter million dollars, while the American recording and publishing rights were worth another three and a half million dollars. Flushed with success, Stigwood gave Andrew and Tim 10 percent of the gross to share; minus his 25-percent commission, that worked out to 7½ percent. It made them both wealthy within a year.

Tim and Andrew were not the only ones getting rich: Stigwood was receiving 50 percent of a show that cost very little to produce (there were no sets to build or truck around and no special costumes), which meant he was realizing, on average, one hundred thousand dollars a week, excluding his management fee from Lloyd Webber and Rice's earnings. By October 1971 rights to *Superstar* had been licensed in France and Scandinavia (where it was produced by Lar Schmidt, then married to Ingrid Bergman), as well as in Germany, Spain, Holland, Australia, South Africa, Israel, Mexico, and South America. The thirty-seven-year-old Australian, who had started out with thirty shillings in his pocket, was now estimated to be worth five million dollars. That kind of money would turn anybody into Savonarola.

The fantastic sums of cash pouring in had opposite effects on Rice and Lloyd Webber, and each reacted in character. During an October 1971 interview with *The New York Times*, Tim proudly said: "We'll make an absolute packet. Nothing wrong with that, is there?" Andrew, typically, was already underestimating his wealth. "Over a period of ten years, we may bring in two or three million," he said for public consumption. "But nothing like what the Beatles made on just one record. Or the Stones."

Wherever *Superstar* was heard, it left a trail of what-it-all-means babble in its wake. In Wheeling, Illinois, the Women's Society of Christian Service of Our Savior's United Methodist Church met on October 6 to discuss the record; in Middletown, New York, the local chapter of the American Guild of Organists made *Superstar* the topic of their dinner discussion on October 11; in Los Angeles, the Holy Faith Episcopal Church offered an audiovisual presentation on October 17, a 35mm-slide show that used the album as the sound track. In choir lofts across America, spontaneous local performances sprang up. On September 26, in Henderson, Texas, the Reverend K. C. Ptomey, Jr., of the First Presbyterian Church, preached a sermon entitled, "What You Always Wanted to Know About 'Jesus Christ, Superstar' But Were Afraid To Ask," as prelude to an October 2 "dramatic musical presentation" of the album.

Newspapers editorialized. The Roanoke, Virginia, *World News* glowed: "After a week, the hum of the rock hymns remains; the Superstar and lesser stars leave a satisfying glow." *The Atlanta Constitution* was unconvinced: "We came away with mixed emotions. And a persistent ringing in the ears." Even Billy Graham, the nation's unofficial nonsectarian chaplain, remarked that "the music, in my opinion, is excellent but the lyrics, while at times reverent, at other intervals border on the sacrilegious . . . to me, the work leaves a great deal to be desired."

The tours were all well and good, but for Andrew and Tim—and Stigwood—the real prize lay ahead: the Mark Hellinger Theatre on Broadway, where *Jesus Christ Superstar* was to have its theatrical premiere on October 12 (by which time sales of the album had topped three million) and, beyond that, Norman Jewison's film version for Universal Studios, which was to start shooting on location in the Holy Land in June 1972. "There is apparently a huge audience for this sort of thing," said Ned Tanen, the vice president of MCA, in the year's understatement. As its popularity grew, *Superstar* seemed to lose some of its shock value: complaints about the subject matter from fundamentalist Christians had abated, while musically, even such mainstream performers as Peggy Lee and Henry Mancini had covered some of the songs. With one million dollars in advance sales for the Broadway opening—then, the biggest advance in history—*Superstar* mania was showing no signs of letting up. The Broadway production, budgeted at seven hundred and fifty thousand dollars, was expected to run for years—by late October it was already sold out through February—and the movie, it was widely predicted, would outgross *Gone with the Wind*.

"My hope is to make *Superstar* a totally spiritual experience, a meditative experience. There's no need to have nude scenes or outrages against the church. It should be a highly mystical experience, an exaltation for the audience."

So said the director, Tom O'Horgan, Stigwood's handpicked choice to put his property on the boards. As hot as *Superstar,* O'Horgan had come out of the avant-garde Café La Mama to direct *Hair*; he had won raves for his productions of *Tom Paine,* about the American patriot, *Futz!,* about a pig, and *Lenny,* about the comic. In his mid-forties, O'Horgan was a man of the sixties, a composer (he wrote the score for the film *Alex in Wonderland*), musician (he once earned a living playing the harp in the Flame Room of the Radisson Hotel in Minneapolis), singer, actor, and director who wore his hair past his shoulders and dressed outrageously; one of his unfinished projects was a rock opera about the takeover of the American government by homosexuals.

O'Horgan was not the first director engaged for *Jesus Christ Superstar.* That distinction belonged to Frank Corsaro, who had made his name both on and off Broadway and at the New York City Opera. Corsaro was a far more plausible choice. The innovative director had practically invented the concept of off Broadway in the late forties with productions of Sartre's *No Exit* and Strindberg's *The Creditors* at the Cherry Lane Theatre and of Shaw's *Heartbreak House* at the Bleecker Street Playhouse in Greenwich Village; he had also staged the New York premieres of Shostakovich's *Katerina Ismailova* (the revised, bowdlerized version of *Lady Macbeth of Mtsensk* that Shostakovich had prepared after Stalin's devastating criticism of his opera) and of Prokofiev's *The Fiery Angel.* Hired along with him for *Jesus Christ Superstar* were the designers Gardner Compton and Emile Ardolino, who had worked multimedia wonders with the Joffrey Ballet's *Astarte,* the New York City Opera's *The Makropoulos Affair,* and *Oh, Calcutta!* Discussions about set design, featuring slides and projections, had already begun, and under terms of an agreement with Stigwood dated June 1, 1971, Corsaro, Compton, and Ardolino were also to collaborate with Rice and Lloyd Webber on the scenario, preparing *Superstar* for the stage.* The distinguishing feature of Corsaro's production was to be an extensive use of television screens, reflecting the media reaction to Christ's life and death.

Over the summer, however, Stigwood seems to have had a change of heart. His productions were often distinctive for their splashy vulgarity, and it is possible that Corsaro was simply taking *Superstar* too seriously. When Corsaro broke several bones in his back in an automobile accident and landed in hospital, Stigwood took the opportunity to replace him and his team. On Monday evening, August 2, Stigwood met with O'Horgan to ask him to come aboard. With Ron Yatter, O'Horgan's agent from the William Morris Agency, Stigwood and O'Horgan met again the following afternoon at three o'clock and O'Horgan sketched out his terms.

On August 5, O'Horgan formally accepted Stigwood's offer to direct the show, contingent on the following demands: a twenty-thousand-dollar fee to be paid prior to the first performance; a 4-percent royalty of the gross weekly box-office receipts and 5 percent of the net profits, if any; the right to direct any and all English-language productions presented anywhere in the world by Stigwood, except those already licensed in Australia and South Africa, with an additional ten-thousand-dollar fee for each, plus royalties; and total creative control over all aspects of the production, including casting, sets, lighting, and costumes. Additionally, the show would have to carry the following credit: "CONCEIVED FOR THE STAGE AND DIRECTED BY TOM O'HORGAN," which was to be used whenever the authors were credited and in the same size type as the authors' credit.

On Saturday, August 7, O'Horgan flew to Ravinia, outside of Chicago, to see *Jesus Christ Superstar* on tour; with him went Robin Wagner, the new set designer, and his friend Harvey Milk.† By August 12, Stigwood had sent O'Horgan both a reel-to-reel copy of the album and a contract, agreeing to the terms but excluding the director from profit participation in either the upcoming *Superstar* film or the concert tours. Rehearsals began the next month.‡

Despite O'Horgan's brave words about wishing a "spiritual experience" on his audience, the production that evolved was anything but meditative. Christ made his entrance emerging, erect, from a silver chalice; he left nailed to a golden triangle. In one scene, he was adorned with a huge coat (shades of *Joseph*) that cost twenty thousand dollars to make. Herod was played as a campy drag queen in platform shoes. In an attempt to reproduce the sound on the album, the cast strolled around the stage leashed to hand microphones, which were passed from one character to another as the occasion demanded—this at a time when most Broadway shows were either lightly miked or not amplified at all. It

---

*Another director who sought the property was Harold Prince. Fresh from his Broadway triumph with Stephen Sondheim's *Company,* Prince sent a telegram expressing his interest in acquiring the rights to produce *Superstar* to Lloyd Webber at his parents' Harrington Court address, where it lay unopened for two weeks. Andrew, who would have welcomed Prince as an alternative to O'Horgan, was in America meeting with Stigwood, and by the time he learned of Prince's interest, it was too late—at least for *Superstar.*

†In November 1977 Milk would achieve fame as the first person ever to be elected to San Francisco's Board of Supervisors on an openly homosexual political platform; exactly one year later, Milk became a martyr to gay liberation when he was murdered in City Hall together with Mayor George Moscone by Dan White, a disaffected former city supervisor.

‡In the fall of 1974, sixteen months after *Superstar* had closed, Corsaro successfully sued the driver and passengers of the other car in the New York State Supreme Court for damages resulting from lost wages. *Superstar* had recouped its investment by August 20, 1972, and gone into profit until closing at the end of June 1973. Under his Stigwood contract, half as generous as O'Horgan's, Corsaro would have received one hundred ninety-five thousand fifteen dollars and seventy cents; under his severance agreement with Stigwood, agreed on to August 18, 1971, he got forty thousand five hundred forty-five dollars and thirteen cents.

was not a directorial conceit but a decision made out of necessity: during rehearsals, O'Horgan had experimented with body mikes, but they kept picking up outside interference—police radios, taxi dispatchers, etc. Three previews had to be canceled, at a cost of thirty-six thousand dollars in lost box-office revenue, while the problems were sorted out.*

After nearly two weeks of previews, *Jesus Christ Superstar* opened on Tuesday, October 12, at seven o'clock in the evening at the Mark Hellinger Theatre on Fifty-first Street, where *My Fair Lady* had once played. The cast included Elliman as the Magdalene, Fenholt (newly married the month before) as Jesus, Dennen as Pilate, and Ben Vereen as Judas. Sets were by Robin Wagner, lighting by Jules Fisher, and costumes by Randy Barcelo; Abe Jacob was the sound engineer, and the conductor was Marc Pressel. Tickets for the theater's 1,581 seats were priced from four dollars to fifteen dollars.†

Although the critics were divided in their estimation of the lyrics and music, they were nearly unanimous concerning the worth (or lack thereof) of O'Horgan's production. Writing in *The New York Times,* Clive Barnes hated almost everything about the show. Rice, he said, "does not have a very happy ear for the English language"—surely a case of the pot calling the kettle black if there ever was one, as Barnes proceeded to demonstrate: "There is a certain air of dogged doggerel about his phrases that too often sounds as limp as a deflated priest." Of Lloyd Webber's music, Barnes wrote, "It is, unhappily, neither innovative nor original," although that judgment did not stop him, a few paragraphs later, from saying that the music was "the best score for an English musical in years." The English-born critic was somewhat amused by O'Horgan's inventive effrontery: "Ever since his beginning at La Mama, Mr. O'Horgan has tried to startle us. Once he startled us with small things, now he startles us with big things. This time, the things got too big. . . . The stage is full of platforms, carriages descend from the heavens, and even the stars over Gethsemane are captured in a blue plastic box. The total effect is brilliant but cheap—like the Christmas decorations of a chic Fifth Avenue store."‡

More reasoned was the opinion of *The New York Times'* Sunday drama critic, Walter Kerr: "Lyricist Tim Rice has found for the rock musical a personal, and I think persuasive, tone of voice. The tone of voice is not merely mod or pop or jauntily idiomatic in an opportunistic way. It sheathes an attitude. It speaks, over and over again, of the inadequate, though forgivable, response ordinary men always do make when confronted by mystery. . . . Andrew Lloyd Webber's score functions well, too, using rock as a frame rather than an obsession. The beat and blare establish an angle of hearing, telling us to cock our ears for the jumpy directness of the lyrics." To make the opera work, Kerr wrote, "all that had to be done was put it on a stage baldly . . . Mr. O'Horgan has adorned it. Oh, my God, how he has adorned it. . . . In both the most obvious and subtlest of ways Mr. O'Horgan is eternally bent on cutting across what is good, or might be good, severing head from body."

Time's Ted Kalem expressed his admiration for both Rice's and Lloyd Webber's contribution but had reservations about O'Horgan's spectacular vision: "A frequently breathless and occasionally stupendous *son et lumière* show, crowded with mechanical contrivances and a headlong rush of happenings." Music critic Alan Rich, in *New York,* lambasted Lloyd Webber's score—"If it is anything related to rock at all, it is on the bottom rung of bubble-gum, and most of it is even below that."—while his colleague, drama critic John Simon, roasted everybody: "What we get at the Mark Hellinger is closer to rock bottom than to rock opera: a mediocre score with less than mediocre lyrics, in an overinflated, megalomaniacal production which, for all its going off like a dozen Roman candles in twelve simultaneously diverging directions, cannot hold a candle to a modest, innocently imaginative, and truly felt little musical like *Godspell.*" Simon went on:

> I shall not even try, in such limited space, to describe what O'Horgan hath wrought in terms of sliding panels and all-engulfing fabrics, pieces of scenery and actors lowered and hoisted through the air, Art Nouveau slide projections, Félicien Ropsish and Aubrey Beardsleyish costumes, creepy objects like inverted metallic elephant trunks with tongues hanging out at the wider end or enormous silver dentures carried about as if they were cymbals, merchants selling what appear to be mummified babies and soldiers in armor cunningly designed to facilitate instant sodomy. Clearly, a man who could invert an elephant's trunk would stop at no imaginable inversion.

Only Douglas Watt in *The New York Daily News* unreservedly praised the production. "A shattering theatrical experience, unlike any other I can recall," he wrote. "[It] seems likely to be around for a long time to come."

---

*In retrospect, the producer's insistence that the show replicate the sonic ambience of the record was foolhardy. At first, O'Horgan wanted to place the orchestra under a plastic bubble, as if it were playing in the recording studio; he had to settle for a Bayreuth-like wooden hood with manhole-sized openings over the pit. Although the aural result was unsatisfactory, Andrew liked O'Horgan's original impulse so much that he copied it later for *Cats* and *Starlight Express.*

†Other musicals during the 1971–1972 season were a revival of two Leonard Bernstein works, *On The Town* and *Candide;* a new show from Anthony Newley and Leslie Bricusse called *It's a Funny Old World We Live In but the World's Not Entirely to Blame;* and the first Israeli musical, a show called *To Live Another Summer—To Pass Another Winter,* described as "a lighthearted treatment of the generation gap as well as the struggle with the Arabs."

‡Platforms and carriages descending from heaven were far from an O'Horgan invention; indeed, they were a staple of baroque opera productions. Further, the window displays in Tiffany's or Saks Fifth Avenue were hardly cheap. To add insult to injury, Barnes misspelled Barry Dennen's surname.

Oblivious to the reviews, a crowd of one thousand invited guests gathered outdoors at Tavern-on-the-Green in Central Park for the post-performance supper. The guest list ranged from Otto Preminger, Tennessee Williams, and Andy Warhol to Jerome Ragni and James Rado, the lyricists of *Hair*. At one point, Ragni bearded Williams and told the playwright that he would love to set one of Williams's plays to music. "I'm too old for you," Williams replied, and Ragni and Rado receded into history. Stigwood celebrated by flying in ten of his relatives from London and Australia and later taking them cruising in the Caribbean on his yacht.

Outside the theater, there was another show going on. Members of several different religious groups, Catholics, Protestants, and Jews alike were picketing, brandishing signs. "Jesus Christ ~~Superstar~~ Lamb of God," proclaimed a typical placard. "Jesus Christ Our Hope ~~Superstar~~," read another. "Christ is not a superstar," said Richard Gallagher, a parishioner at Our Lady of Mount Carmel Catholic church in Queens. "He's the Son of God."

The protests were a reprise of the reaction to the single and to the album — déjà vu all over again. A vocal minority of Catholics objected to the show's implicit denial of Jesus' divinity, while some Protestants were offended by the implication that Mary Magdalene's love for Jesus was more than simply platonic. A group of Baptist ministers in Louisiana denounced the work, while a Baptist pastor in Massachusetts ended a sermon by smashing a copy of the record and advising his congregation to do the same. High-school bands in El Paso, Texas, were forbidden to play any tune from *Superstar*. Father Malcom Boyd, the Episcopal priest and author, said the show had no soul. Even the Mormon hierarchy weighed in from Salt Lake City, calling *Superstar* "a profane and sacrilegious attack upon true Christianity," and adding, "We encourage members of the Church and good men everywhere to oppose this type of entertainment."

Blacks, too, took offense at the casting of Vereen as Judas. "Was it coincidental poetic symbolism that Black actor Ben Vereen plays the role of Judas Iscariot in the much-ballyhooed rock opera *Jesus Christ Superstar*? And incidentally, the fine acting that Vereen puts down might be the only thing of relevance the play has for Black audiences," wrote *Jet* magazine.

The big broadside, though, came from Jews, through the powerful organ of the American Jewish Committee, which (as *Time* phrased it) "soberly considered whether *Jesus Christ Superstar* is good or bad for the Jews and decided that it's bad." The day the show opened, Rabbi Marc H. Tanenbaum sent the news media a seven-page attack on the show prepared for the AJC by Gerald S. Strober, a Presbyterian lay minister with a master's degree in Jewish culture and a consultant for the AJC. Titled "Jesus Christ Superstar: The 'Rock Opera' and Christian-Jewish Relations," the report was a parsing of Rice's text, uncovering anti-Semitic leanings on every page. The show, wrote Strober, "unambiguously lays the primary responsibility for Jesus' suffering and crucifixion to the Jewish priesthood . . . bloodthirstiness is plainly voiced by the priest Annas . . . the current production wordlessly yet unmistakably implicates the priests in the crucifixion sentence upon Jesus. . . . It may be worth noting that in the current performance the role of Judas, a victim of Jewish perfidy, is played by a black man . . . in some cases the emotional coloring is deepened to make Jewish individuals and their acts appear more sinister than the gospel record warrants. . . ." And so on. "*Jesus Christ Superstar*," Strober concluded, "is, if nothing else, insufficiently thoughtful, potentially mischievous and possibly a backward step on the road toward improved Christian-Jewish relations."

A charge of "insufficient thoughtfulness," hedged by the qualifiers "potentially" and "possibly," hardly seems a hanging offense, but Strober's indictment received wide play in the press, both in America and Israel. Quoting Strober, *The Jerusalem Post* called *Superstar* "less than fair" to the Jews, although, the paper admitted, the show "does not repeat the myth of the Jews as Christ-killers condemned by God for all time; it does not claim that all Jews of Jesus' time knew him and forsook him."

In his public statements, Rabbi Tanenbaum was more inflammatory. "The authors," he said, "have written a scenario in which there are heroes and villains, and the Jews are the villains." Tanenbaum hastened to add, however, that censorship "is the last thing we have in mind"; he called it an "educational attempt." His objections were patent nonsense. American Jews had been listening to the *Superstar* album for a year without a hint of trouble. Jewish impresarios had offered it on tour; Jewish public relations men were flogging it across the country; Jewish audiences were flocking to it on Broadway, and Israel was home to one of the most successful touring performances; Dennen, the actor playing Pilate, was Jewish; and 90 percent of the executives of MCA, the recording company, were Jewish, as the Jewish television gossip-columnist Rona Barrett estimated. There was also a certain amount of hypocrisy involved, for the AJC's stand did not prevent it from petitioning the producer for ten free tickets to the show, ostensibly to determine whether *Superstar* would be a fit subject for the committee's weekly half-hour television show, *Jewish Dimension*.

A cooler head belonged to Rabbi Martin J. Zion of Temple Israel of the City of New York. "I had no deep feeling that its presentation was 'anti-Semitic' or that it would adversely affect Christian-Jewish relations," he wrote, pointing out that the show's emphasis on the human nature of Christ "coincides with our Jewish view of Jesus."

To his credit, Stigwood resisted the pressure. He refused to meet with the AJC, which had called on him to change certain details of the staging; under his contract with O'Horgan, he couldn't have even if he had wanted to. Through his (Jewish) press agent, Merle Debuskey,

Stigwood noted that the "Superstar" concept "has been prominent in the public consciousness for some two years," during which time "millions of American Jews have heard it and responded in a salutary manner. I must respect all of this response as well as the minority opinion of one individual. This opinion, I must note, was not expressed either to me or any other member of this production, but was released to the press by the American Jewish Committee. . . . *Jesus Christ Superstar* is in my opinion an affirmation of life, of humanity. It is not a literal representation of the Passion of Christ as revealed by the New Testament. [Indeed, Rice's primary source was not Scripture at all, but Bishop Fulton J. Sheen's *The Life of Christ.*] It views in contemporary style the timelessness of a legend or a myth and the confrontations of a reformer and the establishment. . . ."

Lloyd Webber and Rice were just as adamant. "We're not pro and anti any dogma or sect," said Rice. "These anti-Semitic charges are laughable. Our manager [Land] is Jewish, and he's done more for us than anybody else has. I can't understand people complaining that the Jewish priests are being shown as the bad guys. Everybody in the show—except Pilate—is Jewish. There are some good Jews and some bad Jews." On November 9, Rice and Lloyd Webber went on "The David Frost Show" in America to defend their work.

Once again, though, despite its large advance and its unparalleled PR, *Superstar* was not the success everyone had so widely predicted. Perhaps in reaction to the critical attacks on the production, the box office softened, and when it came time for the Tony Awards, the show was ignored in favor of Sondheim's *Follies,* directed by Prince, and *Two Gentlemen of Verona.* O'Horgan didn't care: "Have you *seen* 'Follies'?" he asked an interviewer. "It's the saddest, most boring show you ever saw in your life."

In retrospect, it seems odd that the salient characteristic of O'Horgan's production—its pronounced gay sensibility—attracted almost no comment at all. One would think that the image of Christ as a phallic symbol might come in for special attention, but each religious group reacted parochially to the thing it feared most: for the Catholics, theology; for the Protestants, sexuality; for the Jews, the slightest recrudescence of anti-Semitism. It is possible, of course, that the production's homoerotic implications went unmarked because, even as late as 1971, nobody was looking for them. Gay liberation was still several years in the future; the avant-garde O'Horgan was ahead of his time in more ways than one.

Tim shrugged off the attacks and went off to Madison Square Garden to attend the "Rock and Roll Spectacular" and see Ricky Nelson get the inspiration for his song "Garden Party." Andrew got angry. The object of his wrath was not the religious organizations, though. It was O'Horgan. The withering review from Barnes infuriated and chastened him all at once; he had seen his worst fears about O'Horgan reproduced in the pages of *The New York Times.* Worse, he began to project how this catastrophe (for so it was already in his mind) would adversely affect his and Tim's chances for success with their next show. It would, he decided, take them years to live this down.

The hiring of O'Horgan was the first wedge between Rice and Lloyd Webber, opening a fissure that would effectively sunder the partnership before the end of the decade. For all their personal closeness at this time, Tim and Andrew were still the proverbial chalk and cheese. Tim, the confident heterosexual, had thought O'Horgan and his rum crew were a little weird—never before had he attended a production meeting at which some of the men were wearing dresses—but otherwise all right.* After a cautiously optimistic beginning, though, Andrew had decided that O'Horgan was all wrong and became increasingly vehement in his opposition. The temper of childhood now asserted itself: the production was the worst disaster of all time, and he would fight it to the death; if it came to London he would personally denounce it in the press; etc., etc. Andrew didn't want O'Horgan's grandiose spectacle, he wanted something simple, ideally in the round, playing against the content of the piece, not exacerbating it.† His antics annoyed both Stigwood and Land, who thought composers should be heard and not seen. Even more annoying, Lloyd Webber was demanding a look at the books and wondering about things like whether he and Tim were getting paid on the gross or the net.

Money was very much on his mind. For some time, Andrew had been living in a basement flat he had bought for four thousand pounds in 1969 at Number 10, Gledhow Gardens, which he shared briefly with his friend David Harrington. (Tim had left Grandma during the summer of 1970 to move in with his girlfriend of the moment, Prudence De Casembroot.) Andrew's neighbors in the Victorian row house would be awakened at all hours by the sounds of Andrew's piano rumbling up through the floorboards, but Lloyd Webber quickly ingratiated himself with them, especially with David Crewe-Read, an antiques dealer with whom he formed a fast, lifelong friendship. Lloyd Webber was quite the gastronome, an accomplished cook who would often prepare dinner in his dining room (a converted coal hole) for Crewe-Read and other friends, or, as the founder and president of something he called the Eating Out Club, he would lead them on a never-ending march through

---

*One afternoon, during an open casting call, Tim dressed in drag and auditioned for Mary Magdalene. He carried on so outrageously that Stigwood, who was in on the joke this time, burst out laughing; the rehearsal pianist, who was not, was so offended by this display of insensitivity on the producer's part that he slammed down the lid of the piano and stormed off.

†The stark, understated production of *Jesus Christ Superstar,* presented by the Shiki Theater in Tokyo became the composer's favorite. There were in fact, two Japanese versions, one played in biblical style and the other in Kabuki dress.

London's dining establishments. By the summer of 1971, however, there were two people again living in the flat at Gledhow Gardens: Andrew and his new wife.

Lloyd Webber had never spent much time with women; he preferred to spend his time working, not chasing girls. But in late 1969, with Tim's example before him, Andrew began to speak of his desire for a "dolly bird" of the kind flocking round Rice. It was high time, he felt, for him to have a steady girl. The problem was, how to meet one? Andrew was an uncomfortable mixer, incapable of small talk and awkward around people of both sexes; he also lisped slightly. Even by the standards of the times, Lloyd Webber cut an eccentric figure in his cinch-waisted, shocking pink velvet jackets, flowered shirts, tight pants, and shoulder-length hair. He asked some of the girls he knew to help him find a suitable companion.

In January 1970 the twenty-one-year-old Lloyd Webber hitched a ride up to Oxford for a party. There he met Sarah Jane Tudor Hugill, a sixteen-year-old schoolgirl. She was pretty, with the baby fat of adolescence still upon her, and she had never met anyone quite like the young composer. With the "Superstar" single behind him, Andrew was already a little famous and, to Sarah, more than a little glamorous. She found herself smitten with him, dazzled really; even so, she was somewhat surprised when, after just a few dates, Andrew suddenly asked her to marry him. Without much hesitation, she accepted.

What was behind Lloyd Webber's haste in proposing to a schoolgirl five years his junior? To his friends, the sudden engagement was Andrew's way of opting out of competition with Tim; Lloyd Webber had never had a steady girl, and when Sarah proved suitable, he decided to call his search to a halt and, like some good businessman, snap her up just as he had snapped up Tim. Further, the few girls Andrew was friendly with—Charlotte Gray and Sally Morgan—were practically the same age as Sarah; Lotte and Sarah, in fact, had attended Queen's Gate School together. Andrew simply didn't know any women his own age.

An immediate wedding was out of the question. Sarah came from a socially conservative, well-off, well-bred country family—her father, Anthony, a research chemist, was an executive with the Tate and Lyle sugar company*—and her parents were steadfastly opposed to such a precipitous union. They could not talk their daughter out of her attachment, but they managed to convince the young lovers that they ought to wait until Sarah was at least eighteen. Maybe by then, they hoped, she would outgrow her schoolgirl's crush.

She didn't. Sarah, in fact, adored Andrew with a child's fierce passion. Whenever they were together she gazed at him with undisguised adoration, and he returned the feelings. He rushed back to England from his first trip to America in the spring of 1970 because he couldn't bear to be without her. On July 24, 1971, a month after Sarah's eighteenth birthday, the couple was married in her parents' village of Ashton Keynes in Wiltshire. The church wedding was conventional but colorful: on the bride's side of the aisle sat members of the staid country middle class, while on the groom's were the longhaired likes of Stigwood, Rice, and Murray Head. Andrew's parents, of course, were there, too; Bill hated big weddings as only a professional organist could, but he went anyway. After the ceremony, Andrew and Sarah left for a honeymoon in Vienna (during which time Stigwood replaced Corsaro with O'Horgan).

Andrew installed his bride in Gledhow Gardens, as both mistress of the house and as his personal assistant. (Tim, by this time, was living in Northumberland Place.) Her husband's career was rapidly taking off, and Sarah Jane Tudor Hugill Lloyd Webber did everything for him. Just before the wedding, Andrew and Sarah bought an eighty-five-thousand-pound country house called Summerleaze in south Wiltshire near Dorset. The house was somewhat dilapidated, and it fell to Sarah to supervise the restoration. She also came with Andrew on his frequent trips to the States, attending to his business and keeping him organized.

There was a lot to keep organized. During the *Superstar* madness Lloyd Webber had somehow found the time to write the score for Stephen Frears's movie *Gumshoe,* starring Albert Finney. Jewison's film version of *Superstar* was in preproduction, with the popular mayor of Jerusalem, Teddy Kolleck, promising full cooperation during the location shooting, as well as 20-percent financial support. Off the success of *Fiddler on the Roof,* the non-Jewish Jewison was hot, which boded well. "I'm on the lookout for an unknown to play—and sing—the lead," said the Canadian director of *The Cincinnati Kid, The Russians Are Coming!,* and *In the Heat of the Night,* who earlier had been touting Topol, his *Fiddler* lead, for *Superstar.* "I just have the feeling in my bones, and my bones are pretty accurate, that we should go with a new face."

Despite Andrew's opposition to O'Horgan's *Superstar* production, the director got the chance to restage his show at the new, 3,828-seat Universal Amphitheater in Universal City, California, perched on a cliffside overlooking the San Fernando Valley near Los Angeles. The show opened on Wednesday, June 28, 1972. By this time, sales of the album had topped four million and the touring companies had earned more than eleven million dollars. The cast featured Ted Neeley as Jesus and Carl Anderson as Judas—both of whom would appear in Jewison's film—as well as Heather MacRae (daughter of Gordon and Sheila) as Mary, and Bruce Scott, ex-husband of Sandy Duncan, as Pilate; the

---

*and later a chief of the Food and Agricultural Organization of the United Nations. There were those who theorized that he also worked for Britain's spy agency, MI6.

conductor was Gordon Lowry Harrell. The production cost four hundred thousand dollars, about half of what it had in New York. Because the amphitheater was then an open-air arena (it is enclosed today), the performance started at eight forty-five, as the sun was starting to set over the Pacific Ocean. (On Fridays and Saturdays there were two shows, at eight thirty and eleven thirty.) The top ticket price was seven and a half dollars. The opening-night invitation made a sartorial suggestion: "Dress: Black Tie or Bizarre."

For Los Angeles, O'Horgan completely revamped his production. One reason, of course, was the vastly different physical circumstances of an outdoor theater nearly in the round. Not even O'Horgan could outdo the spectacular natural setting. Wagner's designs were at once monumental and simple: a giant upturned Christ face, its mouth open wide in a rictus of agony, commanded center stage; it was flanked on either side by disembodied hands whose palms were raised toward the sky. Towering over everything was a huge monolith, wrapped in canvas, that at the end was revealed as the Cross.

True to form, O'Horgan trucked out the show with his customary collection of freaks and monsters, but the production was largely praised. *The Los Angeles Times* dispatched three critics to determine "Is It Opera . . . Rock . . . Art?" Music critic Martin Bernheimer answered yes to the first question, rock critic Robert Hilburn replied no to the second (although he praised O'Horgan), and art critic William Wilson approvingly considered the third: "It belongs to the young and reminds us just how marvelous and awful that moment was when it belonged to us." A dissenting voice belonged to Winfred Blevins of the rival *Herald-Examiner,* who wrote, "the production gives new vividness to the word 'vulgar.' And to the word 'grotesque.'" The show was a hit.

That, however, was little consolation to Lloyd Webber, still nursing his resentment against O'Horgan. His mood improved, however, when Stigwood, using the loophole that exempted the Australian and South African productions from O'Horgan's control, imported Jim Sharman from Australia to stage the London version. Sharman's stripped-down view of *Superstar,* far closer to Andrew's ideal than O'Horgan's, opened at the Palace Theatre, Gilbert and Sullivan's old home, on August 9, 1972. Paul Nicholas played Jesus, with Stephen Tate as Judas, Dana Gillespie as Mary, and John Parker as Pilate; it was conducted by Anthony Bowles, who had been discovered earlier that year leading the Paris production.

After America, the reaction was blissfully tepid and rather dottily British: a group of women sang hymns outside the theater, the National Secular Society handed out leaflets headlined "Jesus Christ Supersham," and an unproduced playwright held a placard reading, "Down with Americanisation and commercialisation of theatre." Although some critics expressed reservations about turning Jesus into a superstar—it sounded so, well, vulgarly *American*—the reviews were generally excellent. "Prediction here is that it should run at least two years," wrote the London correspondent for *The Hollywood Reporter;* in fact, it ran for eight, becoming at the time the longest-running musical in British history. By contrast, O'Horgan's New York production lasted twenty months.

It was time to start looking around for the next project. Andrew and Tim had produced a recording of Prokofiev's *Peter and the Wolf* for Stigwood, narrated by Stigwood's client Frankie Howerd, and Rice was branching out into radio, where his mastery of pop trivia won him a reputation as a bright on-the-air personality. Theatrically, Lloyd Webber and Rice were publicly bandying a few ideas around. There was a movie version of *Peter Pan* in the works for Universal, they said; there was a comedy based on scenes from American history. Tim also had a notion that the life of Eva Perón, the wife of the Argentinian dictator, would make a good topic for a musical. But before that, Andrew insisted, must come a subject that both he and Rice were devoted to, the stories of P. G. Wodehouse. What about something called *Jeeves*?

Entr'acte One: JEEVES COMES A CROPPER

By the middle of 1973 Lloyd Webber's career had begun to develop a distinct pattern that could not have been comforting to the composer. *Joseph and the Amazing Technicolor Dreamcoat* and *Jesus Christ Superstar* had followed similar trajectories in Britain. Both had begun humbly, both had been recorded and released to great fanfare, and, after an initial sale, both had faded badly. If it were not for that gay bar in Amsterdam, the Brazilian discos, and the unaccountable enthusiasms of the Americans. . . . The *Superstar* production on Broadway had reproduced the pattern exactly, too, just as ontogeny recapitulates phylogeny: from Corsaro to O'Horgan to media event to record-setting grand opening to closing, all within two years.

Now the *Superstar* movie was following the same script. At the height of the *Superstar* craze, the idea of a bunch of flower-power freaks running around Israel must have seemed very high-concept in Hollywood — "Hey, kids, let's put on a Passion play!" — but, by the time the film came out in August 1973, passions had cooled considerably. For one thing, the sixties hippies were gone. The long-haired college students who once had been harassed by the crewcuts from the Deep South and the ultrasquare Midwest had mostly cut their locks and gotten jobs; now it was the rural kids who walked around aping Greg Allman and smoking dope.

For another, Americans just weren't interested in *Superstar* any more. It had had its Warholian fifteen minutes of fame, and now no one could quite remember anymore what all the fuss had been about. Even the bogus charge of anti-Semitism raised no more hackles, especially since the film was being made with Israeli cooperation. But the real problem was that on film, *Superstar* was a super snooze. In his review, Howard Thompson of *The New York Times* wrote:

> Broadway and Israel meet head on and disastrously in the movie version of the rock opera "Jesus Christ Superstar," produced in the biblical locale. The mod-pop glitter, the musical frenzy and the neon tubing of this super-hot stage bonanza encasing the Greatest Story are now painfully magnified, laid bare and ultimately parched beneath the blue, majestic Israeli sky, as if by a natural judgment.

Although the settings were spectacular — the movie was shot on location at Vet Guvrin, Silva, Herodion, Avdat (where the Crucifixion scene was filmed), Bet Shean, and the Dead Sea — the rest of the film failed to live up to them. The stars were a bland, passive Ted Neeley as Jesus, who had come from the Los Angeles production — Jewison had found his unknown, all right — Carl Anderson as Judas, also from L.A., and Elliman, whose gig at the Pheasantry had unexpectedly developed into a Mary Magdalene cottage industry. Jewison derived much of his imagery from O'Horgan, particularly his depiction of Herod (a bare-chested, beer-bellied Josh Mostel) as a campy fag with a backup chorus of transvestites.

To demonstrate that this lèse majesté was all in good fun, Jewison framed the opera with a prologue and postlude, showing a gang of hippies driving up in a magic bus, unloading their costumes and props and reenacting the story. Needless to say, this was not Rice's idea. His treatment had called for playing the show straight — a tale of Christ right out of *Ben Hur*. But Jewison wasn't interested in Lew Wallace; Ken

Kesey was more what he had in mind. Melvyn Bragg, the left-wing British writer and, later, television personality, was brought in to share screenplay credit with the director.

The framing conceit, however silly, was not fatal; it was the execution, not the concept, that did the film in. The sight of a multiracial band of Merry Pranksters rambling around the Holy Land was already dated in 1973; today, it seems ridiculous. *Jesus Christ Superstar,* the film, is the *Zabriskie Point* of movie musicals, a cautionary tale of excessive topicality in the face of a fast-moving zeitgeist. "To this viewer," wrote Thompson, "a gaudy rock rhinestone has now shriveled so transparently that by contrast it makes the Greatest Story seem greater than ever." The movie was a flop, gone with the desert's shifting, dry winds.

For Lloyd Webber, this was the gloomy view of his life at the time. One could always look on the bright side: at the age of twenty-five Andrew was already a millionaire. Yet even this silver lining had a cloud: thanks to the confiscatory tax rates in Britain—a top rate of 83 percent on earned income and 98 percent on unearned income—his royalty statements looked better than his bank balance. In 1972, with some of the *Superstar* money, Andrew and Sarah had traded in the basement flat in Gledhow Gardens (sale price: seven thousand pounds) for a seventy-thousand-pound townhouse in Brompton Square, on the north side of Brompton Road, near Holy Trinity Church and the Victoria and Albert Museum.

Lloyd Webber didn't really like the Brompton Square house. The neighborhood was a prime target of burglars, and his home, at Number 37, stood near the end of a long, dark, horseshoe crescent. But he knew the value of London real estate (he had, after all, been studying it all his life) and snapped up the property at what was a bargain price. Spacious and elegant, the Brompton Square house was perfect for entertaining. One night in 1972 the Lloyd Webbers threw a dinner party for rock singer Neil Sedaka, an evening which ended with Sedaka and Tim Rice around the piano, running through the pop repertoire.

Andrew and Sarah didn't stay long in Brompton Square. Their house was broken into once; later, Andrew was informed by the police that he was the target of a bank fraud scheme, which was foiled. The next year, the Lloyd Webbers sold the place for a quick profit of one hundred thousand pounds and used some of the proceeds to buy another country home, located near the village of Kingsclere and the town of Newbury in Hampshire. The manor house was called Sydmonton Court, a huge old pile whose oldest sections dated back to the sixteenth century, but whose most interesting excrescences, as far as Andrew was concerned, were Victorian. The purchase price had been two hundred and twenty thousand pounds, put up mostly by the bank with the house and twenty acres as collateral. With money had come the realization of some of childhood's dreams: the boy who wanted to be the inspector of monuments was now himself the owner of a monument. Two, in fact, since he still owned Summerleaze, a mortgage burden that quickly became so intolerable that Lloyd Webber was forced to sell Summerleaze at a forty-thousand-pound loss.

But not even Sydmonton Court could keep Lloyd Webber content for very long. He needed work. The problem was that Rice did not, at least not in the same way and certainly not at the same pace. In 1974, while on an Italian Riviera holiday with Sarah in Ventimiglia visiting Aunt Vi, Lloyd Webber ran into the film director Ronald Neame, who was then preparing a movie of Frederick Forsyth's 1972 thriller, *The Odessa File,* about an enterprising West German reporter who tracks down a Nazi war criminal. Lloyd Webber, who had known Neame since he was twelve, agreed to compose the score, which he wrote in collaboration with his brother, Julian, and which featured Julian's cello playing. The music was strange and spare and, in the final print, heavily cut. The opening song, "Christmas Dream," meant to evoke the spirit of mainstream pop music circa Christmas 1963, had lyrics by Rice and was sung by Perry Como. ("Watch me now, here I go, all's I need's a little snow," ran the first verse, which was widely—and wrongfully—interpreted in America as a reference to cocaine.) Andrew's music for the song was heavily indebted to Elvis Presley's song "Wooden Heart," right down to its arrangement and German-language middle section. Once again, the film did not do well. Although Maximilian Schell made a suitably oily villain, Jon Voight was miscast as Peter Miller, the Hamburg journalist, and Neame's direction had none of the suspenseful, captivating attention to detail that had marked Fred Zinnemann's film of Forsyth's brilliant first novel, *The Day of the Jackal.* Still, while dabbling with the combination of cello and rock band, Lloyd Webber stumbled upon an ensemble he particularly liked, so he filed away the sound in his head for future reference and got back to thinking about the theater.

His thinking was increasingly focused on an idea that, like *Joseph* and *Superstar,* had originated with Rice: P. G. Wodehouse's unflappable butler, Jeeves. Like almost every other educated Englishman, and quite a few Americans, Rice and Lloyd Webber loved Wodehouse's evocations of a Great Britain that never quite was, a carefree land of silly aristocrats and stalwart help. Understandably to the upwardly mobile Andrew, the new master of Sydmonton Court, the idea of writing a musical about the upper crust in their country houses had a certain appeal.

As far as Rice was concerned, though, their next project had to be the story of Eva Perón. Driving home one evening in 1973, he caught the end of a radio program about her and was immediately smitten: here was another superstar who had done it all and died at thirty-three, and she was blond and beautiful to boot. Any similarity with Jesus, however, ended there; in both her professional and private life, Evita was more like the Magdalene before her conversion. She was an amoral, beautiful bitch, and the more Tim read about her, the more his excitement grew. Tim's obsession with Eva became pronounced; she was all he could talk about. From beyond the grave, Eva cast a spell on the ladies' man that he simply had to resolve. Two weeks after Rice met Jane McIntosh in 1973, he whisked her away to Buenos Aires on a romantic fact-finding mission in Evita's homeland. Jane's companionship proved so congenial that she and Tim were married on August 19, 1974; when their first daughter was born the next year, they named her Eva Jane Florence Rice.

Jane McIntosh was working as a temporary secretary in the office of Capital Radio, London's leading pop-music station, when she met Tim. Rice, by now a celebrity, had his own Saturday-morning oldies show there called "You Don't Know What You've Got," on which he could indulge his love for the great hit songs of the past. By 1974 he also had his own eight-bedroom manor house called Romeyns Court, in Great Milton, Oxfordshire (a bargain at one hundred and twenty-five thousand pounds), where he could indulge his gentlemanly taste for dogs and cricket. The whirlwind courtship and marriage surprised most of their friends: Tim was coming off relationships of some standing with the radiant Juliet Simpkins, whom he knew from his days in the law office, and Pru De Casembroot, who later married the actor David Hemmings (the star of Antonioni's 1966 film, *Blow Up*), as well as uncounted flings of shorter duration. He seemed an unlikely candidate for marriage. Yet he and Jane made a handsome couple: Tim, six feet four inches tall, gangling, his blond hair already starting to thin; Jane, more than a foot shorter, petite, beautiful, composed, her reddish-blond hair and slight burr badges of her Scottish birth and patrimony.

Seduced, Tim just didn't find the sexless Jeeves very interesting any more. Lloyd Webber, however, was proving singularly resistant to Evita's seductive charms and insisted that Tim tackle the stately homes of England before wandering off to the pampas. Reluctantly, the more passive Rice said he would give *Jeeves* a go, while reserving the right to keep on plugging away at Argentina. Throughout 1973, the fissure that had opened between Rice and Lloyd Webber over the hiring of O'Horgan steadily grew wider; the friendship that had seen them spending most of their waking moments together for nearly six years was beginning to fray as both men matured. The Evita-Jeeves dispute symbolized the rift, for two more antithetical characters can hardly be imagined: the hard-edged Argentine whore-turned-plaster-saint and her greedy, grasping husband versus the chinless wonder, Bertie Wooster, and his manservant with a heart of gold.

Marriage was not the only thing drawing the partners inexorably apart. Their country houses—where, like the good English gentry they both aspired to be, Lloyd Webber and Rice spent most of their free time—were not particularly close to each other. And neither, it seems, were their interests anymore. Even though *Jeeves* was Rice's idea, it had paled in the face of the Argentine firecracker; desultorily, Rice worked on a few songs (one was called "Suddenly There's a Valet") and then told Lloyd Webber that he was dropping the project in favor of the show he was calling *Evita*.

From Tim's perspective, the decision made a lot of sense. For one thing, the creation of the show's libretto was limited by the Wodehouse stories. Fiction is always harder to tamper with than fact; one might take liberties with the Good Book, but the Bertie Wooster tales, especially in England, were Holy Writ. For another, *Jeeves* was to be a book musical, with dialogue. Both *Joseph* and *Superstar* had been sung through, their stories already familiar to audiences. *Jeeves* had a plot. Rice looked the situation over and, although he had written three or four songs, sensibly bowed out, hoping Andrew would do the same, so they might get on with *Evita*.*

In his own way, though, Andrew had become just as obsessive about *Jeeves* as Rice had about *Evita*. During the early days of their partnership, Andrew had fretted constantly about losing Rice, whom he saw as his passport to success. Now Tim actually had left him, albeit temporarily. Very well, then, he would show Rice. He would show everybody. *Jeeves* it was to be.

Lloyd Webber's first move was to engage Alan Ayckbourn as the new lyricist. Ayckbourn was Britain's Neil Simon, a skilled chronicler of middle-class sensibilities who was highly regarded for plays such as *Absurd Person Singular* (1972) and his trilogy *The Norman Conquests* (1973). Although he had never written a musical before—indeed, was even said not to like musicals—Ayckbourn was a Wodehouse fan, and he agreed to write the book for *Jeeves;* Andrew, meanwhile, held out the slim hope that Rice could still be persuaded to contribute the song lyrics. With Tim proving adamant, Ayckbourn took on the unfamiliar task of songwriting as well. With the show sketched out in January 1973, Ayckbourn and Lloyd Webber flew to the United States to play the score for the ninety-three-year-old Pelham Grenville Wodehouse at his home in Remsenburg on Long Island and to receive his benediction.†

Despite his quintessentially English name and the Bright Young Things spirit that informed his work, Wodehouse had not lived in England for decades; he had, in fact, been an American citizen since 1955. (Ethel Wodehouse, his wife, ran the local Bide-a-Wee.) Wodehouse's ninety-

---

*Stigwood's management contract with Lloyd Webber and Rice gave him the right to produce anything they wrote, either singly or in tandem, but either man was free not to work if he so chose. The thought that Rice and Lloyd Webber might someday no longer wish to work together had never entered anybody's head.

†The meeting was engineered by Peter Brown, by then president of the Robert Stigwood Organisation in the United States, who had a house in nearby Southampton. Wodehouse did not have a piano, and neither did Brown, so Lloyd Webber and Ayckbourn played the score to the elderly man at the home of one of Brown's friends. The friend was so excited about Wodehouse's visit that she had bought an expensive formal English tea service, but when Wodehouse arrived, all the author wanted was a gin and tonic.

six novels were popular among the anglophilic educated classes in America, though in Britain, Wodehouse was, to some, still anathema for an episode that had taken place during the war. In June 1940 the writer and his wife were arrested by the Germans at their home in Le Touquet, just as they were about to escape. Interred as an enemy alien, Wodehouse, still a British citizen but an American resident, was freed at the urging of the United States government, then not a belligerent. In Berlin, the liberated Wodehouse made five radio broadcasts for the American Broadcasting System, describing his experiences as a prisoner of war: light, witty, and apolitical, they gently gibed the Germans rather than condemning them. In Britain, they caused a furor: Wodehouse had used German broadcasting facilities and thus was technically culpable of collaborating with the enemy. He was advised never to return to England.

The expatriate writer and playwright (eighteen plays) was an experienced musical hand. "Plum" Wodehouse had, after all, written the lyrics to Jerome Kern's song "Bill," which had found its way into *Show Boat;* and, with his collaborator Guy Bolton, had cowritten the book for Cole Porter's *Anything Goes.* He knew what made a good musical, and he also knew that his works had in the past proved singularly resistant to theatrical adaptation. Unfortunately, neither Lloyd Webber nor Ayckbourn nor Eric Thompson, the director, nor Christopher Bruce, the choreographer, shared either his expertise or his feelings. "I have been reading the script with great interest," Wodehouse wrote to Brown on January 9, 1975. "It is certainly unusual, but I have such faith in Alan Acbourne [*sic*] that I am sure it will be all right, though surely much too long at present. Act one 111 pages. Wow!"

In retrospect, Lloyd Webber's hubris in pursuing *Jeeves* says a lot about his character and personality. There was the fierce determination, carried to the point of stubbornness: despite Wodehouse's warnings and Rice's advice, Andrew persisted in believing that the rather twee *Jeeves* books could somehow be the stuff music-theater dreams were made of; "Bumper" Lloyd Webber was not about to be dissuaded by mere expert opinion. There was the self-confidence: so what if Lloyd Webber had never written a piece directly for the stage before? And then there was the sheer cussedness: if everybody told him it was going to be difficult, that only made Lloyd Webber more certain than before that his course was the right one.

As 1975 began, then, the signs were ominous. In February Wodehouse died; at the end, he had finally made the Honours List and went to his grave as Sir P.G., wholly innocent of any complicity in the show now in rehearsal in London. Ayckbourn was struggling with the lyrics; Thompson, who had never staged a musical before, was struggling with the direction; and Lloyd Webber was struggling with everything. To bail himself out of a tough spot—the show needed the sound of a twenties' dance band, something out of the Palm Court, which Lloyd Webber's limited experience and training had not equipped him for—he turned to his musical director, Anthony Bowles, and asked Bowles to do the orchestrations for him, subject to his approval. The problem was, Andrew wanted Bowles's work to go uncredited; according to Bowles, he would even pay extra for the anonymity.

Why Lloyd Webber insisted on retaining the orchestrator's credit for *Jeeves* is a mystery. There was no shame in not orchestrating a musical; Richard Rodgers had employed Robert Russell Bennett for just that purpose, and Stephen Sondheim relied on the services of Jonathan Tunick to give his shows their distinctive sound; even Leonard Bernstein had used an orchestrator on *West Side Story.* But Andrew was adamant. Bowles refused outright, so Lloyd Webber shopped around, getting the same response from two or three others. Lloyd Webber came back to Bowles and begged him to reconsider, offering a joint credit, but by then there was no time; the show was already in auditions. Ultimately, Bowles wound up doing the vocal arrangements, with credit, while the orchestrations were attributed to Lloyd Webber, Keith Amos, Don Walker, and David Cullen. (This was the beginning of a long professional relationship with Cullen, who has since coorchestrated almost all of Lloyd Webber's compositions, including *Cats,* the Broadway version of *Song and Dance,* the full-orchestra arrangement of *Variations, Starlight Express,* and *The Phantom of the Opera.*)

Worse, there were problems with the book. Ayckbourn not only did not know anything about musicals, he didn't trust them, so he wrote a play that would be able to stand without any music whatsoever. "I've tried with *Jeeves* at least to make it dramatically viable," he told the press. "I said to Andrew, 'The only thing I can do is to write a book I could put on the stage if your music didn't happen to arrive in time. I've just got to write something that will work regardless and hope the music comes as a bonus.'"

This, of course, was precisely the wrong way to write a musical, and it condemned *Jeeves* to failure. Ayckbourn's first script was Wagnerian in length, a clever, intricate, and involved play whose plot was original Ayckbourn, although the characters and language were a pastiche of Wodehouse. The action takes place at the East London Club for Unmanageable Boys, where Bertie Wooster is playing a solo banjo concert; his banjo keeps breaking down, and he is forced to tell vignettes to pass the time while Jeeves is sent packing to fetch new strings. This framing structure allowed Ayckbourn to make liberal use not only of Wodehouse's dialogue but also of his descriptive prose; Bertie could stagger back, appalled, and then remark to the audience, "I staggered back, appalled." But if anything, Ayckbourn was too respectful of his source. The first read-through took more than five hours; the first woman did not appear on stage until thirty-five minutes had passed; the first four songs went to Bertie Wooster; and so on. Like the three-night *The Norman Conquests*, a kind of English domestic *Ring* cycle, which was running in the West End, *Jeeves* was an epic. The problem was, it was as long as *Parsifal* and not half as funny.

There also was a problem with the physical production. Originally, the English designer Tony Walton had been hired, but he was also committed to doing *Chicago* for Bob Fosse; when Fosse's heart attack delayed *Chicago*'s opening, a scheduling conflict arose with *Jeeves*, and Walton chose to stay by his old friend's side. At the last minute, Bob Swash, the executive producer of *Jeeves* (Stigwood was spending most of his time in America, and seemed disinterested), engaged someone who went by the single name of Voytek, who imposed a concept on the production. Rather than moving smoothly and magically from place to place, according to the location of Bertie's tales, the play began on a bare stage, upon which Jeeves gradually assembled bits and pieces of a set, so that by the end of the performance the East London Club had been transformed into a glittering, immaculate English country house. Although interesting in its way—"I say, Jeeves, let's put on a show!"—the concept was at odds with both Ayckbourn and Wodehouse, and it deeply offended Lloyd Webber, whose taste was strictly representational.

Rehearsals took place in a theater of war. There were rows between Andrew and Ayckbourn and between Lloyd Webber and Thompson. They fought about cuts, they fought about the ordering of the show's numbers, they fought about the chorus of the Drones Club, the all-male singing sextet that accompanied Bertie, and they fought about the role of the leading female character, Aunt Dahlia—who eventually was written out of the show altogether. During a meeting with Thompson and Walker in Harvey's Restaurant in Bristol, the atmosphere grew especially heated, and Thompson called Lloyd Webber a vulgar expletive. Shattered, Andrew returned to his hotel, sat down on the stairs, and wept. At the first preview in the Hippodrome Bristol in March 1975, *Jeeves* lasted four and three-quarter hours.

Despite a good cast—David Hemmings as Bertie Wooster, Michael Aldridge as the eponymous butler, and Gabrielle Drake as Madeleine Bassett, the ingenue—a morbid air hung over the show. Even after previews had begun, there was no letup in rehearsal, and Thompson (who died in 1982) took to arriving in a muzzy haze. He was used to moving three or four Ayckbourn characters around the stage, not twenty or thirty, and had little idea of what to do with the larger forces a musical comedy demands. As revolution brewed, Bowles and several members of the cast went to Swash and begged him to replace Thompson. "This isn't America," Swash said. "We don't do that sort of thing." Nevertheless, that is what they did; on April 18, the Friday before the show opened at Her Majesty's Theatre, Thompson was fired and replaced by Ayckbourn, which only made things worse. Like a runaway lorry careening down a hill, *Jeeves* was racing to certain doom.

Lloyd Webber was frantic. It was the O'Horgan *Superstar* nightmare all over again: bad because it was happening in England, worse because this time Lloyd Webber had no O'Horgan for a scapegoat, and worst of all because he really believed in the worth of his show. What to do? The sensible course would have been to suspend the previews and see if *Jeeves* could be salvaged. But unless a show doctor was called in, any reappraisal would be made by the same forces that had got *Jeeves* into such a mess in the first place. In a panic, Lloyd Webber telephoned Stigwood in New York and begged him to close the show. Stigwood, who after the *Superstar* experience had already begun to consider Lloyd Webber an annoyance who tended to lose his nerve at crucial moments, refused.

When *Jeeves* opened in London, at the same time as Sondheim's *A Little Night Music*, it was universally panned. "I think musicals are pretty damn boring," Ayckbourn had said, "but I hope this one is a bit different." It wasn't. "*Jeeves* is the all-British musical launched with the unsinkable formula of a Titanic," wrote Jack Tinker in *The Daily Mail*. "It sinks like a stone, fatally holed by an iceberg of immeasurable boredom."* Irving Wardle of *The Times* said, "The effect is like a dream of all the Wooster novels combined into the ultimate ghastly weekend." In *The Evening News*, Felix Barker summed up the show's prospects: "I'm afraid one cannot say Carry On Jeeves with much confidence." In America, *Jeeves* would have closed the next day, or certainly by Saturday, but in Britain, with a far higher economic tolerance for theatrical mediocrity, it managed to stagger on for four-and-a-half weeks, finally expiring on May 24, 1975.

The best way to understand *Jeeves* is to consider it little more than one of Andrew's Westminster schoolboy musicals with a big budget. Those youthful conceptions, after all, comprised Andrew's only previous experience in writing directly for the stage. Further, Wodehouse's stories appeal primarily to adolescents: there is the misogynist Drones Club, a spatted, tuxedoed order of Knights of the Holy Grail; the nattering, monocled perfect fool, Bertie Wooster; the too-cute-by-half collection of English archetypes such as the villainous Sir Roderick Spode, Harold "Stinker" Pinker, and Stiffy Byng; and the coy undercurrent of double-entendre humor—all these underline the fundamental immaturity of *Jeeves*. Far more than the fights among Lloyd Webber, Ayckbourn, and Thompson, it was this quality that did *Jeeves* in.

How bad is *Jeeves*? Absent many key numbers and numerous short interludes, the original cast album is only a vague approximation of the score. Songs such as "Literary Men," "Food of Love," and "Madrigal" are missing from the recording, as are the various connecting instrumental interludes. Still, there is evidence enough. The banjo-playing Bertie and his tiresome Drones are given the worst song Lloyd

---

*Dahlia was to have been played by the actress Betty Marsden, who received equal billing with Hemmings on the *Jeeves* posters, now collectors' items. Tinker ended his review by saying, "My congratulations go to the delightfully talented Betty Marsden who had the luck to be left onshore, not wanted on voyage. A miraculous escape."

Webber ever wrote, a dreadful number called "Banjo Boy," which, incredibly, both opens and closes the show. (This, of course, was dictated by the plot's framework, but a composer in a stronger position than Lloyd Webber was at the time would have put a stake through its heart nonetheless.) Another number, "Spode's Anthem" (called "S.P.O.D.E." on the album) is a Colonel Blimp march à la Elgar with an unaccountable and wildly inappropriate pseudo-Prokofiev bridge.

Emulating Ayckbourn's painfully precious lyrics — "I know the night can't be in vain/The stars shine in God's daisy chain/And even Mister Moon's begun to snore" — Lloyd Webber adopted a mannered, self-conscious style that rejected all traces of the rock idiom in favor of an extended soft shoe. For a role model, he turned to Jerry Herman's score for *Hello, Dolly!*; one of the musical directions in the song "Jeeves Is Past His Prime" reads "heavy *Dolly* style." Many of the songs in *Jeeves* sound alike, the characters are not sufficiently differentiated musically, and for all the fuss over the orchestrations, each number has the same feel as the last; all saxophones, trumpets, and banjos.

Jeeves is not a total loss. "Female of the Species" is a lovely strophic ballad in E-flat major, and the show's best song, "Half a Moment," is a tender, stylish duet. "The Jeeves Waltz," called "Today" on the cast album, is an imaginative dance that modulates from D major to E-flat and finally to G-flat, shifting easily from 6/8 to 3/4. But such moments, or even half-moments, are too infrequent to warrant *Jeeves*'s resuscitation.

Lloyd Webber drew several important lessons from the *Jeeves* fiasco. The first was never to work beyond the level of his expertise. The second was to be sure to have collaborators who knew something about musicals. The third was never to go into rehearsal before the show had all its problems worked out in advance. The fourth was to control as many aspects of the production himself as he could. The fifth was never to write a book musical again; the music must always drive the drama, never the other way around. On the day *Jeeves* closed, the idea for the Sydmonton Festival was born; from then on, Lloyd Webber would try out everything first at his country home, in a little chapel on the property that he converted that summer into a small theater. As a boy, he had learned a lot from his toy theater; now, as a grown-up, he would have a real stage to play with.

To cap the worst year of Lloyd Webber's life, his wife, Sarah, fell ill that summer. Initially, the London doctors diagnosed her complaint as nerves and prescribed tranquilizers. Back at Sydmonton, Sarah worsened, and she was taken to a hospital in nearby Newbury. She lapsed into a coma and was transferred to another hospital in Reading, where a woman doctor recognized her condition as diabetes. Sarah began to come round late in the afternoon, although she had a relapse during the night; ultimately, she spent two weeks in the hospital. Sarah was told that her condition would make pregnancy difficult; she could have children, but she would have to spend a good deal of time in the hospital under direct medical supervision. Undaunted, Sarah said she and Andrew were determined to have children, and the next year she became pregnant with their first child, a daughter, Imogen.

As Lloyd Webber was mulling over his sobering dose of reality therapy, there came a note on Savoy Hotel stationery from Hal Prince, who had seen *Jeeves* while in town directing *A Little Night Music*. Prince had hated the show, but he had been hungering to direct a Lloyd Webber show ever since *Superstar*, and he was just the kind of show doctor that *Jeeves* had needed, so Lloyd Webber was especially receptive to his opinion. "Don't be discouraged, anybody can have a flop," wrote Prince. "This goes with the territory. I hope we work together some day." Prince had one other bit of advice: "Bank the score."

Bank the score; Lloyd Webber didn't need to be told that twice. Ever since *The Likes of Us*, he had been banking scores and periodically raiding them when circumstances demanded. A lyricist couldn't do that, of course, since show lyrics usually have a time-and-place specificity that music need not have; a lyricist had to keep coming up with new verses for a strophic song, but a composer could sit back on cruise control and repeat his melody. Music was malleable, mutable, changeable; it could go into the bank and be drawn out again in a flash. It was all a question of timing.

As the smoke from *Jeeves* cleared, Tim could be discerned beetling away on his Eva Perón musical. In the midst of the Bristol debacle, Andrew had already begun to sketch out his new tunes.

Chapter Four: OH, WHAT A CIRCUS

It was a chastened Lloyd Webber who came back to Rice in the middle of 1975 and said he was ready to sign on for *Evita*. He had been itching to show his erstwhile partner that he could succeed without him, and he had failed. Chafing under the unfavorable monetary arrangement of his contract with Stigwood, he had been hankering for greater personal control over his business dealings, and now his need for Stigwood was greater than ever. More than anything else, Lloyd Webber wanted to be at the center of the London theater world, and here he was, just another composer with a flop on his hands.

Now that the horror show was over, though, Andrew felt a great sense of relief. He had always trusted Tim's instincts, and in the case of Eva Perón Tim was never surer about anything. While Andrew had been losing his shirt on *Jeeves*—the production cost more than two hundred thousand pounds, all of it down the drain—Tim had been busy with *Evita*. After his visit to Buenos Aires, Rice had read just about everything there was to read on the life of the Rainbow of Argentina. He had a plot, he had a script, and he had some lyrics. There wasn't going to be any book, no dialogue at all; Lloyd Webber had learned his lesson from *Jeeves*, and Tim had no ambitions as a playwright. They both agreed that the best way for them to tell a story was operatically, entirely through music. Now all Andrew had to do was write the score.

Despite the failure of *Jeeves*, not all was gloom and doom as Lloyd Webber and Rice set to work in earnest on *Evita*. Recapitulating their experience in the Herefordshire hotel during the writing of *Superstar*, they headed down to Biarritz in France in the summer of 1975 to rough out *Evita*, but in five days they succeeded more in exploring the fine restaurants than actually composing; after a while, when it became clear that, beyond a rough draft of Act One, no productive work was being accomplished, they were joined by Sarah and Jane. Despite *Jeeves*, there were steady offers coming in to compose for the operatic stage: the English National Opera in particular was eager to have a Lloyd Webber work in its repertoire, while productions of *Joseph and the Amazing Technicolor Dreamcoat* were starting to pop up in schools all over the world. Andrew also had found an especially able personal assistant in a young woman named Bridget Hayward, one of those formidable English girls whose perfect accent and haughty glare could freeze a visiting Yank in his tracks, make him impulsively declare that the Revolution was all a gigantic misunderstanding, and have him beg for the Restoration.

Although it was on the proscribed list in Argentina and elsewhere in South America, *Jesus Christ Superstar* was becoming a hit in various unlikely places, such as Catholic Spain. Even if something was lost in the translation, *Superstar,* it seemed, was resonating:

JESUCRÍSTO SUPERSTAR
Oficina de Producción
Madrid 25th November 1975

Mr. David Land*
Superstar Ventures
London-England

Dear Mr. Land:

Thank you for your letter of 11th November. I am a bit surprised you did not now the date opening because we send you a cable with the new date, and another one with the great news and reviws that it was a great, great success. Better, impossible. More than six minutes of clapping and bravos at the end with everybody standing up and in trance. It was and memorable opening, and we should like very much that Tim and Andrew will saw it. We wait for them in few days just when our political situation could be more stablishes with the new king.

Unfortunally, the box office is not very strong, in part of the situation of the country. We did a great effort, but not in the right moment with Franco's dying and everything, and the fear of the people going anywhere. We hope, anyway, that slowly everything coul be fixed in the right place. It is a lovely production of Superstar, and in a few days I'll send you programs, posters, fotographs, critics just to have and idea of what we have done.

We are working like mad on the record, and we want to finish it this week, to realese it in two more weeks. The sad accident of Teddy Batista reatrd even the record. But it will be a fantastic record and we hope to do a great deal here and in America. Of course, as soon as I can I'll send all the copies you wnat, and with any charge. All of you are the fathers of the creature, like we said in Spain.

So, wait till soon for more news. And thsks again.

Ignacio Artime
Generalísimo, 16
Madrid 16
Spain

Artime's optimism proved well-founded. By the middle of March 1976 *Superstar* had become the most popular musical ever presented in Spain, grossing more than six hundred and fifty thousand dollars since its November 6, 1975, opening. It had not been an easy path to success. Although the director Jaime Azpilicueta had held the rights to the show for four years, Generalissimo Francisco Franco's censors were not about to allow an obviously blasphemous entertainment such as *Superstar* to take the boards. Not until after Jewison's film played in Spanish movie theaters for a year and a half did they finally relent, although officials closely supervised the goings-on in the converted Alcala Palace cinema in Madrid.

As well they might have, for the Spanish production, as originally conceived, was far more inflammatory than O'Horgan's. Out, by censor's orders, went the swastikas painted on the high priests, out went the machine guns on the stage, out went the screen-projected newspaper headlines proclaiming Christ's revolutionary spirit. Police were stationed in the theater for every performance but, undaunted, audiences flocked to it ten times a week, up to sixteen hundred people at a time at a top ticket price of four hundred pesetas (about six dollars and fifty cents). Teddy Bautista, a prominent Spanish singer and composer, sang the role of Judas and also served as the musical director. After the show closed in Madrid, it toured Spain, and the Spanish-language recording sold more than seventy-five thousand copies in just six weeks. True, in Argentina the Buenos Aires theater where *Superstar* was to have played had burned down mysteriously, and the movie house where the film played was firebombed, but maybe the Spanish success of *Superstar* was a good omen for the Argentine project.

Or maybe Lloyd Webber had finally matured. Whatever the case, he threw himself into the *Evita* score with a passion and commitment that was extraordinary even by his own obsessive standards. After the bromides of *Jeeves,* Rice's politically aware text for *Evita* struck a chord in Andrew. Look around, Tim mused: England in 1975 was a mess. The country was paralyzed by strikes that were verging on class warfare, the Labour government under Prime Minister Harold Wilson was ineffectual, unwilling to crack down on its constituency and unable to control it.

---

*Having been bought out by Stigwood, the affable Land stayed on with direct day-to-day management responsibility for Lloyd Webber and Rice. Land liked Tim and Tim liked him, but Land was finding Lloyd Webber's constant carping about money wearisome, just as Desmond Elliott had six years before.

The end of the first act of Evita *in Hal Prince's memorable 1978 London production. Elaine Paige is Evita and Joss Ackland is Perón.*

Prince's task was to take a popular album and turn it into a show, which he did brilliantly.

90

*P*aige kicks up her heels in the "Buenos Aires" number.

A rehearsal for the same scene.

P̲aige with David Essex, who played Che.

S̲iobhan McCarthy as Perón's mistress. Her song, "Another Suitcase in Another Hall," is one of Evita's highlights.

In the fall of 1979 Prince brought Evita to Broadway, casting Patti
LuPone in the title role (top). The director toned down the London
version's pro-Evita stance to create a spare, almost Brechtian staging.
Opposite, top: LuPone as Evita at the height of her fame. Opposite,
bottom: Mandy Patinkin as Che.

The Casa Rosada scene, Evita's finest
moment in London.

A phalanx of army officers in Larry Fuller's
imaginative Broadway choreography.

The Evita *curtain.*

"The Art of the Possible," a new number requested by Prince that depicted Perón's rise to power as a deadly game of musical chairs.

SONG
AND
DANCE

Song and Dance, *seen in both London and New York in the 1980s, was constructed from two earlier, separate works: the* Variations *for cello and rock band of 1978 and the song-cycle* Tell Me on a Sunday *of 1979. Right: Bernadette Peters on Broadway, where the show ran for 474 performances. Below: Marti Webb, for whom* Tell Me on a Sunday *was written, singing in the Palace Theatre.*

And now look at Argentina in the forties: strikes, social unrest, an impotent government. Argentina was not so very far off, either; to Americans, South America may have been one vast Hispanic barrio, but to the more sophisticated English, Argentina was a country with close ties to England and Europe. Until the arrival of Perón, it was a prosperous, heavily urbanized nation nursing a fragile democracy. It had a sizable English and English-speaking minority and, in fact, was not predominantly Spanish at all: due to massive immigration in the nineteenth and early twentieth centuries, the largest ethnic group in Argentina was the Italians, with pockets of Germans, French, Swiss, Poles, Russians, and Portuguese; with nearly half a million Jews, Argentina had the fifth largest Jewish population in the world. The few blacks that the Argentines had imported as slaves had been absorbed into the general population, and, owing to a policy of ruthless extermination, there were hardly any Indians. Argentina was, for all intents and purposes, a white European country, with a glamorous opera house in the Teatro Colón and a gracious capital city that called itself the Paris of South America. It was not really so very foreign after all, and in the story of a charismatic populist who clawed her way to power by manipulating the trade unions, both Lloyd Webber and Rice sensed the presence of a cautionary tale.

Which is not to say that they agreed on how to present their story. For two years, Tim had been in love with Evita. (And why not? She was a beautiful petite blond of the type he most admired.) Not so Andrew. He found Evita repulsive, dangerous. The sexuality that attracted Tim made Andrew uncomfortable. Jeeves, Bertie Wooster, et al. had been so bland, so bloodless, so, well, English; Evita was as hot as molten lava. To capture her, Lloyd Webber would have to step outside his own aloof personality, dig down deep, and try to project, musically, what had made her so irresistible to millions. "I know you think she's a bitch," Rice told him, "but make her wonderful."

He did: the resulting score was a turning point in Lloyd Webber's career—the first real evidence that here was not simply a minor British talent with a knack for catching a pop wave, but a serious composer of depth, talent, and technique working in tandem with a lyricist of style and substance. Everything that the pair had learned from *Joseph* and, more important, from *Superstar* jelled. Freed from his Bible studies, Rice could impart more bite and bounce to his lyrics; liberated from his strange-bedfellows' apprenticeship to Elvis and Prokofiev, Lloyd Webber was free to experiment and synthesize, to seek, and find, an original, vital melodic language that stamped his music as his own—and not as a collection of disparate influences. *Evita* is a masterpiece.

Like *Superstar*, *Evita* from the first was intended as an opera. And like *Superstar*, it too began its life not in the delivery room of a public theater but in the intensive-care surroundings of the recording studio. Once burned, twice shy: Lloyd Webber was not about to take the stage with anything he did not consider ready. With *Superstar* he had evolved his orchestrations as he went, slowly, painfully, and expensively, but by *Evita* he had learned much, and, with his father's active encouragement, he confidently set about preparing the score. It was the first time since childhood that Bill had helped his son musically. Then it was simply a matter of notation; now Bill drew on his own considerable technical resources to advise Andrew on instrumentation (he suggested the Paraguayan harp, for example), and which doublings to avoid— the nuts and bolts of an effective orchestral score. Unlike *Jeeves*, this time there would be nothing left to chance, no strangers' kindnesses or competence to depend on. *Evita* would succeed or fail on the merits of Andrew's music and Tim's words.

Rice's first draft had been largely factual and biographical, but Lloyd Webber insisted that a mere retelling of Eva's rise and fall was not enough. For *Evita* to work it needed a hook—a dominant idea that would crystallize the whole show into a few minutes of overwhelming emotional power. For inspiration, Andrew thought back to his school days at Westminster when, on one of his many forays into the London theaters, he saw Judy Garland perform in *The Talk of the Town* variety show at what is now the Hippodrome. Garland by this time was near the end, a pathetic, drug-addicted woman living on past glory. She showed up nearly an hour late for her performance, and when she sang her signature tune, "Over the Rainbow," the crowd hooted in derision and threw coins onto the stage. She could not continue and retired to her dressing room, defeated and broken. This, then, was just the image Lloyd Webber sought: the spectacle of a woman whose most potent weapon had, in the end, been turned against her, the echoes of the melody taunting her with remembrances of things past. If Citizen Kane's mantra had been "Rosebud," Evita's would be "Rainbow." Focusing intently, the partners developed the Final Broadcast, a scene in which Evita, wracked with cancer, tells the people of Argentina that (under pressure from Perón's generals) she will decline the office of vice president—to the strains of an anthem that, earlier in the show, had proclaimed her triumph.

Dying heroines expiring to past glories is a sound operatic tradition. At the close of Wagner's *Tristan und Isolde*, the soprano summons up musically the interrupted duet she had sung in Act Two with her lover and, with her death, consummates it. In the last act of *La Bohème*, the orchestra poignantly recalls the high spirits of the Bohemians and Mimi and Rodolfo's love duet from Act One, while Mimi herself manages one last gasp of her first-act aria, "*Sì, mi chiamano Mimi.*"*

---

*Lloyd Webber's knowledge of opera, while gleaned largely secondhand through recordings, was wide. Under his father's influence, he had become a Puccini fan at an early age, and from the Italian master he had learned the value of the *coup de théatre*. In *La Bohème* it comes as Mimi collapses in the garret; in *Tosca*, when the heroine leaps from the top of the Castel Sant' Angelo. And in *Evita*, it is "Don't Cry for Me, Argentina."

With the hook they were looking for, Rice and Lloyd Webber worked on *Evita* throughout the second half of 1975 and nearly all of 1976. Their method of working might best be described by the axiom, *"Prima la musica, doppo le parole"* — the age-old issue of which deserves pride of place, the words or the music (and the subject of Richard Strauss's opera *Capriccio*). Andrew's tunes usually came first, and then Tim's words, although sometimes they worked the other way around. The first song they finished and recorded was Evita's anthem, which had the working title of "It's Only Your Lover Returning." This was less a song than an old-fashioned scena for soprano, an extended aria in which Evita tries to justify her cynical philosophy to the people of Argentina. To sing it, Tim and Andrew engaged Julie Covington, a slight, boyish singer and actress with close-cropped hair and a big voice, whose career had been launched earlier in the year by the television series *Rock Follies*, a show about an all-female rock band.

The idea for the hit song was sound, but both Tim and Andrew agreed that the first line was not quite right, though "It's Only Your Lover Returning" certainly made sense in the context of the rest of the lyric:

> *The truth is I never left you*
> *All through my wild days*
> *My mad existence*
> *I kept my promise*
> *Don't keep your distance*

They sent Covington back into the studio to dub in a new first line, "All Through My Crazy and Wild Days," but that was even worse. Tim tried one more time. There was a phrase he had used elsewhere in the text, in the funeral scene with which the opera began, and in the Final Broadcast at the end; now, just before the single was to be released, he made it the first line and the title of the show's central song: "Don't Cry for Me, Argentina." So what if it didn't make much sense? It had the right feel.

For the crucial role of Che — the Guevara-cum-Everyman who is the show's ironic commentator — Andrew wanted Murray Head, his Judas on *Jesus Christ Superstar*. Bowles, the musical director who had been with Lloyd Webber since the London production of *Superstar* in 1972, balked. He disliked Head's singing and recommended instead an Irishman who went by the name of C. T. Wilkinson, a choice that found strong favor with Rice as well. Lloyd Webber, however, was adamant. Andrew told Bowles to rehearse the rest of the cast — Covington, Barbara Dickson as Perón's mistress, Paul Jones as Perón — while he, Lloyd Webber, would coach Head privately. Just before recording was to begin, Lloyd Webber asked Bowles where Wilkinson was: Head was not good enough, and they had bought out his contract. So Colm Wilkinson, who later created the role of Jean Valjean in *Les Misérables*, became the first Che. And shortly after *Evita* opened on stage in London, Bowles was summarily fired. He never worked with Lloyd Webber again. His place was taken by David Caddick, a student of Bill's who came highly recommended.

Evita was first presented publicly during the summer of 1976 to Andrew's guests at Sydmonton Court. In London, Lloyd Webber had sold the Brompton Square house for one hundred and seventy thousand pounds and was living with Sarah in the garden and ground floors of a maisonette flat at 51 Eaton Place (he later bought another flat, which he used as an office, at 11 West Eaton Place), but his heart — like Tim's — was in the country. The festival, an offspring of the *Jeeves* catastrophe, had begun in embryo the year before (Julian had played a cello concert), but *Evita* was the first new Lloyd Webber work tried out, as it were, in his own backyard, fifty-eight miles southwest of London.

For a composer coming off a flop, Sydmonton Court was a major financial extravagance. Even though manor houses were selling for a song in the wake of the British stock-market crash and the lowest ebb of the Labour government, the house still cost a fortune to keep running, and the acreage that came with it required looking after as well.* Andrew, however, was determined to hang on to it, no matter what the cost, and he redoubled his efforts to make *Evita* the hit that both he and Tim dearly wanted it to be.

Evita was not performed live that summer. Instead, the invited audience of friends and colleagues witnessed an audiovisual slide show whose sound track consisted of the album that Lloyd Webber and Rice were then producing. Reaction, gleaned informally from those present, was enthusiastic, and it sent the pair back into the studio once again, to polish their new creation.

---

*At first Lloyd Webber owned 20 acres, of which only 5 were his directly to control. Over the years, as his fortunes waxed, he gradually bought up more of the surrounding countryside. By 1984, he owned 65 acres; by 1988, the grounds had expanded to 1,350 acres, and he still wanted more. Sydmonton Court's history may be gleaned from a description that Lloyd Webber wrote for his Sydmonton Festival program. Here again is the voice of the would-be inspector of ancient monuments:

> The earliest visible parts of Sydmonton Court date from the sixteenth century. These can be seen in the stepped gables on the South Front and in the brickwork of the North Front. The old exterior of the sixteenth century house can be seen in the Stone Hall. The wings on either side of the South Courtyard are eighteenth century, but the windows onto the courtyard obviously date from the major reorganisation of the house in the early 1950s. At that date the effects of a period of disuse and the wartime accommodation of several hundred US Servicemen were put to right and a large Victorian wing was demolished. . . . At first glance the North Face looks eighteenth century in date, but it is clearly a late Victorian "Georgianisation" with windows inserted into the sixteenth century brickwork.

Although *Evita* was going well, the partnership was in its last stages. Rice and Lloyd Webber had worked smoothly together during the writing, but in the recording studio they fought constantly, over everything from the size of the orchestra needed to realize the composer's vision—the London Philharmonic was playing the score*—to the smallest aspects of the orchestration. Once, when Tim criticized a particularly egregious example of the orchestra smothering his words, Lloyd Webber exploded and started screaming at Rice. Tim walked out: why should he stick around to be abused? Besides, there was a cricket match he wanted to attend.

"A songwriting partnership is like a marriage," wrote Richard Rodgers, who spent twenty-five years with Lorenz Hart and another eighteen with Oscar Hammerstein II. "Apart from just liking each other, a lyricist and a composer should be able to spend long periods of time together—around the clock if need be—without getting on each other's nerves. Their goals, outlooks and basic philosophies should be similar, so that the song they create is accepted as a spontaneous emotional expression emanating from a single source."

That, at least, was the ideal. But the quarrels between Lloyd Webber and Rice were hardly unprecedented in the annals of music theater. The relationship between composer and lyricist is often a yin-yang affair, each seeking in the other those traits that he lacks. But that didn't mean they had to like each other: Gilbert and Sullivan (in part due to the machinations of D'Oyly Carte) had cordially detested one another and communicated only by mail. Rodgers survived collaborations with the brilliant but tortured alcoholic Hart and the more placid but painfully slow Hammerstein with his equanimity intact but faltered when he tried to work with the mercurial Alan Jay Lerner. In opera, Verdi's relations with his librettists were often contentious, and the petit-bourgeois Richard Strauss and the elegant Hugo von Hofmannsthal were as temperamentally different as night and day. Closer to Rice and Lloyd Webber's generation, the two primary Beatles, Lennon and McCartney, had offered further proof of this maxim: the one (Lennon) sarcastic, biting, cynical, yet beneath it all passionate and concerned; the other (McCartney) sentimental and often saccharine, yet underneath difficult and demanding.

Rice and Lloyd Webber were no different. As they grew older—grew up, really—characteristics that could be glossed over in the flush of late adolescence took on greater import in prosperous adulthood. Andrew was little changed; there were still the volcanic flashes of temper, the harsh words and dire threats directed most often at those he felt would not or could not retaliate, tempered by his genuine solicitousness and bonhomie at other times, his fondness for lashing back the old vino rosso with some of the Kensington lads or hieing off to the East End to cheer on the pitiful Leyton Orient Football Club with Julian and John Lill.

Tim, however, had grown more complex. On the surface he was still the perfect public-school gentleman, with a quick wit, a gracious command of the mother tongue, and a gentility that suited the lord of Romeyns Court. Down deeper, though, was a fundamental disquiet in the soul, an existential misanthropy that had already surfaced in his lyrics. In Tim's universe, lovers used each other, no one could be trusted, and in the end they all came to grief. In *Superstar*, Christ had died but had not risen; now in *Evita*, La Perón would climb out of her coffin in a futile search for salvation.

After six months of work, the first fruits of *Evita* were ready. "Don't Cry for Me, Argentina" was released by MCA—having gambled and won big on *Superstar*, MCA was only too happy to give *Evita* a major push—in October 1976, backed with the exuberant "Rainbow High." Unlike "Jesus Christ Superstar," the single started strong and stayed strong, climbing rapidly up the charts to number one. The song whose title was almost an afterthought proved to be the hit single that Lloyd Webber and, especially, Rice had been seeking since the mid-sixties. The next month, the double album of *Evita* appeared, and it too was a smash, quickly going gold. A month later, the album spun off a second single, "Another Suitcase in Another Hall," an uncomplicated but touching ballad for Perón's deposed teenage mistress that was one of *Evita*'s few moments of repose; the "B" side was the harrowing "Requiem for Evita," the album's opening number. Maybe other Britons, too, shared Andrew and Tim's dark view of what was going on in their country.

Certainly Derek Jewell did. The man who had "discovered" Rice and Lloyd Webber at Central Hall gave the *Evita* album a glowing notice in *The Sunday Times*. "*Evita* is a quite marvelous modern opera, exceeding in stature even *Jesus Christ Superstar*," wrote the by-now not-quite-objective critic. "Lloyd Webber's score, so full of glorious melodies apart from the well-known 'Don't Cry for Me, Argentina,' is an unparalleled fusion of twentieth-century musical experience. Echoes of the past: Tchaikovsky, Puccini and church choral music shimmer hauntingly through, but it is the interweaving of pop, rock, jazz, Broadway, Latin and other elements which makes the brew so astonishingly potent. . . . Lloyd Webber is perhaps the most remarkable musical child of his generation. He has heard much, sensitively absorbed it, and produced his own completely original and personal synthesis."

Yet the real reason for *Evita*'s success is to be found in its quality. Far more than *Superstar*, *Evita* had a polished, finished gloss. It was no ad-hoc affair, evolving as it went along, as *Superstar* had been, but a fully formed dramatic entity: an opera, as surely as Strauss's *Salome* or *Elektra*—or Sullivan's *Ivanhoe*—was an opera, but one conceived directly for disc.

---

*Unlike their American counterparts, the major London orchestras are flexible organizations that do a great deal of recording in addition to playing concerts. The LPO's participation in *Evita* did not imply any artistic endorsement.

Writing directly for recordings before essaying the West End had distinct commercial advantages, but the decision to put *Evita* on wax before a director ever got near it was not motivated solely by remunerative considerations. In the late sixties and seventies, many composers in the rock and classical fields were conceiving their music for records. The Beatles had invented the idea of a "concept" album with *Sergeant Pepper's Lonely Hearts Club Band* and, later, the magnificent *Abbey Road,* compositions that could not be performed live. Simultaneously, electronic-music composers such as Morton Subotnik were circumventing the performer-middleman with direct-to-tape pieces such as *Golden Apples of the Sun* and *Silver Apples of the Moon,* two works commissioned by the enterprising Tracey Sterne of Nonesuch Records.

To composers, recordings held out the prospect of realizing their visions perfectly, without making them worry about the vagaries of live performance. Why they should want to do so had its origins in the textual-fidelity movement that had gripped music since World War II. Following the baleful influence of Arturo Toscanini, who proclaimed himself the servant of the composer (never mind that Toscanini was not above touching up orchestrations here and there and even adding notes from time to time), conductors and performers made playing exactly what was written the raison d'être of their existence. As creativity waned and the standard repertoire hardened, it became ever more imperative to play just the notes, ma'am; indeed, a lesser generation of music critics began using faithfulness to the printed score as a benchmark by which to judge artistry. So it was a short leap, then, for composers to hit upon the idea of eliminating, or at least neutralizing, the performer altogether. Neither Lloyd Webber nor Rice was willing to go that far; they, after all, wanted to see *Evita* on the stage. But by recording their show first and then shopping it around, they ensured that its form and most of its content would be theirs forever, no matter who directed it.

Enter Hal Prince. Shortly before *Evita* was released, Prince got a call from Lloyd Webber, asking him if he would like to hear the new score. Prince said yes, and Andrew flew to Prince's house in Majorca, bringing with him a tape of the album. The English National Opera's director, Lord Harewood, the queen's cousin, had offered to stage *Evita* at the London Coliseum, but Andrew wasn't ready for the opera house, no matter how populist.* Andrew said no, thanks; he wanted *Evita* to be heard eight times a week, not just the eight times or so it would be performed annually in an operatic repertoire system. He wanted Hal.

They listened to the music, and Prince was impressed. He sensed the potential right away, but realized that he would have to face the same fundamental problem that O'Horgan had: how to put on the stage a work that, at this point, existed only in the aural imagination? Prince told Lloyd Webber that he liked the material—any opera that began with a funeral couldn't be all bad—but that he wasn't sure they had a show yet; and besides, it would be a couple of years before the busy director would be able to stage it.

Prince knew whereof he spoke. Unlike O'Horgan he was no avant-garde wonder, but a highly respected veteran whose Broadway career stretched back to *The Pajama Game* in 1954. Tall, bearded, and perpetually tanned, Prince had a long string of hits and succès d'estimes behind him in both musical comedy and opera, including most of Stephen Sondheim's works: *A Funny Thing Happened on the Way to the Forum, Company, Follies, A Little Night Music, Pacific Overtures,* and the piece he was working on when Lloyd Webber came calling, *Sweeney Todd.* In addition, he had staged *West Side Story, Cabaret, Fiddler on the Roof,* and *On the Twentieth Century,* as well as Puccini's *La Fanciulla del West* for the Lyric Opera of Chicago and Weill's *Silver Lake* for the New York City Opera. If anybody could make a smash out of *Evita,* it was Prince.

After hearing the album, Prince sat down and wrote a three-thousand-word memo to Lloyd Webber outlining his suggestions, among them a notion to have Evita played by three different actresses, each to reveal different facets of her nature. About a week later, he got a curt, almost peremptory, reply from Andrew and Tim, thanking him for his interest and saying that they were postponing all theatrical considerations until the album was launched. Rice and Lloyd Webber quarreled over Prince; "Who is this mush?" asked Tim derisively. But Andrew eventually prevailed. Seven months later, Rice and Lloyd Webber arrived at Prince's office in Manhattan, handed him the finished album, and said they were now ready for him to direct it. Although Prince's nose was a little out of joint—they had just gone ahead and done it their way after all—he had to admire the chutzpah. Of course he would direct it, he told them. *Evita* was on its way.

Working with the score in one hand and the libretto in the other, Prince began to visualize the scenes. It was not Rice's intention to write a docudrama, historically correct in its every particular; instead, he was seeking the essence of what made Evita such a glamorous figure in her time. Luckily, Prince was not a cerebral, what-is-my-motivation-for-this director; instead, he was interested in making stunning stage pictures. They were perfect for each other. Despite his initial reservations, Prince did not have to make extensive changes. To give the staging specificity, the director insisted that the Che character be identifiable as Guevara, the revolutionary, and not as an amorphous, Brechtian Everyman (recall that Judas, too, had begun life as Everyman on the "Jesus Christ Superstar" single). And he made one major cut, dropping Che's rock basher, "The Lady's Got Potential," and requesting in its place a new song that would make explicit Perón's rise to power, "The Art

---

*The ENO bears much the same relationship to the Royal Opera House, Covent Garden, as the New York City Opera, during its feisty City Center days, once did to the Metropolitan Opera—an enterprising house willing to experiment with its repertoire and to offer home-grown singers the chance to sing big roles for the first time.

of the Possible." Because "The Lady's Got Potential" had a dramatically irrelevant subplot about insecticide (!), some other lyrics had to be changed, some scenes extended, and others shortened; to make Lloyd Webber's hard-won orchestrations suitable for the theater (the London Philharmonic would not be playing in the pit), the veteran composer and arranger Hershy Kay was called in. Kay followed Lloyd Webber's original orchestrations closely and retained most of the score's distinctive sound—the drum riffs in "Perón's Latest Flame," the wailing saxophone in the "Charity Concert" duet between Evita and Perón, and the harp whose announcement of the Death motive comes just after the lovers have first met. Contrary to some later press reports, the score did not need extensive revision, addition, or subtraction: *Evita* on the stage was substantially the same as *Evita* on disc.

Later in his career, Lloyd Webber would write more sophisticated, better integrated scores, but *Evita* has a hard, flinty beauty about it that is unique in his output. The criticism that the score is "about as Latin as steak and kidney pie" misses the point: Lloyd Webber was not trying to be Xavier Cugat or even Edmundo Ros; that way lay parody. Although there are Latin forms in *Evita*, the music makes no pretense to being authentically Spanish or South American, merely modern.

The opera begins in "A Cinema in Buenos Aires," which is showing one of Evita's movies. The feature is interrupted by the announcement of Evita's death, on July 26, 1952, which occasions an outburst of national grief and mourning in the "Requiem for Evita." The daring of Lloyd Webber's score is immediately evident: the first four bars of the highly dissonant E-minor opening are in 4/4, 5/4, 4/4, and 9/8; abruptly shifting meter continues to distinguish the music for the remainder of the show. The theme of Evita's "Lament," which will close the show, is proclaimed loudly in the orchestra, and as the wailing rises to a climax, it is rudely interrupted by the first real song, Che's "Oh, What a Circus," a slick tango in E major whose pliant, ironically lyrical melody stands in stark contrast to the funeral:

> *Oh what a circus! O what a show!*
> *Argentina has gone to town*
> *Over the death of an actress called Eva Perón*
> *We've all gone crazy*
> *Mourning all day and mourning all night*
> *Falling over ourselves to get all of the misery right*

The figure of Che will stalk the show, standing outside the action but always offering a bitter, ironic commentary on it. He berates his fellow Argentines for idolizing a corrupt social-climbing prostitute: "Sing you fools! But you got it wrong/Enjoy your prayers because you haven't got long/Your queen is dead, your king is through/She's not coming back to you." And he apostrophizes the dead Evita, too, to the strains of the song that will become her anthem later in the opera: "You let down your people Evita/You were supposed to have been immortal/That's all they wanted/Not much to ask for/But in the end you/Could not deliver." Evita rises from her coffin and, in D-flat major (a key that Lloyd Webber often reserves for his most important songs), sings a verse of "Don't Cry for Me, Argentina."

The story then flashes back to the young Evita's meeting with a popular singer, Agustín Magaldi, whom she sees as her ticket out of the pampas and on to the big city. He sings "On This Night of a Thousand Stars," a deliberately clichéd tango pastiche, to which Evita replies, in pairs of 5/8 and 6/8 bars: "I wanna be a part of B.A., Buenos Aires, Big Apple." Magaldi, taken aback by this show of independence by a bit of fluff he thought was a one-night stand in a tank town, warns her, "Eva, beware of the city," but she is not to be dissuaded. To the tune of Magaldi's warning, Evita goes to town.

The next number, "Buenos Aires," is one of Lloyd Webber's most accomplished songs, a complex samba of tremendous drive, energy, and power that brilliantly captures Evita's force of will:

> *What's new Buenos Aires?*
> *I'm new—I wanna say I'm just a little stuck on you*
> *You'll be on me too!*

Nominally in C major, the song is as slippery as Evita herself, periodically dropping into C-flat and darting up into A-flat. For the bridge ("And if ever I go too far/It's because of the things you are/Beautiful town—I love you"), Andrew reached into his drawer, retrieving the first song he and Tim had written for Ross Hannaman, "Down Through Summer" (the first of several self-borrowings that turn up in *Evita*). After a brief dance interlude, the song ends with Evita's promising, in a descending series of polychords, that B.A. is going to get "just a little touch of star quality."

"Good Night and Thank You" is an ironic G-major lullaby in a lilting 6/8; Evita bids farewell to a succession of lovers as she rises, horizontally, up through the ranks. Tim's cynical view of the impermanence of love and the inevitability of betrayal is given full voice here:

> *There is no one, no one at all*
> *Never has been and never will be a lover*
> *Male or female*
> *Who hasn't an eye on*
> *In fact they rely on*
> *Tricks they can try on their partner*
> *They're hoping their lover will help them or keep them*
> *Support them, promote them*
> *Don't blame them*
> *You're the same*

On the record, the next song is "The Lady's Got Potential," a fine rocker and bitter commentary by Che ("The greatest social climber since Cinderella," he calls Evita) that on stage was excised and replaced with "The Art of the Possible," a dour meditation for Perón and his rivals on the nature of political power. In "Charity Concert," Evita and Perón meet for the first time and are immediately attracted to one another. She has had him, the rising star of Argentine politics, in her sights all along; "I'd be surprisingly good for you," she sings. The sinuous melody in E minor is marked by a flatted fifth—B-flat instead of B-natural—but its kinship to the funeral music is unmistakable; Evita is doomed, and at the end of the scene the harp is heard softly intoning the Death motive.

Evita moves in with Perón and ousts his teenage mistress, who is given one of the show's hits, "Another Suitcase in Another Hall." The world-weary lyric is far too sophisticated for a fifteen-year-old schoolgirl—"I don't expect my love affairs to last for long/Never fool myself that my dreams will come true"—and her character never reappears, but even if it is shameless song plugging, the poignant melody offers the show's first moment of repose—indeed, the first and last moment of genuine human feeling or emotion. Part of the melodic line is derived from the song "Summer Day," from *Jeeves;* harmonically, "Another Suitcase" is remarkably simple, moving from C major to F to G7 and back to C— musical child's play that captures the girl's immaturity far better than the words.

Evita is not accepted by the aristocracy nor by the military, and in the marchlike "Perón's Latest Flame," the two groups declare their hostility. "We should all be on our guard," sing the officers, "She should get into her head/She should not get out of bed/She should know that she's not paid/To be loud but to be laid/Slut!—Dangerous Jade!" When Che, pretending to be a reporter, rushes up to Evita and asks, "Whom did you sleep—dine—with yesterday?" Lloyd Webber quotes a snatch from another song from *Jeeves,* "Eulalie," but it is only a passing, one-bar reference and may have been unintentional.

A segue leads to the stirring first-act finale, "A New Argentina." Under Evita's influence, a weak, vacillating Perón has quit the army to lead a populist uprising of workers, promising universal suffrage, nationalized industries, shorter hours, higher wages, and more public spending— all promises the historical Perón delivered on. The chorus is a rousing A-major march in 12/8; on the record, it ends quietly with Evita musing, "Would I have done what I did/If I hadn't thought, if I hadn't known/We would take the country," but on stage Prince brought back the shirtless ones for a final shout of "A new Argentina! The chains of the masses untied/A new Argentina! The voice of the people/Cannot be and will not be and must not be denied!"

Act Two opens with the scene on the balcony of the Casa Rosada. Perón and Evita have triumphed; just who is the real people's choice can be gleaned from the shouts of the crowd, in which the chants of "Perón" are gradually overcome by the chants of "Evita." This freely tonal passage is suddenly swamped by a great outburst from the orchestra, in the pivotal key of D-flat, introducing Evita's aria, "Don't Cry for Me, Argentina." Anyone who thinks this number is meant as Evita's apotheosis cannot have listened very closely to the lyrics; far from celebrating her, the song is her cynical apologia for her greedy rise:

> *It won't be easy, you'll think it strange*
> *When I try to explain how I feel*
> *That I still need your love after all that I've done*
> *You won't believe me*
> *All you will see is a girl you once knew*
> *Although she's dressed up to the nines*
> *At sixes and sevens with you*

I had to let it happen, I had to change
Couldn't stay all my life down at heel
Looking out of the window, staying out of the sun
So I chose freedom
Running around trying everything new
But nothing impressed me at all
I never expected it to

After she finishes—and receives the multitude's plaudits—Evita turns to Perón. "Just listen to that!" she says. "The voice of Argentina! We are adored! We are loved!" The scene closes with an extended section of *Sprechstimme* for Evita as she whips the crowd into a frenzy ("Evita Perón! La Santa Perónista!") with her vow to redistribute income and tear down the wall of privilege that has separated the peasants from the oligarchs. Whether Arnold Schoenberg had Eva Perón in mind when he developed his method of half-speaking, half-singing is moot, but the device works most effectively.

"High Flying, Adored" is a song for Che, a gentle F-major tune in 4/4 with a fine lyrical bent and a Schubert-like strophic structure, distinguished by a sharp modulation to D major when Evita takes the verse; like "Don't Cry for Me, Argentina," it is meant ironically. "Rainbow High" follows, a C-minor barcarole in 6/8 and 9/8. Depending on the point of view of the critic, Rice's lyrics for this song either proclaim his talent or reveal him for a hack:

I came from the people
They need to adore me
So Christian Dior me
From my head to my toes

——

I'm their savior!
That's what they call me
So Lauren Bacall me
Anything goes

There is a nice moment when, at the word "I'm their savior!" Evita suddenly ratchets the key up a half-step to C-sharp minor; when it drops down again, it is in C major, and Evita closes the number with a brief recollection of "Buenos Aires"'s "little touch of star quality."

"Rainbow Tour" is a narrative for Perón, recounting Evita's grand tour of Europe in 1947. In an E-major ditty in 4/4, the dictator recounts his wife's off-stage travels through Spain, Italy, Portugal, France, and Switzerland, which began triumphantly but gradually wore down. The song is periodically interrupted by echoes of an angular interjection from "On This Night of a Thousand Stars"; once it meant Evita was getting started, but now it is associated with her rejection by European society ("Did you hear that? They called me a whore!"). Evita has reached her apogee; now, her thousand stars are beginning to fade.

"The Actress Hasn't Learned" is her reproach to fate. Still despising the aristocrats, Evita excoriates them and proclaims her solidarity with the working class to the melody of "Another Suitcase"—a musical indication that she, too, is on her way out. Che takes up the thread with "And the Money Kept Rolling In," a brisk D-minor commentary in 7/8 on the crooked Foundation Eva Perón. Prince and Fuller much extended the song on stage, turning it into an exhilarating dance number. The people, however, are oblivious to the evidence that the Peróns are skimming cash and stashing it in Switzerland, and they celebrate Evita in "Santa Evita," an F-major children's prayer whose harmonic pattern is identical to "Another Suitcase"; later, the workers take up her anthem and turn it into a forceful march as they proclaim Evita a saint.

With Evita visibly failing, Che takes his leave of her in the "Waltz for Eva and Che." The cynical theme of lovers' betrayal, first heard when Evita met Magaldi, is here applied to Evita's relationship with Argentina, and the melody of the middle section of "Buenos Aires" (or "Down Through Summer") is heard once again. Then she was looking forward to conquering the city; now, Evita laments the cancer-ravaged physical condition that makes her campaign so difficult to continue.

Perón reflects on his wife's health in "She Is a Diamond"; his touching G-minor soliloquy is a variation of the "I'd Be Surprisingly Good for You" melody of their first meeting. "Dice Are Rolling," itself a reminiscence of Perón's grab for power, is a scene for Perón and Evita in which she iterates her determination to be vice president, conducted in a stark recitative that recalls the deliberations of the high priests in *Jesus Christ Superstar*. The Betrayal motive makes an appearance as does, more ominously, the Death motive.

The dying Evita, however, cannot overcome the objections of the military leaders who force her to stand down. In "Eva's Final Broadcast," she effectively abdicates, to the strains of "Don't Cry for Me, Argentina"; it is a bitter replay of the Casa Rosada scene that opened the second act. A "montage" of the opera's themes passes in review as Evita lies on her deathbed, dimly heard remembrances of past glories. Her final song, "Lament," is a B-flat minor dirge that picks up the big orchestral melody first heard at the beginning of the show. In it, Evita assesses her Faustian bargain—bright, intense fame at the expense of a long life:

> *The choice was mine and mine completely*
> *I could have any prize that I desired*
> *I could burn with the splendor of the brightest fire*
> *Or else, or else I could choose time*

So Evita dies, a brief, blazing comet in the southern skies. Like another great seducer, Don Giovanni, she is unrepentant to the end.

As the embalmers come on to begin their grisly work, the last word, on stage, belongs to Che. For the first time, he speaks without musical accompaniment: "Money was raised to build a tomb, a monument to Evita. Only the pedestal was completed and Evita's body disappeared for seventeen years." It is an unsatisfactory ending on several counts. The record closed, more effectively, with the song of the embalmers, sung to the same tune to which Evita had been Christian Diored and Lauren Bacalled in "Rainbow High."

But the real problem with Che's little speech is that it begs the question. What happened to the body? The truth is, as they say, stranger than fiction. Evita, who weighed only eighty pounds at her death in 1952, was indeed embalmed, by Dr. Pedro Ara, the Spanish cultural attaché in Buenos Aires. For nearly two and a half years, Evita's corpse lay in state at the Ministry of Labor. When Perón was ousted in a 1955 coup shortly after being excommunicated by the Vatican for, among other transgressions, taking a thirteen-year-old mistress and legalizing divorce and prostitution, the head of army intelligence seized the body.

No one, though, knew what to do with it. One officer, Major Antonio Aranda, kept it in his bedroom; fearing intruders, Aranda slept with a loaded pistol under his pillow—a precaution with tragic consequences when Aranda accidentally shot and killed his pregnant wife while she was headed to the bathroom. The corpse then spent some time in a storeroom, in a packing case labeled "Radio Sets"; the case was eventually shipped to Bonn, West Germany, and from there, the body now in a coffin, to Rome. In Italy, it was received by a nun who was told it contained the remains of one Maria Maggi, an Italian widow who had died in Argentina.

In 1971, with Argentina in a state of political and economic collapse, the generals called on Perón to return from his exile in Spain. Evita's body was exhumed and driven to her husband in Madrid. There the coffin was opened, in the presence of Perón, his new wife, Isabel, and Dr. Ara: aside from some tattered clothing and a broken fingertip, Evita was in mint condition. Perón's return to the Argentine presidency in 1973 was short-lived; he died of a heart attack on July 1, 1974, and he and Evita were buried in a private cemetery. Evita's macabre, posthumous Rainbow Tour was over.

After the nightmares of *Superstar* and *Jeeves,* the theatrical production of *Evita* was a dream..There were four weeks of rehearsals, nine previews, and then the show opened on June 21, 1978, at the Prince Edward Theatre in Old Compton Street. Tim's instinct was right: from the time the premiere was announced, London was bewitched by *Evita.* The search for the leading lady made headlines; Covington had always said that she would not play the role on stage, and in this she was adamant; she had even refused to promote "Don't Cry for Me, Argentina" after the single was released because, in her judgment, it could not properly be understood out of context. (She was right.) Covington had ambitions to play serious roles at the National Theatre and in opera—two months after *Evita* opened, she was performing in Kurt Weill's *The Seven Deadly Sins*—and she simply did not want to be typecast as a pop singer. When extensive open calls and private auditions proved fruitless, Rice in desperation took Covington out for an expensive dinner. The show couldn't go on without her, Tim said, she simply had to do it, would she reconsider, would she *please* be his Evita? He was practically on his knees. After the cheese, Covington gave her reply: thanks, but no thanks.

The choice fell upon a thirty-year-old unknown, Elaine Paige, whom Tim and Andrew had first encountered singing in the chorus of the London *Jesus Christ Superstar.* "The third angel sings well," Lloyd Webber had noted in his audition notes. Paige had been bouncing around the West End and appearing in television commercials; she was in Blackpool, shooting a play for television, when her agent called and suggested she audition for *Evita*. At first, Paige balked. She didn't want to do any more musicals; it was success on the legitimate stage she was after. Her agent persisted: "Buy the album and listen to it," she said. "Then tell me what you think." Paige bought, heard, and was conquered.

At Paige's audition, Rice, Lloyd Webber, and Prince loved her right away. The tiny lady—she stood under five feet tall—with the big mezzo voice had just the right combination of gritty street smarts and unbridled sexuality they were looking for. At her audition, Elaine sang "Don't Cry for Me, Argentina." When Andrew asked her for "Rainbow High," she looked at him without batting an eye and said, "Oh, fuck, I haven't got the music." Lloyd Webber knew he had found his Evita. On opening night, in the best showbiz tradition, the chorus girl became a star as the audience gave Paige a ten-minute ovation at her curtain call.*

Prince's direction was brilliant. Featuring rock singer David Essex as Che and actor Josh Ackland as Perón and designed by Timothy O'Brien and Tazeena Firth of the National Theatre, the show had a hard, cold glint that complemented the score's fundamental (and, for Andrew, unprecedented) cynicism. "Goodnight and Thank You," which chronicles Evita's sexually propelled rise to the top, was a revolving door of lovers, with Evita emerging after each encounter in ever more resplendent deshabille. "The Art of the Possible," Prince's addition, was played as a game of musical chairs among Perón and his fellow officers, each hungry for power. "A New Argentina," the first finale, brought an angry chorus of Evita's *descamisados* to the front of the stage, placards waving and banners flying. And that was just Act One.

The critics split, but the cheers outweighed the jeers. Jewell, by now Rice and Lloyd Webber's foremost proponent in the press, wrote: "In Tim Rice, Lloyd Webber has a partner of perfection. Rice writes trenchant, witty, modern lyrics superbly married to Lloyd Webber's ambitious score—a score skillfully orchestrated." *The Sunday Times* drama critic, John Peter, noted that "the music is immensely more interesting and sophisticated than that of *Jesus Christ Superstar*. Its recurring themes weld it together into an echoing whole, and its moments of bleak dissonance hint at something sinister and inhuman. Evil is the most difficult thing to communicate through music, and Lloyd Webber's pounding idiom, made up of rock, tango, and ballad, is exhilarating, almost seductive. Evita would have approved."

Prince's guiding philosophy in putting *Evita* on the stage was simple: *Evita* was an opera.† Prince was speaking from practical experience. In New York, he had a critical hit on his hands with Sondheim's finest work, *Sweeney Todd*, the story of the Demon Barber of Fleet Street; even though Sondheim's earlier *Pacific Overtures* had not fared as well, Prince's production had revealed both works for the genuine serious music dramas they were. Scalpers were getting several hundred pounds for a pair of seats to *Evita* on a Saturday night, and the show was quickly sold out months in advance.

There were, however, some strong dissenting voices. Some critics raised the question of whether Rice and Lloyd Webber had somehow glamorized Eva Perón and, in so doing, celebrated fascism. The formidable Bernard Levin of *The Times* called *Evita* "one of the most disagreeable evenings I have ever spent in my life, in or out of the theater." Levin was infuriated by Rice and Lloyd Webber's presumption in calling their work an opera; in his view, it was an affront to the holy shades of Mozart and Wagner:

> There is a still greater corruption at the heart of this odious artifact, symbolized by the fact that it calls itself an opera, and has been accepted as such by people who have never set foot in an opera house, merely because the clichés between the songs ("Let's Get This Show on the Road"—"This Crazy Defeatist Talk"—"What, Commit Political Suicide?") are sung instead of spoken, and the score includes, among the appropriate "slow tango feel" and similar expressions, such markings as "poco a poco diminuendo."

Levin finished with a blast: "Next we'll have a musical about Hitler," a cheap shot that ignored the fact that there already was a musical about Hitler—"Springtime for Hitler" in Mel Brooks's comic masterpiece, *The Producers*.

Tim, as usual, had a ready answer for the charge of incorrect politics. "If your subject happens to be one of the most glamorous women who ever lived, you will inevitably be accused of glamorizing her," he said. "The only political messages we hope will emerge are that extremists are dangerous and attractive ones even more so."

Some of the same objections were raised when the show opened in the United States. Rice and Lloyd Webber already had had a taste of what the American critics might think from a review of the London production by Frank Rich, then writing for *Time*:

> *Evita*'s a cold and uninvolving show that does little to expand the traditional musical comedy format or our understanding of a bizarre historical figure. . . . Rice's libretto never aspires to much more than a comic-book version of history . . . he's so agog he

---

*The vocal demands of Evita were hard on Paige; she missed ten of the first fifty performances with a throat ailment and by September had relinquished two of the eight weekly shows to her understudy, Susannah Fellows.

†"To me, opera is and always has been musical theater of its time in a form with limited dialogue," Prince told Jeanne Miller of *The San Francisco Examiner* when the show tried out on the West Coast in mid-1979, prior to its fall Broadway opening. "Puccini and Verdi were pop composers of their era and even today lots of people say that they wrote organ-grinder music for the monkeys to dance to and the audience to hum. The snobbish lines of rigidity have brought a certain amount of awed reverence to that genre and have therefore mired contemporary composers in those traditions. But those operas were the showbiz musicals of their times."

might as well be describing the career of Judy Garland. . . . [Paige] is a strident actress who fails to convey Evita's erotic magnetism. . . . Despite its synthetic Latinisms, flip dissonance and references to Lennon-McCartney songs, Webber's music is evocative and often catchy . . . but Prince is capable of sinking to Rice's simplistic level: Argentina's aristocratic class is symbolized by a phalanx of chorus people who seem to have stepped out of the "Ascot Gavotte" number of *My Fair Lady.* The director also cannibalizes his own previous work. *Evita's* portentous first-act finale is a dead ringer for that of *Cabaret* ("Tomorrow Belongs to Me"). The show's neo-Brechtian lighting scheme and montage finale also recall that 1966 production.

Producer Robert Stigwood, Rich noted, "plans to bring *Evita* to Broadway next year, where its London reception is not likely to be repeated." Even in a highly favorable notice in *Saturday Review,* Martin Gottfried attributed the success of the London *Evita* not to Rice and Lloyd Webber, but to Prince and, amazingly, to Kay. "Rice's lyrics," said Gottfried, "merely provided an excuse for Prince's elevation of the entire project to a new dimension. Webber's music, quasi-opera, set to relentless rock-and-roll rhythms, has been rescued by Hershy Kay. It has not only been relieved of the monotonous drum beating but has been fleshed out and deepened to become a new kind of theater music, with crashing dissonances underlining light melodies."

This, of course, was ignorance speaking. Still, the omens for *Evita* in New York initially were not good. Unlike in Britain, where sales of the album had topped two hundred and fifty thousand copies, the record had not done at all well in the United States. It is a truism in American journalism that no one has ever paid a nickel to read a word about Latin America, and the same, it seemed, might be true for a musical on a Latin subject. When Lloyd Webber and Rice came to New York in March 1977 to perform a cabaret program of their songs at the Ballroom in Chelsea, John Rockwell of *The New York Times* wrote: "Particularly, they would like us to appreciate their new *Evita,* which is a hit in their native England, but a failure so far in this country." The program, said Rockwell, was "an interesting, sometimes attractive affair, but it suggests that after twelve years together, both men have still to realize their full potential."

But *Evita's* rise was just as irresistible in the United States as it had been in Britain. Actors Equity, the actor's union, was balking at allowing Paige to recreate her British triumph on Broadway, so a spirited competition on the part of various Evita hopefuls ensued, much of it waged in the press: Stigwood wanted Ann-Margret for the part said the press agents; no he didn't, he wanted Raquel Welch; no, Charo. During auditions, among those who turned up were Meryl Streep, Tovah Feldshuh, and Julie Budd.

As in London, the part went instead to another unknown, a pert Long Islander named Patti LuPone. LuPone's "overnight" success, like Paige's, was a long time coming: the twenty-seven-year-old actress had been a member of John Houseman's Acting Company at the Juilliard School and had had parts in the Stephen Schwartz musical *Working* and in David Mamet's plays *The Water Engine* and *The Woods.* For her audition, three days before she was to leave for California to start filming in Stephen Spielberg's *1941,* LuPone dressed in a business suit, her hair pulled back in a bun, Evita-style. She sang "Don't Cry for Me, Argentina" movingly; halfway through "Rainbow High" Prince interrupted her and said, "I want to pursue this." LuPone was so happy that she impulsively lifted a chair she had been using as a prop over her head. Trudging to her final callback through the snowdrifts of a rare Manhattan blizzard, LuPone appeared wet and bedraggled, but she sang like an angel. Two days later, on the set in California, she got a call from her agent. "Congratulations. . . ."

With LuPone in the title role, Mandy Patinkin as Che, and Bob Gunton as Perón, *Evita* opened on May 8, 1979, at the Music Center in Los Angeles. The guests at the premiere were a motley Hollywood lot of stars, has-beens, and never-weres; "This show would have been a real hit if only they had gotten Eva Perón to come tonight," one of the glitterati said to Lloyd Webber. Despite Rich's prediction, *Evita* was a great, great success — better, impossible — grossing $264,074 in its first week, a house record, only to surpass that total in the second week with $269,536 — this in the face of the gasoline shortage that brought southern California traffic to a halt. Two months later, the production moved up the coast to San Francisco, debuting at the Orpheum Theater on July 17.

The reviews in both cities were generally favorable. In *The San Francisco Examiner,* Miller called the show "an extraordinary and often electrifying rock opera . . . compelling and filled with excitement." In the morning *San Francisco Chronicle,* drama critic Bernard Weiner was somewhat more skeptical: " 'Evita' is not as good as I had hoped — mainly because of its book; remember that the show began as a record album, not a piece for the theater — but director Harold Prince's staging, and many of the music numbers, are so spectacular as to make one almost forget the built-in deficiencies." Weiner was disturbed by the show's lack of a book: "What was the lure of Perónism? Of Evita? How did they use their power?"*

The most considered of the West Coast reviews was William Murray's, in *New West* (later, *California*) magazine. "*Evita,*" wrote Murray, "is,

---

*The drama critics' childlike insistence on dialogue would be amusing if it did not bespeak such a blissful unawareness of operatic history and practice. In opera — indeed, any kind of music drama, including musicals — it is the *music* that tells the story, not the words. Further, both on the West Coast and in New York, some drama critics wrote about *Evita* as if they had never heard, or even heard of, the album, which had been in release for some time.

first of all, not a musical comedy at all but an opera, pure and simple":

It has no spoken dialogue, no truly individualized numbers, and it depends for its effects on a complete blending of music and drama in the Wagnerian tradition. It cannot even qualify as a rock opera, like *Tommy,* because its score, even at its most rhythmic, is a complex musical tapestry made up of quite traditional orchestral and vocal elements. The choral work is especially stunning, comparable in spots to the best of Benjamin Britten, and it clearly establishes Andrew Lloyd Webber, only 31 years old, as a composer of great promise.

With an advance sale of nearly two and a half million dollars, *Evita* opened at the Broadway Theatre in New York on September 25, 1979, after two weeks of previews. Although Prince had somewhat revised the production to make Evita seem less a saint than a sinner, the American critics were even more offended than the British by what they saw as the authors' sanitizing of Evita; from their reactions, one would think Rice had written *Adolf Hitler Superstar.* If Andrew had worried that *Superstar* had cost him and Tim whatever reserves of good will the New York drama critics possessed, the reviews proved him right.

New York:
In *Evita* you have Webber's junky tunes (except for two or three that are quite nice, although derivative) and Rice's either strained or flat lyrics, and, instead of singing, electronics.... What sort of chaps are these authors who can exalt with equal enthusiasm Jesus Christ the last time round and Eva Perón this time? If you want to help fill the coffers of these two amoral, barely talented whippersnappers and their knowing or duped accomplices, by all means see this artfully produced monument to human indecency. The bad taste of the offering should linger in your mouth. [John Simon]

Newsweek:
Soft... Andrew Lloyd Webber's work here is much too genteel and anglo for its hot Latin subject... Tim Rice's lyrics lurch from blandness to vulgarity... LuPone doesn't transmit the driving force, the astonishing charisma that made an ambitious trollop into a tremendous political force and a folk saint. [Jack Kroll]

Time:
The Rice-Lloyd Webber score is inferior to their work in *Jesus Christ Superstar.* While ingratiatingly melodic for the most part, Lloyd Webber's tunes seem to have been composed by the British equivalent of ASCAP anonymous. Rice's lyrics too often rely on straw-clutching rhymes. The dying Eva plaintively asks, "What is the good of the strongest heart/In a body that's falling apart?" [T. E. Kalem]

The New York Times:
Though the Rice-Webber score sometimes sounds as though Max Steiner had arranged it for Carmen Miranda, there are waltzes and polkas and threatening marches to keep us alert for tricky tempo-shifts; the lyrics, however, lack the odd and very human perceptions that often distinguished *Jesus Christ Superstar.* [Walter Kerr]

Predictably, Prince's real and imagined contributions were cheered by all and sundry: "dazzling," "brilliant precision," "telling... shrewd."* The critics' real ire was reserved not so much for *Evita*'s quality as for its politics—the show's alleged glorification of fascism.

This was a sensitive subject in New York. New York City is the biggest Jewish city on earth, a place where fascism means only one thing, Nazism, with all its resonances. One simply cannot discuss fascism dispassionately in New York; Lloyd Webber and Ayckbourn had lampooned the British fascist leader Sir Oswald Mosley and his Black Shirts in *Jeeves,* in the character of Sir Roderick Spode, *Führer* of the Black Shorts. But in the United States fascism was no laughing matter. John Simon put the case against *Evita* most eloquently:

It is perfectly useless to say that Evita is not held up for approbation; a protagonist who displays cunning, energy, wit, and, above all, phenomenal success will always seduce the unthinking masses, whether they be shirtless Argentines or bedizened Broadwayites. What the real-life Eva accomplished on a large scale the stage Evita reproduces in miniature, but stench is stench on any scale. I am not arguing, of course, that anyone seeing *Evita* will rush out and do likewise, but I am saying that a show like this ends up glorifying a base opportunist and Fascist, just as certain books by Capote and Mailer end up magnifying and dignifying murderers. It is particularly melancholy to note the number of Jews involved in the producing of *Evita,* starting with its director;

---

*Seduced by the lure of personal celebrity, many New York City drama critics, even those working for reputable publications, have long since recognized the value of a quote line, or "blurb." A critic does not get his review posted prominently outside the theater or emblazoned on a bus card or quoted in the ads by being relentlessly negative. *Time*'s critic, William A. Henry III, for example, was once described by the irreverent *Spy* magazine as "the critic nice enough to write his own blurbs."

how would these people feel about a musical whose protagonist was Stalin, Hitler, or that other Eva, Braun—even assuming that the show would include a choric Mandelstam or fictionalized Einstein to berate that protagonist?

The answer to that question, I am afraid, is available in the movie *The Producers,* in which a crazy Nazi writes a passionate tribute to his idol that as a gimmicked-up Broadway musical, *Springtime for Hitler,* has theatergoers laughing their asinine heads off and becomes the hit of the town. I should not at all be surprised if this "Springtime for Evita" (as even Clive Barnes saw fit to dub the blatantly pro-Evita London version) ends up doing just as well. Let no one doubt that ability of life to imitate anti-art.

Simon's was an honorable position, but it ignored one crucial fact: it is not the duty of art to concern itself with fidelity to life. Every time a work of art on a historical subject, whether a film, book, play or opera, is criticized for falsifying its inspiration, the artist's right to transform experience is implicitly denied; this kind of criticism would reduce all art to photorealism.

Further, the obloquy missed the point. Tim had told Andrew to make Evita wonderful, and Lloyd Webber had: one could not complain simultaneously of "Webber's junky tunes" and cry that Evita was glamorized. For the first time, Andrew's music equaled or surpassed Tim's words. If Evita seems glamorized, it is through the power of the music, though Lloyd Webber's score seems to have been subtler than his listeners were capable of recognizing. "I cannot imagine any intelligent person going to *Evita* and coming away with anything but the idea that she was a fairly grisly piece of work," Lloyd Webber told the press, but few heeded him. Even a passing ability to read a score would have disabused the critics of any such notions, but when it comes to reviewing musicals, drama critics are the blind men trying to describe an elephant.

Despite the critical brickbats, *Evita* was a hit on Broadway, running for 1,567 performances (more than twice as many as *Superstar*); Lloyd Webber was proving himself to be that most valuable of commodities, the critic-proof show composer. (Lloyd Webber felt that the turning point for *Evita* came with the Soviet invasion of Afghanistan in late 1979. The heightened awareness of the evils of totalitarianism, whether of the fascist or communist variety, brought people into the theater. That, at least, was his theory.) Ironically, the show won the New York Drama Critics Circle Award as the best musical of the season—there was hypocrisy for you—as well as seven Tony Awards, including best director for Prince, best actress in a musical for LuPone, best book, best score, and best musical; in 1981, the Broadway cast album won a Grammy Award, and that same year Paramount Pictures bought the film rights, beginning a production odyssey that would last as long as that of Evita's corpse. Lloyd Webber was now a force to be reckoned with. *Superstar* had won him the Drama Desk Award as the most promising composer of the 1971–1972 season; now the promise had been fulfilled.

What to do next? Restless as ever, Andrew had written a series of variations for cello and rock band for his brother, Julian, and was already at work on a song cycle for female voice. He was also mulling over a one-act opera on Charles Dickens's short story *The Signal-Man* and had an embryonic notion that the competition between Puccini and Ruggero Leoncavallo, both of whom wrote an operatic version of Murger's *Scenes de la vie de bohème,* might be of interest. At a chance meeting in a Milan café, the two composers discovered they were both working on operas based on Murger's novel. Friendship instantly turned to enmity; "Let the public decide," declared Puccini, and the public did. For his part, Tim was eager to get on with a musical about an international chess match between a Russian and an American, and Andrew made some brave noises to the press about writing the score. *Evita,* however, proved to be the last major Lloyd Webber–Rice musical. Success finally his, Lloyd Webber was ready to step out on his own.

Two years before *Evita* opened in London, Lloyd Webber was already thinking about his next project. Not for him was Rice's long artistic gestation period; he could not imagine spending, as Tim had, five years on a project like *Evita*. While waiting for Prince to begin work, Lloyd Webber had started casting about for something else to do.

During the creative hiatus, he took the opportunity to get reacquainted with his brother, Julian. He and Julian had not been close since the childhood days with the toy theater; the three-year difference in their ages, coupled with Andrew's departure for boarding school when Julian was nine, had meant they had not spent their adolescence together, and their interests had diverged. Julian had been a fervently committed classical musician since he was thirteen, uninterested in the pop world he used to share with his brother. He didn't care about gold records or Elvis or the Everlys any more; Elgar was his ideal. At twenty-six, Julian was emerging as the finest British cellist of his generation, having made his debut at the Wigmore Hall even before his graduation from the Royal College of Music in 1972.

Julian had been after Andrew for some time to write a cello piece for him. Andrew had said he would, but so far nothing had come of it. The brothers celebrated their rapprochement by indulging some of the tastes of their youth, specifically by attending football games at Orient. Talk about the East London Home for Unmanageable Boys: British football stadiums are veritable madhouses, crammed with screaming, shouting, singing fans who stand on the terraces and cheer their team and brimming with brawling, drunken droogies who periodically go on violent rampages, smashing and bashing anything that gets in their way. The image of the relentlessly middle-class Andrew and Julian, two gentle musicians, sitting in the stands surrounded by a howling, bloodthirsty mob is more than a little comical and incongruous.

Still, the atmosphere resulted in the next major Lloyd Webber piece, *Variations*. During his rise to prominence, Andrew's enthusiasm for Orient, one of the league's lesser lights, had waned considerably; at the end of the 1976–1977 season the club needed a tie or a win in its final match to avoid dropping out of the second division and into football purdah.* Julian, the fan, bet his brother, the apostate, that Orient would stay up; if Julian was right, then Andrew would finally have to write that cello piece he had been promising. On May 17, Orient managed a 1–1 tie with Hull, and shortly thereafter Andrew was back at his desk. And into his drawer.

Rather quickly, he decided he would use Paganini's famous Twenty-Fourth Caprice for Solo Violin as his subject. In so doing, Lloyd Webber was positively inviting invidious comparison, for the bouncy little tune in A minor had been the font of inspiration for many composers, among them Liszt, Brahms, and Rachmaninoff. Brahms had composed two books of "Paganini" Variations for the piano, while the dour Russian had put the theme at the center of one of his most popular concert pieces, the *Rhapsody on a Theme of Paganini* for piano and orchestra. Given the widespread attention the new work would receive in Britain, it was either presumptuous or bold of Lloyd Webber to use the same theme in his first "serious" instrumental composition.

Undaunted, he set to work. Few Lloyd Webber pieces were ever composed altogether fresh, and *Variations* was no different. Back in the days of *The Likes of Us*, Andrew had written a tune that he especially admired, but Dr. Barnardo's boys had never had the chance to sing it; it

---

*British football—soccer—is not as incomprehensible to Americans as cricket, but it comes close. The equivalent to Orient's precarious position would be if a major-league baseball team got so bad (the 1988 Baltimore Orioles, for example) that it dropped out of the majors altogether and fell into Triple A.

would come in handy now. There was another lost melody, this one in A major, that he had used in *Jeeves,* but the song didn't work—the lyrics weren't right and there was something wrong with the tune—and it had been cut during tryouts. Now, he reached for both songs again.

To the nonmusician, Lloyd Webber's inexhaustible drawer may seem the crassest kind of opportunism, proof positive of his limited ability and acquisitive musical nature that his detractors allege. Yet musical recycling has a perfectly respectable pedigree. Rossini, for example, unapologetically borrowed the overture to *The Barber of Seville* from two of his earlier operas; Beethoven used the same material in his three overtures to his opera *Leonore* (only to discard them all, fashion a wholly different fourth overture, and retitle the piece *Fidelio*). The test is not any given piece of material's provenance, but how it is employed. The tune from *The Likes of Us* was transformed from a rather harsh, relentless boys' bleat into a moment of great lyrical repose by the simple expedient of slowing it down. With the *Jeeves* song, Lloyd Webber did not merely reuse the same melody exactly; instead, he varied it through the simple but effective means of register displacement, so that what originally had been a bland, unattractive sequence with a tight melodic compass became a fluid, pliable, and memorable tune. The change was not major: instead of having the melody go C-sharp–B–C-sharp–B–C-sharp–A–B on its way down to the dominant note, E, Lloyd Webber also made the top of the melody an E. Thus: C-sharp–B–C-sharp–B–C-sharp–E–B. It was just the difference of a perfect fifth, but it was all the difference.

With this, the fifth variation, as the centerpiece and the "Barnardo" song as the pivotal eighteenth variation (a tip of the hat to Rachmaninoff, whose own eighteenth variation is the lyric high point of the *Rhapsody on a Theme of Paganini*), the rest of the work proceeded with Lloyd Webber's usual alacrity. Speed in composition does not necessarily mean sloppiness; instead it is even more likely to indicate inspiration. Many Broadway composers worked, and work, at a lightning tempo; Gershwin wrote his short opera, *Blue Monday,* in five days, and his magnum opus, *Porgy and Bess,* in only twenty months. Julian was away on tour, so consultations were relegated to long-distance telephone calls.

By August 1977 *Variations* was ready for performance at the Sydmonton Festival. The piece was enterprisingly conceived as a dialogue for cello and rock band, a real crossover work that would combine classical techniques of variation with the sound and feel of a tight jazz-rock ensemble. To play it, Andrew had assembled a crack group of musicians through his connection with MCA: David Caddick and Rod Argent on keyboards, John Hiseman on drums, and Barbara Thompson on winds.

Crossover music was a hybrid whose history stretched back to Ravel's Piano Concerto in G Major and Gershwin's *Rhapsody in Blue.* Since jazz became an international musical language after the turn of the century, serious composers had sought somehow to fuse it with symphonic and operatic practices. It was not just a one-way street, for jazzmen, too, had tried to make the blend: Benny Goodman commissioned a Clarinet Concerto from Aaron Copland, and Stravinsky had written his *Ebony* Concerto for Woody Herman; in the fifties and sixties the Modern Jazz Quartet and the Dave Brubeck Quartet had each essayed various forms of "fusion," or "third-stream," music. So, once again, although it may have seemed opportunistic to some, Lloyd Webber was working in a historically legitimate tradition.

Julian found much to admire in the piece; to the press, he described it as the finest British chamber writing since Benjamin Britten. Despite his brother's inexperience in writing for solo cello, Julian had only a few suggestions, mostly involving the use of double stops in the last variation; the *scordatura* of the piece's final note—tuning the cello's lower string down from a C to an A—was Andrew's idea. (Kodaly did something similar in his masterpiece, the Sonata for Solo Cello.)

The first performance, however, nearly destroyed the brothers' newfound fraternity. Julian and the band were scheduled to perform *Variations* as the second half of a morning concert that was to begin at eleven-thirty; the first half would consist of Julian's playing of a couple of cello sonatas, accompanied by his regular pianist, Yitkin Seow. (Other works on the festival program that year were Bill Lloyd Webber's hymn "See Israel's Gentle Shepherd," written for Imogen's christening, and a version of the life of Byron starring Gary Bond, who had played Joseph in the 1973 London production of *Joseph and the Amazing Technicolor Dreamcoat.*) Seow, however, was delayed in arriving from Belfast, where he had performed the night before, and did not reach Sydmonton until the afternoon; Julian and the ensemble played *Variations* twice, once on each half of the program. Seow's absence had let them get two readings of the new piece under their belts, valuable preparation before recording was to begin, but Julian's older brother did not see it quite that way. Andrew, always a nervous wreck at the premiere of any new work, was furious. He didn't want to hear about Seow's airline problems, he wanted him at Sydmonton on time. When Seow belatedly arrived, a boiling Andrew was so angry that he refused to speak to the poor pianist and commanded that he be sent away immediately. This exhibition of bad manners brought Julian into the row, to the defense of his colleague; Julian shouted that if Andrew was going to be like that then he, Julian, wanted nothing more to do with the project: to hell with the *Variations,* he was leaving too. Only the timely mediation of Julian's wife, Celia, managed to defuse the tension.

And so they went into the studio, to commit *Variations* to disc. The forces were nearly the same: Julian, Argent, Thompson, and Hiseman were joined by the other members of Hiseman's Colosseum II rock band: Don Airey, keyboards, John Mole, bass, and Gary Moore, guitar. Julian by this time was a veteran recording artist known for his championing of British music—not only repertoire pieces such as the Elgar Cello Concerto but more obscure works, such as Frank Bridge's *Concerto Elegiaco* and the piano trios of John Ireland, which he had recorded. Accustomed to the hurried schedule of most tight-budgeted classical recordings, Julian found the more leisurely pace of rock performers a refreshing change. He and Andrew and the band spent several weeks in the studio, and the record was released in Britain on January 3, 1978. It was an immediate hit; by January 4, it had already climbed to number eight on the charts, on its way to gold within five weeks. (America, however, was a different story: there, the album sank, unremarked and unadmired.)

The purely instrumental version of *Variations* exists in two separate forms, the original conception for cello and rock band and the full orchestra arrangement that David Cullen prepared for a London premiere in October 1985. They are substantially alike, the orchestral version dropping a redundant variation and adding some counterpoint to fill out the piece's overall texture.

Variations opens not with the Paganini theme but with a variation of it (so does the Rachmaninoff *Rhapsody*) for the ensemble, mysterious and evocative. The cello then enters with the familiar theme, stated unaccompanied, and the first four numbered variations follow in quick succession, each in the home key of A minor. At the fifth variation, the key switches to A major and the *Jeeves* song is heard, sung out by the solo cello. Variation six is a stuttering ragtime, while number seven introduces a brisk basso ostinato figure (here in 7/8) that will reappear later in the piece.

At variation eight, the storm clouds lift as another, gentler ostinato takes over in the upper registers, to accompany the work's opening figuration; Lloyd Webber later hijacked this riff for the beginning of *Starlight Express*. After a brief cadenza for the soloist, variation nine is a bluesy dance. The mood shifts abruptly in the tenth variation, a soft waltz for cello and piano that recalls the melody of *Joseph and the Amazing Technicolor Dreamcoat*'s best song, "Close Every Door." Variations eleven through fifteen are linked, moving from angular Prokofiev-like dissonance (eleven) to a brisk allegro in alternating 4/4 and 7/8 meter (twelve) to a Brubeckian 5/4 (thirteen) that features the distinctive, leaping melodic sixth of *Evita*'s "Rainbow High" to a syncopated dance (fourteen) to a dotted-rhythm fifteenth variation called "The Tributes"; the tributes in question going to Lloyd Webber's rock archetypes and, inevitably, to Prokofiev.

The sixteenth variation brings back an echo of the bass ostinato first heard in the seventh variation, over which the Paganini theme rings out loudly, finally emerging as a sailor's hornpipe. In the first version of *Variations*, numbers thirteen and fourteen are then reprised, but not in the orchestral version, which proceeds directly to variation seventeen: eight slow, enigmatic bars of shifting polychords. The haze gradually dissolves to reveal the eighteenth (or "Barnardo") variation, couched in Lloyd Webber's "important" key of D-flat. Variation nineteen is a brief transition to the kinetic energy of the twentieth, replete with flowing sixteenth notes, in which the first half of the Paganini theme is proclaimed in the bass while its second half serves as a counterpoint in the treble. This leads directly into a restatement of the fifth variation, the piece's "hit tune," ornamented by winds and punctuated by brass chords.

This unexpected song, though, is cut off in full flower by a jazzy G-minor boogie in the bass that ends abruptly at the mysterious twenty-second variation, whose rhythm and clashing minor ninths are derived, whether consciously or unconsciously, from the slow movement of the Shostakovich Fifteenth Symphony. The last variation, number twenty-three, begins portentously with the cello pitted against apocalyptic A-minor chords, but it then transforms itself into a gallop and rushes home, to the final low A on the cello. Here *Variations* ended—for the time being.

Although Lloyd Webber was widely perceived in Britain to be a wealthy man—and by any conventional standard he was—it was not until *Variations* that he was able to protect and maximize his income. Even though he was rich, Lloyd Webber thought he was broke; for a time, overextended by his real-estate purchases, he even contemplated declaring bankruptcy. Andrew was still under contract to Stigwood, but that ten-year agreement, negotiated with Myers and Land in the disadvantageous days of 1969, was nearing its end, and more than ever Lloyd Webber was chafing under its terms. The 10-percent royalty that he and Tim split on their works was subject to high taxation under the Labour government; further, it was not really 10 percent at all, since they paid one-fourth of it back to Stigwood as a management fee (and, on *Joseph*, another fifth to Novello music publishers, a relic of the grand rights that Desmond Elliott had let slip away). Before the tax laws were changed in the sixties, performing artists had been able to shelter some of their income by declaring royalties a capital gain, but that loophole was no longer available. A producer, however, could: if Lloyd Webber could set himself up as his own managing agent, he could immediately lower his effective tax rate from the high 90s to 30 percent.

Thus was conceived, in 1977, the Really Useful Company, Ltd., a corporate entity that would protect any of Lloyd Webber's income that was not directly related to his Stigwood salary and royalties or his work with Rice. (The name of the corporation was derived from Wilbert Awdry's series of children's books about trains, one of Andrew's childhood favorites.) It was through the Really Useful Company that Lloyd Webber signed the recording contract for *Variations* with MCA, and the recording bore his name as both composer and producer. At the same time, Lloyd Webber set up a publishing company, Steampower Music, Ltd., to handle a project he had in mind for an animated cartoon about railway trains based on the story of Cinderella.*

His foray into his own business ventures came as no surprise to Stigwood. Relations between the two had worsened steadily, and Lloyd Webber was barely tolerated around the offices of the Stigwood Group. He was always wanting to look at the books, to see this contract or that, worrying about percentages of the gross versus percentages of the net. Although he and Rice had made Stigwood a lot of money, Stigwood by this time had moved on to other, more lucrative ventures, successfully producing the films *Saturday Night Fever* and *Grease*. Truth to tell, he was sick of Andrew Lloyd Webber and wished he would just go away. When the Lloyd Webber–Rice contract came up for renewal in 1979, Lloyd Webber asked the RSG to help capitalize the Really Useful Company in return for equity, but Stigwood's henchman, Freddie Gershon, and Lloyd Webber had a most unpleasant final meeting. The upshot was that in May, Andrew and Tim were once again on their own.

(For a time, Lloyd Webber contemplated suing Stigwood over what he felt were the inequities in their contract, especially Stigwood's acting as both agent and manager—selling Rice and Lloyd Webber to himself and taking a 25-percent cut for his trouble. Lloyd Webber was dissuaded by counsel, who told him that the courts would not look kindly on the complaint by a couple of literate public-school boys that they had not understood what they were signing.)

To run his new company, Lloyd Webber hired Brian Brolly, the former MCA executive who had backed him and Rice on the *Superstar* album when they were just a couple of nobodies. After leaving MCA, Brolly had caught on with ex-Beatle Paul McCartney, negotiating several of McCartney's biggest coups, including the purchase of the rights to the Buddy Holly copyrights; the income from "That'll Be the Day" alone could practically let a man live comfortably for life. But, although he paid Brolly well, Paul would not give Brian the thing he most wanted—a stake in McCartney's company, MPL, Ltd.—and Brolly put the word out he was ready to jump ship for the right offer. At a dinner party, Lloyd Webber asked his friend John Eastman, Paul's brother-in-law and a lawyer, if he should go after Brolly, and Eastman said yes. In 1978, for a 30-percent share in the Really Useful Company, Brian Brolly came on board. David Land, who had been with Andrew and Tim since the beginning, was left out. Stigwood was furious. "You're making an old man [Land] very unhappy," he shouted at Lloyd Webber. But what was done was done.

Andrew may never have been happier than when he was surrounded by four accountants, two lawyers, and a tax expert, as a bitter Land said later, and he was clearly in his element at home in Sydmonton, but his heart was still in the theater. In 1979 he and Tim briefly discussed the idea of writing a song cycle for female voice about an English girl and the problems in her love life. Tim liked the idea and had sketched out two or three song lyrics; he even had a certain female singer in mind while doing so because, during the London run of *Evita*, he and Elaine Paige had become lovers. It was an intense, passionate relationship: for Tim, Elaine was Evita come to life in all her glamour and glory, and he found her irresistible. None of Tim's friends could understand it; not because they didn't like Paige, but because no one had an unkind word for Jane Rice, the mother of his two children (their son, Donald, had been born in 1978). Andrew was especially disapproving, and relations between the two men worsened.

A few songs were sketched, but Andrew got tired of Tim's leisurely pace and latched on to Don Black, who had won an Oscar for his lyrics for the title song of the film "Born Free." Black was a pro, who had written lyrics for several of the James Bond movies, including *Thunderball* and *Diamonds Are Forever*, as well as for musicals, such as *Bar Mitzvah Boy*, which he wrote with Jule Styne and, with fellow Bondsman John Barry, *Billy*, based on Keith Waterhouse's *Billy Liar. Billy* had featured Elaine Paige as Rita, one of the women in the mendacious hero's life. Black had come to Lloyd Webber's attention courtesy of Hal Prince, who recommended that he see *Bar Mitzvah Boy;* "Wander along and take a look at it," said Prince. "There's an intelligent lyricist lurking there."

The result of their collaboration was *Tell Me on a Sunday*, written for Marti Webb, who had been one of Paige's successors in the London *Evita*. The subject—the trials and romantic tribulations of an English girl adrift in Manhattan—was Black's idea. Why were so many English women abandoning their homeland for America? What were the problems they faced upon arrival? What were the cultural differences they discovered in dating American men? The idea was interesting, a kind of updated, feminized Connecticut Yankee in reverse, and Lloyd Webber set to work.

Tell Me on a Sunday premiered at Sydmonton in September 1979 and was later performed on the BBC as a television special. In this, its first incarnation, it was a dour, unlovable piece. The nameless heroine is a human trampoline, her affairs with various younger lovers,

---

*Lloyd Webber loved trains. Like many Europeans, he had an idealized view of the American railroad. His image was that of the great nineteenth- and the early-twentieth-century locomotives that surged across North America and welded a country out of a continent—not the decrepit wrecks that were then shambling along the Boston–Washington corridor. In the attic at Sydmonton, Lloyd Webber had a huge model-railroad set, to go along with his collection of pinball machines and other games; he could spend hours up there, a pinball wizard that would put Tommy to shame.

Hollywood producers, and married men inevitably coming to grief, yet she springs back up, ready for more abuse. "It's not the end of the world," is her motto, sung when she picks herself up off the floor and soldiers on to the next disaster; the cycle's last lyric is "It's not the end of the world to be free/It's not the end of the world to be me."

Fairly unpromising stuff, made worse by the dreary anonymity of it all. The only one of the woman's lovers who is dignified with a name is Sheldon Bloom, the movie mogul, at whom the girl throws herself with abandon:

> Let me move in and let's get this show rolling
> I'll talk to your plants I'll even go bowling
> There is nothing I wouldn't do
> I'll be the perfect little lady for you
> Sheldon Bloom
> Make some room

(Although Bloom is a stereotypical Hollywood Jew, this time Lloyd Webber was immune to charges of anti-Semitism, for Black was Jewish.)

The original *Tell Me on a Sunday* has a few redeeming social values. "You Made Me Think You Were in Love" is a gentle swinger whose melody in part originated with the "Summer Day" number in *Jeeves*. "Capped Teeth and Caesar Salad," a send-up of the manners and mores of Beverly Hills, an admittedly stationary target, has wit and bite. The linking recitative, which begins with "Let Me Finish" and runs throughout the piece, is smoother and more accomplished than the recitative in either *Superstar* or *Evita*. And the title song, which is our punching bag's—er, heroine's—plea to her next torturer, is one of Lloyd Webber's most eloquent meditative ballads, set to one of Black's better lyrics:

> Don't write a letter
> When you want to leave
> Don't call me at 3 A.M. from a friend's apartment
> I'd like to choose how I hear the news
> Take me to a park that's covered with trees
> Tell me on a Sunday please.
>
> Let me down easy
> No big song and dance
> No long faces no long looks
> No deep conversation
> I know the way we should spend that day
> Take me to a zoo that's got chimpanzees
> Tell me on a Sunday please.
>
> Don't want to know who's to blame
> It won't help knowing
> Don't want to fight day and night
> Bad enough you're going.
>
> Don't leave in silence
> With no word at all
> Don't get drunk and slam the door
> That's no way to end this
> I know how I want you to say goodbye
> Find a circus ring with a flying trapeze
> Tell me on a Sunday please.

Well, maybe not the bit about chimpanzees. One of the problems with the first version of *Tell Me on a Sunday* was that, to American ears, the lyrics just didn't ring true. Not only was the girl a masochist, she seemed to have flunked geography as well. The very first verse of the first song, "Take That Look Off Your Face," contains the following infelicity: "He's doing some deal up in Baltimore now/I hate it when he's away."

Even Clara from Clapham (our heroine is actually a Muswell Hillbilly), if she has been off the boat for more than five minutes, would never say such a thing: to New Yorkers, Baltimore is *down,* New England is *up,* the rest of the United States is *out,* and Europe is *over.* Later, in "Capped Teeth," she sings that "every man and beast/came from out East," when a Californian would say "*back* East."

The 1980 record album, whose cover depicted Webb spray painting its title across the Manhattan skyline, did well—well enough for Lloyd Webber to start thinking how he could put *Tell Me on a Sunday* on stage. By itself, of course, it was impossible; too short, too depressing, too unfocused. But in combination with another piece, one just might be able to make something of it. Two one-acters, a kind of Lloyd Webberian *Cav 'n' Pag.* That was the ticket. Now the question was: what to pair it with?

Several likely candidates, and one unlikely one, came to mind. Although he hadn't yet written a note of it, *The Signal-Man* was one possibility; two gloomy Guses on the same evening could work, as the Mascagni and Leoncavallo yoking had amply demonstrated. And speaking of Italian opera in general and Leoncavallo in particular, there was still Andrew's notion to construct a short opera from the rivalry between Puccini and Leoncavallo.

Lloyd Webber's notion was to compose imaginary outtakes from the music each composer might have written—Puccini playing Mimi's aria, "*Si, mi chiamano Mimi,*" but with an entirely different melody, for example. He had even gone so far as to jot down a Pucciniesque melody, in homage to a composer he had long admired.*

The idea seemed promising, but he had one other thought as well. A dedicated cat fancier (Julian, on the other hand, was a great admirer of turtles and kept a pair named Boosey and Hawkes as pets), Lloyd Webber had long admired T. S. Eliot's *Old Possum's Book of Practical Cats,* a collection of whimsical verse for children that found the American-born poet in an unbuttoned mood. "Old Possum" was one of Eliot's nicknames, and the poems betrayed their creator's Midwestern origins in their peculiarly American turns of phrase. The Eliot poetry was far from a dramatic narrative, though, and Lloyd Webber was more inclined toward a suite of the *Cats* poems, not a full-fledged evening in the theater.

Ultimately, he rejected all three possibilities. A closer solution was at hand, suggested by a young impresario he had recently met named Cameron Mackintosh: the *Variations.* What was that his heroine had sung in *Tell Me on a Sunday?* "No big song and dance." He had the songs. What if *Variations* were the dance? And what if he put them both together, on the same evening? So what if they were thematically unrelated? One could call the ad-hoc show "A Concert for the Theater," or some such. Better yet, *Song and Dance.*

But first, *Cats.*

---

*And who was, in fact, a recycler after his own heart; the music to Rodolfo's first words in *La Bohème,* "Nei cieli bigi," was retrieved from an aborted opera, *La Lupa.*

Chapter Five: JELLICLES CAN AND JELLICLES DO

Cats, which opened at the New London Theatre on May 11, 1981, was the signal event in Lloyd Webber's life. Before *Cats,* he was the young composer who, with his partner Tim Rice, had ridden a hit record to fame and a hit show to fortune, following up *Superstar* with the solid, if still controversial, achievement of *Evita.* After *Cats,* he was wealthy beyond the dreams of avarice and the centerpiece and chief tangible asset of an entertainment empire that stretched around the world. Before *Cats,* he was a kind of British Marvin Hamlisch, a successful theater professional without a high public profile; after it, he was what he had always wanted to be: master of the West End, conqueror of Broadway—in short, Andrew Lloyd Webber, Superstar.

The raw statistics of *Cats* are impressive: on February 21, 1989, *Cats* passed Hamlisch's *A Chorus Line* to become the most profitable theatrical venture in history, having amassed a net profit of fifty-eight and a half million dollars worldwide, forty-four million dollars of that total in North America (and twenty million of that on Broadway), for a return on investment to the show's backers of eleven to one. In a highly speculative industry, in which "angels" routinely lose their shirts, if not their wings, *Cats* was a spectacular achievement, not the least for Lloyd Webber and the producer, Cameron Mackintosh, who, with a few other royalty participants, shared 25 percent of the gross profits—in this case, about fourteen million dollars.

More than six years into its run in New York, *Cats* was still selling out, grossing three hundred thousand dollars a week and posting a weekly net profit of about forty-five thousand dollars. The gross from productions in the United States and Canada was more than four hundred million dollars; the first national touring company, which ran from 1983 to 1987, netted nearly eight million dollars, and the first bus-and-truck company, which took the show to the American hinterlands between 1986 and 1988, earned ten million dollars. And all this for a musical whose prospects were considered so dim that it took the financial contributions of more than two hundred small investors to first get it on the boards.

The effect of *Cats* on Lloyd Webber's life, though, goes far beyond money. In the darkest days of late 1980, when he had to mortgage Sydmonton for a second time to invest seventy-five thousand pounds in *Cats,* Lloyd Webber was gambling everything he owned in a bid to transform his life. If *Cats* had failed, as *Jeeves* had, he probably would have gone back to Rice and begged for another libretto; he would have forfeited his country estate and thus notions of country-squire grandeur; and, very likely, he would have stayed married to his first wife. But when *Cats* succeeded, it transformed his existence.

On November 4, 1980, Lloyd Webber, accompanied by his aide Bridget ("Biddy") Hayward, wandered into the New London Theatre in Drury Lane—by reputation the unluckiest theater in London and then in use as a television studio and conference center. Andrew thought he was headed there at the request of Thames Television for consultation on a musical matter. Instead, he was the surprised victim of Eamonn Andrews's "This Is Your Life," the British version of the long-running American program.

The show is a remarkable symbolic document. Never very comfortable in public, Lloyd Webber endured the ordeal with his face set in a grim rictus, sinking back into his chair in an attempt to make himself as small and inconspicuous as possible. The shoulder-length hair and velvet suits of his mod days were a thing of the past; the father of two small children (Imogen had been born on March 31, 1977, and Nicholas Alastair on July 22, 1979) was now given over sartorially to the English Rumpled Look, tousle-headed and usually tieless. The only time that Andrew really seemed to enjoy himself on the show was when Don Everly, half of the Everly Brothers, popped out of the wings for a quick hello; most of the time, the only part of him that showed any emotion was his brown, sloping cat's eyes, which darted around the studio, taking it all in, forecasting, calculating, plotting.

One by one, the guests came out from behind a screen, each to tell a little Webberian anecdote. His wife, Sarah, recalled their first dinner date, when she, the teenager, wondered if he was going to make her pay her share; Jean and Bill told the world what a troublesome child "Bumper" had been, and Edmundo Ros got on the horn from his home in Spain, glad to have been of service in soothing the little savage's breast. Julian told the already shopworn anecdote of the Orient football bet, Tim Rice talked about moving in with Andrew's granny because the price was right, and a by-now mollified David Land reminisced about the pop museum idea of so long ago.

Gary Bond came on to tell the story of how Lloyd Webber and Sarah joined him for a holiday on the Greek island of Mykonos after *Joseph* had opened in the West End; Lloyd Webber had arrived wearing his trademark velvet suit while everyone else on the beach was naked. Bond called him "a very loyal friend." Paul Nicholas, who had played Jesus in the recently closed London *Superstar*—in sum, the show had run for 3,357 performances, a British record—noted that they had not worked together for eight years. "Nothing personal, I hope," he said. Elaine Paige arrived, as did David Essex, who had been the Che to Elaine's Evita, and Marti Webb and Stephanie Lawrence, both replacement Evitas, were also on hand. The actor Robert Powell chatted about a board game Andrew had once inflicted on his friends, called, appropriately, "Insanity." Near the end, Hal Prince came on from his office in New York, ruing his failure to get a hold of *Superstar*, reveling in his *Evita* triumph. "I finish with one question," Prince said. "What do we do next?"

That was the question on Eamonn Andrews's mind as well, but he was thinking about Lloyd Webber and Rice. As well he should; "This Is Your Life"'s subtitle that evening might well have been "And Not Yours, Tim Rice." If the program's producers had set out deliberately to insult Tim, who sat through the show with a tight little smile of bemusement, they could not have done a better job. If there was any sense that Lloyd Webber owed any of his success to his partner—indeed, that Rice had conceived all three hit shows—it was very well hidden. (Andrews had first asked Rice to be the guest of honor, but Jane Rice had turned the request down flat.)

Rice and Lloyd Webber hardly looked at each other during the program. Their only spontaneous exchange came during Land's narrative— "He managed to get hold of Elvis's guitar and the busted trousers of . . ."—which was interrupted by a quick flash from Lloyd Webber, who cracked, ". . . Tim Rice!" So the old sexual jealousy was still operative. When Andrews asked Lloyd Webber what his and Rice's next project would be, the composer replied, "It's a closely guarded secret." He still didn't feel free to abandon Tim entirely.

Nevertheless, it is instructive to consider the fate of each of the show's participants vis-à-vis Lloyd Webber: with very few exceptions, from that moment on few of them would have any further effect on Andrew's fortunes. During the program, Bill Lloyd Webber sat slumped in his chair, his chin resting on his chest. Body language was very revealing in the Lloyd Webber family—there was Jean's prim control, Andrew's protective hunch, and Julian's modest self-effacement—and Bill's posture eloquently bespoke a man both tired and sick, and sick and tired. Some fathers would take vicarious revenge in witnessing a public celebration of their son's triumph in a field that fate had closed to them, but Bill seemed to take no pleasure in it at all. After his "Bumper" story, he sat almost motionless, contemplating, perhaps, not his son's victory but his own defeat. Nor were other family members immune from the changes that would shortly sweep Andrew's life. By 1984 Sarah Hugill would officially be the ex–Mrs. Lloyd Webber and Sydmonton Court would have a new mistress.

As far as performers were concerned, Nicholas would appear in *Cats* and then would disappear; there would be no major roles forthcoming for Bond; and it would take an accident for Paige to get into Lloyd Webber's next show. Land was already gone, of course, and Prince would have to wait six years until he directed another Lloyd Webber musical. What *did* have a future, however, was the space, the New London Theatre itself, which, as luck would have it, had been built by Sefton Myers. As Andrew looked around, he decided that the theater-in-the-round would be perfect for *Cats*.

Lloyd Webber had first encountered Eliot's whimsy as a child, when Jean (who was even madder about cats than he was) would read the poems to him. In 1972, during all the to-ing and fro-ing to America that accompanied *Jesus Christ Superstar*, he found *Old Possum's Book of Practical Cats* at an airport bookshop and devoured it on the flight. They may have been meant as poems for children, but they sounded like song lyrics to him; Lloyd Webber made his first musical sketches after *Evita* opened in London and had privately played a few of the tunes for some friends in his London flat. Not surprisingly, they encouraged him to continue.

Published in October 1939, between the verse play *The Family Reunion* and the essay *The Idea of a Christian Society*, *Old Possum's Book of Practical Cats*—"Old Possum" was a nickname given Eliot by Ezra Pound—was widely regarded as a lesser effort by the St. Louis–born poet who had transformed himself into a pillar of the English establishment. "Pleasant, inoffensive and unremarkable," the Eliot scholar

Burton Raffel had said of the book. *Practical Cats* may have found the Nobel Prize-winning writer slumming along Tottenham Court Road, but Eliot took the verses seriously; they were, after all, written for his two young godchildren. Further, not all was high-minded poetasting in the world of Thomas Stearns Eliot. The whoopee cushion was not unknown in the Eliot household, and the august poet once wrote a fan letter to Groucho Marx; at Harvard, he had penned a slightly salacious mock epic called *King Bobo and His Big Black Queen,* "whose bum was as big as a soup tureen." Even *The Waste Land,* his most famous poem, contained the line, "O O O O that Shakespherian Rag," and Eliot had essayed the theater in the uncompleted play *Sweeney Agonistes.* With Tim drifting away—"Andrew can't wait to work," Mackintosh observed, "and Tim can't wait until the work is done"—he was still in need of a librettist. They didn't come any tonier than old T. S.

During the summer of 1980, at Sydmonton, Lloyd Webber unveiled his settings in front of his invited audience. *Cats* was not offered as a musical, but as a song-cycle, much like *Tell Me on a Sunday,* which had made its debut at Sydmonton (along with Edward Duke's one-man show *Jeeves Takes Charge* and Rod Argent's song *Tomorrow Shall Be My Dancing Day*) the year before; the other work that year was a *Missa Brevis* by Michael Stuckey. This was not the first time that the *Cats* poems had been treated musically. During Eliot's lifetime, British composer Alan Rawsthorne had written a melodrama in which actor Robert Donat read the poems over Rawsthorne's instrumental music. Eliot had cautiously endorsed the endeavor, saying: "I like the idea that they are read against the musical background and not themselves set to music. But I am not at all sure yet what I think of it, and, of course, I should have to hear them all." Earlier, Eliot had turned down a request from Walt Disney to use the poems in an animated feature; they were hard-scrabble alley cats, he said, not cute little anthropomorphs.

Despite the successful Sydmonton performance, the notion of presenting *Cats* as a musical was still very far off: with no story line and no main character, *Cats* appeared to be no more than an animadversion. Still, Andrew had taken the precaution of inviting Valerie Eliot, the poet's widow, to the festival that summer. Ever since Dean Sullivan had gone to bat for "Superstar," benediction had been important to Lloyd Webber (if only Eva Perón could have made the L. A. opening . . .) and if Mrs. Eliot would vet his settings, then, who knew, something might come of it after all. To Lloyd Webber's delight, Valerie Eliot did much more than vet them, she positively rhapsodized about them. Eliot would have loved the songs, she said. Would Andrew like to see an unpublished eight-line fragment about Grizabella the Glamour Cat that Eliot had left out of the work because he felt it was too depressing for children? Would he like to see some of Eliot's correspondence about the *Practical Cats*? He would very much indeed.

Valerie Eliot was nearly forty years younger than her husband when they were married in 1957, he for the second time. She had been his secretary; during their eight years of marriage, which ended with Eliot's death in 1965, she was his confidante and editor of his letters. She knew how important a part of his makeup Old Possum was, and she was delighted to assist Lloyd Webber in any way she could.

And so was producer Cameron Mackintosh. Lloyd Webber's relationship with Mackintosh, a confirmed bachelor whose youthful appearance was enhanced by his modest stature and a suggestion of not-quite-melted baby fat, was of fairly recent vintage. Mackintosh, the son of a half-Scottish timber merchant and his Maltese wife, grew up in comfortable middle-class surroundings in north London and in Hertfordshire. The parallels between Mackintosh's early life and Lloyd Webber's were striking. Andrew and Cameron were contemporaries, both passionate about the musical theater and both pursuing it with a single-mindedness that bordered on the obsessive. Like Andrew's, Cameron's father was a musician, an amateur trumpeter who played under the name Spike Mackintosh in a band called the Troglodytes. Like Andrew, Cameron had been introduced to the theater by an aunt, who took him to the Bristol Old Vic to see Julian Slade's *Salad Days* in 1954, when he was eight years old. At first he resisted, but once exposed to the magic of stagecraft, he was quickly hooked; three weeks later, sporting the Scottish kilt, he was back at the show in London's Adelphi Theatre, where his presumption in demanding to meet Slade was rewarded by a backstage tour. And like Andrew, Cameron had created a toy theater in his home, this one a puppet show for which he wrote the scripts and his brother Robert pulled the strings.

Most stagestruck youths want to be actors: Mackintosh wanted to be a producer. His first job came in 1965, as an eighteen-year-old stagehand for *Camelot* at the Theatre Royal in Drury Lane, for which he earned seven pounds a week; he managed to scrape up an additional seven pounds a week by cleaning the auditorium after performances. From the beginning, Mackintosh displayed his zest for self-promotion. Even though it cost him half his salary, he took a two-room flat in Half Moon Street, Mayfair, figuring it was better to pay a little more for the right address than to save three quid a week and live in, say, Highgate. He traveled by taxi, not tube, always arriving for work impeccably dressed. Look at me, Mackintosh was saying to the world, I am going places.

Up the production ladder he climbed, reopening the Kenton Theatre in Henley with five plays. In 1969 he stormed the West End with a revival of Cole Porter's *Anything Goes;* it was a disaster, closing almost immediately, and his backers lost everything. "If you survive this, you'll survive anything," Bernard Delfont, the theater's owner, told him. Another catastrophe followed in 1970, a theatrical version of the popular British radio show *The Dales,* whose wheels came off at the Winter Garden in Blackpool, leaving Mackintosh fifteen thousand pounds in debt to the National Westminster Bank.

Undaunted, Mackintosh pressed on, raising money and putting on shows until in 1976 he scored a breakthrough with a production of *Side by Side* by Sondheim at the Mermaid Theatre, which ran for 781 performances, earning more than one hundred thousand pounds on an investment of six thousand. This was followed by revivals of Bart's *Oliver!,* Schwartz's *Godspell,* and, in 1979, a touring version of Jim Sharman's production of *The Rocky Horror Show.*

Mackintosh was a born impresario, whose powers of persuasion were made more effective by his gentle appearance. He was no cigar-chomping bully, pounding his desk and screaming "You'll never work in this town again!" at some hapless actor. Mackintosh could charm money out of Midas, and he had a flair for publicity not seen since Barnum. Who else could squeeze backing for provincial touring productions of *Oklahoma!* and *My Fair Lady* (starring Anna Neagle) out of the Arts Council of Great Britain? Mackintosh could, and did.

He was, in other words, a man after Lloyd Webber's heart, and it seemed only natural he and Andrew eventually would form an alliance. Yet their first meeting was contentious. At the 1978 Society of West End Theatre Awards, at which *Evita* was named best musical, Lloyd Webber was offended by the way his music was presented. Mackintosh, the producer, had asked for only one song, "Don't Cry for Me, Argentina," but Andrew insisted on a medley. Lloyd Webber got his medley, but the sound system went horribly wrong, and it threw the volatile composer into a rage: the show would have been fine if a pro like Hal Prince had produced it, he declared to anyone who would listen. Fortified by claret, Mackintosh wanted to go to Lloyd Webber's house and punch him in the nose.

In January 1980, with tempers cooled, Lloyd Webber telephoned Mackintosh and invited the producer to lunch at his club, the Savile. Another thing the two found they had in common was a fondness for the grape, and a bibulous afternoon ensued, the upshot of which was that they discovered they liked each other; better, they needed each other; best of all, they could do business together. Mackintosh and Lloyd Webber were two hungry men, and not just for the repast provided by the Savile. Lloyd Webber may have been selfish, prickly, and difficult, but he had always known how to forge a marriage of convenience when it was necessary to advance his career. For his part, Mackintosh looked across the lunch table and saw a man as self-possessed as himself, a composer who, despite his reputation in Britain, was still chasing the big score. Back in 1965, when Tim Rice had first met Andrew, he remembered thinking to himself, "This guy's going to make it"; now, fifteen years later, Mackintosh was having the same reaction.

What Mackintosh grasped immediately was that Lloyd Webber represented the future of the musical theater. Although it was nice to revel in glorious reminiscence of the great days of Rodgers and Hammerstein, those days were gone for good, and there was no use trying to recapture them. For some reason, composers and critics in America could not get this simple principle into their heads, as the annual yammering about the Decline of Broadway proved. America was supposed to be a young country, brimming with fresh ideas, but on Broadway everybody was either old (the ninety-two-year-old George Abbott, for example, was still active) or acted old. Here it was, 1980, and no other Broadway composer had yet admitted that Elvis or the Beatles ever existed. In the United States, it seemed, both the theater people and the classical-music crowd had the same snobbish attitude toward the pop music of the fifties, sixties, and seventies: they just wished it would go away and leave them alone. The Great White Way, it seemed to Mackintosh, was a great white vacuum, waiting to be filled.

Valerie Eliot's revelation of the "Grizabella" poem got both Lloyd Webber and Mackintosh to thinking that maybe there was more to *Cats* than a song cycle. At Mackintosh's suggestion, Lloyd Webber enlisted Trevor Nunn, the dashing director of the Royal Shakespeare Company, to help him in fashioning *Cats* for the stage. Nunn was an unusual choice, for despite his formidable theatrical credentials his experience in the commercial musical theater was limited to a musical version of *A Comedy of Errors* at Stratford in 1977 and a revival of George S. Kaufman's *Once in a Lifetime* in 1979, which ended with a fifteen-minute singing and dancing tribute to the Hollywood musicals of the thirties. A *Jeeves* lesson was being violated, but Nunn knew language, didn't need a trot to decipher Eliot's multiplicitous references to London people, places, and things, and certainly knew the scope and sweep of British culture. Andrew thought Nunn was right for the show in a way that Hal Prince could never have been.

In one of Eliot's letters, there was a throwaway reference to something the poet called "the Heaviside Layer," a kind of animal heaven to which a worthy cat (or dog) might be transported. This, coupled with the "Grizabella" fragment, was the peg Nunn was looking to hang the show on. One could not put a string of unrelated poems on the stage, but if there was a semblance of a plot, no matter how tenuous, well, maybe something could be done. Consider the poem:

> *She haunted many a low resort*
> *Near the grimy road of Tottenham Court*
> *She flitted about the no-man's land*
> *From "The Rising Sun" to the "Friend At Hand."*

And the postman sighed as he scratched his head
You'd really have thought she'd ought to be dead.
And who would ever suppose that that
Was Grizabella the Glamour Cat?

What if the drab Grizabella was to become the cat who would find her redemptive feline apotheosis? Eliot's poetry may not have been very deep—its metaphysical point was that, in the end, cats are much like you and me—but there was some amusing social commentary running through it. The quick-witted Nunn seized on this quality, put Grizabella at its center, and, presto, like one of Mister Mistoffelees's conjuring tricks, the cat was out of the bag.

Still, *Cats* was at root a small idea that badly needed expansion. Nunn was no professional songwriter, but he had written the texts for the songs in *A Comedy of Errors* at Stratford, and he took pride in his way with words. There was no opening number, so Nunn, assisted by the lyricist Richard Stilgoe, got to work on the Prologue, cobbling together a pastiche that was made up of quotations from Eliot's collected works. This, the "Jellicle Songs for Jellicle Cats," was intended to set the tone and the place—the night of the Jellicle Ball, when the cats gather to choose the one of their number who will be transported to the Heaviside Layer.

Early on, the decision was made to make *Cats* a spectacular; if there could not be bread, then let there be circuses. Quickly, Nunn assembled the production team. From the Royal Shakespeare Company came John Napier, the designer with whom he had created the eight-and-a-half-hour epic *Nicholas Nickleby,* to fashion a kitty Disneyland-in-the-round. (So much for Eliot's rejection of Uncle Walt.) Gillian Lynne, who had assisted Nunn with his two previous musical efforts with the RSC, was called upon to put the cast through its paces.

The decision to hire a British choreographer was a calculated dare: everyone knew that the English couldn't write musicals, and they were positively certain that the Brits couldn't do dance musicals. Lynne was no kitten: she had joined the Royal Ballet in 1944, performing with the company for more than seven years before she abandoned classical dance for musical comedy. She choreographed Anthony Newley's *The Roar of the Greasepaint, The Smell of the Crowd* on Broadway in 1964, *Pickwick* in 1965, and *How Now Dow Jones* in 1968 and had directed *My Fair Lady* and *Tomfoolery* for Mackintosh. Because the story of *Cats* would be told largely through dance, Lynne's title was Associate Director. In casting *Cats,* the creative team was looking for singers who could dance and dancers who could sing, not actors and actresses, and very few West Enders were likely to qualify. The biggest name they had was Judi Dench, whom they cast as Grizabella.

At an open audition call early in 1981, Sarah Brightman showed up. Andrew had been twigged to Brightman by choreographer Arlene Phillips, whom he had met in 1977 over a meal at the Grill Room of the Savoy Hotel. Phillips had boosted Sarah to fame as the lead singer in her rock-dance group, Hot Gossip, which was made up of black boys and white girls. Brightman was twenty-one years old, slender, and slinky, her hair cut in the spiky punk style then fashionable and colored blue; with Hot Gossip, she had had a big hit with "I Lost My Heart to a Starship Trooper." Brightman had quit Hot Gossip after three years to seek a career in the legitimate theater and had been out of work for a while when she appeared at the open call. She sang a couple of lines and was dismissed, so she was surprised when a few days later she got a telephone call from Biddy Hayward asking her to meet Andrew at his Eaton Place flat.

None of Lloyd Webber's friends suspected there was anything wrong with his marriage, but after nearly nine years a vague dissatisfaction had started to set in. Sarah had been the best helpmeet a man could want, functioning as wife, mother, lover, and majordomo. She had spent months in the hospital bearing their two children. During the "This Is Your Life" program, she had beamed with pride at the celebration of her husband's work and at the end of the show Imogen and Nicholas had been brought out to cuddle with their daddy. If Andrew was an unhappy husband, he did not let on. Besides, what fueled him was success, not sex, and so far he had resisted all temptation to fool around in a profession in which fooling around came with the territory.

But Sarah Brightman was different. Sarah Hugill was a pretty, domesticated homemaker; Brightman was a forbidden fruit, ripe and luscious. There was about her more than a whiff of forbidden sexuality. Her racy image in Hot Gossip—and before that, with the television dance company Pan's People—all fishnet-stockinged legs and heaving bosom, was only part of her attraction. Even more important, she was, like Andrew, entirely a creature of the theater. Her mother, Paula, had started her dancing at the age of three, and Sarah had made her debut at thirteen, playing one of Queen Victoria's daughters in a West End production of *I and Albert.* She attended three theatrical schools, among them Elmhurst, but dropped out when she was sixteen. At eighteen, she had eloped with Andrew Graham-Stewart, the manager of the rock group Tangerine Dream, but neglected to tell her parents about the wedding for two years, even though she left Graham-Stewart and moved back home after a few months; the Brightmans, who resided in Bournemouth (Grenville Brightman, Sarah's father, was a property developer), thought she had simply been living with her boyfriend.

Sex and entertainment ran in the family: in the early sixties Paula Brightman had been one of the attractions at the famous Murray's Cabaret Club, which occupied a basement in Beak Street, Soho. Murray's was in the vanguard of Swinging London; one of the musicians who played there for many years called it "an upholstered sewer." Under British law, the bare-breasted showgirls had to stand motionless on the stage (whereas, in America, they had to keep moving), but on the floor the hostesses moved easily among the rich, powerful crowd. Although Percival "Pops" Murray was a master of the casting couch, for propriety's sake he forbade his girls from mingling with the clientele after hours. That rule seems to have been honored mainly in the breech: in 1963 two of Murray's girls, Christine Keeler and Mandy Rice-Davies, met John Profumo and Stephen Ward and helped bring down Harold MacMillan's Tory government. (Keeler, however, was adamant that Murray's was not a bordello; "other clubs were knocking shops," she said, "but not Murray's.") In a photograph of Murray's girls from the period—the women are scantily attired as harem girls—Paula's raven hair and liquid dark eyes, two attributes she passed on to her look-alike daughter, along with her vivacious personality, command immediate attention.

Sarah was a looker like her mother, but for a long time Andrew was interested only in her voice. Lloyd Webber's Eaton Place auditions were no casting-couch tryouts; he liked to get a good look at his principals, to gauge their abilities and effect up close as well as from a distance. Phillips was right: the girl could sing, with a pure, untrained soprano that sounded a little like a boy's, yet she obviously moved like a woman. Although Lloyd Webber liked Brightman, she had to return and audition four or five times before she got the secondary role of Jemima. Casting *Cats* in London was tricky, because while the British could muster the thirty or so first-rate singer-dancers the show needed, there were not the sixty or ninety or one hundred and twenty choristers an open call would uncover in New York. In sporting parlance, England had a good first string but no bench. Still, by February, the show was cast. *Cats* was starting to howl.

In November and December 1980 Napier had fashioned a scale model of the theater they proposed to use—the New London—but in January an attack of cold feet on the part of the theater's owners, who decided to stick to industrial trade shows rather than risk their steady income on what seemed to them a preposterous idea, had resulted in the withdrawal of their offer to let the space. A mini-crisis ensued, accompanied by a frantic, fruitless search for another suitable theater, and it was only through the timely arm-twisting of Bernard Delfont that the New London became available once again.

Now another problem arose: nobody wanted to invest in *Cats*. Even with the names of Cameron Mackintosh, Andrew Lloyd Webber, and Trevor Nunn attached to the project, Mackintosh's usual suspects took one look at *Cats* and said no thank you. Their reasoning was sound. As Lloyd Webber described it to an interviewer several years later:

> I can give you the objections and they sound a convincing lot. Andrew Lloyd Webber without Robert Stigwood; without Tim Rice; working with a dead poet; with a whole load of songs about cats; asking us to believe that people dressed up as cats are going to work; working with Trevor Nunn from the Royal Shakespeare Company, who's never done a musical in his life; working in the New London, the theatre with the worst track record in London; asking us to believe that twenty English people can do a dance show when England had never been able to put together any kind of fashionable dance entertainment before. It was just a recipe for disaster. But we knew in the rehearsal room that even if we lost everything, we'd attempted something that hadn't been done before.

Mackintosh needed five hundred thousand pounds to get *Cats* on its way. (Having learned his lesson, the producer never invested his own money in a show.) In desperation, he placed an advertisement in the financial newspapers, inviting the general public to put up a minimum of seven hundred and fifty pounds for a stake in *Cats*. In the end nearly two hundred and twenty individuals contributed, including one man who gambled his life's savings—five thousand pounds—on his faith in Lloyd Webber, Nunn, and Eliot. Typically, Mackintosh took the dire straits as a photo opportunity and got a picture in *The Evening Standard* of his cat, Bouncer, putting his paw to a seventy-five-pound investment.

Bouncer's faith in his master's judgment was all well and good, but there was one thing still missing: a hit song. Two weeks into rehearsals, Nunn still felt the show needed the Big Tune, a song that everyone would walk out humming; it would give the evening a unity and a focus that it badly needed. Writing from preexisting lyrics was something new for Lloyd Webber, who had been used to evolving words and music as he and Rice had gone along. Usually, his music had come first, but Eliot's verse was all but immutable: its rhythms would dictate the musical meter, its phrases would dictate the shapes of the melody. For all their many attractions, however, Eliot's words had yet to call forth a "Superstar" or "Don't Cry for Me, Argentina."

Nunn wanted something, he wanted something big, and he wanted something now. Andrew headed to the keyboard, and to the drawer. His Puccini-Leoncavallo opera had come to nought, but he had written a Puccini-like melody as part of his outtakes idea. One day, in rehearsal, he played the melody for Nunn, who asked him what it was. "It's a very extravagant emotional theme," Lloyd Webber said. "Make it more emotional, more extravagant, and we'll have it in *Cats*," Nunn said. The song was "Memory." When Lloyd Webber played it later for the cast, Nunn solemnly intoned to all and sundry: "What is the date? The hour? Remember, because you have just heard a smash hit by Lloyd Webber."

Indeed, the melody was so Pucciniesque that Andrew worried it might be a real Puccini tune. He asked his father, "Did I steal it?" Bill assured him that he had not, and added: "It's going to be worth two million dollars to you, you fool."

Now they had the tune, but no words. They were fresh out of Eliot. What they needed was a lyricist who could capture Grizabella's down-and-out despair, someone witty, someone clever, someone imaginative. Someone, in other words, very like Tim Rice.

At first, Rice turned them down flat. But then Judi Dench, the Grizabella, injured herself badly in rehearsal, tearing her Achilles tendon, and Elaine Paige came on as a last-minute replacement. This got Tim's attention, for a couple of reasons. One, obviously, was personal, but the other was business. Judi Dench couldn't sing very well, but Elaine could, and Tim, like Bill, smelled a hit.

So, as it turns out, did Elaine. Driving home late one evening, Paige was struck by an instrumental melody that the announcer identified only as a "theme" from Andrew Lloyd Webber's new show, *Cats,* then in rehearsals. With the right lyrics, she thought, the song could be big, very big. The melody was interrupted by the midnight news, so Paige had just enough time to rush into her house and put a blank cassette in the tape deck and await its promised replay. As she ran up to her front door, a black cat she had never seen before stood by the walk; "Come on, kitty, cross my path," thought Elaine — in the antipodean realm of show-business mythology, a sign of good luck — and sure enough the cat did.

Inside, Paige taped the song and went to bed that night thinking that she would call Lloyd Webber in the morning and beg him to let her record the song. Instead, she was awakened by a phone call from Mackintosh, telling her that Dench could not go on and asking Elaine to please, four days before the first preview, join the cast of *Cats* as Grizabella. She had got the part, and a new pet, too, for the black cat stayed.

Rice, however, was not so lucky. What Tim didn't know was that Nunn had already written a lyric for the new song, and that he would be competing with the director for a spot in the show. Nunn had holed up in Hampstead one weekend and read through Eliot's collected verses twice, trying to imbue himself with the dead poet's style and spirit. From the poem "Rhapsody on a Windy Night" came the notion of memory, which became the title of the song Nunn was writing:

> *Memory, turn your face to the moonlight*
> *Let your memory lead you*
> *Open up, enter in*
> *If you find there the meaning of what happiness is*
> *Then a new life will begin*

Rice's lyric, written in a thirty-six hour white heat, began:

> *Street lights, and the darkness between them*
> *Like the good and bad sides,*
> *Of a life almost done.*
> *Shake the memory of my passions returning to me*
> *None forgotten, no not one.*

At first, Rice's lyric was greeted with relief by all. Paige had been singing a different version of the Nunn lyric each night; during one preview she dried completely, and the orchestra had to repeat its interlude until she remembered which particular lines she was supposed to be singing. Tim's words would put an end to the memory-a-day she had been enduring.

The final decision as to which lyric to use was nominally Nunn's. He was not exactly a disinterested party — if the song became a hit, as it seemed sure to do, the lyricist stood to make a great deal of money.* He felt, though, that Rice had characterized Grizabella as entirely human and that her suicide threat later in the song was too depressing. Worst of all, Nunn thought that Rice's lyric was bewildering the audiences, and "Memory" was not getting the show-stopping reception it deserved. "Memory" just had to work; it was the climax of the show. Nunn took his concern to Mackintosh. The producer, director and, et tu, Lloyd Webber huddled and over a weekend decided that Nunn's, not Rice's, would be the lyric they would use. On Friday, Paige was singing her lover's words; on Monday, she was singing her director's.

Rice was mortified; he knew he should never have gotten involved with *Cats* in the first place, but his pride was wounded. Nunn claimed he had telephoned Tim and asked for twenty-seven different modifications, which Rice refused; Tim retorted that no one had asked him for any revisions and that, as a professional, he would have been only too happy to comply if they had. There were threats of legal action. The London

---

*As indeed he did: Nunn's association with Lloyd Webber made him a millionaire. In the year ending April 1985, records show that Nunn earned 1,123,780 pounds from just three foreign productions of *Cats* in the United States, Hungary, and Japan. "Memory" has probably pulled in 1 million pounds in publishing royalties.

press, of course, had a field day. *Schadenfreude* is catnip to journalists, and the news that the two millionaire songwriters had fallen out became for a time Topic A. Yet, like a married couple that can't stand each other but delays divorce for the sake of the children (or out of sheer inertia), Rice and Lloyd Webber continued to tease the public all through 1981. As late as December, they were said to be working on Tim's latest passion, his show about chess players: "That is," Rice said to *The New York Post*, "if I can get past his secretary."

Although Lloyd Webber was adamant that *Cats* was about cats and nothing but cats—"Hal, it's about cats," he said to Prince during preliminary discussions, when he was still casting about for a director—it is tempting to see the show as something more: Lloyd Webber's *Enigma* Variations, say, with some of the cats representing people in his life. Indeed, one hopes it is more, for *Cats* is no *Evita*, nor even a *Jesus Christ Superstar;* in many ways it is a regression to the spirit and technique of *Joseph*, without that early show's freshness. Although there are the inevitable stretches of 13/8 time signatures, the score has (dare one suggest) a doggedness about it that may be a function of its being, for long stretches, entirely in 4/4 (so is *Lohengrin*, the only thing Wagner and Lloyd Webber have in common) and very often in the key of B-flat major. Many of the tunes are dull and unvaried, and one production number, "Of the Awe-full Battle of the Pekes and the Pollicles," rivals *Jeeves*'s "Banjo Boy" as the composer's worst effort. If *Superstar* is a piece for which one's admiration grows upon familiarity with the score, *Cats* is one that suffers.

Cats is fundamentally a suite. The "plot" of Grizabella's redemption—and the even lamer subplot concerning the catnapping of Old Deuteronomy—notwithstanding, the structure of *Cats,* as it finally evolved, exists for only one reason: to plug "Memory," a song that is reprised three times before it is ever heard in full. "What if *Cats* really is now and forever," wondered the American television talk show host David Letterman; if it is, it is a triumph of special effects and marketing over content and emotion.

And yet, there is something about *Cats* that has deservedly won it fame and success. Perhaps it is the sheer audacity of the undertaking, or its size and scope. Maybe it is the subject matter, for cat fanciers are numerous and fierce in their affections. Whatever the case, in mid-1989 it overtook *Jesus Christ Superstar* as the longest-running musical in British history; worldwide, it has played in thirteen countries, including West Germany, where it opened in Hamburg in March 1983; Austria, where it debuted at the Theater an der Wien in November 1983 and moved to the Ronacher Theater in October 1988, still going strong; and France, a country long resistant to musicals, where it began a run at the Théâtre de Paris on February 23, 1989.

The show begins promisingly enough with a brisk Overture, which states the insistent, chromatic cats' theme in a swinging 6/8 and very quickly develops into a three-voice fugue before the music finds a home key in B-flat and scoots toward a chattering conclusion. The Eliot pastiche, "Jellicle Songs for Jellicle Cats," brings the cast slithering into the aisles and up onto the stage as the alley cats gather to prepare for the Jellicle Ball. The song makes extensive use of a device, syncopation, that marks the score throughout (otherwise, the relentless march of common time would put the audience to sleep): "*Jel*-licles are *and Jel*/licles do, Jelli-*cles* do and Jellicles *would*/Jellicles would and *Jel-/*licles can, Jelli-*cles* can and Jellicles *do*." In the middle, the song is interrupted by an ecclesiastical chorus in B-flat:

> *The mystical divinity of unashamed felinity*
> *Round the cathedral rang "Vivat"*
> *Life to the everlasting cat.*

"The Naming of Cats" follows. It is intoned rather than sung, a *sprechstimme* recitation of the archest of the Eliot poems. It, too, lands in B-flat until a modulation at the end prepares the way for the E-major song of "The Old Gumbie Cat" (in 4/4). This is a music-hall tap dance, delivered by a narrator and chorus and punctuated by interjections by Jennyanydots, the Gumbie Cat herself. It could be a portrait of Jean, the composer's mother:

> *But when the day's hustle and bustle is done*
> *Then the Gumbie Cat's work is but hardly begun.*
> *And when all the family's in bed and asleep*
> *She tucks up her skirts to the basement to creep.*

> *She is deeply concerned with the ways of the mice—*
> *Their behaviour's not good and their manners not nice;*
> *So when she has got them lined up on the matting,*
> *She teaches them music, crocheting and tatting.*

"The Rum Tum Tugger," which follows in the related key of A major, is a typical Lloyd Webber homage to a rock model, this one to Mick Jagger of the Rolling Stones. It is even more heavily, and cleverly, syncopated than "Jellicle Songs for Jellicle Cats," which makes it sound more rhythmically complex than it really is. In setting the poems as songs, some of Eliot's words had to be slightly changed—the Tugger's "If you offer him a pheasant he would rather have grouse," becomes "If you offer me a pheasant I'd rather have grouse"—but their essential integrity is preserved. The contrary cat's song is interrupted by a drop into the parallel minor as Grizabella comes trudging on, carrying her heavy load of existential angst, over a dotted-rhythm ground bass.

Grizabella's gloom, however, is just a passing shudder. The next song, "Bustopher Jones," is a good-natured hymn to the Cat About Town in E major (and 4/4), that captures the fat cat's St. James Street pomposity. The key changes to F major as Bustopher sings, in a reference sure to baffle Americans, "My visits are occasional to the senior educational/and it is against the rules/For any one cat to belong to both that/and the joint superior schools." (There is a passing reference in the text to the Drones Club which, thank God, does not call forth a musical reminiscence of "Banjo Boy.") For no apparent reason, one of the cat's phrases will later turn into a theme for Old Deuteronomy, the patriarchal cat whose plodding basso music is squarely in the tradition of such operatic holy bores as Mozart's Sarastro and Verdi's Padre Guardiano, although not nearly as distinguished.

The villainous Macavity's music slinks by, a first cousin to Henry Mancini's theme for the Pink Panther, and then "Mungojerrie and Rumpelteazer" (F major, 4/4) prance on. In London, their song was a Johnny two-note (G and A), but Lloyd Webber discarded it for America and replaced it with a better, more fluid melody. "Old Deuteronomy"'s tune is, aside from "Memory," the most memorable of the evening, a graceful, flowing F-major meditation in 6/8, whose soothing effect is immediately negated by "The Pekes and the Pollicles," a cat-eat-dog set-to that should have been put to sleep in previews. This undistinguished piece is made immediately redundant by a real production number, "The Jellicle Ball," an extended ballet in which Lynne's dancing cats get to strut their stuff; it is basically an exhilarating reprise and extension of the Overture, punctuated by the Old Deuteronomy theme and, for some reason, the trumpet call from Stravinsky's ballet *Petrouchka*.

The final number before intermission is "Grizabella the Glamour Cat." The trudging motive is sounded in the bass as the fallen strumpet drags herself across the stage; a cor anglais muses sadly; and then the voice of "Memory" is heard in the land. It is just a B-flat–major tease, though, for it ends as quickly as it began, and the lights dim to one of the Overture's themes.

The second act begins with "The Moments of Happiness," an E-minor dirge intoned by Old Deuteronomy, brightened, if that is the right word, by a D-major snatch of "Memory." A long number then ensues. "Gus the Theatre Cat," an old, broken-down actor, mutters into his beer about the glory days of the theater, when cats were cats:

> *And I say: now these kittens, they do not get trained*
> *As we did in the days when Victoria reigned.*
> *They never get drilled in a regular troupe*
> *And they think they are smart, just to jump through a hoop.*

Gus's recollections bring about a scenic transformation as the elderly thespian relives his moment of glory as Growltiger, the fearsome pirate. In London, this quite brilliant set piece was holed below the water line almost immediately by "The Ballad of Billy McCaw," a barroom vaudeville that conjured up the bad old days of English musicals. For America, Lloyd Webber, against his wishes, cut the "ballad" entirely and expanded on a Puccinian tune (in his "important" key of D-flat major) found elsewhere in the scene, turning it into a very deft and entertaining parody of the first-act duet in *Madama Butterfly: "In una tepida notte,"* sing the lovers Growltiger and Griddlebone, as a murderous band of Siamese prepares to storm the ship and make the pirate walk the plank.

"Skimbleshanks the Railway Cat" starts promisingly enough, in a brisk 13/8, but after only four bars the composer loses his nerve and regresses to 4/4; the melody recalls Prokofiev's *Lieutenant Kije* Suite (which, in fact, was among the music Eliot liked to listen to while he was writing the *Cats* poems, and Lloyd Webber picked up the rhythmic similarity). "Macavity: The Mystery Cat," Eliot's homage to the Sherlock Holmes stories and their archvillain, Professor Moriarty ("the Napoleon of crime"), is told not by the fiend in feline shape, but by his terrified victims in a bluesy 4/4, relying on the "spooky" cliché of a diminished chord to provide the basic musical material; it is succeeded quickly by a fight scene, at the conclusion of which Macavity appears to electrocute himself—an event perhaps not regretted by the audience.

"Magical Mister Mistoffelees" is a star turn for the principal male dancer; Macavity had kidnapped Old Deuteronomy, but Mistoffelees conjures the geezer back up from whatever cat hell Macavity had consigned him to. This scene is succeeded by, yes, Grizabella and, at long last, "Memory."

"Memory," the staple of a million elevators and hotel lounges, has become so omnipresent that it is hard to hear it with fresh ears.* It

---

*"Memory" has provoked more than six hundred covers, one of them a hit for Barbra Streisand. No one, it seems, is neutral to this ubiquitous song. To the despair of cocktail pianists everywhere, it has become the most requested tune of the 1980s; at a dance in Palm Beach, a woman jumped up onto a table when the band struck it up and shouted to the audience, "Quiet you fools! This is a work of art!" Writing in *The Washington Post*, lounge pianist John Eaton, noting "Memory's" more than passing resemblance to a phrase from Ravel's *Bolero*, called it "an outrageous piece of fakery."

begins, not with Grizabella finally singing it, but with yet another reprise by a cat who warbles an incantation in D major before Grizabella propels her weary bones one last time across the floor, in B-flat minor. The Magdalene of cats then launches into it in a full-throated B-flat major:

> *Midnight, not a sound from the pavement*
> *Has the moon lost her memory?*
> *She is smiling alone.*
> *In the lamplight the withered leaves collect at my feet*
> *And the wind begins to moan.*
>
> *Memory, all alone in the moonlight*
> *I can smile at the old days*
> *I was beautiful then*
> *I remember the time I knew what happiness was*
> *Let the memory live again.*

At the song's climax, which follows—"Touch me, it's so easy to leave me/All alone with the memory/Of my days in the sun"—Lloyd Webber modulates to, and ends in, his favorite key of D-flat major.

The song should perhaps be called "Mem'ry," for its prosody is all wrong: the word "memory" is set to two notes, not three. Further, the song is constructed from sheer repetition, for the melody never changes; the brief middle section seems more pro forma than anything else; although it is in 12/8 (with one 10/8 bar thrown in to make the phrasing come out right), that is still four beats to the bar. What makes "Memory" so irresistible, though, is its chord structure, I–VI–IV–III–II–VI–V–I, a standard romantic-era harmonic progression that emphasizes the IV chord—an E-flat chord in the key of B-flat major. This plagal half-cadence is a favorite Lloyd Webber melodic device, but it is often found in British music, both folk and "serious"; Vaughan Williams, for one, used it frequently. In "Memory" it clicked, to produce a hit of awesome proportions. Coward's dictum of the potency of cheap music was never more appropriate.

After this aria, *Cats* tumbles rapidly downhill, even as Grizabella ascends to meet her maker. "The Journey to the Heaviside Layer" is a chirpy little chant in G major (and, of course, 4/4), switching quickly back to B-flat so that "The Addressing of Cats" can begin in the home key:

> *You've heard of several kinds of cat*
> *And my opinion now is that*
> *You should need no interpreter*
> *To understand our character*
> *You've learned enough to take the view*
> *That cats are much like me and you*

[Since a cat is singing, Eliot's line does not make much sense.]

> *You've seen us both at work and games*
> *And learnt about our proper names*
> *Our habits and our habitat but*
> *How would you address a cat?*
> *So first, your memory I'll jog*
> *And say: a cat is not a dog*

To this we've come. Then, as if some Rum Tum Tugger had suddenly taken command of the score, the music lurches contrarily into B major—a key not heard once in the entire show—and there, mercifully, *Cats* ends.

When *Cats* opened, the London critics were divided as to its merits. Everybody agreed it was a pastiche, but there the consensus ended. Irving Wardle of *The Times* called it "a vast input of talent which never succeeds in taking fire with an organic work. Lloyd Webber's music exploits two thematic motifs as dramatic binding agents and draws on a wide range of popular styles to characterize the separate numbers: blues, waltzes, a pathetic old music hall ballad for Gus the Theatre Cat, a chugging patter number for Skimbleshanks and a massed chorale for the finale of Old Deuteronomy. The orchestration strikes me as more remarkable than the basic material, but it is powerfully melodic theater music."

Michael Billington of *The Guardian,* however, loved the show: "Many hands have made *Cats* work, but in the end one comes back to Lloyd Webber's remarkable ability to find tunes that fit each specific feeling. The highest compliment I can pay is that I don't think the poet himself would have felt that his material had been tarnished or betrayed." Succinctly, Robert Cushman of *The Observer* wrote: "*Cats* isn't perfect. Don't miss it."

Just as Andrew and Tim had put the ghosts of Rodgers and Hammerstein behind them by forgetting all about the Broadway model and forging ahead with *Superstar* and *Evita* on their own terms, so Lloyd Webber and Mackintosh had stumbled onto a new formula for musical theater success. The trouble with Broadway—the trouble with the Shuberts and the Nederlanders and the others—was that they were too shortsighted. Their world was delimited by New Haven, Philadelphia, Washington, and "the Coast." London was a transatlantic rival, France was a place you went on vacation, and as for Germany, forget about it. Mackintosh, however, saw all those places as potential markets, and Japan too.

It is simply not true that the musical did not travel well; it was the *book* musical, whose disappearance the American drama critics were forever bemoaning, that was difficult to export. (The nostalgia for a lost golden age was memorably articulated in the March 27, 1989, issue of *Newsweek,* in a review of the Smithsonian Institution's *American Musical Theater* record collection. "The set climaxes with Broadway's glory years—roughly, from *Oklahoma!* in 1943 to *My Fair Lady* in 1956," wrote Jim Miller, the magazine's pop-music critic. "And it ends, wisely, with the aptly titled 'Sunrise, Sunset' from *Fiddler on the Roof* in 1964. By then, the musical had achieved its classical form—only to be set reeling by the popularity of rock, which gave minstrelsy a new lease on life and sent Broadway into a commercial and artistic tailspin from which it has never fully recovered.")

Opera, the original bookless musical, more than travels well, it is a permanent international floating crap game; cultures as disparate as those of northern India, Canada, and Japan take readily to Mozart, Puccini, and Wagner. Indeed, it is the operas that *are* localized book musicals—*singspiels* like Weber's *Der Freischütz* and even Mozart's *Abduction from the Seraglio*—that tend to be hothouse flowers. (*The Magic Flute* is an exception.) Further, Hollywood had shown that American films and television shows, with their high production values, played from Bristol to Bangladesh. What Mackintosh, Nunn, and Lloyd Webber were doing was synthesizing the two, evolving an all-purpose, exportable, international entertainment marked by brilliant scenic design and told entirely through music.*

To Mackintosh, Lloyd Webber seemed ideally suited to the task. His musicals already had a wide following, not only up and down Britain, where small productions of *Joseph and the Amazing Technicolor Dreamcoat* and touring versions of *Jesus Christ Superstar* were forever rambling, but in the world at large: by the time *Cats* opened on Broadway, there would be *Josephs* in South Africa and Australia, and *Evitas* in Israel, Austria, and Japan. There was already an established international market for the music of Andrew Lloyd Webber.

What Lloyd Webber needed to do was improve. Certainly, *Cats* had struck a chord in Britain, but as a composer Lloyd Webber still had a long way to go. Andrew had musical credentials far more impressive than some prominent Broadway composers of the past—Irving Berlin, who could play the piano only in one key and relied on a gear-shift mechanism to modulate, for example—but in a sense he was too educated to be a natural and too natural to be educated. Jonathan Tunick, Sondheim's orchestrator and musical alter ego, could score the pants off Lloyd Webber; so could Bennett, Rodgers's orchestrator. Their scores had a glow and a patina that Andrew's lacked. And look at George Gershwin. Even Lloyd Webber admitted he had a long way to go before he came close to replicating the artistic success of something like *Porgy and Bess.*

True, Lloyd Webber's music brimmed with unusual time signatures, and the use of 5/4 in "Everything's Alright" really worked very well. There was even a fugue in the *Cats* Overture. But elsewhere, as in the *Variations,* the offbeat bars seemed pasted on rather than an organic development of the material, and they were performed with a grim, Doggett-like determination. You could practically hear the musicians counting: "*one*-two-three-four-five-six-seven, *one*-two-three-four-five-six-seven. . . ." Tony Bowles had had a nice feel for Andrew's music: his London *Superstar* was a far more relaxed, lyrical affair than the frantic original double album, and his *Evita* was silken smooth. But he, of course, had been fired. Despite the runaway triumph of *Cats* in England, the critical jury was still out on Lloyd Webber, especially in America, where *Cats* was giving rise to growing suspicion that Lloyd Webber was merely a canny pastiche artist, feeding off the inspiration of others.

The fact was that Lloyd Webber was an agglutinative composer, not a thief. Inhabiting the strange twilight zone between amateurism and expertise (a land wherein has dwelt, and continues to dwell, many of Britain's most distinguished figures), he could not honestly tell when a tune sounded right because it sounded right or because he heard it somewhere else before. Musicians are like sponges; once a melody registers

---

*Cats was far from the only bookless musical on Broadway. The dreadful *Dreamgirls,* a condescending minstrel show, had no real dialogue; neither did Sondheim's masterpiece, *Sweeney Todd.*

on the brain it is filed away and never really forgotten, although its provenance may be. From his earliest songs—from "1969" and "Probably on Thursday"—Lloyd Webber's music had echoed its creator's musical upbringing and experience. If he was ever to be taken seriously, he would have to synthesize something new and vital from it, not merely something popular. *Evita* was the model he needed to emulate, not *Cats*.

No one could deny, however, that what Lloyd Webber did have, in spades, was a grasp of contemporary musical technology. Some press accounts painted him as hopelessly unmechanical, but that was not true. Andrew was a born techie; the den at Sydmonton brimmed with tape decks, synthesizers, and video equipment, which he could play like a virtuoso. As his fit over the quality of Abe Jacob's sound design for the New York *Cats* would amply demonstrate, Lloyd Webber knew exactly the kind of quality he wanted and exactly how to get it. He was familiar with synthesizers, body mikes, and bass amplifiers, and he could run a sound-mixing board with the best of them. Andrew knew the nuts and bolts as no other Broadway composer did. That and his natural head for business, not his compositional technique, was his leg up.

The new Mackintosh–Lloyd Webber art form, of which *Cats* was the first manifestation, did not depend on star names—Lloyd Webber shows neither needed stars nor made them; the composer was the star.* Nor was their appeal culture-specific. No one was as potty about animals as the English, but everybody loved cats (or hated them—a best-seller that year was Simon Bond's *101 Uses for a Dead Cat,* another example of Lloyd Webber's uncanny ability to catch the zeitgeist express). What Mackintosh was selling was a product, a trademark, and he marketed it as aggressively as Coca-Cola. In collaboration with the British theatrical advertising agency, Dewynters, Mackintosh inundated London and, later, the world, with *Cats* icons and paraphernalia. From Forty-second Street to the Ginza, *Cats* promotion was standardized: there was the same pair of sloping yellow cat's eyes peering from every poster, the same *Cats* t-shirts, the same *Cats* watches; about the only thing there wasn't was *Cats* kitty litter. In New York, Lloyd Webber had been accused of sending over prepackaged musicals since *Jesus Christ Superstar,* but the *Cats* hype, once it was certain that the show was a hit in London, was the genuine article.

In New York, Broadway's biggest billboard was painted black and dotted only with the pair of yellow eyes; the same icon went up outside the Winter Garden Theatre (whose façade was painted black) four months before the show arrived. On television, there was the ubiquitous logo again, with the voice-over: "Isn't the curiosity killing you?" All summer, every weekend, advertisement-bearing airplanes covered the New York metropolitan area from the Jersey shore to Montauk Point, and teaser ads ran in the Sunday papers each week. Fred Nathan, a savvy young press agent, swamped magazines as disparate as *Penthouse, Esquire, Vogue, Smithsonian,* and *Life* with feature stories. Even the record-high ticket prices—a forty-five-dollar top—were a perverse kind of selling point, for the more expensive something was the more New Yorkers, inured to price-gouging in every facet of their lives, liked it. By the time the show opened, on October 7, 1982, it did so with (once again) the largest advance sale in Broadway history: six million two hundred thousand dollars, two thirds of it already paid in full.

Unlike in Britain, it took only four major backers to provide *Cats* with its four-and-a-half-million-dollar budget: the Shubert Organization (Gerald Schoenfeld, chairman, and Bernard B. Jacobs, president), ABC Entertainment, Metromedia Corporation, and Geffen Records. Because the American version was being presented under different auspices—Mackintosh, the Really Useful Company, David Geffen (who issued the cast album on his record label), and the Shuberts—contracts and guarantees had to be renegotiated with the creative team. With a sure hit in his pocket, Lloyd Webber was tough; Jacobs, a Broadway veteran, was taken aback by what he viewed as greed remarkable even by the standards of show business.

At a cost of two and a half million dollars, the Winter Garden Theatre, on Broadway near Fiftieth Street, was gutted to accommodate Napier's unit-set junkyard, in which the detritus of human civilization is seen from a cat's perspective. Although it could not be performed in the round, the New York production was in many ways closer to Napier's original sketches than the New London's.

Napier at first suggested that the Winter Garden's proscenium be removed, but practicality dictated otherwise, so instead he extended the stage by twenty-four feet, out over the orchestra pit, and wrapped seats around both sides of the extension. The proscenium arch also necessitated changing the show's penultimate scene. In London, Grizabella had made her heavenly exit up a grand staircase that emerged from the New London's back wall, but in New York her apotheosis had to take place center stage, that the whole audience might see it. The stairway had to emerge, miraculously, from the ceiling, so the technical coordinators, Peter Feller and Arthur Siccardi, broke through the Winter Garden's ceiling, built a shed to house the mechanism that would operate the stairs and then rebuilt and reinforced the roof.

Indeed, safety first was the production motto, reinforced by the strict New York City fire codes. Everything was firetested until it surpassed the city standard several times over. Engineers were called in to tell the producers where it would be safe to suspend the lights and false ceiling, which together weighed more than ten tons. A new sprinkler system was installed, and fire walls rebuilt. The theater's granite foundation was drilled to install the panto spring-trap that would shoot Alonzo the Rumpus Cat up through the floor, and hydraulics were installed to operate both the folding upstage wall (four tons), which dropped down for "Growltiger's Last Stand," and the levitating truck tire,

---

*Elaine Paige was the exception, but she was a star only in Britain, not in America. In New York, the names of Streisand, Liza Minelli, and Ann Reinking were briefly floated for Grizabella, but in the end the part went to actress Betty Buckley, then best known for her role in the television series "Eight Is Enough."

which conducts Grizabella twelve feet above the stage floor and twenty-five feet downstage to meet her stairway to paradise.

To furnish the dump, Costume Armor, Inc., manufactured 665 separate items of oversize trash, including Coke cans, Martel cognac bottles, Turtle Wax jars, Uncle Ben's Rice boxes, a half-gallon container of Dellwood Dairy milk, cigarette packs, Kirin and Moosehead beer bottles, silverware, Dixie cups, eggshells, fish bones, pots and pans, and a football, among other urban jetsam, all constructed of Kydex, Nomex (fireproof paper), or fireproof wood. Even the stage required special attention. In London, the dancers were wearing it out, so in New York it was reconstructed with Benelex, a hard surface, to which was attached a large painted groundcloth. The lighting plan of David Hersey, the American-born designer who had worked on both *Evita* and *Nickleby,* called for four thousand festoon bulbs, a fiber-optic system in the ceiling to create the illusion of a vast, starry night, and three hundred pairs of blinking cats' eyes. At center stage was a huge ring of lights that, as the show began, slowly rose into the air like the mothership from Steven Spielberg's *Close Encounters of the Third Kind* or, Spielberg's hit that year, *E.T.*

Impressive, yes, but was all this really necessary? *Cats,* after all, had started out as a character suite in the composer's living room; now it had metastasized even beyond its London incarnation. The American cast was slightly smaller: although it featured eight acrobats instead of two, several of the cats were conflated and others renamed (Jemima, for example, had become Sillabub), and Lloyd Webber rewrote and expanded the score. He provided the new melody for the "Mungojerrie and Rumpelteazer" song and reconceived the "Growltiger" play-within-a-play, substituting the *Madama Butterfly* parody. Did the critics say he relied too heavily on Puccini? Very well, then, he would throw the criticism back in their faces. It was a private joke in which he was sure to have the last laugh.

Before the show crossed the Atlantic, there had been a rumor that Lynne would be replaced by an American choreographer, such as Michael Bennett, but here she was. *Cats* was a marathon. Everyone was on stage almost all the time, and costume changes had to be effected in less than a minute. Naturally, there were tensions. Lloyd Webber's explosion over the sound system was just one temper tantrum among many. (In London, after previews had already begun, Lloyd Webber and Lynne began to go at each other. *Cats* was the worst show he had ever seen, Andrew shouted, and he was going to remove the score and go home. Lynne shouted right back: if he removed the score they would just go ahead and do the show to counts. Afterwards, leaving the theater, Lynne saw a small, forlorn figure sitting alone in the dark auditorium. "It will be all right, won't it, Gilly?" said Lloyd Webber.)

The day *Cats* opened on Broadway, October 7, 1982, Andrew Lloyd Webber became the first man in the history of the musical theater to have three shows running simultaneously on Broadway and in the West End. In New York, *Evita* was still hanging on, and *Joseph and the Amazing Technicolor Dreamcoat* had moved uptown from the East Village; in London, he was holding forth with *Cats, Evita,* and a new show called *Song and Dance,* a combination of *Tell Me on a Sunday* and *Variations* that Mackintosh had talked him into while they were both crossing the Atlantic on the *Queen Elizabeth II* in the summer of 1981; with Marti Webb and dancer Wayne Sleep (who had been Mr. Mistoffelees in London's *Cats*), it had opened at the Palace Theatre in April.

Contrary to the popular belief that in the United States everyone loves a winner, the American critics loaded their shotguns and went cat hunting. "No show is critic-proof," was a favorite saying of Bernie Jacobs; *Cats* was about to test his maxim.

"Not quite purr-fect," headlined *The Daily News.* "It's quite a musical but hardly purr-fect," mewed the the copycat *New York Post. The Boston Globe* proclaimed, "The performers are wonderful, but 'Cats' is a dog," while the *The Village Voice* settled for "Kitty Litter." (In a remarkable example of editorial clumsiness, Edwin Wilson's review in *The Wall Street Journal* was titled, "Tim Webber Brings His Curious 'Cats' to Broadway," which must have made the absent Rice feel good.)

"The razzle-dazzle of 'Cats,' a British cat cantata set in a junkyard that swept into the Winter Garden last night glittering like a few hundred Christmas trees, may be enough to keep you in your seat for two-and-a-half hours, if not exactly on the edge of it," wrote *The Daily News*'s Douglas Watt. "But in spite of some effective moments, it makes for a strained and eventually wearing evening." Barnes of *The New York Post* wrote in his lead: "One thing is certain. The new Broadway musical *Cats,* which purred into what is left of the Winter Garden Theatre last night, is a towering triumph for two men: the director Trevor Nunn and the designer John Napier. The British import does well by two other men—the composer Andrew Lloyd Webber and the posthumous lyricist T. S. Eliot—and one woman, choreographer Gillian Lynne."

In a piece headlined, "O That Anthropomorphical Rag," *Time*'s T. E. Kalem articulated the consensus: "*Cats* is a musical that sweeps you off your feet but not into its arms. It is a triumph of motion over emotion, of EQ (energy quotient) over IQ. One could say at the end of the evening what someone says during the show. 'We had the experience but missed the meaning.' In *Cats,* the spectacle is the substance." More viciously, *The Village Voice*'s Michael Feingold wrote, "To sit through [*Cats*] is to realize that something has just peed on your pants leg. . . . It ought to be retitled *101 Uses for a Dead Musical.*"

The usually savage John Simon was kinder than expected. "There is something for everyone—even dog lovers—in *Cats,*" he wrote in *New York* magazine, "a kind of whiskered Disneyland full of sound and furry [*sic*]. You may justly feel that it is slight and overblown, that it is wasteful . . . and terribly arch, but you cannot help experiencing surges of childish jubilation, as cleverness after sleek cleverness rubs against your shins." Lloyd Webber's tunes, "purrloined" as they might be, "manage to work as a score," while Nunn's "canny and effervescent" direction creates "a delightful albeit trivial *Gesamt*almost*kunstwerk.*"

The crucial review, however, belonged to Frank Rich, the recently appointed chief drama critic of *The New York Times.* Rich had come from *Time,* where he had been one of the magazine's two film critics. A contemporary of Lloyd Webber, Rich was bright and smart and a good writer. But in temperament he was no different from the other New Yorkers who pined for the lost glory days of Rodgers and Hammerstein, the last link to whom was represented by Rich's idol, Sondheim; despite his youth, Rich brought the nostalgic sensibility of a man twice his age to bear on his reviews.

Rich, however, loved the magic of the theater, and it was this aspect of *Cats* that won him over. It bothered him only a little that *Cats,* despite all of Nunn's bravado about the Deeper Meaning of Life, was content-free. For Rich, *Cats* was a guilty pleasure:

> It's not that this collection of anthropomorphic variety turns is a brilliant musical or that it powerfully stirs the emotions or that it has an idea in its head. Nor is the probable appeal of "Cats" a function of the publicity that has accompanied the show's every purr since it first stalked London seventeen months ago. No, the reason why people will hunger to see "Cats" is far more simple and primal than that: it's a musical that transports the audience into a complete fantasy world that could only exist in the theater and yet, these days, only rarely does. Whatever the other failings and excesses, even banalities, of "Cats," it believes in purely theatrical magic, and on that faith it unquestionably delivers.

Ironically, in light of the later hostility between Rich — soon to be dubbed "the Butcher of Broadway" by the British press — and Lloyd Webber, it was this review that established the legend of Webberian invincibility. Robert Brustein may have written in *The New Republic* that "with the help of talent, imagination, and a little taste, *Cats* could have been effective as a small cabaret piece," but that was just the point. Let the Feingolds of the world deride him — "[Lloyd Webber's] music is such inane, characterless drivel that only a generation of stoned clones and TV drones could have summoned it up." Let the amateur tune detectives hunt through his music, arresting its influences: "[The music corroborates] my longstanding theory that Webber, whose father was Dean of the Royal College of Music" — not quite right, Feingold! — "always tries in his scores to recreate a childhood experience of wandering along the august corridors of that institution, picking up random snatches of whatever was being played or sung in its practice rooms." (Aside from the mistake about Bill, this theory was remarkably close to the unconscious mark.) It didn't matter any more. They said *Cats* couldn't be done, that Andrew was nothing without Rice, that he was nothing without Stigwood.

And yet he had done it. He didn't need Rice, and his bank account sure didn't need Stigwood. He had showed them. He had showed them all. Well done, Webber! Nothing, and no one, could stop him now. Maybe he *was* critic-proof. One of his friends said that Andrew could, if he felt like it, write a musical about a deck of cards. But he had a better idea: a musical about trains. At least trains moved.

Kittens frolicking in a cosmic junkyard: Cats *in London, 1981.*

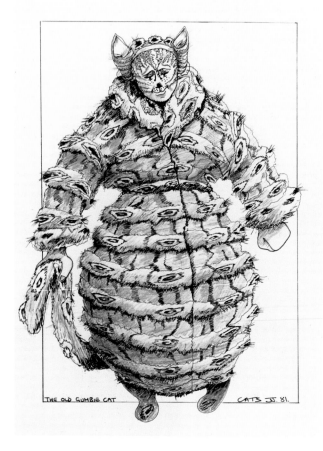

Left:

Two of designer John Napier's costume designs for the show. *Above: Old Deuteronomy. Below: The Old Gumbie Cat.*

The London set for Cats, *under construction by Kimpton Walker, the builders.*
The scope of the production is clearly visible as workmen realize Napier's vision.

Above:

A *kitten in the London production of* Cats.

Opposite, top:

In *rehearsal for* Cats. *In a calculated gamble, British choreographer Gillian Lynne, who had assisted director Trevor Nunn on his two previous forays into musical theater with the Royal Shakespeare Company, was chosen to turn people into convincing felines.*

Opposite, bottom:

Lynne *with one of her dancers.*

No one thought the British could successfully mount a dance musical. When Lloyd Webber went looking for backers, the big West End angels turned him down flat. In the end, Cats was financed by more than two hundred small investors. One man put up his entire life savings of five thousand pounds.

Right:

The original London Cats cast. Sarah Brightman, whom Lloyd Webber first met during auditions, is Jemima (fourth from the left).

Opposite:

Elaine Paige, who created the role of Grizabella, was not the producers' first choice. But when Judi Dench injured herself in a fall, Paige stepped in.

In New York, the Cats *creative team relaxes: (from left) Napier, Nunn, lighting designer David Hersey, Lynne, and Lloyd Webber.*

The New York cast poses for a poster shot.

138

The "Growltiger's Last Stand" scene in New York, where it was turned into a parody of Puccini's Madama Butterfly.

The Jellicle Ball.

Old Deuteronomy on his way to the Heaviside Layer at the end of the Broadway production.
Nunn found a reference to the "cat heaven" in Eliot and made it the climax of the show.

From the start, Cats *was about cats and nothing but. There was no hidden program or larger meaning.*

Skimbleshanks, the Railway Cat, in Hamburg (top) and in New York (above).

Did you ever see a train skating? Above: A choo-choo en pointe.

Some of the skaters in action.

Building the Starlight set in London.

At first, Lloyd Webber's idea for Starlight Express *was to write a show for children about a Cinderella-like steam train. In 1977 he recorded the single* "Engine of Love." *"No resistance to my pistons" sang Earl Jordan and the Steam Team.*

Below:

Two *of John Napier's renderings for the costumes. As the idea—and Lloyd Webber's reputation—grew, so did* Starlight Express, *until it became the biggest, most expensive musical of all time.*

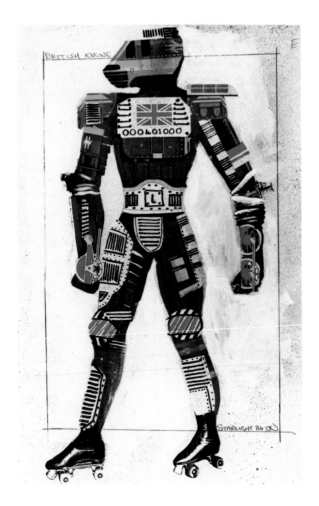

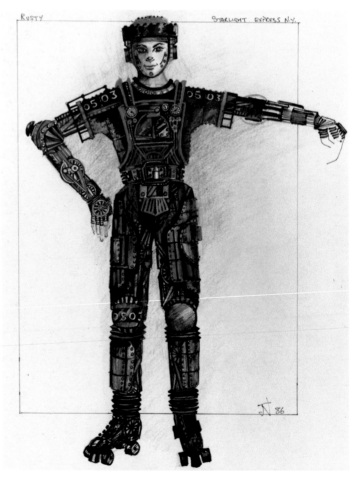

Choreographer Arlene Phillips, director Trevor Nunn, Lloyd Webber, and Stephanie Lawrence, who played Pearl in the London production.

Lawrence with members of the London cast. Ray Shell, who played Rusty, is at far right.

The finale of Starlight Express *on Broadway (left). Hovering above the cast is the giant railroad trestle, which moved and rotated during the show's five races. In London the skaters surrounded the audience, but in New York the tracks projected only a few yards into the house. Top: In both cities the dance steps were tricky and intricate. Above: Poppa, the old steam train, and the Rocky Brothers.*

Overleaf:

The New York production was critically disdained and closed after less than two years. By that time, even the composer had realized Starlight Express, *however spectacular, was too big for its own good.*

R̶ocky I, II, III, *and* IV *on Broadway. In London, there were only three*
Rockys, but then Sylvester Stallone's fourth boxing movie came out.

*S*tarlight Express *found favor in West Germany, where it played in Bochum. Above: Greaseball, the Elvis Presley–like leader of the diesel trains.*

REQUIEM

The Requiem *Mass was Lloyd Webber's bid for serious bona fides. Lorin Maazel leads the Orchestra of St. Luke's at the premiere in Manhattan.*

Lloyd Webber, tenor Placido Domingo, soprano Sarah Brightman, boy soprano Paul Miles-Kingston, and Maazel take their bows.

Chapter Six: U.N.C.O.U.P.L.E.D.

Lloyd Webber's elation as *Cats* took Manhattan was short-lived, for on October 29, 1982, his father died in London at the age of sixty-eight.

Bill had been having trouble with his high blood pressure and with his prostate for some time. After returning from New York, where he had attended the *Cats* premiere, and playing a memorial service at Central Hall on Monday, October 11, he entered the hospital the next day. At first, there seemed to be no immediate cause for concern, but after an operation Bill began to have trouble with clots in his blood and Jean steeled herself for the worst. On the day of his death, a Friday, he seemed in good spirits on the telephone; the tubes had been taken out, he said, and he was headed off for a bath. A few hours later, Jean got a telephone call from the doctors who told her to come quickly and to bring her sons. She rang Andrew at Sydmonton, and Julian drove her to the hospital, but by the time they got there, Bill was gone. His kidneys had failed, and then his heart. He died three weeks and a day after he had witnessed his son's greatest triumph.

Andrew and his father had not been close. Bill was a difficult man to know, always away playing in church, teaching, or locked up in his study at Harrington Court—or simply inhabiting that private world in which he was a great and celebrated composer. His wants were simple, as were his pleasures; when Andrew was searching for a present to give his parents, the most they would accept was a refrigerator to replace the one that hadn't worked properly in generations.

Yet Bill's guidance and support had been crucial. After witnessing the *Superstar* fiasco in New York, it was Bill who consoled Andrew in his room at the Pierre Hotel; "These people don't understand anything," he said. He had also encouraged and aided John Lill, and he took pride in Julian's development. Once, after Julian had appeared on "The Marti Caine Show," where the program's attractive hostess greeted her guests in a revealing dress, Julian got an angry letter from a member of the congregation at Central Hall saying his presence on the show was "a disgrace to his father's name." Yet Bill had watched the broadcast with his son, chuckling and enjoying it greatly. He was no prude.

And he was no snob, either. Consider, for example, his elder son's passion for pop music of the early sixties. While the rebellious posturings of the Beatles and the Rolling Stones seem in retrospect far less threatening than the heavy metal shenanigans of Motley Crüe and Twisted Sister, parents then viewed rock and roll with alarm. Not Bill; he may have preferred Mozart and Puccini but if Elvis and the Everlys were what Andrew wanted to listen to, that was fine with him; the boy would come round to Mozart and Puccini eventually. Not many professional academic musicians are that tolerant or enlightened regarding their offspring.

So, at the end of the day, Bill had a lot to be proud of. Andrew was the most financially successful British composer since, probably, Handel; Julian, the best British cellist since God knew when; and John, practically Bill's foster son, the leading English pianist of his generation. As a father, he had given a good account of himself, after all.

Jean took Bill's death with her customary equanimity. Jean was a firm believer in euthanasia; if Bill was going to suffer, then his death was a relief. Jean had a fatalistic view of life, a legacy of her brother Alastair's untimely demise; further, she was kindly disposed toward spiritualism. In 1976 Julian suffered a mysterious finger ailment that made it virtually impossible for him to play the cello. Doctors were baffled, but then Jean remembered reading about Rosemary Brown, the London psychic who had recently drawn the world's attention—and derision—by her claim that composers such as Schubert and Chopin were dictating their music to her from beyond. Brown gently pressed Julian's fingertip and advised him to rub warm olive oil on it every day. Sure enough, over the next few weeks, the sharp, stabbing pain disappeared, never to return. While Jean didn't claim to see the shades of people past, she was sensitive toward psychic phenomena; after Bill's death, she was sure the cats could see him, benignly haunting the flat. And she was sure that, on some level, he was still communicating with her, causing her to wonder about and concern herself with things she had never considered before.

Bill's death was followed two months later by another departure, when Biddy Hayward, who had been Andrew's secretary and personal assistant for nearly a decade, quit. Lloyd Webber had always been a difficult man to work for, but after *Cats* he was even worse. Being Lloyd Webber's p.a. meant being on call nearly twenty-four hours a day. The explosive success of *Cats* had made him a public figure in Britain, his name began popping up in Nigel Dempster's column, and the tabloids began to routinely refer to him as "millionaire-composer Andrew Lloyd Webber." Lloyd Webber, however, was no better suited to handling the press than he had been at the time of *Jesus Christ Superstar*, and his growing celebrity made him sometimes bully those who wouldn't, or couldn't, fight back. In sum, he was a personal assistant's nightmare, and Biddy decided she needed a break. Tidily, Hayward first found a replacement for herself, and then in December 1982 she left.

(The hiring of the new woman, Sue Knight, was typical of Lloyd Webber's impatience. One afternoon, Knight got a call from an employment agency with whom she had left her resumé, telling her there was a position available with Lloyd Webber. Knight, whose background was in record promotion, first interviewed with Hayward on a Monday, then returned the next day to speak with Lloyd Webber. On Wednesday, she met with Sarah Lloyd Webber and on Thursday with Andrew and Brian Brolly. The next day she got a call from Brolly, asking if she could start the following Monday. Once Andrew had decided Knight was right for the job, he wanted her right away and was not about to let niceties like two-weeks' notice get in the way. She was at work within a week.)

As 1983 got underway, the most important change of all in Andrew's life was in the offing. During Sarah Brightman's year-long run in *Cats*, nothing romantic or sexual had occurred between her and the composer, but when Lloyd Webber chanced to read a review by Milton Shulman of Brightman's performance in Charles Strouse's children's opera *Nightingale* and decided impulsively to go and see her, the pent-up sparks began to fly. Here was a singer, the kind he had always dreamed of, with a fresh, young voice of distinctive timbre and great promise. And she had been in *Cats*! Why had he not noticed her before? He would have given her something special to sing, but even though she had been right there in his own living room he just had missed the special talent that he was hearing now. And she was beautiful, too. Lloyd Webber found himself powerfully attracted to Sarah Brightman; suddenly, he was in the grip of a passion he had never really known before.

They had dinner together soon after and found they had a lot in common, particularly a passion for the musical theater; she wanted to make it, and he wanted to remake it. As the relationship warmed and grew, they went off to Italy for a weekend, where they talked over their pasts. Sarah told Andrew about her husband (also an Andrew), and he told her about his wife (also a Sarah). Yes, he had loved Sarah, and yes she had loved him, probably even more. But, as far as he was concerned, it was over; Sarah had been right for him once, but no longer. Suddenly, Lloyd Webber blurted, "Now, what are we going to do about getting married?" It was a proposal, and Brightman accepted.

It is tempting to see, in the speed and unilaterality with which Lloyd Webber decided to remarry, a repeat both of Sue Knight's hiring and of his wooing of Sarah Hugill. Life was an audition to Lloyd Webber, and once he had the right person for the part, he was ready to sign her up. Brightman's divorce would not be a problem. Even though she was still legally married, she had only lived with Graham-Stewart for a short time, and they had no property to speak of. Lloyd Webber's marital status, however, was far more solid; moreover, there was the potentially thorny question of community property to be decided. He and his wife had been married for more than a decade, during which time, with her assistance and acumen, he had become rich and famous. During the horrible period when nobody would invest in *Cats*, Sarah Lloyd Webber had personally telephoned friends, keeping a list of those who gave and those who didn't. Even if she consented to his desire for a divorce, of which she currently had no inkling, it was not going to be pleasant.

Lloyd Webber's desire for Sarah Brightman was another expression of the great changes that were sweeping his life. By entertainment-industry standards, he was a virgin; the idea that some women found money and success a powerful aphrodisiac was just beginning to dawn on him. In 1980 he had flown to Los Angeles to appear on "The Merv Griffin Show" and to promote the Metromedia showing of the BBC's *Tell Me on a Sunday* program with Marti Webb. At the studio, he encountered a young woman who attached herself to him and later that evening tagged along with Lloyd Webber as he dined with friends. After a while, it became clear to everybody—finally even to Andrew himself—what this really useful groupie was after. It may have been the first time in his life he had been unfaithful to Sarah, and the effect on him had been profound. So *this* is what success got you!

Up to then, Andrew had been something of a prude; he vocally disapproved of Rice's affair with Elaine Paige, for example. But thereafter, friends noticed a change in him, a new awareness and self-confidence. He was no longer the shy, skinny, funny-looking boy at Westminster. He was not handsome, and he would never be able to do anything with his hair, but there were many things about him that women found appealing, starting with his great brown sloping cat's eyes. He moved like a cat, too, light and soundless on his feet, and he had the quick reflexes of a cat as well. No one went into the attic at Sydmonton to challenge him at, say, board hockey, and expected to come back down victorious.

The most attractive thing about him was his mind. Many women love a winner, and suddenly Lloyd Webber had the look of one. He liked to pretend that his memory was terrible, and in some ways it was; he was hard-pressed to remember the birthdays of his children. But numbers stuck in his mind like melodies; he had a head for figures, but, more important, he had a head for figuring out what to do with figures. By late 1982 he was earning about a million pounds a year, and Margaret Thatcher's rise to prime minister meant that he was getting to keep most of it. (In 1979, just before the general election that swept the Tories to power, he had briefly threatened to move to the United States.) What was more, he now knew how to spend money to make money. Even though it had cost a lot, the *Cats* promotion budget was solid gold; once the show opened and was a hit, the producers didn't have to spend anything on advertising. Lloyd Webber was a born businessman, smart enough not to invest his own money in his shows when he could invest that of others and reap the profits just the same.

This realization, which gradually dawned on him as *Cats* took off, came as something of a surprise, for Andrew had always regarded himself as, first and last, a musician. But Mackintosh had proved remarkably inspirational. All his life Andrew had been used to hearing why something could not be done; the Circumlocution Office's philosophy of How Not To Do It that Dickens had described in *Little Dorrit* was still operational in many British minds. You couldn't stage *Superstar,* it was blasphemous; *Evita* was evil; nobody would pay to see a show about cats. Mackintosh and Lloyd Webber, however, thought the way Americans were supposed to; they were asking, "Why not?" when everybody else was asking, "Why?" And they were taking the answers to the bank. Although it may have been partly unconscious, it was during this post-*Cats* period that Lloyd Webber remade his life from the top down. He did not have to reinvent himself so much as realize the potential that had lain inside him all along.

He wasted little time. On April 18, 1983, Lloyd Webber dipped his toe into the cold waters of the West End with Denise Deegan's play *Daisy Pulls It off* at the Globe Theatre, the first time his Really Useful Company had produced something he had not written. The evening was another first as well, for it was the first time he had appeared in public with Sarah Brightman. Andrew was seen at the premiere with his wife on his arm, but he attended the cast party afterward with Brightman. Sarah Lloyd Webber knew the blow was coming and had not wanted a public scene or humiliation, so she went straight home after the show. The next day, Lloyd Webber announced that he would leave his wife of nearly twelve years and marry Brightman.

Fleet Street, that last bastion of middle-class sensibility, went wild. In Britain, successful men simply didn't ditch their long-suffering wives—they had met when she was *sixteen,* for God's sake. It was all very well to keep "a bit on the side" (as the army officers had sung in *Evita*), but to move her to the center. . . . It was too much. On that day was born the image of Brightman the Jezebel homewrecker, the sexy showgirl who had broken up the Lloyd Webbers' happy family. Her past was picked over and amplified; reporters were shocked—*shocked!*—to discover that she had once danced in fishnets with the racially mixed Hot Gossip troupe. From then on, Andrew and Sarah, or "Sarah II," as she was immediately dubbed, became media staples, their comings and goings watched, their trash pawed through, their rows breathlessly reported or vividly imagined. They became, in short, modern celebrities.

The caricatures were the cruelest. Even before the puppet show "Spitting Image" launched its devastating neutron strikes on everyone from the Royal Family to the First Family, not sparing Mr. and Mrs. Lloyd Webber ("Introducing Sarah Brightman," nattered a host, "without whose presence no Royal Gala would be perfect . . . ly terrible."), the newspaper cartoonists set to work. Andrew's large head, unruly bangs, feline eyes, and personal fortune were a natural target; almost inevitably, he was portrayed in drawings as a Fat Cat, licking a saucer clean of Really Useful Cream.

Well, it was true: he wasn't the best-looking man in the world, but now he had something he had wanted since his teens—the dollybird of his dreams—and he didn't care what anybody else thought. Take that, Tim Rice: you don't get *all* the girls. True, he did have a lot of money (in September 1983 the satiric magazine *Private Eye* did a number on him under the heading, "Lloyd Webber Buys the Bank of England"), but Andrew was very British in his attitude toward wealth: one didn't flaunt it, like those vulgar Americans. Besides, he was not personally extravagant. He had no interest in clothes, as anybody could plainly see; his Carnaby Street days were long gone, and now he usually trooped around in patterned sweaters and slacks. He didn't much fancy driving cars. What he liked best about having a lot of money was that it made him master of his own destiny. He would never have to rely on a Stigwood again, never have to worry about an agent signing away the grand rights to one of his shows, never be gripped by that four-o'-clock-in-the-morning cold sweat when a show wasn't going right. He could simply close it. Couldn't he?

But he was mad about Brightman, for he loved her both as a woman and as a singer. Her Hot Gossip days were far behind her; Sarah was now studying voice seriously at the Royal College of Music and talked of singing opera. He found himself wishing that Bill could have known her; Bill would have loved the way Sarah could sing Rachmaninoff in Russian, loved her light, musical voice and her gentle laugh. Even before his legal separation from Sarah Lloyd Webber came through, on July 26, 1983, Andrew had put a diamond on Brightman's finger. She moved into the flat at 51 Eaton Place, while Sarah Lloyd Webber and the children took over the office premises at 11 West Eaton Place; Andrew bought another house, at 20 Greek Street, Soho, to use as his office.

Lloyd Webber and Sarah Brightman could not marry right away, for there were still the various decrees to await and the business with the lawyers. Sarah Lloyd Webber had given her husband his freedom, but it was going to cost him, and from August until March of 1984 solicitors shuttled between them. His first offer of half a million pounds was rejected; although press estimates of the final settlement ranged up to seven million pounds, the truth was somewhat more modest: seven hundred and fifty thousand pounds in cash and property, including the house on West Eaton Place, plus three hundred thousand pounds in trust for Imogen and Nicholas. (Later, Lloyd Webber purchased a house in Oxfordshire for his ex-wife, placing it in the name of their children.) The 1983 Sydmonton Festival was delayed until September, while Sarah I moved out of the country manor she had personally decorated; but by Christmas of that year it was the Brightmans who were signing the guest register, not the Hugills.

At Sydmonton that September, the Lloyd Webber work of the moment was a show called *Aspects of Love,* which was subtitled "A Cabaret by Andrew Lloyd Webber and Trevor Nunn." Marti Webb and Sarah Brightman were the featured performers. The show was based on the 1955 novella of the same name by David Garnett, a minor member of the Bloomsbury Group. In 1980, during rehearsals for *Cats,* Lloyd Webber had given Nunn the 105-page book and asked him to read it with an eye to getting it on stage eventually. Nunn did and wrote Lloyd Webber a letter saying he thought it would offer a remarkable opportunity for Andrew to write a score of Mozartean proportions (and, for the librettist, Da Pontean possibilities). There were just five main characters, and it seemed to Nunn that each could be characterized musically in a very specific way. In closing, Nunn offered to write the book for the show.

Andrew wrote back and said no thanks; this was an opera he wanted to write with Tim Rice—Tim, in fact, had introduced him to the book—and he and Rice took off for the south of France in the region near Pau, where much of *Aspects* is set, for three days of eating and drinking; in the end no work was done. Rice had heard about *Aspects* from the film producer Peter Shaw, who was trying to interest him in writing a script. Tim had decided against the movie project, but he had sent the novella along to Hal Prince, to see what the director thought of it. Prince said he had already directed a show about the intertwined love lives of a small circle of people called *A Little Night Music,* and he didn't want to repeat himself.

The project languished until 1982, when Nunn, Rice, and Lloyd Webber gathered at the Caprice restaurant (or at Andrew's flat; recollections differ) to talk over ideas. Right away, there were disagreements. Nunn said he thought Alex, the young Englishman, was the principal character, the one through whose eyes the audience would see the action. Rice said no, it was Rose, the French actress with whom Alex falls in love but who leaves him for Alex's uncle, George. They agreed to spend the next three weeks or so working on a libretto, to see how it all might work out. Lloyd Webber had already written a couple of tunes for the show, including a song called "It's a Miracle."

A short time later, though, Lloyd Webber got a note from Rice. It said he was dropping out of the project. *Aspects* seemed thinner to him every time he read it, and he had started to think there was nothing there. Besides, Tim was busy with *Blondel,* the show he had written with composer Stephen Oliver that was *Come Back Richard* come back to life. It even had a song in it called "Saladin Days."

Lloyd Webber was very upset. *Aspects* was the project he hoped would bring him and Tim back together again. Certainly, Garnett's novella seemed a perfect subject for Rice, a story of betrayals and reconciliations—the saga of a lovestruck young man who grows older and wiser in the ways of amour. Unlike Tim, Andrew grew more enthusiastic about the book each time he read it, and when Rice turned him down, Nunn had never seen Lloyd Webber so close to tears. Andrew approached several other lyricists, among them Don Black, before Brian Brolly was dispatched to ask Nunn if he would try his hand at it.

Nunn decamped to the Bahamas, where he wrote fourteen songs and, upon his return to London, three more. Although the two men got along well, Lloyd Webber seemed cool toward Nunn's work; the content of the songs was all right, he told the director, but there was no "hook," nothing from which to fashion a catchy title—in short, no hit. Andrew wanted hits.

Still, the 1983 Sydmonton performance went off as planned, with Webb and Brightman singing about ten of the songs. One of the tunes that summer was called "Married Man," which Andrew soon orchestrated and recorded with Brightman and the London Philharmonic Orchestra. It was intended as the show's opening number, a song for the character of Giulietta, an Italian sculptress who is George's mistress and, at the end of the book, Alex's wife. The record could not be released, for obvious reasons; Lloyd Webber's lawyers felt that a song with that title sung by Brightman in the midst of the difficult divorce negotiations simply could not be made public (although she sang it later that year in a concert at the Barbican Centre). So into the drawer "Married Man" went, to await its rebirth a few years later. Indeed, the whole of *Aspects of Love* went into the drawer.

Andrew had another idea. His father's death had affected him greatly, and the notion dawned on him of writing a Requiem Mass in Bill's honor. English church music had always been a part of the Lloyd Webberian musical aesthetic—what was "Old Deuteronomy" if not some High Church cantor?—and, besides, he felt it was time for him to establish his "serious" bona fides. They didn't come much more serious than requiems, and Sarah's pure voice would be perfect in a religious setting—a nice counterweight to her former iconography, too. He simply had to find some project for her, to show her off to the world. Maybe, he thought, even *Aspects of Love* somewhere down the line, if he could ever talk Tim into it.

In the midst of all this artistic and personal turmoil, Lloyd Webber acquired something else he had always wanted: a theater to call his own. In 1982 he had bid about a million pounds for the Aldwych Theatre, but he was topped by the Nederlanders. Later, he blew a bid on the Old Vic when the price he was prepared to pay—five hundred thousand pounds—was prematurely made public and the Canadian Ed Mirvish bought it for fifty thousand pounds more. Lloyd Webber and Nunn had an idea of starting a musical theater school, and it seemed to them that either the Aldwych, which sits in the street of the same name, right off the Strand, or the Old Vic, across Waterloo Bridge in south London, would have been perfect.

So when the Palace Theatre, just down Greek Street, came on the market, he snapped up the freehold on August 23, 1983, for a crisp one million three hundred thousand pounds, all of it lent by banks, plus an additional two hundred thousand pounds to Emile Littler, the former owner, to relinquish the lease. Andrew was delighted with his new toy. The Palace, a terra-cotta Victorian wonder that commanded Cambridge Circus, had been built by Richard D'Oyly Carte with some of the fortune he made as Gilbert and Sullivan's producer. As the Royal English Opera House, it opened on January 31, 1891, with Sullivan's opera *Ivanhoe*, the first of what the impresario had hoped would be a series of native British operas. *Ivanhoe* ran for 155 performances—a remarkable number, by modern standards—but it was not the success that D'Oyly Carte had hoped for. Nor were the native British operatic talents he had hoped to encourage forthcoming. There weren't any. After *Ivanhoe* closed, a French opera took its place, and the next season saw Sarah Bernhardt in Sardou's play *Cleopatra*. In December 1892 the hall's name was changed to the Palace Theatre of Variety; Pavlova danced there in 1910, and the theater was the site of the first Royal Command Variety Performance in 1912. Later, the Palace became known as one of London's leading houses for musicals. Shows as disparate as *No, No Nanette*, Ivor Novello's *King's Rhapsody*, and Rodgers and Hammerstein's *The Sound of Music* were hits there. Even closer to Andrew's heart, though, was the Palace's biggest hit of all: *Jesus Christ Superstar*, which had held court for nine years and 3,358 performances. Not to mention that the theater's current occupant was Lloyd Webber's *Song and Dance*.

The Palace was Andrew's boyhood dream come true. Run-down as it was and defaced by neon, it was still all his: a theater to call his own. (For a time in 1964, when Littler sold it to a property company, it appeared the theater might be torn down. Indeed, Littler had retained his lease to ensure participation in any future profits should the site ever be redeveloped, but preservation societies had frustrated that notion.) Even before the deal was struck, Andrew was on the phone to Biddy Hayward: "If I buy the Palace, will you come back and run it?" he asked her. She thought a while, and then said yes, returning to his employ in December 1983. The Palace, Lloyd Webber announced, would be used exclusively for musical theater, and he made noises about running a real opera in the house sometime during the 1985–1986 season. The school idea, though, was put aside for the moment, for the Palace was a destination theater, a place where you took a show, not whence you transferred one.

Song and Dance had opened on April 7, 1982. On the surface, the idea of linking *Tell Me on a Sunday* with *Variations* was preposterous, since, against all Webberian odds, they had nothing whatsoever in common—neither thematic material nor common point of origin. A year after *Cats* opened in London, though, Lloyd Webber was walking on water. Anthony Van Laast choreographed the *Variations* (by this time familiar to British television watchers as the theme for Melvyn Bragg's "South Bank Show," a popular arts program), and John Caird directed.

Waste not, want not: Lloyd Webber glued the two pieces together principally by adding words to the *Variations'* big tune, the fifth variation, the one he had retrieved from *Jeeves,* and by having the still-nameless girl wander on stage at the end of the *Dance* section to sing it. The song was called "When You Want to Fall in Love," and Caird's staging indicated that poor Marti Webb had at last found a man in the person of Wayne Sleep, the dancer from the Royal Ballet. Some of the lyrics were changed, the order of the songs was slightly rearranged, and the first part of the "Sheldon Bloom" song was broken out and reprised as a separate number called "Married Man" (no melodic relation to the forbidden song from *Aspects*). Most significant, there was also a new ballad that was clearly intended as one of the show's three lyric high points, along with "Tell Me on a Sunday" and the poignant "Nothing Like We've Ever Known." The importance Lloyd Webber attached to the new song, "The Last Man in My Life," may be gleaned from the key scheme: the melody begins in C major, but by the time the verse is reprised, it has modulated to D-flat major:

> *I'm a lady when you kiss me*
> *I'm a child when you are leaving*
> *I'm a woman every time our bodies meet, complete.*
>
> *Long lost feelings stir inside me*
> *Used to think nights were for sleeping*
> *Being wanted is a thrill I never knew, 'till you.*

Song and Dance was, of course, a hit, running until March 1984, when the Palace was closed for a couple of months to allow Lloyd Webber's engineers to start the massive task of restoring the theater before moving in a revival of Rodgers and Hart's *On Your Toes* in June. *Song and Dance* had done well—it had run for 795 performances—but there was something unsatisfactory about it. All the deficiencies of the original album—the mawkish story, the heroine's unattractive personality, exacerbated by Webb's mediocre singing—still obscured the *Song* half, and when *Song and Dance* finally came to New York on September 18, 1985, it was with a drastically rewritten book and lyrics by Black and the American lyricist and stage director Richard Maltby, Jr. Reviewing the London version in *The Financial Times*, Michael Coveney offered: "It is a very long time since I have sat through a more ostentatious, less theatrically coherent evening."

When Lloyd Webber closed *Song and Dance* in London, though, he had something other than fixing up the Palace on his mind. Indeed, his urgent attention was devoted to the Apollo Victoria Theatre, near Victoria Station, where his new musical *Starlight Express* was unveiled on March 27, 1984.

"Unveiled" is the right word, for the premiere of *Starlight Express* was the high-water mark of Webberian gigantism, a production on such a vast scale that it made *Cats* look like an off-Broadway three-hander. As was by now his custom, Lloyd Webber had first tried out *Starlight* at Sydmonton in 1982—Andrew had begun to compose the score almost as soon as *Cats* was safely out of the bag in London—along with Derek Jewell's Duke Ellington anthology, *Duke.* As he had with *Cats,* Lloyd Webber assembled a production team to realize his vision. Again, the director was Nunn, the designer Napier, and the lighting man was Hersey. Arlene Phillips, the leader of Hot Gossip, was brought in as the choreographer; the lyricist was Richard Stilgoe, who had contributed to *Cats.*

What they evolved, by the time casting began in the fall of 1983, was a far cry from Lloyd Webber's original trot for an iron-horse Cinderella. As far back as *Jesus Christ Superstar* he had been toying with the idea of a show about trains, and in 1973 Lloyd Webber was asked to compose the music for a series of television cartoons based on Wilbert Awdry's "Thomas the Tank Engine" stories, familiar in America as "The Little Engine That Could." A few frames of a cartoon had been animated and some music written, but then the project was dropped. In 1977 Andrew had recorded a couple of pieces for MCA: "Engine of Love," performed by Earl and the Steam Team, and the instrumental "Steamin'." Earl Jordan was an American soul singer he had met a couple of years before whose ability to sing a three-note chord that sounded like a locomotive's whistle Lloyd Webber found delightful.

How suitable for children the train project really was may be gleaned from some of Peter Reeves's lyrics to "Engine of Love." (Reeves had been the Narrator in the Frank Dunlop production of *Joseph.*) A black female chorus shouts out "Ride it, ride it, ride it on the Steam Train," while the engine swaggers, "No resistance to my pistons":

> *Engine of Love,*
> *Take me with you baby*

Just pull me along
Right along the line

'Cause you're my
Engine of Love
Thrill me with your motion
And I'll follow you
Your track hand in mine.

About 1975 *Starlight Express* had made an intermediate stop along the way when another television company asked Lloyd Webber if he would be interested in writing music for a cartoon version of the Cinderella story. That, too, came to nothing, but in 1982, Lloyd Webber took his children for a ride on the restored Valley Railroad in south central Connecticut, not far from the Goodspeed Opera House, which presents classic musicals in a historic setting. Again, the urge to write a piece about trains came over him. This time, the Cinderella notion was combined with the train motif and thus evolved a story about a steam engine whose ugly sisters were a diesel and an electric train and whose fairy godmother was a magical train called the Midnight Special. As Lloyd Webber explained: "The midnight train lent the steam engine special equipment on condition it was all back by midnight, so the Special could leave on time. In his haste to get back on time the steam engine dropped a piston. The Prince went around America to find the engine which the piston fitted, etc., etc." In the early eighties, after the wedding of Prince Charles and Lady Diana, the final sequence was changed: Charles and Diana were the Prince and Princess Charming, seeking the mysterious silver engine that, in its haste, had dropped its cowcatcher.

With the production team in place, the project was reconceived again, this time on a scale that would have done Inigo Jones proud. The first impulse was to have the actors driven on stage in little trains, from which they would pop out and act like human beings, but then Nunn had a better idea: what if the actors themselves moved on wheels? What if they were on roller skates? The central conceit of *Starlight Express* was thus that people could be transformed into railroad trains by putting them on skates and sending them scooting around a specially designed set. This would be no proscenium musical, but a vast experience-in-the-round, like a ride at Disneyland—*Cats* goes to Space Mountain. If a camel is a horse designed by a committee, then *Starlight Express* was a children's musical designed by the Sun King.

To begin with, there was the set. The havoc Napier had wreaked on the Winter Garden in New York was nothing compared with his devastation of the Apollo Victoria, the theater chosen as *Starlight*'s site after other locations such as the Roundhouse (where *Joseph* had once played), various warehouses around London, and even the deserted shell of the Bourne and Hollingworth department store were considered. As a sign of the hubris that attended every aspect of the project, nearly half the theater's 2,700 seats were ripped out, leaving room for only 1,400 spectators per performance. To create the roller derby he envisioned, Napier hired the London firm of Kimpton Walker, which he had used for *Cats*, to build the production. The show's budget was two million pounds (which it overran by about 20 percent); one million four hundred thousand pounds alone were spent on transforming the theater. (As with the Winter Garden, there was a clause in the contract stipulating the restoration of the theater to its original configuration once the show closed.) With costs like this, the show had to run for forty-three weeks at full capacity before backers would see any return on their investment.

Some raw statistics give an idea of the scale of this remarkable undertaking. The set incorporated two and a half acres of sheetboard, sixty tons of steel, six miles of timber, nine thousand feet of trussing, six thousand light bulbs, and seven hundred and fifty gallons of paint and varnish. The central skating bowl required techniques normally applied to casting the hull of an ocean-going yacht. The planning specs themselves covered thirty-six typewritten pages and four hundred pages of designs and drawings. It was the largest set ever put into a London theater—and it was made to order within six weeks.

But what did it look like? The skating bowl was where the stage should have been, and a skating oval was extended out into the stalls; some lucky patrons got to sit right in the middle of the action. (Retractable crash barriers were raised during races, to prevent injuries.) Another, larger track completely encircled the stalls along the auditorium's inner walls and rose up to dress-circle level, while a third track ascended to the upper circle, so that even the folks in Nosebleed Hollow could be part of the action. Still, it was impossible for everyone to see everything all the time, so three large television screens were strategically placed for all to follow the fun.

The centerpiece of the set was a huge gantry bridge that linked the two halves of the upper track. This vast, rotating trestle was a cousin to the flying tire and magic staircase of *Cats*, but even more impressive. The sight of this behemoth, rising, falling, rotating, opening, and closing as the skaters whizzed across it at speeds up to forty miles an hour invariably elicited gasps of astonishment from the audience, along with the loudest applause of the evening.

Nunn's skating idea had been inspired by the virtuosos he had seen doing their thing in New York's Central Park. The likelihood of finding forty dancing roller skaters in England was even smaller than finding thirty singer-dancers, but that did not faze Nunn or Phillips, who drilled her troops at the Tropical Palace, a former movie theater in north London: "If you fall, get up," she told them. "If you're hurt, get out of the way." Ever since he saw Hot Gossip in action, Lloyd Webber had wanted to work with Phillips—for a while, he thought of asking her to choreograph the *Dance* section of *Song and Dance*. But aside from a forgettable show called *Fire Angel*, this would be her musical theater debut.

How far they had come from the days, not so very long ago, when it took the life savings of the hoi polloi to get *Cats* on track. *Starlight Express* was the most expensive musical ever staged in Britain, and its finances, along with those of its composer, elicited as much comment as the piece itself. Napier, for one, felt obliged to defend what the producers had wrought. "It's not just buying toys," he told *The Sunday Times*. "When people accuse us of squandering money they tend to forget we are giving skilled people full employment, with British equipment and know-how, proving that we can do it better than the Americans." In addition to its other charms, then, *Starlight* was a great day for England.

Lloyd Webber, too, came under the microscope. Ever since *Superstar* he had been downplaying his personal worth—"Andrew thought he was broke when he was down to his last three million pounds," cracked an acquaintance. *The Sunday Times* estimated his fortune at around twenty million pounds, to which Lloyd Webber responded in character: "I couldn't even afford to invest in *Starlight* myself," he said, forgetting to add that, like Mackintosh, it was against his business principles to invest in his own shows, especially now that he didn't have to.

The transformation of Lloyd Webber into a public personality was now complete. Gerald Scarfe, the noted caricaturist, sketched Andrew's head as the locomotive of a money-laden train, rolling down "The No Story Line" on its way "To the Points." A black cat was jumping across the track in front of him—shades of Elaine Paige—and the caption read, "This is the Webber Train crossing the border/Bringing the cheque and the postal order."

All this, then, and music too. In writing the score, Lloyd Webber was frankly seeking a hit; amazingly, "Don't Cry for Me Argentina" was his first and last number-one single (the *Evita* album reached number four on the BBC chart, the only one that really mattered); not even "Memory" had made it to the top of the pops. This irritated him. Even though by now he was fully a creature of the theater, the teenager who with Rice had desperately sought a number-one hit was still a part of his makeup, and if he could achieve it on his own, so much the better.

As a result, Lloyd Webber and Stilgoe were tinkering with the score right up to the premiere, adding songs and dropping them. Frequently, they worked together in restaurants, scribbling words and music on napkins or manuscript paper and singing quietly to each other. Stilgoe was a Liverpudlian, raised on religious songs such as "I Know That My Redeemer Liveth," which he sang in church, and on rockers such as "Rip It Up," which he sang at the Cavern, the legendary rock club that spawned the Beatles. Moreover, Stilgoe was at one time a cabaret performer who wrote the Royal Variety Show in 1983, and he also specialized in writing for children. No one pretended that Stilgoe was a lyricist in Rice's league, much less T. S. Eliot's, yet Lloyd Webber was, to his credit, determined that Stilgoe's name be prominently associated with what the world viewed as exclusively his undertaking. ("One senses that Britain's Rodgers, having found his Hart in Tim Rice, is still looking for his Hammerstein," noted *The Observer*.) Everybody was calling the new show "Andrew Lloyd Webber's *Starlight Express*," but in a letter to Brian Brolly written on January 13, 1984, Andrew told the head of the Really Useful Company how he wanted the show publicized:

> Dear Brian,
>
> I appreciate the reasons for the change in the advertising of "Starlight Express" and I understand that the creative team feels it reasonable that my name be used exclusively for the promotion at this early stage.
>
> However, everybody knows that I am very concerned about the over-use of my name and am not that keen to bring it forward. I believe it wrong not to now introduce Richard Stilgoe into the advertising. Therefore, I propose that the advertising should now read "Andrew Lloyd Webber and Richard Stilgoe's new musical Starlight Express." I believe that to be a very good idea on all levels.
>
> Yours sincerely,
>
> Andrew Lloyd Webber

Even so, Stilgoe was almost invisible once it came time to promote *Starlight Express*. The British media love a photo opportunity as much as their American cousins, so when Lloyd Webber and Nunn posed aboard the steam locomotive William H. Austen, which had been conveniently parked outside the Apollo Victoria before the show opened as a mute testimonial to the wonders that awaited the public within, the papers snapped it up. There was the director of the Royal Shakespeare Company sporting a conductor's hat, while a broadly smiling Lloyd Webber beamed down on him from the choo-choo above.

Five days before the premiere, on his thirty-sixth birthday, Lloyd Webber took Sarah Brightman as his bride. The ceremony was performed in the magistrate's office in Kingsclere, the Berkshire village near Sydmonton Court, in front of Sarah's mother and David and Lisa Crewe-Read. It was a snap decision, inspired in its timing by the fact that Andrew's final divorce decree had come through two days earlier; further, he and Sarah would be presented to the queen that evening after the gala preview performance of *Starlight Express,* and Andrew was determined that it would be as Mrs. Lloyd Webber that Sarah met royalty. "Are you sure you want to go through with it?" Sarah asked him on the way to Kingsclere. "Don't be stupid," he replied.

That evening, which was also a benefit for the Centre for World Development Education, the queen arrived at the theater in a crystal-embroidered coral pink chiffon evening dress, accompanied by the duke of Edinburgh. Along with Andrew and Sarah, Stilgoe, Napier, Phillips, and Hersey were also presented, and after the performance the queen and the duke went on stage to meet the members of the cast.

The next week, *Starlight Express* made its public debut. Ushers uniformed as railroad employees guided the patrons past chugging model trains that circled the auditorium and squeezed them into seats near the red and yellow "Wall of Death" outer skating track or, for the stout of heart and lucky of ticket, in the center island itself. The lights dimmed, and the resounding tritone blast of a train whistle rang out. Out of the murky gloom came a stab of oncoming headlights. Nine men in black-leather outfits hurtled out of the fog and launched into "Rolling Stock," the show's first number.

From the start, the central paradox of *Starlight Express* was apparent: a celebration of the power of steam over diesel and electricity, it was completely dependent on modern technology. As if to underscore the fragility of its electronic lifeline, the gods of the theater gave the first-nighters an object lesson: just as Lon Satton, who played the wise old engine Poppa, started to sing, "There are dark days ahead when the power goes dead"—at that very moment—the power went dead as Satton's body mike was overcome by interference from the BBC television truck parked outside. Stephanie Lawrence, playing Pearl, the female lead, threw Satton a hand mike, and he finished the show like something out of an O'Horgan production, trailing a wire behind him. Lloyd Webber, never comfortable on first nights, nearly jumped from his seat. It was the *Jesus Christ Superstar* nightmare coming back to haunt him again! Afterwards, at the opening-night cast party, Lloyd Webber was still steaming, his hair plastered sweatily over his forehead.

The next day, the reviews rolled in. "Andrew Lloyd Webber's new show, with pert lyrics by Richard Stilgoe and book by nobody who is named, marks the apotheosis of the High Tech masque," wrote Michael Ratcliffe in *The Observer* in a perceptive review headlined "Rollermouse Rock":

> It celebrates the arts of lighting and design through the remarkable talents of David Hersey and John Napier, who with the director Trevor Nunn have devised an elaborate and original presentation which completely controls and takes over the show. Is the *show* any good? No. The mountain labours marvellously for more than two hours and brings forth a mouse.

> It is not so much that the show gets lost in an orgy of roller-skating, rather that it scarcely shows up at all. Putting actors, singers and dancers on little wheels does not in itself make them simulate more plausibly the great trains of transcontinental America [*what* great trains of transcontinental America?] than if they performed on their own strong feet; but it does prescribe the nature of their movements and compel them to tear round Napier's three tracks through the auditorium in heats for a race whose rules are never made clear.

Lloyd Webber's score, wrote Ratcliffe, "seems to me much the least interesting he has done."

In *The Financial Times,* Coveney wrote that "the musical, in its best moments, surges out and around the building like a stage version of *Rollerball* and ironically establishes the value of steam engines at the expense of the diesels. This then disappointingly unravels as a Thatcherite message of self-improvement, finding what you have within you and jolly well pulling yourself together. This side of the show, which becomes preponderant in the second act along with some unsatisfactorily untying of rivalries and romances, I can live without." *Starlight Express,* Coveney decided, was "clearly *Cats II.*"

Irving Wardle of *The Times*: "Andrew Lloyd-Webber [*sic*] now ranks not only as the transatlantic king of popular music theatre but also as its reigning Medici; and both roles are combined in this translation of the Rev. W. Audrey's [*sic*] modest little steam engine stories into the most spectacular commercial production (not excluding *Cats*) since Sir Oswald Stoll ran his own private train into the Coliseum."

The Daily Telegraph's man, John Barber, began: "As spectacle, overwhelming, as engineering, phenomenal. You have to see it—and then you won't believe it. But whether 'Starlight Express' adds to the reputation of its composer (Andrew Lloyd Webber) and director (Trevor Nunn) is a question. This is only playing trains on a gargantuan scale. But, my goodness, it is fun. . . . I found 'Cats' the better show; it has greater variety, far more humanity. But this is unquestionably an astonishing experience, which will turn every decent sensationalist into a little boy in a paradise nursery."

In his review, headlined "The Blockbuster That Ran Out Of Steam," Michael Billington summed up:

> "Starlight Express" is a hymn to the age of the steam train. But the ultimate irony is that it takes a £1.4-million John Napier set, a multiple-level roller-skating track, and a Spielbergian flow of special effects to celebrate a pre-electric heaven. Not, in fact, since Lionel Bart's "Blitz" has London seen a musical where the technology so totally dwarfed the minuscule content.
>
> In "Cats," the balance between spectacle and emotion was well-nigh perfect and the final ascent to the skies lifted the spirits. But here when the cast finally hymn the "Light at the End of the Tunnel," I was reminded of Raymond Briggs's classic remark that what that often signified was simply an oncoming train.

If so, it was an oncoming train loaded with sterling and greenbacks. *Starlight* was already sold out months in advance; as Milton Shulman predicted in *The Evening Standard,* "'Starlight Express' will make Mr. Webber even more filthy rich than he already is."

Everyone, it seems, admired the spectacle, or at least respected the expertise behind it, but the show's actual content had few defenders. Rather surprisingly, the raffish weekly magazine *Time Out* liked it. "There is so much *going on* in this show: such superb choreography by Arlene Phillips, such a variety and flow of musical and visual styles, such thump and gaffump and locked-carriage tenderness in Lloyd Webber's writing, that the whole damn thing just carries you away."

Lloyd Webber's foremost champion was, of course, Derek Jewell. By now, Jewell had lost all objectivity concerning his former discovery; how else to account for sentiments (published in *The Sunday Times* of April 1, 1984) like "*Starlight* is not the best music Webber has written, but it is without doubt the most accomplished"?

> In "Starlight," Webber is writing hits: discrete commercial hits. That's no secret. He's said that's his aim, that he's in love with American train sounds. "Starlight" is American music. Listen, as the overture ends, and Greaseball's gang appear hazed in loco-motive searchlight. The tritone "whoo-whoo" of the railroad whistle, the churning beat, is pure Duke Ellington. Play Duke's "Happy-Go-Lucky Local" to hear one Webber influence. "In the South, firemen play blues on the whistle—big smeary things like a goddam woman singing in the night," as Ellington observed.
>
> Webber's evocation of trains is as brilliant as Duke's. His best music is that overture, prefacing the rocking "Rolling Stock"— reprised, naturally, since ALW knows a good tune when he's written one—his contrapuntal writing, and the superb *moto perpetuo* of the train races. That's *real* Webber, like the "Memory" contender at the end, "Only He."
>
> For the rest, this ecstatic genius Webber is simply taking on (and beating) the Americans at their own game: busting out "The Blues" with lusty Lon Satton, or gospel or disco-electric or country-style—Stilgoe's best lyric "U.N.C.O.U.P.L.E.D.," wonderfully sung Dolly-like by Frances Ruffelle. It's as if, having won three Grand Nationals, Webber's showing how stylishly he can succeed in big-money chases at Ascot.

It is always sad to see a critic go into the tank, but here Jewell jumped in with both feet. Although Lloyd Webber had even less to do with Ellington than with Wagner, Jewell couldn't resist trying to link the two at every opportunity. In another piece, he portrayed Lloyd Webber sitting at the keyboard, hitting tritones on the piano and invoking the sacred shade of the dear departed Duke—even though, as he had to admit, "no one has yet cast Webber as an Ellington fan." Except, of course, Derek Jewell.

The truth is, not only does *Starlight Express* bear no resemblance to Ellington, neither does it much resemble Lloyd Webber. It is, in fact, the least of his scores, a collection of tunes, some of them quite charming, in search of a theme. It doesn't matter, as Lloyd Webber was constantly reminding everyone, that it was supposed to be for children; that it was meant as a simple fairy tale; that it was, in short, more like *Joseph* in spirit than *Cats.* It didn't matter because it wasn't. Sociologically, *Starlight* was regressive: the locomotives were all male—no resistance to their pistons—while the coaches were all female. As staged in London, it was also racially patronizing. The steam engines were played by black actors, the diesels by whites; Electra, the bisexual electric train whose theme song is "AC/DC," was also black. (Not only the creative team was insensitive; in his review, Shulman wrote of the plot that "intellectually it would not tax the imagination of a retarded eight-year-old.")

Coveney was right: *Starlight Express* is *Cats II* — or "*Cats* on Tracks," as it was promptly anointed — but not half so good. There is an Old Deuteronomy train in the person of Poppa, a Grizabella train in the form of Belle, the "sleeping car with the heart of gold." There is the technique of plugging the big tune ("Starlight Express") just before intermission and then repeating it in the second act. As in *Cats*, *Starlight*'s first act is a series of genre pieces while the second act works out the plot, such as it was.

Elements from earlier Lloyd Webber shows make appearances too: the Elvis impersonator from *Joseph* is reprised as Greaseball, and the extraneous ballad for a minor character (reminiscent of "Another Suitcase in Another Hall" from *Evita*) reappears, this time called "There's Me," sung by the caboose, C. B. (The first time this tune appears, it is, of course, in D-flat major.) The song that opens Act Two, "The Rap," owes something to the opening number of Bernstein's *West Side Story*, but lacks its model's gritty street smarts. In the end, all the electronic razzle-dazzle could not disguise the fact that *Starlight Express* was an overblown and overhyped, yet tired and perfunctory show that was unworthy of the composer of *Evita* or the director of *Nicholas Nickleby*.

The score does not warrant close inspection. It begins with a short overture, whose rolling ostinato is a first cousin to the eighth variation of *Variations*. The theme of the Starlight Express is briefly heard, and then, with a hard-rock chug, "Rolling Stock," the ensemble for the diesel train Greaseball and his gang, gets the show started. However much the melody (coincidentally) resembles Jerome Kern's discarded "It's Getting Hotter in the North Every Day," this arresting opening turns out to be the high point of the show. On the stage, Phillips's choreography quickly ran out of steam, necessarily hampered by the limited steps at her disposal. The touted train races — there are a mind-numbing five in all — were impossible to differentiate: a chaotic mass of entangled skaters gamely trying to get to the finish line before the music stopped; one could not tell who won or why, much less care. A game without rules is a Caucus Race — "All have won and all must have prizes," as Alice learned in Wonderland. The hero, Rusty, was a sexless, ineffectual shrimp, while the invocation of the Starlight Express was a poor imitation of the Heaviside Layer. Even the moving railroad bridge got boring. *Starlight Express* was a two-hour-and-twenty-minute-long train wreck.

Some critics admired Stilgoe's lyrics, although it is hard to understand why. Stilgoe picked up Reeves's sophomoric double-entendres in "Engine of Love" and made a whole evening out of them. In "A Lotta Locomotion," the female coaches are anthropomorphosed in crude sexual terms: "Buffy at your service/ever open wide/my microwave is cooking/to warm you from inside./A lotta locomotion/will do the trick/come and bite my burgers/I'm hot and cheap and quick." The refrain of Electra's disco ballad, "AC/DC," goes "AC/DC its OK by me. I can switch and change my frequency." (The 7/8 time signature, however, gives the song a kinky momentum that fits the subject.) "He Whistled at Me," a song for Pearl, which is what melodically became of "Engine of Love," has the refrain, "Nobody can do it like a steam train." When Dinah becomes disenchanted with Electra, she uncouples from him with the observation, "He never whistles at me/it's damaging my status/I don't think he can whistle at me/he lacks the apparatus." And so on.

Elsewhere the words are simply flat. One song is built, stupefyingly, around the eponymous refrain, "Freight is Great." The "Starlight Express" anthem begins:

> *When your goodnights have been said*
> *And you are lying in bed*
> *With the covers pulled up tight*
> *And though you count every sheep*
> *You get the feeling that sleep is going*
> *To stay away tonight*

If Tim Rice's "Memory" lyric had made Grizabella too human, what about this? Railroad trains do not count sheep, although they sometimes run them over. Probably the best lyric is that to the song "U.N.C.O.U.P.L.E.D.," a Tammy Wynette knockoff, although its curious punctuation leaves something to be desired:

> *Now I'm just U.N.C.O.U.P.L.E.D.*
> *I can't seem to stop C.R.Y.I.N.G.*
> *People look at me and think*
> *"There she goes, the missing link,"*
> *She's been U.N.C.O.U.P.L.E.D.*

And I'm just U.N.C.O.U.P.L.E.D.
But I'll get my R.E.V.E.N.G.E.
He'll come crawling back one day
Then I'll turn to him and say
Go away you B.A.S.T.A.R.D.

Oddly, some of the best musical moments come in the interminable train races, in which Lloyd Webber displays his cleverness in combining themes: one had a better idea of who was ahead listening to the music than by watching the massive television screens. Even here, Lloyd Webber nullifies some of the effect by instrumentally reprising songs that have not yet been heard, such as Electra's "No Comeback," whose melody is first sounded in Race One, yet is meant to illustrate the evil train's discomfiture at the end.

The show's best song, in part because it is the least pretentious and lyrically inoffensive, is "There's Me," a lovely tune sung by the utterly unappealing, treacherous red caboose, C. B. It is another of Lloyd Webber's Schubert-like constructions, akin to "High Flying, Adored" in *Evita*. Short, pointed, and poignant, it relies heavily on the plagal cadence to make its effect. Despite Jewell's optimism, the show's big ballad, "Only He/Only You," is no "Memory." It lacks the apparatus.

Starlight found an audience in England, where by September 1986 it had racked up its one-thousandth performance; to celebrate, Lloyd Webber threw a champagne party at the Roof Gardens in Derry Street. Six months later, three years after its London opening, *Starlight Express* finally came to New York, opening on March 15, 1987, at the Gershwin Theatre (formerly the Uris), three days after Nunn's other unwieldy technological spectacular that season, *Les Misérables,* opened at the Broadway Theatre. *Starlight* had taken a roundabout route to Broadway, for at first the idea had been to present the musical as a touring arena show. The cost of the production, the most expensive ever on Broadway, was eight million dollars, two and a half million for the set alone. Although Bernie Jacobs and Gerald Schoenfeld had attended *Starlight* at its London premiere, under the impression that they had an ongoing arrangement with Lloyd Webber, in the end the Shuberts did not get the show; instead, it went to the rival Nederlander organization. Most of the money (five million dollars) was put up by MCA, with the other three million dollars coming from the New Zealand investment company of Strada Holdings. The producers were Lord Lew Grade (Bernard Delfont's half-brother) and Martin Starger, an independent who had produced *Sly Fox* on Broadway as well as Robert Altman's film *Nashville.*

Starlight Express was even worse in America than it had been in Britain. "This is quite deliberately based on the same basic, unspoken contract as Disneyland," Nunn was quoted as saying in *The Wall Street Journal.* "That is: 'Here is my money; hit me with the experience.'" What he forgot was that in the United States a "Mickey Mouse" production has a bad connotation. In London, *Starlight* at least had the courage of its original convictions—a Briton's idealized view of America, offered to like-minded other Britons—but in New York the set was "Americanized," dotted with place names like "Kalamazoo" and "Cincinnati" to show that this really was the U.S. of A. The Gershwin could not be torn apart like the Apollo Victoria (shades of the *Cats* problems), so although the proscenium set was larger—one hundred and twenty feet wide—the exhilarating Sens-surround race track of London was in New York a poor relation, extending only a few rows beyond the proscenium. The score had been reworked, for the worse, by Andrew and Phil Ramone: chopped up, reorchestrated, and generally made a hash of. Played by an invisible band (à la *Cats*), it sounded terrible.

To his credit, Lloyd Webber knew he had an embarrassment on his hands in America, but—just as with *Jeeves*—there was nothing he could do about it. When *Jeeves* closed, it did not really hurt his reputation, for anybody could have a flop; when *Starlight* didn't, at least not right away, it wounded it badly. Then it was because he was powerless; now it was because he was too powerful. In retrospect, if *Starlight* had laid an egg straight off, Lloyd Webber probably would not have had to run the critical gantlet that he did for his next major show, *The Phantom of the Opera.* The myth of invincibility would have been shattered; he would have been proved a mere mortal, like everybody else. Everybody loves a loser. When it didn't, he became fair game—better, he became big game.

In a remarkable disclaimer, Lloyd Webber appended the following program note to the American version of *Starlight Express*:

At the 1982 Sydmonton Festival *Starlight* was finally performed with the intention that it might become a concert for schools. Here it was heard by Trevor Nunn. First there was a plan that it should open the new Barbican Centre in London as a concert sung by all the schools of the City of London, but the ever-resourceful Mr. Nunn had other ideas. He felt the story should be more about competition, that for children today it should be more of a pop score and above all that it could be a staged event because trains could happen through roller skates. Frankly some of us had doubts so the first act was "workshopped" in 1983 [at Notre Dame Hall]. It was great fun so the button was pushed on the London production of *Starlight Express* which opened in March 1984.

I hope Trevor and my other collaborators will forgive me for saying that despite the commercial success the show has had in London, something of the joy and sense of pure fun that was the original intention seemed to get lost and *Starlight Express* was not quite what we intended.

It was, in short, all Trevor's fault. The Nunns of the world had made him do it.

This admission was all the ammo the American critics needed. They sacked *Starlight Express* like the Wild Bunch robbing a Wells Fargo Bank train. Frank Rich had already hated the show in London; *Starlight,* he wrote then, "is a dud, joyless and mechanical. Money substitutes for creativity; machinery and deafening noise replace theatrical magic." Rich predicted that "American parents may also be far more sensitive than their British counterparts to this show's patronization of women and blacks. The hideously costumed female train cars in 'Starlight' all seem to be hookers. . . .The black cars are heroes, but Mr. Lloyd Webber's pastiche versions of rap, blues, gospel and Michael Jackson are pure white bread."

So Rich was loaded and ready when *Starlight* finally came to town:

> In a full-page program note, the composer Andrew Lloyd Webber modestly explains that he conceived his musical, "Starlight Express," as an entertainment "event" for children who love trains. Over two numbing hours later, you may find yourself wondering exactly whose children he had in mind. A confusing jamboree of piercing noise, routine roller-skating, misogyny and Orwellian special effects, "Starlight Express" is the perfect gift for the kid who has everything except parents.
>
> Instead of aspiring to his usual Puccini variations, Mr. Lloyd Webber has gone "funky," English style, by writing pastiche versions of American pop music — with an emphasis on blues, gospel and rap. Short of a Lennon Sisters medley of the Supremes' greatest hits, soul music couldn't get much more soulless than this.

In *The Wall Street Journal,* Edwin Wilson wrote: "The show has an arresting appearance, and it has plenty of sound, but if you go to 'Starlight Express' expecting content, you will be disabused of your preconceptions. What attempts there are at telling a story and plumbing emotional depths, or even shallows, are pathetic. The only reason to see 'Starlight Express' is for the skating and for the visual effects, which, though they grow a bit monotonous, are spectacular." Not quite two years later, despite a four-million-dollar advance sale, *Starlight Express* closed on January 8, 1989, after 761 performances — a hit for anyone but Lloyd Webber. In London, however, it continued to roll merrily along, celebrating its fifth anniversary in the spring of 1989.

So much for Jewell's theory that Lloyd Webber was beating the Americans at their own game. It may have sounded that way in England, even to someone who knew something about real black American music, as Jewell did, but it certainly didn't play that way in the United States. If anybody bought the original cast album, he or she has yet to admit it.

On November 21, 1985, Jewell died at the age of fifty-eight. To the end, he was Lloyd Webber's staunchest defender. Although American critics take a prim attitude toward fraternizing with artists, the British have few such scruples; it is common, even honorable, for a British music critic to meet with composers and performers privately, to socialize with them and to become identified publicly as a supporter. In England, the critic and the artist are in league together for the good of their art (in theory, anyway); they do not have the natural adversarial relationship they do in the United States. Jewell simply carried collegiality to excess.

Five months before his death, Jewell wrote Andrew a letter, thanking him and Sarah Brightman for a dinner party that Jewell and his wife Liz, had attended. Over the course of the dinner, Lloyd Webber had described his plan for his next show, and Jewell greeted the idea with his customary enthusiasm:

> I was fascinated by all that you had to say about the Phantom. The idea of Lloyd Webber's "shabby little shocker" [a reference to the musicologist Joseph Kerman's famous characterization of Puccini's *Tosca*] is a brilliant one. I want to write about that as you get closer to a final shape before anyone else does.
>
> There are at least two other things which inevitably whizzed across my mind as we talked. The first is to write a proper piece about all the performances of the Requiem which are being done, contrasting these plus the album's continuing success in America and elsewhere with some of the snotty things some of the critics have said. . . .

Penultimately there is that idea which floated in the air of doing a possible book on the number of times that critics have got it wrong! This I am extraordinarily interested in. When you've got a moment, is it something we could do together? I know a good deal about it from the pop angle but I'm not nearly as knowledgeable as you on the classical stuff. Anyway, what about doing it together? We would then have a rival publication to the Rice Book of Hit Singles. But let's think about it.

Jewell's book never became a reality, but both of the projects Lloyd Webber had talked about did. He had been looking to write a work for Sarah to sing, and now he had not one, but two of them: dark, brooding, mysterious pieces that would show off her high soprano to best advantage. One would take place in church, the other in the bowels of the Paris Opera, where a lovelorn composer was wooing a beautiful young soprano with a new opera he was writing just for her. And any relation to any person, living or dead, was purely coincidental.

Precisely where Lloyd Webber derived the inspiration for his next major work, the *Requiem*, is unclear. It seems to have had many fathers. In 1978 Humphrey Burton, the director of arts programming for the BBC had asked Andrew to compose a requiem for the victims of the Troubles in Northern Ireland, but with *Evita* and the *Variations* happening that year, nothing came of it.

Still, the idea of a requiem stayed in the back of Lloyd Webber's mind, and when his father died in 1982 he decided to act on it. A second stimulus was the continuing struggle in Northern Ireland; when the Irish Republican Army set off a bomb outside Harrods in Knightsbridge at Christmastime in 1982, the explosion killed Philip Geddes, a young journalist from *The Daily Express*, whom Andrew knew slightly. A third incentive was a piece in *The New York Times* that Lloyd Webber read about a young Cambodian boy who was forced to choose between killing his mutilated sister or being killed himself. According to Lloyd Webber, all of these events played a role in calling forth and shaping the *Requiem*.

Church music was, obviously, a far from unknown commodity in the Lloyd Webber household. Bill wrote reams of it; at Westminster, in the shadow of the abbey, Andrew had heard lots of it. Every educated British musician was raised on English church music, and the urge to write a Mass was a common one. From the days of Weelkes and Wilbye through those of the Lutheran Handel or the Catholic Elgar, sacred music has been a significant part of British musical life. Ralph Vaughan Williams, Elgar's successor in the front rank of English composers, had written a Mass in G Minor for unaccompanied choir, and in the early sixties Benjamin Britten had fashioned the *War Requiem* (though not from liturgical texts but from the poetry of Wilfrid Owen). At age ten, Lloyd Webber had attended a memorial service for Vaughan Williams, and at thirteen he had witnessed the premiere of the *War Requiem*. So the pedigree of his own *Requiem* was anything but commercial.

Whether his purpose was entirely spiritual, however, is moot. With *Starlight Express* up and running in London by the spring of 1984, Lloyd Webber was casting around for new ideas, preferably those that would involve his new wife. He couldn't wait to show off Brightman to the world. There had been a thought of putting her into *Starlight*—Sarah really could roller-skate very well—but that was soon enough dismissed: *Starlight* had no starring roles, and he wanted something bigger for her.

There were several candidates. One was already at hand, the *Song* part of *Song and Dance.* He had just closed the show in London, of course, but there was always television, and so he put Sarah on the *Song* set and filmed her performing the *Tell Me on a Sunday* cycle for later broadcast in both Britain and the United States. Sarah looked the part, but at twenty-three she was young and vocally immature; she had only been studying seriously for a short time, and it showed. Like most young singers, Brightman was still learning just what her voice could do: what its comfortable range was, how high it could be pushed, where its bottom lay, and so forth. Written for the limited range of Marti Webb, *Song* showed off neither her soaring top—she could climb up to a high D—nor her solid chest voice. It was not the right piece for her.

The *Aspects of Love* that Lloyd Webber was still fiddling with seemed more like it. But he still had no real sense of which way the musical ought to go. The music he had composed for *Aspects*, it now seemed to him, was all wrong for the subject; it was too brooding, too dark, too romantic. *Aspects* demanded a more sophisticated score. Maybe he should put it in *Phantom*, but that would take a while to retool. So, as

Sherlock Holmes always said, when you have eliminated the impossible, whatever is left—no matter how improbable— must be the truth. The *Requiem* it would be.

It was a gamble. Ever since *Jesus Christ Superstar,* Lloyd Webber's admirers had sought to cast him as a serious composer whose scores, although certainly entertaining , were also seriously meant. Now it was time for him to prove it. He needed to show the world that *Starlight Express* had been an aberration, a Toonerville Trolley that had gone berserk and turned into the Twentieth Century Limited, and the *Requiem* was just the vehicle to do it. The artistic failure of *Starlight* had gotten him to thinking that writing hit songs was now beyond, or unworthy of, him; maybe he should forget all about that aspect of songwriting and, at the risk of his commercial success, start concentrating on intrinsically musical qualities.

What is more, it would be a welcome challenge. Andrew needed to stretch himself, to expand both his technical reach and his emotional grasp. *Starlight Express* had been a rewrite of *Cats,* as everybody noticed; that train was traveling backward, not forward. To sit down and compose a piece of abstract music would not be easy, but it would be good for him. Writing for an operatic soprano wouldn't hurt either. Most composers his age would have done that years ago, in their student days at conservatory, but he had missed out on all that; his *Lehrjahre* were blatantly—and, of course, profitably—public, for all to see.

A requiem was a nice compromise, part abstract music and part theater, as Mozart, Berlioz, and Verdi had proved. Few texts, after all, were more overtly dramatic than the Dies Irae. After some thought, Lloyd Webber settled for the classic Roman Catholic Latin liturgy that had served so many composers so well over so many years; Bill would have liked that. Of specifically Northern Irish influence, there was none, but the Cambodian story surfaced in the unusual scoring of the piece, for boy soprano and female soprano—"the resonance," as Lloyd Webber said later, "for the idea that the soprano should be young and therefore have a special connection with the solo boy." To another interviewer he added: "I decided this would be about the manipulation of children in war." There would also be a tenor, representing the world at large, but no alto and no bass. Nor would there be any violins in the orchestra, a precedent already established by Brahms and Gabriel Fauré in their requiems.

A short first draft was tried out at Sydmonton during the summer of 1984. Sarah sang the soprano role, William Kendall was the tenor, and Paul Miles-Kingston took the boy soprano part; the chorus was the Winchester Cathedral Choir, led by Martin Neary. (The Kings House School Choir, a children's chorus directed by Michael Stuckey, a young man who had been Alan Doggett's lover, sang at the Sunday religious service in Ecchinswell that traditionally concluded the festival; Kings House had appeared at Sydmonton each year since 1978.) Reaction was positive, so Lloyd Webber set about in earnest on the piece, working on it over the next six months with an eye to a New York premiere in February 1985. Almost nothing was allowed to interfere with the *Requiem*: once having settled on it, Lloyd Webber devoted nearly his full time to the project. By October the *Requiem* was complete, and by Christmas the orchestration was finished. Much of the scoring was done by David Cullen, whom Andrew thanked in a program note to the EMI/Angel recording, "For his transcription of the score into something legible from my indecipherable manuscripts and also for his help during its frequent re-orchestration."

The *Requiem* is perhaps the most underrated and misunderstood of all Lloyd Webber's scores, not excluding *Evita.* In evaluating the work, it is important to keep in mind its place in the composer's oeuvre: the *Requiem* is part heartfelt outpouring, part calculated tailoring of a work to a specific voice, and part technical exercise in writing and scoring for large conventional forces. Which one of these elements preponderates, of course, is partly in the ear of the beholder, but the one thing the *Requiem* is not is a cheap, cynical ploy—this despite the fact that, ironically and regrettably, the "Pie Jesu" movement later became a hit single. (Take that, *Starlight Express.*) Lloyd Webber said of it: "I don't know what place it will find in the music of today, but to me it is the most personal of all my compositions."

The premiere, on February 24, 1985, before one thousand invited guests at Saint Thomas Episcopal Church at Fifty-third Street and Fifth Avenue in midtown Manhattan, was a glamorous affair. (The British premiere took place two months later, on April 21, in Westminster Abbey.) The New York City performance was attended by the likes of Edward Heath, the former British prime minister, who covered it for *The Financial Times,* writer Kurt Vonnegut, composer Charles Strouse, and starlet Susan Anton. Bernie Jacobs was there, and so was Robert Stigwood. The Public Broadcasting Service and the BBC filmed the evening for later presentation on their *Great Performances* and *Omnibus* programs, respectively. Brightman, Miles-Kingston, and the Winchester Cathedral Choir reprised their Sydmonton roles. They were joined by the Saint Thomas Choir (Saint Thomas was the only church in America to maintain its own choir school) and the Orchestra of Saint Luke's. The tenor part was sung by Placido Domingo, whom Lloyd Webber had known for several years socially and who had been after the composer to write something for him, while the conductor, another friend, was Lorin Maazel, the former music director of the Cleveland Orchestra and later, briefly, of the Vienna State Opera. As befits a requiem, the atmosphere was solemn, perhaps excessively so (nobody, after all, had died, at least not recently). Tickets were thirty-five dollars apiece, the money going to the Holy Apostles Church Soup Kitchen for the Homeless and Poor in New York City. The *Requiem* is a forty-seven-minute work, so at the first performance it was preceded by three brief choral pieces: the visiting Winchester choir sang Purcell's "Jehovah, quam multi sunt" and "Hear My Prayer," conducted by Neary, while the Saint Thomas Choir performed Bach's "Singet dem Herrn," led by Gerre Hancock. Then came *Requiem*.

The piece begins with a low chord sounded by the piano and brass, an A–E–B sonority that, in context, is at first ambiguous: is the key A minor, with an added second (B)? Or E minor with an added fourth (A)? Quickly, it proves to be the former; the added second chord will dictate the work's harmonic language. The boy soprano enters, intoning "Requiem aeternam" to a modal tune that is one of the piece's principal themes. After a brief choral interlude, the soprano and tenor pick up the tune at "Kyrie eleison," the soprano ascending to a high D, the tenor to high B-flat.

The "Dies Irae," which is usually the excuse for a composer to unleash his mightiest forces to depict the Day of Wrath, is disappointingly muted. Part of the problem is the beginning, an open-fifth trumpet leap that sounds distressingly like Roman gladiator music from a biblical epic. Another problem is the rhythm, which switches between 6/8 and 4/4 and prevents any real forward momentum from developing; the choral writing, too, is tight and crabbed. The music turns contemplative as the tenor enters with "Judex ergo," a G-minor tune whose initial melodic compass is a major seventh but which, at the words "mors stupebit," suddenly rises up to high B-flat for both soprano and tenor in the *Requiem*'s first emotional climax. The "Rex Tremendae" begins with the same rising fifth that opened the "Dies Irae," this time proclaimed by the men's chorus, but then reverts to the boy soprano's opening melody and ends quietly on the words "salva me."

The next section, for solo soprano, is the "Recordare," which starts with an organ meditation on an angular tune in 6/4 that is picked up by the singer and spun out in a long, pretty line with a piquant leap of a minor seventh at its end. Again, the music flies high, twice to a high B-natural and then, at the end, to a high C-sharp before settling on a high B that is part of an unequivocal E-major sonority emphasized by a trombone cadence. Verdi made the "Ingemisco" a tenor aria, and it is here too, a sobbing, Italianate number that lies comfortably and communicates effectively. The mood changes abruptly with a brisk, nightmarish Prokofievian march at the words "confutatis maledictis" that reprises a melody from the "tuba mirum" section of the "Dies Irae." The march, though, ends as abruptly as it began, and the chorus return to hymn the "Lacrymosa," a direct repetition of the tenor's "Judex ergo" tune. Another reprise comes next, the "Ingemisco" sob, now set to the words "huic ergo," but this too fades out in the work's most effective close, a sequence of dropping sevenths for the soprano at the words "dona eis" that climbs back up to a quiet, floated high A-flat amen.

After a short choral anthem, the choppy, episodic "Offertorium" breaks into a brief instrumental fughetto, then resumes its choral ruminations, bubbling through a "Hostias" and finally landing back on the open fifths at "transire ad vitam," before subsiding again. The syncopated "Hosanna" follows, the first and only intrusion of Broadway in the score. It is a joyful noise, made by the tenor, which soars to a high B-flat and is then picked up by the chorus and turned into a vocal version of the little fugue heard earlier. The counterpoint does not last long, as the toe-tapping "Hosannah" melody reasserts itself—sometimes, friskily, in 7/8 instead of 4/4—over a background of woodwinds, drums, and, for punctuation, brass. The song climaxes when it suddenly clashes with the soprano and her mysterious "Recordare" theme, set to the words "Dies irae, dies illa," and the movement ends quietly with the "Recordare" theme in the orchestra.

All this, though, has been merely a prelude to the Requiem's "hit tune," the "Pie Jesu," sung by the soprano and the boy. It is one of Lloyd Webber's most finely wrought compositions, in no small measure because it makes an art of its utter simplicity. Written in A-flat (and not, surprisingly, in D-flat), it blends the two soprano voices beautifully, combining them in thirds the way Mozart does in his writing for the two sisters in *Cosi fan tutte*. The full chorus then enters, also in A-flat (the movement never modulates), at the words "Agnus Dei," then retires so that the two treble voices may finish pianissimo. "Pie Jesu" is the *Requiem*'s "Memory," but closer in spirit to the "In trutina menis" aria from Orff's *Carmina Burana* than to anything by Puccini.

"Lux Aeterna," intoned by the chorus soprano, leads directly to the tenor's spiritually disquieted "Libera Me." The music swells as the chorus and the soprano enter, and there is a short reminiscence of the "tuba mirum" march music. But this tune has now lost its steam, and it subsides gently into the opening modal theme, stark bare fourths and fifths. The boy enters and reclaims his song; not even one last violent outburst from the orchestra can dissuade him, and he sings through it, repeating the word "perpetua" over and over as the *Requiem* gradually fades away.

From a technical point of view, it is easy to see what is wrong with the *Requiem*: the solo writing lies too high (the piece would be more effective transposed down a full third), it is short-winded in its development, often static in its harmony and muddied in orchestration. The fundamentally diatonic added-note harmony wears on the ear, and not even the radiance of the "Pie Jesu" can completely dispel the aural gloom. Yet one must also point out what is right with it: the *Requiem* has a size and scope that not many contemporary composers attempt anymore, an honesty of spirit that, however naïve, is refreshing, and a willingness to go for the big effect. It is bold music, with vivid, striking moments that rival in their emotional force passages in Britten's *War Requiem*: the "mors stupebit" climax of the "Dies Irae," the otherworldliness of the "Recordare," the healing balm of the "Pie Jesu." It is honorable music, intended honorably.

The critical response to the *Requiem* in the United States, however, illustrated the composer's by-now inescapable dilemma; at the time of *Superstar*, Lloyd Webber had been criticized for his "operatic" pretensions by the drama critics; now, it was his turn to be criticized for his pop-music pedigree by the music critics. Writing in *The New York Times*, Bernard Holland put his finger on it:

> Twentieth-century music is so beset by quarrelsome factions that composers who mediate between them deserve our full attention. Andrew Lloyd Webber, maker of "Cats," "Evita" and other successful popular entertainments, took his skills into a very different world of style last night and brought us a Requiem, one of the most solemn and ancient of musical forms.

> Mr. Lloyd Webber's Requiem, unfortunately, tells us nothing new. What he does manage to do with his smooth, graceful melodic lines and familiar dramatic props is to accommodate the ideas of a great many other composers and do so very graciously. Thus Ravel and Fauré, Orff and Prokofiev—all ground into a fine homogeneity by a tradition of movie composer and easy listening arrangements—paraded past us in graceful salute. There were the tried-and-true bendings of traditional harmony, Mr. Domingo's quasi-Hebraic melodies from biblical Hollywood in the Lacrymosa, and everywhere pedal points rumbling ominously. Mr. Lloyd Webber's democratic orchestration—which ignored violins but embraced a wide range of wind and percussion instruments—promised much but fell back too often on massive claps of thunder and other coups de théâtre, most of which startled rather than moved.

> Thus Mr. Lloyd Webber was least effective when he tried the hardest. The intended force of the Dies Irae merely grated, while the massive outburst that interrupted the boy soprano at the final lines served to vulgarize his sweet singing, not to set it off. In the gospel energy of the Hosanna and the natural folksiness of the Pie Jesu, on the other hand, Mr. Lloyd Webber seemed to emerge from beneath his pretensions and offer us music to enjoy.

Another critic with an open mind was Andrew Porter, the South African–born, London-trained critic of *The New Yorker*. Ferociously erudite, in a way that few American critics were, Porter was of the friend-in-court school, especially when it came to things British, and his review, published in the March 11, 1985, issue of the magazine, was judicious:

> [Lloyd Webber's] Requiem is not exactly a distinguished piece of music, but it is a "felt" work and an honest one. The effects are obvious, but they are effective. Lloyd Webber—as the success of his theatre pieces attests—has a flair for lyric invention, for tunes that catch. The Requiem begins with a motif—a falling E–B–E motto—that moves into a well-devised theme. He is not a composer on a grand scale; he thinks of a tune and then plugs it. . . .This is unchallenging music—unless the challenge is to a listener to set aside any ideas of development, difficulty and such subtlety as informs the varied repetitions of the Agnus Dei in Verdi's Requiem.

In his review for the *FT*, Edward Heath wrote that the *Requiem* "made a profound impact on those present. It was received with prolonged applause from a large and distinguished audience, most of whom, after all, had not known beforehand what to expect. . . .The *Requiem* creates its effect as much through its simplicity as through its technical ingenuity. There are moments of sheer beauty which will linger long in the memory." Heath, himself an amateur organist, then went on to thoughtfully and professionally examine the piece, movement by movement. His tack was descriptive, rather than analytic or critical, yet an American could only read his notice with awe, trying to imagine, say, President Ronald Reagan doing something similar.

Others, however, were less impressed. Michael Kimmelman of *The Philadelphia Inquirer* said the *Requiem"* was "so concertedly serious it seemed more like a parody, as if the composer lacked the compositional depth to do justice to the form. Instead, Lloyd Webber has composed a work that is like a grim *Cats*. There are catchy melodies colored by just enough dissonance to make it clear that they are supposed to be serious, but not enough character to make them truly interesting."

Martin Bernheimer of *The Los Angeles Times* had liked *Jesus Christ Superstar*, but he listened to the *Requiem* and changed his tune, calling it "sanctimonious whoopee." The *Requiem*," said Bernheimer, "aspires to the pure fragrance of churchly incense, but it ends up reeking of cheap perfume. No one can accuse Lloyd Webber of writing music that is ugly or monochromatic or ill-intentioned or inaccessible. One can accuse him, however, of writing music that gives eclecticism a bad name."

The most virulent denunciation came from Peter Davis in *New York* magazine. "It is depressing to see so much money and media hype squandered on such a pretentious and crushingly trivial hunk of junk," wrote Davis. "Perhaps the saddest part of this sorry enterprise is the presence of Maazel and Domingo. Both musicians surely knew what they were doing when they agreed to perform, record, and videotape this drivel—but then, the lure of receiving so much media attention must have been irresistible."

Davis raised a good point: what about all the hype and media attention? How could a work by a composer with no track record in serious music attract performers of the caliber of Domingo and Maazel, be premiered in such august surroundings, be videotaped for almost immediate broadcast (in Britain, the *Requiem* was shown on April 3, introduced by Humphrey Burton; in America, it aired two days later, on Good Friday), and be recorded by a major label, even if its composer's name was Andrew Lloyd Webber? The answer spoke volumes, not only about Lloyd Webber the composer but also of Lloyd Webber the businessman.

In October 1984 Peter Brown had pitched Andrew for the *Requiem* account and had got it. Brown and Lloyd Webber had been friends for years. Brown had been at the meeting at Stigwood's house on that day back in 1969; later, he had headed Stigwood's American operation before being ousted in a 1976 power struggle. He had gone to Los Angeles, a city that adored resident Brits, expunged the last traces of his Liverpool accent, and been reborn as a smooth and very successful PR man. Brown had the foresight to keep his palatial bachelor apartment on Central Park West, easing his way for his return to New York in 1984 when he founded the public relations firm of Brown and Powers Associates.

Brown played the American media like a harp. He seemed to know everybody, moving easily at the highest levels of government, commerce, and the entertainment business. At a Peter Brown party, one was likely to encounter anyone from Bess Myerson, the former beauty queen turned New York City commissioner, to Edward Acker, the chairman of Pan American Air Lines, to Elaine Strich, the Broadway actress (who had made a cameo appearance as a voice on the telephone on the original recording of *Tell Me on a Sunday*). Although an Englishman to his bootstraps, Brown understood the American media in a way that eluded most Britons, and he was just the man to try to improve Lloyd Webber's American image.

So Brown took Andrew to school. You can't treat the American critics the way you treat British ones. In England, Andrew was always ready to hector an editor, fire off a letter to a writer, or sue a tabloid, as the need arose, but that sort of browbeating didn't work in the United States. In England, there were two basic breeds of journalist. There were men like Derek Jewell, whom you could pat on the head or chuck under the chin secure in the knowledge that they might nip at you from time to time but never bite back. And there were the curs of Fleet Street, mean little bastards who hunted in packs, snarling and snapping until you gave them a good kick and they went slinking away. The American media, though, were more domesticated. As long as you fed them regularly and treated them with some respect they remained good tempered, if somewhat independent and unpredictable; starve them for too long and they would eventually eat the baby. Various presidents of the United States could testify to that.

Brown may have been right about America, but Andrew saw no reason to change his approach in his own country. The following letter, from Lloyd Webber to Philip Norman of *The Sunday Times* is typical of the way Lloyd Webber had always handled the press in England:

31st January 1986

Philip Norman, Esq.
The Sunday Times
P.O. Box 7
200 Gray's Inn Road
London WC1X 8E2

Dear Philip:

It is a long time since I've seen you and it would be nice to meet up again.

Somebody has sent me a comment you made, which I presume referred to my "Pie Jesu" from my Requiem, in the Sunday Times, in which you said it was distressing to see choir boys in their fuffs singing pseudo anthems by myself whilst Britain has more problems with child abuse than at any time in the recent past.

I just thought I should bring to your attention that when it was suggested that the "Pie Jesu" be issued as a single recording, I immediately arranged to donate all my royalties from the production of the record to Save The Children.

With best wishes.

Yours sincerely,

Andrew Lloyd Webber

One would never do that in the United States. There, the press would think its vaunted objectivity was being compromised. Better just to be nice, ignoring the criticism and accommodating the requests for interviews and free tickets.

Still, it was all true: the "Pie Jesu" *was* a hit, and so was the *Requiem* album. Released shortly after the premiere, the single had entered the charts at number fourteen, while the album had debuted at number eleven. The *Requiem*'s popularity was no fluke. A full four years later, the *Requiem* album was still on the Classical Top 20 in Britain. In mid-March 1989 it was holding steady at number six, between the Albinoni *Adagio* and the late Jacqueline Du Pré's recording of the Elgar *Cello Concerto* made with her husband, Daniel Barenboim. The Lloyd Webber family was also represented on the classical charts by Julian, whose recording of the same Elgar concerto was at number three. (And Julian's *Elgar* was just behind Du Pré's earlier recording of the piece, with Barbirolli. The English can't get enough of Elgar.)

Nor was the record unappreciated in America. In February 1986 it won a Grammy Award as the best classical album of 1985, which went on the shelf at Sydmonton alongside Lloyd Webber's three Tony Awards (one for *Evita,* two for *Cats*) and his three Drama Desk awards. That same year, the *Requiem* was turned into a dance for the American Ballet Theater by Sir Kenneth MacMillan, the company's newly appointed artistic associate director.

In short, the success of the *Requiem* bespoke significant marketing muscle, which is where the Really Useful Company was living up to its name. Lloyd Webber had not composed the *Requiem* in an ivory tower and then sent it off to a publisher, hoping for the best. Even before the score was finished, Brian Brolly had swung into action, lining up the BBC (whose producer, Ian Squires, brought Maazel on board), arranging the premiere in New York, setting up the EMI recording and publishing the vocal and orchestral scores. In the winter of 1984–1985, movie director Stephen Frears made a video of the "Pie Jesu," using as footage film of children in war; it was aired twice on the television show "Entertainment Tonight," and within seven weeks the album was number one on the Billboard charts. Within a few months of the Saint Thomas's performance, the market was flooded with videocassettes, albums, singles, and sheet music. The beauty of it was that one could still take the high road while raking in the cash, donating performance proceeds to charities like the soup kitchen in New York or, at the British premiere, to charities associated with the Sussex emergency services and the Royal Sussex County Hospital, which had treated the victims of the October 1984 bombing of the Grand Hotel in Brighton by the Irish Republican Army that very nearly claimed the life of Mrs. Thatcher. So, in the end, the Irish theme had come full circle.

Lloyd Webber took the bad reviews hard. He had presented the *Requiem* seriously, and here it was being thrown back in his face. It almost didn't matter that Maazel had stood up for him; in an interview with *Women's Wear Daily* (that, delightfully, posthumously promoted Bill Lloyd Webber to "dean of the Royal Academy of Music"), Maazel had responded to the charge that Lloyd Webber's music was derivative. "No one can possibly write great music on his own," the conductor said. "A composer needs others to stimulate him, to firm up his fancy. Even in Beethoven you can hear the composers he admired—Weber, Gluck, as well as Haydn. I think this is a piece that's really inspired, an important statement."

(Endorsement of the work's quality later came from another, unexpected quarter. "As soon as I saw this score I decided to do it," said conductor Dimitri Kitayenko of the Moscow Philharmonic; to great acclaim, he performed the *Requiem* in Tchaikovsky Hall in January 1989 assisted by the Latvian State Choir under Imants Cepitis. "What I like is the work's obvious emotion," said Cepitis. "Today, composers of choral music—both here and, I think, in the West—are usually too afraid of writing tunes which express emotion so openly." Lloyd Webber's music was far from unknown in the Soviet Union. In May 1988 the Vienna cast of *Cats* brought the show to Moscow for two sold-out weeks, and *Jesus Christ Superstar*—*Jayzus Kreestus Superstar*—had been an underground hit in pre-*glasnost* days.)

Despite its flaws, the *Requiem* was a pivotal work in Lloyd Webber's career. He had frankly offered both *Superstar* and *Evita* as operas, and no one had believed him; they could not get past the Elvisisms. Now, at last, he had thrown aside all pretense of being a pop composer—that had died with *Starlight Express*—and was testing the limits of his talent. In a way, the *Requiem* was the graduation exercise he had never written at the Royal College of Music; Bill would have been proud.

Whatever the ultimate fate of the *Requiem,* the piece had accomplished its most important objective. Even more important than writing something for Sarah, it had given Andrew the technical tools that he would need for his next major work for the theater. The reviews were worrying, of course. He was beginning to think that no one in America was ever going to like him, which was one of the reasons he was forever blowing hot and cold about living in New York some day. Although Andrew now had money, property, and reputation, none of that could buy him what he most craved: respect.

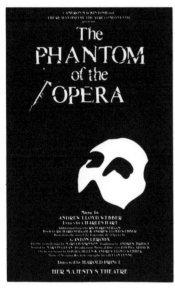

In late 1984, while browsing in a secondhand bookshop in New York City, Lloyd Webber stumbled across a copy of Gaston Leroux's 1910 novel, *Le Fantome de l'opéra*. To most people, if they thought about it at all, Leroux's perfumed thriller about a hideously deformed Svengali and his beautiful operatic Trilby was an unread work of once-popular literature best known as the basis of Lon Chaney's 1926 silent-movie version and of the talkie remakes starring Claude Rains and Herbert Lom. It was no more likely to be made into a successful musical than, say, the life of Eva Perón or the poetry of T. S. Eliot.

Andrew, however, saw it differently: to him, it was the romantic opera plot he had been looking for. He had been thinking about *Phantom* for several months. Just after she married Andrew, Sarah Brightman had been asked to star as the heroine Christine Daaé in playwright Ken Hill's musical adaptation of *The Phantom of the Opera* being staged at Stratford East in London, and Andrew and Cameron Mackintosh went round to see it. It was a speculative visit, for not only did they want to judge whether Hill's *Phantom* was a suitable vehicle for Sarah, they were also considering producing the show.*

Hill's concept was to combine the Leroux story with real operatic excerpts of the period. After seeing it, Lloyd Webber and Mackintosh sought the advice of director Jim Sharman, who had made *Superstar* a hit in London and had later won cult status as the director of *The Rocky Horror Show*. Sharman said he thought Hill's *Phantom* was too much of a comic romp and that it wouldn't be interesting unless Andrew wrote the music himself. Mackintosh and Lloyd Webber agreed, and they dropped the project. (In September 1988 Hill's show crossed the Atlantic to play in San Francisco. Plans for a Broadway opening never materialized.)

Still, the idea of a musical about the phantom stayed with Lloyd Webber, and the more he thought about it, the better it seemed. He was tired of hearing the accusation that his musicals were devoid of real emotions, that he didn't write shows about people, only about gods, demigods, cats, and trains—tired of it, and more than a little conscious of its truth. For the fact was that Lloyd Webber *was* cool and aloof, at times brusque or even rude. Part of this was appearances: Andrew was naturally shy around strangers, and his British reserve came in handy as a defense against unwanted familiarity. In particular, he could not understand those glad-handing, back-slapping Americans who were always trying to reach out and touch someone. He held the world at arm's length, and, the more successful he got, the more he wanted to keep it that way. Another part of his reputation for remoteness, however, was real. Lloyd Webber loved Sarah Brightman, but he spoke of her coolly,

---

* Having pulled it off with *Daisy Pulls It off* the year before, the Really Useful Company was seeking other non–Lloyd Webber material. In 1984 the company offered Melvyn Bragg and Howard Goodall's *The Hired Man*, followed by Ken Ludwig's *Lend Me a Tenor* in 1986, and Willy Russell's *Shirley Valentine* in 1988. In 1989 the latter two productions were successfully transferred to Broadway.

and although the newlyweds periodically sat for some silly "living and loving together" press stories, one rarely saw them displaying affection in public. His late father he regarded dispassionately, almost as if Bill had been someone else's dad. The volatile temper—usually triggered when Andrew felt particularly pressed or criticized—was often his only visible emotion, the only time the molten core ever bubbled to the surface; but it was when he talked about his childhood and the way his mother had always seemed to care more about John Lill or her Gibraltar boys than about him or Julian, that the hurt really showed.

At first, he thought *Aspects of Love* was going to give him the emotional release he was looking for. The David Garnett novella—the story of a libidinous extended family who wage war upon each other with that most lethal of weapons, sex—seemed tailor-made for venting his emotions. *Aspects,* however, wasn't turning out as he had hoped. In 1983 he had written much of the score for his "cabaret" to words by Trevor Nunn, but the music and the text had seemed at odds and, much as he loved his tunes, he knew they weren't going to work for this particular story. But they would come in handy someday; that's what drawers were for.

Why weren't the tunes right? Even discounting the social infelicity of "Married Man," the song Sarah Brightman had sung at the 1983 Sydmonton Festival while Andrew was still married to his first wife, Lloyd Webber realized that the melodies he had composed for the cabaret were too gaudy for the finely shaded text; he needed a bigger, larger-than-life story to hang them on. In 1985 he was thirty-seven years old, and he had been working in the theater for nearly half his life. He knew when a show wasn't working, and *Aspects of Love* was not working.

He also knew that some considered his whole career a matter of luck and timing, like hitting a number on the roulette wheel at Deauville four times in a row (how quickly they forgot about *Jeeves*). In his heart, he knew they were wrong. Lloyd Webber was proud of his hard-won technique, proud of his theatrical savvy. Where was the luck? Each time they said it couldn't be done—that Christ was no subject for an opera, that Evita was a she-devil, that the British could never produce a successful dance musical, especially one about cats, that trains was an impossible subject for a show—and he had done it. In Britain he was a celebrity, and talk was starting that a knighthood was in his future. Didn't that prove something?

The fact was that art and commerce had long been wrestling within Lloyd Webber's breast, with victory usually going to the latter. No matter how hard he tried, it seemed, he just couldn't help himself; in the end, the marketer always took over from the artist. The "Pie Jesu" was only one example, just the kind of thing that left him open to accusations of media hype. Because, at the end of the day (a British locution Lloyd Webber much favored), his shows *were* generally accompanied by a lot of attention, fuss, hype—not all of it of his own devising, to be sure, but laid at his door nonetheless.

Although America had been paying the rent since the *Jesus Christ Superstar* album and, latterly, the Broadway production of *Cats,* many of the important critics there still remained remarkably resistant to the charms of Lloyd Webber's shows, which hurt the composer's pride; they couldn't get past the hype. Ever since the *Superstar* album miracle and the O'Horgan stage debacle, Andrew had been obsessed with his reputation in the United States. Did the Americans like him or didn't they? The critics were so inconsistent, so hard to figure out, blasting *Superstar* and hammering *Evita,* then turning around and awarding the latter show a fistful of prizes and praising the *Joseph* revival on Broadway. And *Cats,* what was one to make of its reception? Some called it irresistible, and others were allergic to it—"Something has just peed on your pants leg," indeed. Still, the money kept rolling in.

For some time, Lloyd Webber had been thinking about moving to New York. Back in the bad old days of the Labour government, he had contemplated leaving England for tax reasons, but Mrs. Thatcher's reforms had alleviated the fiduciary cause of his distress; a bright lad could make, and keep, some proper money in England now. New York had its attractions, though. In 1976 he had seen an apartment on the top floor of one of the best buildings on Central Park West. In the depths of Manhattan's real-estate slump the price was a bargain at one hundred and ten thousand dollars—a decade later the apartment would be worth ten times that—but his accountant talked him out of purchasing it because the man didn't think Andrew should get involved with paying taxes in the United States.

Now Lloyd Webber's thoughts were turning toward New York again. In 1984 he and Sarah moved out of his old flat in Eaton Place and moved to 45 Green Street, in Mayfair, where they lived in the top two floors of an apartment complex built in the 1920s. Of course, they had Sydmonton Court as well, but Andrew thought that maybe it was time to start looking for a little pied-à-terre in Manhattan as well; Sarah liked New York. She was, in fact, one of those English girls for whom Manhattan was irresistible, just like the heroine of *Tell Me on a Sunday.**
Lloyd Webber had a soft spot for that piece and for its theatrical form, *Song and Dance,* and he wanted to take it to America. He realized, however, that the London version of *Song and Dance* was not suitable for export, for the problems with *Tell Me on a Sunday* had only been glossed over, not corrected.

---

*Earlier in 1984, Brightman released "Unexpected Song" and "Come Back with the Same Look in Your Eyes" as a single for RCA, the performances taken from her video of the show, which had been taped before a live audience in the Palace Theatre.

As luck would have it, Lloyd Webber, accompanied by Nunn, that year caught a delightful show on Broadway called *Baby*, with music by David Shire and lyrics and direction by Richard Maltby, Jr. Impressed, Andrew invited Maltby to England, ostensibly to talk over a new project but in reality to sound him out about revising and directing *Song and Dance* for America. The first half of the show, Lloyd Webber pointed out, is told entirely in song, so it would be helpful if the director were also a lyricist: "Someone like you, Richard," Andrew said.

Maltby knew he had a big job on his hands, not the least of which was to adapt, change, and throw out, if need be, large chunks of Black's original text. No theater professional is renowned for his or her selflessness, but the soft-spoken, gentle Black was not given to fits of egomania, and he agreed to work with Maltby on the revisions, or at least not to get in his way. The first order of business was to make the lead character more real and more sympathetic, so in short order she was given a name (Emma), a profession (milliner), and a boyfriend named Joe (from Nebraska). The order of the *Sunday* songs was rearranged once again ("Take That Look off Your Face," for example, was restored to its original album position as the first song of the show), and new songs were written, including the belter, "English Girls," and "So Much to Do in New York." Oddly, one of the best songs of the London stage version, "The Last Man in My Life," was dropped. For the *Dance* section, choreographer Peter Martins of the New York City Ballet was enlisted to refashion the movement entirely. To tie the two sections together more effectively, Lloyd Webber injected some of the *Variations* tunes into the *Song* half. The final stroke was the casting: Bernadette Peters, New York City's favorite Kewpie doll, as Emma, with dancer Christopher d'Amboise as Joe, the midwestern cowboy.

The all-American *Song and Dance* was tried out at a workshop production in New York in March 1985; four months later it went to the summer theater festival in Williamstown, Massachusetts, for a week. Previews at the Royale Theater in Manhattan started on September 4, and the show officially opened on September 18, 1985.

By now, it came as no surprise to Lloyd Webber that the show should fail to find favor with Frank Rich of *The New York Times.* "Empty material remains empty, no matter how talented those who perform it," Rich began:

> Describing herself as "a girl who lets men take advantage," Emma devotes most of her 20-odd songs to sulking about her misadventures with various, unseen men who take her to bed and then kick her into the street. The authors treat her almost as shabbily. They don't bother to examine Emma—they merely exploit her. For all the time we spend with this woman, we learn little about her beyond her sexual activities. She is an empty-headed tramp with a heart of gold, exhumed from the graveyard of sexist stereotypes, and her mechanically told story might as well be the song delivered by Perón's discarded mistress in Mr. Lloyd Webber's "Evita" ("Another Suitcase, Another Hall") played over and over, as if on a maddening film loop.

Of the music, Rich wrote: "As is this composer's wont, the better songs are reprised so often that one can never be quite sure whether they are here to stay or are simply refusing to leave." The critic did, however, have kind words for Peters, an actress beyond criticism in New York.

Another notice, another hell. Rich's view was echoed by most other major critics: loved her, hated it. In *New York*, John Simon leveled the show. "This Emma could be Emma Hamilton, Emma Woodhouse, Emma Bovary, or even that concept envisioned by the poet Christian Morgenstern when he wrote that all sea gulls look as if their name were Emma," said Simon, although he too raved about Peters: "She not only sings, acts and (in the bottom half) dances to perfection, she also, superlatively, *is.*" *Time*'s Bill Henry was even more severe in his condemnation of Lloyd Webber: "No celestial choirs appear to sing in Lloyd Webber's ears, no muse or demon seems to haunt him, and his concoctions cannot bear close logical inspection. But he can beguile even sophisticated viewers into believing for the moment that they are witnessing highflying art." *Song and Dance* ran for 474 Broadway performances, except for *Jeeves* the fewest ever for a Lloyd Webber show, closing on November 8, 1986.

Song and Dance, though, was a mere bagatelle, compared with his next show. After talking it over with Mackintosh, whose advice he valued highly, Lloyd Webber decided to go ahead with his own version of *The Phantom of the Opera.* Brazenly, his first impulse was to appropriate Hill's idea of quoting real operas. Leroux's novel is rife with operatic references, especially to Gounod's *Faust*, and Andrew thought it might be fun to quote from *Faust* and other operas of the late nineteenth century, connecting them with filler material of his own device. Indeed, the first public press release he issued on the new project said that "the score for *The Phantom of the Opera* will include both existing and original music." (There was the Leoncavallo–Puccini opera notion again.)

During the autumn of 1984, while at work on the *Requiem*, Lloyd Webber, with Mackintosh, cobbled together a score of operatic greatest hits from Gounod, Delibes, and others, but this ridiculous idea was soon recognized for the lazy folly it would have been, and Andrew discarded it. Having devoured the novel, Lloyd Webber was surprised to find that the original *Phantom* story (which takes place in 1896—the same year as the premiere of *La Bohème*; there was the Puccini connection again) bore little resemblance to the later movie versions with which he was familiar. The protagonist was no vengeful composer, disfigured after having acid thrown in his face, but a savant—architect, ventriloquist, magician, composer—hopelessly, even insanely, in love with a beautiful young girl whom he sees as his passport to physical happiness and musical immortality.

This was it, the opera plot he had always wanted. Not only did it offer him the chance to write about human beings (granted that one of them was a congenitally deformed genius, a second a pliable ingenue, and a third an empty-headed aristocrat), it gave him a perfect excuse to cast Sarah Brightman with her high, pure, virginal soprano voice as the heroine, Christine. Furthermore, the large forces that the *Phantom* demanded would offer him the chance to write more complex ensembles than he ever had before, while the full-blooded nature of the story required a symphony orchestra to match. His mind made up, Lloyd Webber promised Mackintosh that as soon as the *Requiem* was finished, he would make *The Phantom of the Opera* his next priority.

Following his by now familiar modus operandi, he set about recycling the music from the aborted *Aspects of Love*. Songs first conceived to accompany a text set in Paris and the Pyrenees would be applied to the gargoyle who lurked in the bowels of the magnificent Palais Garnier—the Paris Opéra. One of the tunes from *Aspects*, "It's a Miracle," held the melodic seeds of two *Phantom* songs: "Angel of Music" and "Wishing You Were Somehow Here Again." As the show's title song, Lloyd Webber decided to reuse a rock-and-roll number that producer Mike Batt had recorded for him as a demo track in late 1984, when *Phantom* was still a pastiche idea.

Now it was time to go shopping for a lyricist. Andrew knew that Rice was not interested, for Tim by this time was working with Benny Andersson and Björn Ulvaeus of the Swedish rock group ABBA, who were composing the music for his long-planned show *Chess*. Lloyd Webber wrote to Alan Jay Lerner, and asked the veteran if he would be interested, and he was delighted when Lerner said yes. It was another boyhood dream come true: the chance to work with, as the cliché had it, one of Broadway's living legends. The lyricist of *My Fair Lady* and *Camelot* and the composer of *Cats* and *Starlight Express* seemed an unlikely match over an unlikely subject, but Lerner was impressed with Lloyd Webber's obvious passion for *Phantom* and confirmed his judgment about the stageworthiness of the story. "Don't ask why, dear boy," he told Andrew. "It just works."

Lerner, however, was able to write only a few lines before ill health forced him to give up the project (he died of cancer on June 14, 1986). So Lloyd Webber turned instead to Richard Stilgoe, his collaborator on *Starlight Express*. Stilgoe and Batt worked up some words for "The Phantom of the Opera," a song that Andrew was already eyeing as the show's first single, to be issued even before the musical was completed.*

Stilgoe also began work on a libretto, and by the summer of 1985 enough had been written to present a draft of the first act of *The Phantom of the Opera* at the Sydmonton Festival, mocked up by Lloyd Webber and the designer Maria Björnson. Even in the confined space of the Sydmonton chapel, Björnson was able to approximate such *coups de théâtre* as the plummeting chandelier that ends the act. Thirty-six years old in mid-1985, Björnson was a noted theater and opera designer (whose credits included *Der Rosenkavalier* for the Royal Opera House, *Die Walküre* for the English National Opera), who, by coincidence, lived in the flat next door to Lloyd Webber's old Gledhow Gardens haunts. An intense, driven woman, she was unmarried and lived alone. "I don't have a personal life," she told *The Daily Mail*. "My life centres on the theatre."

Nunn was surprised, to say the least, when he heard the music: here were the tunes for his songs from *Aspects of Love*, now recycled with completely different words, without even a by-your-leave. So that was how Lloyd Webber fired people: so much for Nunn as the lyricist for *Aspects*. It was a hard lesson to learn, and a hard, brutally public way to learn it—"It was a bitter pill for me to swallow," Nunn said later—but the director swallowed both the pill and his pride. He could smell another hit and hoped Andrew would let him be part of it.

Although the 1985 Sydmonton performance was *Phantom* in broad outline, musically it was still more rock than opera, and Lloyd Webber found himself once more dissatisfied with it. He was, in fact, dissatisfied with nearly everything about it (aside from Björnson's contribution): book, lyrics, and music. The cast, which included Colm Wilkinson (the original Che on records) as the Phantom, was largely drawn from Mackintosh's forthcoming production of an obscure French musical by Alain Boublil and Claude-Michel Schoenberg called *Les Misérables*.† Aside from Sarah Brightman as Christine, they would not be available. Quietly, Lloyd Webber resolved to take the opportunity to change nearly everything about *Phantom*.

---

*The song, featuring Brightman and Steve Harley, the former lead singer of the rock group Cockney Rebel, was released in January 1986, nine months before *The Phantom of the Opera* opened in London. It got as high as number seven on the charts.

†Directed by Trevor Nunn and John Caird and first performed on October 8, 1985, at the Barbican Theatre under the auspices of the Royal Shakespeare Company, *Les Misérables* moved to the Palace Theatre on December 4. Some RSC supporters were outraged by what they viewed as Mackintosh and Nunn's blatant use of the Barbican as a tryout venue from which to judge the musical's commercial potential. The RSC spent three hundred thousand pounds mounting the show and did not recoup its outlay; Mackintosh and Nunn, however, profited handsomely from the show that Mackintosh predicted would outgross *Cats* worldwide. In May 1986 Nunn resigned as RSC director. *Les Misérables* came to America in March 1987, where it repeated its success.

Some time back, Andrew had mentioned his idea to Hal Prince, and Prince was responsive. Even though Nunn was clearly angling for the assignment—indeed, had some proprietary interest—Hal, Lloyd Webber decided, was the better man for the job. Trevor was always looking for motivation, but hadn't Lerner specifically advised against doing that? Prince, on the other hand, was a master of beautiful stage pictures. He wouldn't give a damn about the Phantom's motivation or the holes in the plot; on the contrary, the steamy decadence of the story was perfect for him. In Lloyd Webber's opinion, Hal was right for *Phantom* in the way he had been wrong for *Cats* (although with that show, admittedly, it had been Prince who had asked if there was a larger meaning behind the show, and Nunn who had accepted it at face value). When Andrew had first broached the subject of *Phantom*, Hal had perked up and said, "Great! A romantic musical. Let's do it." That was just the response Andrew was looking for. Prince it would be.

Prince had been invited to attend the 1985 Sydmonton Festival, but he had turned down the offer. He didn't want any preconceptions cluttering up his mind before he had a chance to think the project through for himself. At his home in Majorca, Prince looked over the score and the libretto, and his heart sank a little. The verses struck him as poor, and there was no second act at all, but he still believed in the possibilities of the story. *Phantom*, it seemed to him, should not be a cheap horror show, but a serious piece about repressed sexuality. In August he flew to Paris to have a look at the Opéra, seeking inspiration. He went to the right place.

"If you seek my monument," said Sir Christopher Wren, architect of St. Paul's Cathedral in London, "look around you." Charles Garnier, the designer of the Opéra (his only other notable surviving building is the Casino àt Monte Carlo), could well make the same boast. Everything about the Paris Opera House is monumental. There are 2,531 doors, opened by 7,593 keys; more than six miles of underground passageways; fourteen furnaces pump heat into the house through four hundred and fifty grates; the building covers a site of nearly three acres and rises seventeen stories. For Garnier, who won the commission in a competition, too much was never enough—except in the auditorium, which seats only 2,156.

But what makes the Opéra different from any other opera house in the world is the dark subterranean lagoon that lies beneath it. More a reservoir than a lake, the visitor can see it through the dusty sub-sub-sub-basement gratings: a murky pool, 130,663.55 cubic feet of greenish water, nearly 6 feet deep, that is pumped out and replaced every ten years or so. When work on the Opéra began in 1861, at the height of the Second Empire, Garnier and his team of more than one hundred assistant architects hit water beneath the wide boulevards of Baron Haussmann's new, improved Paris. Working day and night, they spent nearly eight months pumping it out. To keep the foundation dry, Garnier designed a unique double-walled waterproof basement of concrete, cement, brick, and bitumen. When the architect calculated that ballast would be necessary to support the enormous weight of the structure above, he flooded the basement, and sediment from the water seeped into any cracks, sealing them.

The roof of the massive building is hardly less interesting. A flight of precipitous metal steps—there are no handrails—leads to the apex of the inverted V at its top. Here, rude graffiti proclaims a visit to this aerie by the Rats—not rodents, but the little ballet girls whose nineteenth-century forebears used to collect the ropes of the suicides who would string themselves up in a nook or cranny of the Opéra, disconsolate over the end of a love affair with a ballerina or singer. Possession of the ropes was thought to bring good luck. On the rooftop are two snorting statues of Pegasus and a radiant Apollo, whose golden lyre (a motif repeated throughout the house) does double duty as a lightning rod. The view is unimpeded from the Eiffel Tower to the Tour Montparnasse; according to Leroux, "[Christine] breathed freely over Paris, the whole valley of which was seen at work below."

Indeed, Leroux's book is remarkably accurate in its description of Garnier's Opéra, right down to the double set of managers the opera house routinely had in the nineteenth century—one to oversee the artistic side and the other to keep an eye on business matters. Leroux was a prominent journalist, and he had a pass that let him come and go in the Opéra as he pleased. He knew the mystery of the place. Along the miles of dark hallways, in the abandoned underground stone stables where the smell of horseflesh still lingers, things went bump in the night. "The Opéra ghost really existed," Leroux wrote in the novel's opening sentence. "He was not, as was long believed, a creature of the imagination of the artists, the superstition of the managers, or a product of the absurd and impressionable brains of the young ladies of the ballet, their mothers, the box-keepers, the cloak-room attendants or the concierge. Yes, he existed in flesh and blood. . . ."

In fact, the legend of the phantom originated with a distraught swain, rejected by one of the ballerinas, who committed suicide in the old opera house, which was then in the rue Le Peletier; the unhappy lover willed his skeleton to the props department, so he could always be near his beloved. Leroux picked up the legend and amplified it (the discovery of bones belonging to some poor unfortunates who had been killed there during the Paris Commune uprising only added to the frisson), weaving his story of the vengeful Erik and the vulnerable Christine in and around the Opéra's manifest physical reality.

Consider, for example, the real-life mystery of the cellars, which is mentioned a couple of times in the novel. Leroux wrote: "Before burying the phonographic records of the artist's voice, the workmen laid bare a corpse . . . near the little well, in the place where the Angel of Music first held Christine Daaé fainting in his trembling arms, on the night when he carried her down to the cellars of the opera house." The place is exactly as Leroux described: affixed to a sheer metal door without a doorknob is a plaque that reads: "Gift of M. Alfred Clark, 28 June, 1907. The room in which are contained the gramophone records." No one is exactly sure what is in this room, but it seems that the spot where Erik died—wearing "the plain gold ring . . . which Christine Daaé had certainly slipped on his finger, when she came to bury him in accordance with her promise"—is a time capsule, not to be opened until 2007. Clark was the director of the Berliner Record Company in Paris in the first decade of the twentieth century, so it is likely that the sealed vault contains a representative sample of his company's wares of the period.* Prince took all this in eagerly. He liked the dark, gloomy, romantic atmosphere and wanted to capture it in his production. He had no worries about Björnson, whose portfolio had been sent to him in Paris; now it was up to Lloyd Webber to reproduce it in his music. If Andrew did, they would have a big hit on their hands. Both Prince and Lloyd Webber sensed that the moment for the megamusical had passed (*Starlight Express* and Dave Clark's *Time* had seen to that), but romance is something that never goes out of style. Mix it up with a little Grand Guignol, as Prince and Sondheim had done in *Sweeney Todd,* and you wouldn't be able to keep 'em away. The love interest was important: *Todd* had been a critical success but had not played as long as expected, in part owing to a lack of warmth. The hero and the girl in that show had been attractive enough, but the bloodthirsty barber and his amoral paramour had gotten all of the best tunes. Lloyd Webber would have to be careful that his phantom didn't walk off with the show.

Sanguine about his chances for success, Prince returned to New York.† Almost immediately, he was visited by Mackintosh, who took Prince to lunch. There was a ticklish situation back in London, the English producer began, and Prince sensed what was coming. Trevor, you see, had thought *The Phantom of the Opera* had been promised to him and, well, er, Mackintosh and Lloyd Webber thought they had better let Nunn have it. Terribly sorry about this but. . . .Angry and hurt, Prince got to his feet and left the restaurant, leaving Mackintosh still sputtering apologies across the table.

Back in his office, Prince gathered up all his notes on *Phantom* and stuffed them into an envelope. "Put this in a file where you can get your hands on it quickly," he said to his assistant. "They'll be back." Sure enough, they were. A few weeks later, Prince got a call from Lloyd Webber's office in London. There had been a terrible mistake, the show was Prince's all along, Mr. Lloyd Webber had personally intervened in favor of Prince and, well, er, would Mr. Prince please reconsider directing the show after all? Mr. Prince would.

If any incident demonstrated Lloyd Webber's commanding position in the musical theater, it was this one. With hardly an apology, he could play fast and loose with two of the most prominent directors in the English-speaking theater—and make them dance to his tune. Lloyd Webber was a changeable sort, the Rum Tum Tugger of composers, but he was also fervent in his desire to get the best man for the job. For some reason, he and Nunn had had a falling out—according to some witnesses, they practically came to blows—most likely over the artistic wasteland of *Starlight Express.* Maybe it had something to do with Nunn's resentment over the cavalier way Lloyd Webber had treated their songs for *Aspects of Love,* summarily snatching the music out from under Nunn's words and reusing it in *Phantom.* Whatever the case, Prince was back on the scene.

But they still needed a lyricist. Stilgoe, whose limited gifts were not up to the poetic demands of the story, was concentrating on the book, plotting out the show in collaboration with the composer. In April 1986 Lloyd Webber once again found himself in the position of casting about for a songwriter, but this time he was out of ideas. Fortunately, Mackintosh was not. A year earlier, the impresario had been a judge in the competition for the Vivian Ellis Prize, given by the Performing Rights Society to encourage young composers and librettists. One of the finalists was Charles Hart, a twenty-four-year-old Londoner who had entered an unproduced show about Moll Flanders, for which he had written both words and music. Hart did not win, but Mackintosh was impressed. "A good lyricist is a rare beast," he said to Hart. "Would you be interested in writing some on-spec lyrics to one of Andrew Lloyd Webber's tunes?"

Hart was, but a year passed before Mackintosh was heard from again, during which time Hart bumped around, working as an assistant musical director on forgettable shows such as *Adrian Mole* and *Blockheads.* Suddenly, Mackintosh reappeared, delivering a cassette tape to Hart of the maestro playing an unnamed Lloyd Webber tune and asking him to outfit it with words. Hart did, thrice over: "Look at Us," "Knowing Him," and, the title that eventually stuck, "Think of Me." Both Mackintosh and Lloyd Webber were delighted, and Hart was duly

---

*Since the author made this discovery on a visit to Paris in 1987, the Opéra has been petitioned to open the room in the interests of scholarship and preservation. As late as 1989, however, the administration remained adamant in its intention to honor Clark's wishes and keep the room sealed.

†Prince needed a hit. After bombing with *Merrily We Roll Along* in 1981, his long-term professional relationship with Stephen Sondheim had come to at least a temporary end. Lloyd Webber knew it, too. Responding to the common criticism that his own shows were nothing without clever stage direction, Andrew snapped to an interviewer early in 1985: "They said *Evita* was nothing without Hal Prince. But what was Hal Prince done since *Evita* that's been successful?" Prince's string of flops included *Merrily, A Doll's House,* and *Grind.*

summoned to meet Mackintosh and Lloyd Webber in the latter's office on the fourth floor of the Palace Theatre. By this time *The Phantom of the Opera* was well underway; Brightman and Harley had a hit with the Lloyd Webber–Stilgoe title track, which had been heavily promoted by means of a video directed by the flamboyant Ken Russell, and Sarah and the ageless Cliff Richard's version of the duet "All I Ask of You" was scheduled for a May release. It was rather late in the day to be hiring a lyricist.

Nevertheless, Lloyd Webber and Mackintosh were quickly convinced they had found their man. They had asked Hart to read Leroux's novel and to be prepared to discuss it. During the interview, they peppered him with questions: what did Hart think of the property? Could it be made into a musical? What did he think he could add to it? Andrew, as always, was intense, brusque, and hyperactive, his words sometimes tumbling out so fast that his tongue tripped over them, and he made the novice nervous. Throughout the meeting, Hart had been struggling with his coffee cup in a desperate attempt to pick it up and actually drink some of its contents without spilling it. Solicitously, Lloyd Webber asked him if he would like some more but then proceeded to top off the coffee with fresh tea. Too polite and too terrified to say anything, Hart swallowed hard and drank it down. He got the job, and within three months the lyrics were ready.

Although the broad outline of Leroux's tale was maintained—the Phantom would be the polymath his author had envisaged, not merely a vindictive and demented composer—the plot was streamlined, and some major characters, such as the Persian, were eliminated. The crucial change, though, was the decision to reprise the Phantom's dramatic unmasking at the end and make it pathetically public. This led to Lloyd Webber's idea of actually composing the work only alluded to in the book, Erik's opera *Don Juan Triumphant,* and to his notion of writing pastiches of composers whose works might have been in the Opéra's repertoire at the time—Meyerbeer, for example, and Salieri. Thus, Lloyd Webber's *Phantom* began to take on solid form.

About this time, press reports began to filter out about the latest Lloyd Webber project. By now, Andrew was such a public figure in Britain that nothing he did remained secret very long. Part of this was due to his own volubility: although he had a well-deserved reputation in the media for prickliness, he was also constitutionally incapable of keeping a secret. But, to an even greater extent, it was due to the well-oiled publicity and marketing machine that the Really Useful Company had become. For the fiscal year ending June 30, 1985, the company reported a profit of nearly four million dollars on revenues of more than seventeen million dollars, up almost a million and a half dollars from the year before. The Little Engine That Could, did.

On January 6, 1986, therefore, Brian Brolly, the managing director, and Lloyd Webber, the executive director, took the Really Useful Company public as the Really Useful Group, plc. The corporate logo was a Swiss army knife. Four million shares were offered at a price of three pounds and thirty pence per share, or about four dollars and fifty-nine cents. Lloyd Webber, who sold just under three million shares, made more than ten million dollars from the offering, while still retaining a 40-percent stake in the company he had founded eight years before; Brolly owned 15 percent. For the City, the offering was something of a flier, since the assets of the group consisted of the rights to Lloyd Webber's shows from *Cats* on, the Palace Theatre, and, later, its offices in the restored Soho townhouse at 20 Greek Street. As part of the deal, Lloyd Webber signed a contract giving the Really Useful Group exclusive rights to his services for seven years, for which he would receive 5 percent of the box-office receipts. As an executive director of the new company, Lloyd Webber was also paid a salary of forty thousand pounds a year, but he resigned that position in September 1986, just before *Phantom* opened, to take a thirty-thousand-pound cut in pay as a nonexecutive director on the nine-member board. To Lloyd Webber's great joy, Tim Rice agreed to join the board as another nonexecutive director. Rice was full of hope that this gesture meant he and Andrew would work together again, and the talk began once again that the erstwhile partners might reunite some day.

The hope, in fact, was realized. In the summer of 1986 Lloyd Webber and Rice collaborated on a short piece for the queen's sixtieth birthday, commissioned by the queen's youngest son, Prince Edward.* The work was called *Cricket,* after Rice's special passion. Directed by Trevor Nunn, the June 18 performance took place at Windsor Castle. There were eleven songs, with titles such as "The Summer Game," "Fools Like Me," and "The Final Stand." The cast included Ian Charleson, John Savident, and Sarah Payne, and the band was made up of the same musicians who had played on *Variations*: Rod Argent, Jon Hiseman, John Mole, and Barbara Thompson. Later in the summer, *Cricket* was reprised at Sydmonton and again in the fall in London at a dinner for Tim's favorite charity, the Lord's Taverners.

Cricket, however, proved nothing more than a diversion for Andrew. *Phantom* was the real business at hand. That same summer, the English papers were full of stories about Lloyd Webber's new musical. On one thing they all agreed: this time the composer did not want to offer his show "pre-sold with a lot of advance hype," as he put it. "I wanted to write from my heart rather than with my head," he explained. Although the Webber head rarely nodded, even when the heart was engaged, *The Phantom of the Opera* was to be Lloyd Webber's most daring

---

*In January 1988, Prince Edward, using the name Edward Windsor, joined the staff of the Really Useful Group as a production assistant, the lowest rung of the theatrical ladder.

and sophisticated score, and it perceptibly changed his reputation. Musicians who had remained resistant to the charms of his melodies suddenly began to take notice, and those for whom opera was not by definition a dead art form quickly realized that here, indeed, was a serious new work.

After less than two weeks of previews, two of which were canceled (at a cost of thirty thousand pounds and considerable goodwill from those holding tickets) due to technical problems, *The Phantom of the Opera* opened on Thursday, October 9, 1986, at Her Majesty's Theatre in Haymarket—the site of the *Jeeves* disaster. The joint producers were Cameron Mackintosh and the Really Useful Theatre Company, Ltd.—a sign that the Really Useful Group still needed Mackintosh's expertise. Mackintosh's clout was such that, in June, the show's advertising was changed from the "Andrew Lloyd Webber/Hal Prince musical" to "Cameron Mackintosh and The Really Useful Theatre Company, Ltd. Present. . . ." Hyped or not, the public needed no convincing. It took to *The Phantom* at once, cherishing it for its electric pacing, its romantic, tear-jerking story, and its Spielbergian roller-coaster ride of scenic chills, thrills, and spills. Lerner was right: don't ask why, it just works.*
The Phantom of the Opera opens with a short prologue, set among the dusty artifacts of the fictional Opéra Populaire, which are being auctioned off. Raoul, the seventy-year-old Vicomte de Chagny, first buys a poster from an old production of the opera *Hannibal* by "Chalumeau." The auctioneer brings out a papier-mâché monkey playing a barrel organ, and Raoul's reminiscences are immediately triggered when the music box plays a tune that later becomes the choral number that will begin the second act, "Masquerade":

> *A collector's*
> *piece indeed . . .*
> *every detail*
> *exactly as she said . . .*

> *She often*
> *spoke of you my friend . . .*
> *your velvet lining*
> *and your figurine of lead . . .*

> *Will you still play, when*
> *all the rest of us are dead . . .*

The auctioneer continues, coming to his prize: "A chandelier in pieces. Some of you may recall the strange affair of the Phantom of the Opera: a mystery never fully explained. We are told, ladies and gentlemen, that this is the very chandelier which figures in the famous disaster." Restored and equipped with electric lights, the chandelier is once again functional, the auctioneer explains, while beneath his spoken words the orchestra ruminates on a tune that will be associated with the Phantom's lair. "Perhaps we may frighten away the ghost of so many years ago with a little illumination, gentlemen?"

With a flash of light, the draperies fall away and the chandelier, modeled to look like the real one in the Paris Opera House, rises and begins its ascent to the roof of the theater.† The thunderous chords of the Overture give immediate evidence that *The Phantom of the Opera* is to be a funhouse ride: Andrew Lloyd Webber in the Temple of Doom. A blasting B-flat-minor chord descends stepwise to G-flat major, then back up again, while the bass line pounds out a gloomy theme that evokes the air of mystery that surrounds the Phantom. The music swells to a climax then suddenly falls away to reveal the first scene—a rehearsal of *Hannibal*.

The charge of being a pastiche artist had dogged Lloyd Webber for so long that it must have amused him to embrace it wholeheartedly in the work that, paradoxically, turned out to be his most original score. The *Hannibal* scene is mock-Meyerbeer (an inside joke since Meyerbeer is practically synonymous with second-rate, overblown opera), and it introduces the principals: the temperamental prima donna, Carlotta Giudicelli, the portly primo uomo, Ubaldo Piangi (another joke, since *piangere* in Italian means "to cry"), the two theater owners, Messrs. Firmin and André, the slightly sinister Madame Giry, her daughter Meg, and the chorus girl, Christine Daaé.

---

* Steven Spielberg, for one, didn't ask. As soon as the *Phantom* opened in London, there were reports that the director had optioned the movie rights.
† This seemed one of Prince's few miscalculations, since it vitiated the shock of the chandelier's fall at the end of the act.

As the rehearsal breaks up, Firmin and André, who have just taken over the direction of the house, request to hear "Elissa's third-act aria" from *Hannibal,* to which Carlotta graciously assents. The ballad, more Balfe than Meyerbeer, is "Think of Me," and it begins with a simple piano accompaniment, marked "like Schubert" in the score:

> *Think of me,*
> *think of me fondly,*
> *when we've said*
> *goodbye.*
> *Remember me*
> *once in a while —*
> *please promise me*
> *you'll try.*
>
> *When you find*
> *that, once*
> *again, you long to take your heart back*
> *and be free —*
> *if you*
> *ever find*
> *a moment*
> *spare a thought*
> *for me . . .*

Carlotta, however, gets no farther than the word "heart" in the second verse, for just at that moment a painted backdrop crashes down, terrifying the soprano and causing her to storm off, and evoking a round of "He's here! The Phantom of the Opera" squeals from the chorus girls. Madame Giry steps forward to tell the new managers that the Opera Ghost welcomes them to his domain and commands them to leave Box Five empty at each performance for his personal use — and, of course, to continue to remit his salary of twenty thousand francs a month.

Carlotta's discomfiture proves to be Christine's opportunity, and she steps up, at Meg Giry's urging, to sing "Think of Me." In mid-verse, the scene is transformed into the Opera Gala, at which Christine hits a final high B-flat and is hailed by the crowd as a brilliant new discovery. In the audience is the company's patron, the Vicomte de Chagny, who at once recognizes Christine as his playmate from childhood. As Christine heads for her dressing room after the show, she hears a strange, unearthly voice, half whispering, half singing: *"Bravi, bravi, bravissimi."* Turning, she sees only Meg, to whom she explains the source of her newly revealed artistry in the song "Angel of Music": She has an unseen teacher who predicts great things for her.

"Angel of Music" is in D-flat, the key that means "resonance" to Lloyd Webber. The tune sprang from the discarded "It's a Miracle" of *Aspects of Love,* a dotted-rhythm roundelay in 6/8 in which Christine psychologically equates her dead father (an itinerant Swedish violinist) with her invisible tutor. When Raoul comes backstage to greet her, waiting outside her room until she has changed, the voice of the Phantom is heard again, to the tune of "Angel of Music":

> *Insolent boy!*
> *This slave*
> *of fashion,*
> *basking in your*
> *glory!*
>
> *Ignorant fool!*
> *This brave*
> *young suitor,*
> *sharing in my*
> *triumph!*

In the show's first *coup de théâtre*, Christine looks into her mirror and suddenly sees the Phantom there, impeccably attired in formal clothes, a half-mask covering his face. He beckons and she steps into the mirror, vanishing.

Down they go, into the heart of darkness, the Phantom leading Christine by hand as, in another scenic coup, they descend into the depths of the Opera House and sail across its underground lake. Their song is "The Phantom of the Opera," a G-minor rocker that was a holdover from the 1985 Sydmonton version. (This song's even earlier first draft was called "I Walk the Floor," a Nunn inspiration during the brief time in which he was *Phantom*'s director that was meant to show off Brightman's chest voice and lower register, in contrast to her high, pure soprano. The notion was that she would be a sleepwalker, who sang high only in her sleep.*) The Phantom's ghostly chromatic chords stalk the song as he tells Christine that she is now irrevocably in his thrall:

> *Sing once*
> *again with me*
> *our strange*
> *duet . . .*
> *My power*
> *over you*
> *grows stronger*
> *yet . . .*

They are in the Phantom's lair. Since he first heard Christine sing, the Phantom has needed her for his music, and he pours out his feelings in his credo, "The Music of the Night." This song was "Married Man" of the first *Aspects*, but unaware of its origin, few could imagine that the ravishing lullaby was not created specifically for this moment. In the key of C-sharp major, the enharmonic equivalent of D-flat (since, on the piano, C-sharp and D-Flat are the same note), the Phantom invites Christine to join him in darkness:

> *Floating, falling,*
> *sweet intoxication!*
> *Touch me, trust me,*
> *savour each sensation!*
> *Let the dream begin,*
> *let your darker side give in*
> *to the power of*
> *the music that I write—*
> *the power of*
> *the music of the night . . .*
> *You alone*
> *can make my song take flight—*
> *help me make the music of the night . . .*

The ending of the song is extraordinary. As the Phantom holds the tonic note, a C-sharp, the orchestra slides slowly from an F-sharp chord to a D-sharp minor to a D minor to a C major, finally alighting back on a C-sharp minor sonority: the same sequence of chords that will end the show. Poignant and piquant all at once, psychologically insightful and dramatically correct, it is the moment when the audience collectively realizes that it has come to the right place.

The next morning, Christine awakes to find the Phantom busily at work composing his opera. She sneaks behind him and rips off his mask. "Damn you!" he screams at her. "You little prying Pandora, you little demon—is this what you wanted to see!" Christine alone sees the Phantom's face at this point; the audience receives only a glimpse of his deformity before the Phantom hastily covers himself again.

As Christine is returned to the world above, the worried theater managers wonder where she went in a comic duet, "Notes." This scene and the ensemble that follows is Lloyd Webber's most expert writing, gradually adding characters—Raoul, Carlotta, Madame and Meg Giry, and Piangi—until a fine ensemble is achieved. In a series of messages, the Phantom has demanded that Christine play the lead in the company's

---

*In 1988, an amateur songwriter named John Brett sued Lloyd Webber, claiming that the melodies of "The Phantom of the Opera" and "Angel of Music" had been pirated from songs Brett had submitted in 1985 to Rice and Elaine Paige—an absurd contention since (a) the Sydmonton *Phantom* had taken place nearly a month before Brett said he sent in his songs and (b) both Lloyd Webber numbers dated from the 1983 version of *Aspects of Love*.

forthcoming production of *Il Muto* by one "Albrizzio," but in the glorious septet, "Prima Donna," the managers try to reassure their angry diva of her place in their affections. The deft writing of this gracious C-major waltz, which modulates to B-flat halfway through, is expert and varied. Lloyd Webber had come a long way from "Banjo Boy."*

Their resistance, however, proves foolhardy when, during *Il Muto*, the Phantom, an expert ventriloquist, suddenly makes it appear that Carlotta is croaking like a frog. "Behold! She is singing to bring down the chandelier!" cries the Phantom from one of his aeries. Flustered, Carlotta decamps at once, and the managers call for the ballet until such time as Christine can change costumes and take over the lead. But the ballet is interrupted by a grisly occurrence, when the body of the stagehand Joseph Buquet suddenly dangles on stage at the end of a rope as an object lesson to those who would defy the Phantom. The distinctive whole-tone scale that is associated with the Phantom's music, and with *Don Juan Triumphant* in particular, now rings out.

Amid confusion, Christine and Raoul flee to the roof, the one place in the Opera House that they might be safe. There they sing the love duet "All I Ask of You," once again written in the key of D-flat. (Unlike *Cats*, the key scheme of *Phantom* does not become monotonous, despite its heavy reliance on the darker flat keys. Lloyd Webber modulates frequently, and both the chromatic and whole-tone scales associated with the Phantom often result in a deliberately ambiguous tonality.) Richard Rodgers may have been Andrew's idol, but there is precious little overt Rodgers influence in his music—except for this song:

> *Then say you'll share with*
> *me one*
> *love, one lifetime . . .*
> *let me lead you*
> *from your solitude . . .*
>
> *Say you need me*
> *with you*
> *here, beside you . . .*
> *anywhere you go,*
> *let me go too—*
> *Christine,*
> *that's all I ask*
> *of you . . .*

As the duet ends, the lovers exchange their first kiss; unseen, the Phantom is watching them. He is crushed by Christine's avowal of love for Raoul and, to the melody of the duet, he mourns:

> *I gave you my music . . .*
> *made your song take wing . . .*
> *and now, how you've*
> *repaid me:*
> *denied me*
> *and betrayed me . . .*

Angered, he takes his revenge. The scene cuts swiftly to the performance of *Il Muto* in which Christine is singing the lead. As the performers take their bows, the Phantom swings the massive chandelier back and forth, laughing maniacally. With a demented shout of "Go!!" he sends the fixture plummeting to the stage. With this incredible coup, the first act of *Phantom* ends.†

---

*At Prince's suggestion, the septet, originally a sextet (Meg Giry was added to it later), replaced an unsuitable comic number called "Box Five."

†Like much of *Phantom*, the incident of the chandelier, which is found in Leroux, is grounded in fact. On May 20, 1896, a counterweight—not the seven-ton, 400-bulbed chandelier itself, built by Lacarriere and Delatour—fell at the end of the first act of *Thétis and Pélée* (not *Faust*, as in the book) at exactly 8:57 p.m., killing a fifty-six-year-old concierge from the rue Rochechouart named Madame Chomette. It was the unhappy lady's first, and last, visit to the opera. The next day, the papers trumpeted: "Two Hundred Kilos on the Head of a Concierge!" although in fact it was more nearly eight hundred.

Act Two takes place six months later, at a New Year's Eve masked ball on the grand staircase of the Opera House. A brief bit of stage business for the two managers leads directly to "Masquerade," an impressive C-major choral number and, later, dance:

> *Masquerade!*
> *Grinning yellows,*
> *spinning reds . . .*
> *Masquerade!*
> *Take your fill—*
> *let the spectacle*
> *astound you!*

The merriment is abruptly broken off when a reveler attired as Poe's Red Death materializes at the top of the stairs. Musically, the clash of revelry and horror is represented by the cadence: the chorus, now singing in E-flat, is undercut by a crashing C-minor chord for the Phantom, followed by his funhouse chromatic slide. (Lloyd Webber had previously used this cadence near the end of *Requiem.*) The Phantom announces that he has written an opera and directs the managers to produce it. Spying a chain around Christine's neck, which holds her engagement ring from Raoul, he cries: "Your chains are still mine—you will sing for me!"

In a backstage corridor, Raoul collars Madame Giry, the Phantom's go-between, and demands that she tell him what she knows. Giry briefly tells Erik's history, sticking close to Leroux—a circus freak, deformed from birth, who was also a prodigy: scholar, architect, and musician alike, who had taken up residence in the building he helped construct, the Opera House.

The next scene takes place in the managers' office, rhythmically tricky in 15/16 and 7/8 ("Ludicrous! Have you seen the score?") that leads to a reprise of "Notes." Raoul argues that they should stage the Phantom's opera and set a trap for the composer. Christine, however, demurs. To a sinuous, free-floating melody that is more expansive than most of Lloyd Webber's tunes, she sings: "Can I betray the man who once inspired my voice? Do I become his prey? Do I have any choice? . . . Oh, God—If I agree what horrors wait for me in this, the Phantom's opera . . .?"

Despite her qualms, *Don Juan Triumphant* goes into rehearsal. There is some amusing byplay concerning Piangi, who finds the whole-tone scale impossible to sing and insists on a more conventional melody.* This causes an uproar among the chorus, which is also struggling with its music; just as the rehearsal is threatening to deteriorate completely, the piano suddenly comes to life and plays the passage by itself. The ghostly manifestation sends Christine into a trance, and she rushes off, to the graveyard in Perros where her father is buried, to seek solace. There follows one of the score's big numbers, Christine's "Wishing You Were Somehow Here Again." It begins in G minor but moves to the parallel major almost immediately; throughout it continues to shift back and forth between the major and the minor:

> *Wishing you were*
> *somehow here again . . .*
> *wishing you were*
> *somehow near . . .*
> *Sometimes it seemed,*
> *if I just dreamed,*
> *somehow you would*
> *be here . . .*

Naturally, the Phantom is nearby. (Why? Don't ask, dear boy. He just is.) Preying on Christine's vulnerability and confusion regarding her father and the father figures in her life, he attempts to lure her back: "Wandering child . . . so lost . . . so helpless," he sings seductively, to the melody of "Angel of Music." Raoul now turns up, too, and a war for Christine's body and soul ensues (a fine trio, based on "Angel of Music"), in which Raoul emerges victorious. Hurling imprecations and magic fireballs alike, the Phantom curses: "Now let it be war upon you *both*!"

The action moves back to the Opera House. Raoul and the managers have positioned police marksmen around the theater, ready for anything. *Don Juan Triumphant* begins, with a massive chorus like something out of Britten's *Peter Grimes* (here, the ghost of Bill Lloyd

---

*Use of the whole-tone scale was considered innovative and daring in the late nineteenth century; it figures prominently in the works of Debussy. Even today, it still sounds different and difficult to some: "If the Phantom is supposed to be such a brilliant musician," a woman wrote to Lloyd Webber, "why does he write such horrible music?"

Michael Crawford as the Phantom of the Opera.

Phantom *included several operatic pastiches. Top: A scene from* Hannibal, *the mock-Meyerbeer grand opera that opens the show. Above: Piangi and Carlotta study with incomprehension the score of the Phantom's own opera,* Don Juan Triumphant. *Right: Christine (Sarah Brightman) hears the ghostly voice of the Angel of Music in her dressing room.*

Opposite:

On one of Björnson's most dazzling sets, the big choral number "Masquerade" *opens the second act. The Japanese production, at the Nissei Theater in Tokyo (opposite, bottom), reproduced the New York and London versions almost exactly.*

188

Attired as the Red Death in homage to Poe, the Phantom arrives at the ball, bearing the score of his opera, Don Juan Triumphant.

Opposite, top:
Three of Björnson's fanciful designs for the "Masquerade" scene.

Opposite, bottom:
Brightman and costar Steve Barton rehearse a sequence in London. Gillian Lynne was the choreographer.

To enable the Phantom to scramble high above the audience's head, Bjornson designed a false proscenium to set before the theater's genuine one. The Phantom is everywhere, and try as they might, the lovers cannot escape him. Right: "The very chandelier which figures in the famous disaster." It comes crashing down at the end of Act 1.

There really is a lake beneath the Paris Opera House, which novelist Gaston
Leroux used as the setting for his 1910 thriller. Here, the Phantom ferries
Christine across the lake to a rendezvous in his ghostly abode.

The Phantom unmasked. In a scene familiar to all horror-movie aficionados, Christine sneaks up behind him while he is playing the organ and whisks the mask from his face. Later in the show, he will be unmasked in even more dramatic fashion.

Opposite, top:

The point of no return. In the show's final trio, Christine begs the Phantom to spare the life of her lover, Raoul (Barton).

Opposite, bottom:

On opening night of Phantom in New York, Barton, director Hal Prince, Crawford, Lloyd Webber, and Brightman hear the cheers.

For a 1988 piece in Vanity Fair, *Brightman posed in the Paris Opera House, wearing some of the costumes she wore in the show. Above, Brightman in the Phantom's underground domain. The cobwebs were added by the photographer for effect.*

Crawford, Brightman, and Lloyd Webber. Behind them *is the chandelier.*

*Brightman, in costume as Christine, sits atop the
Opera House with Paris at her feet. The acrophobic Lloyd
Webber could hardly bear to watch the photo shoot.*

CRICKET

In 1986 Lloyd Webber briefly reunited with his old partner Tim Rice for a royal command performance in Windsor Castle. Here Prince Philip, Nunn, Lloyd Webber, Queen Elizabeth, and Rice pose with members of the cast. The young man in the tuxedo at far right is Really Useful Group production assistant Edward Windsor, better known as the queen's youngest son, Prince Edward.

CRICKET
MUSIC BY ANDREW LLOYD WEBBER
LYRICS BY TIM RICE
DIRECTED BY TREVOR NUNN
1st PERFORMANCE WINDSOR CASTLE, 18 JUNE 1986

CHESS

After splitting up with Lloyd Webber following Evita in 1978, Rice went on to write Blondel with composer Stephen Oliver in 1983 and Chess with Benny Andersson and Björn Ulvaeus of ABBA fame. The 1986 Chess production in London (below and bottom) was to have been directed by Michael Bennett, but ill health forced him to step down, and Trevor Nunn took his place.

ASPECTS OF LOVE

*R*omance of the rails: Rose (Ann Crumb) and Alex (Michael Ball) on the train from Paris to Pau.

Above left:

Alex and George.

Above:

Giulietta, the Italian sculptress who is George's mistress.

Left:

Sixteen years after their first meeting, Alex goes backstage to see Rose, now a famous actress.

The dangerous liaisons among Alex, Rose, George, Jenny, and Giulietta form the plot of Aspects of Love. *Above: Rose and Alex at George's villa in Pau. Right: Alex and George, who are both in love with the same woman.*

Webber surely disapproved). It is followed by a brief conversation between Don Juan and his manservant, Passarino, in which they exchange cloaks in order to further the Don's chances of the successful seduction of a serving wench. Piangi disappears behind a curtain and, with a tug of the Phantom's deadly Punjab lasso, steps into eternity.

The Phantom emerges, clad as the Don, and sings what is very likely the show's best song after "Music of the Night," "The Point of No Return." Christine is playing the role of Aminta, the Don's prospective conquest. At the Don's first words, however, Christine looks up and recognizes the Phantom behind the costume of cowl and cape. "The Point of No Return" becomes an F-minor duet:

> *Past the point*
> *of no return*
> *the final threshold—*
> *the bridge is crossed, so stand*
> *and watch it burn . . .*
> *We've passed the point*
> *of no return . . .*

Dropping all pretense now, the Phantom turns to Christine and begs her to marry him. To the tune of "All I Ask of You," he sings:

> *Say you'll share with*
> *me one*
> *love, one lifetime . . .*
> *Lead me, save me*
> *from my solitude . . .*
>
> *Say you want me*
> *with you,*
> *here beside you . . .*
> *Anywhere you go*
> *let me go too—*
> *Christine,*
> *that's all I ask of . . .*

The Phantom never makes it to the word *you,* for at that moment, Christine calmly removes his mask and wig and displays him, in all his hideous unadornment, to the audience. The Phantom, so dominant to this point, visibly shrinks: at the very moment he is revealed as a monster, he becomes a pitiable, harmless child. In the tumult that follows his unmasking and the discovery of Piangi's body, the Phantom, clutching Christine tightly, escapes to his netherworld, pursued by Raoul.

In the Phantom's den, the final confrontation takes place. The Phantom places a bridal veil on Christine's head. "Pity comes too late—turn around and face your fate: an eternity of *this* before your eyes!" Christine draws herself up and coolly replies:

> *This haunted face*
> *holds no horror*
> *for me now . . .*
> *It's in your soul*
> *that the true*
> *distortion lies . . .*

Raoul arrives, and the Phantom quickly takes him prisoner. The Phantom offers Christine a choice: if she will marry him, Raoul will be set free; if not, he will die. Summoning her willpower, she sings:

> *Pitiful creature*
> *of darkness . . .*

*What kind of life
have you known . . . ?*

*God give me the courage
to show you
you are not
alone . . .*

Fearlessly, she kisses him, full on the lips.

Shattered by the first gesture of affection he has ever received, the Phantom frees the lovers. With a vengeful populace on its way to rescue Christine, the Phantom bids farewell to her:

*You alone
can make my song take flight —
it's over now, the music of the night . . .*

Dejected and beaten, the Phantom sits on the throne in his sitting room. He wraps his cloak around him and, as his pursuers arrive, vanishes while the orchestra thunders out "The Music of the Night." The last image is of Meg, who pulls aside the cape to find only the Phantom's mask left behind; the final music is the sliding chordal sequence that concludes the song, this time, of course, notated in D-flat: G-flat, E-flat minor, D minor, C major, and one last resonant D-flat major.

From the key structure alone, it is clear that Lloyd Webber himself considered *Phantom* his most important score. And so it was. *Phantom*, in fact, represents such a leap beyond anything he had done to that point that it can only be explained as one of those periodic quantum leaps that every real artist makes in his art. When one takes into account that *Phantom* is also Lloyd Webber's theatrical successor to *Starlight Express,* its quality is even more astonishing. Which is not to say it was not also popular: four of its songs landed high on the charts in Britain, including "The Phantom of the Opera," "The Music of the Night," "All I Ask of You," and "Wishing You Were Somehow Here Again." But, for the first time in Lloyd Webber's life, art finally had superseded commerce.*

Not that *Phantom* is perfect. The miscalculation of the chandelier has already been noted, but a more serious problem involves the lyrics. While Hart occasionally had an effective flight of fancy, too often he settled for the pedestrian cliché, with the result that *Phantom* tends to come bumping back to earth just as it is about to soar: "You have truly made my night," "I trust her midnight oil is well and truly burned," even "The point of no return"—close your eyes and it could be Robin St. Clare Barrow all over again.

In writing the show, Lloyd Webber had already partly cast it, for Christine was specifically written for Brightman. By this time, the Lloyd Webbers' marriage was a routine subject for the newspapers, and the fact that Lloyd Webber had written the show for Sarah touched off a frenzy of "investigative" marital reporting. Throughout 1986 and into 1987, there were reports of fierce rows between man and wife during rehearsal. In August 1986 *The News of the World* reported that Sarah had called Andrew "a slug in flared trousers." (Incorrect, said Andrew. "Actually, I haven't worn flared trousers since 1968," adding, typically: "Whoever put that story about was totally irresponsible. Apart from making it up, they could have endangered the whole £2-million project.") In December, the press had another field day when Sarah was rushed to the hospital with stomach pains: "Sarah fainted after row with Andrew," ran one account, claiming that a panicked Lloyd Webber had screamed "She's dying!" to the ambulance attendants. Brightman was released after half an hour, blaming her condition on wild mushrooms she had eaten at a restaurant that day.

Even more dramatically, *The News of the World* breathlessly trumpeted the "Double Love Life of the Phantom Beauty." The March 1987 story alleged that Brightman had been carrying on with rock composer Mike Moran since before her wedding to Andrew. "Once, after the

---

*Although not for long. Within months, there were *Phantom* souvenir books, *Phantom* jewelry, even a perfume called *Esprit de Phantom,* which by 1989 was the third best-selling perfume in America. There one also detects the hand of Mackintosh.

Lloyd Webbers were married, Mike looked tired and I asked what he'd been up to," the paper quoted an unnamed "friend." "He smiled and said: 'Sarah was round last night and we were at it all night.'" (Nonsense, said Andrew: "Neither of us, quite simply, could find the time to have an affair with someone else. The honest truth is that we are ludicrously happy.")

The stories infuriated both Lloyd Webbers and a call from the lawyer quickly followed in their wake. On February 7, 1987, after a report that the *Phantom* cast was relieved when illness forced a fractious Brightman to miss a few performances, *The Star* printed the following retraction:

> Following our article on Friday, January 30, Michael Crawford has asked it to be made clear that he is totally unaware of any animosity at all among the cast backstage at 'The Phantom of the Opera' and that he himself looked forward to Sarah Brightman's return to the show after her recent bout of flu.
>
> The Star and its readers are great admirers of Sarah Brightman, who is a highly regarded professional in her field. We apologise to Miss Brightman if our story implied otherwise.
>
> The Star accepts that there is no truth whatsoever in the allegations made in the article and has agreed to pay to Sarah Brightman a substantial sum in damages (which she will donate to charity) and her legal costs.

For the title role, Steve Harley had hoped to be tapped, but instead the part had gone to the forty-four-year-old Michael Crawford, an against-type masterstroke. In the press, Lloyd Webber attempted to placate the disappointed rocker. "Both Steve and I felt that with the way my score was going he wouldn't have been right for it," said Andrew. "But I'm seriously thinking of writing a major musical for him." Which, of course, was moonshine. Crawford, born in Salisbury as Michael Dumbell Smith, had once been voted the funniest man on British television, thanks to his role as Frank Spencer in the popular series "Some Mothers Do 'Ave 'Em." But having seen him play the leads in *Billy, Flowers for Algernon,* and *Barnum,* Lloyd Webber knew that he could sing; Crawford had, in fact, been trained by Britten and had appeared in both *Noye's Fludde* and *Let's Make an Opera.* He also shared a voice teacher with Brightman. (In America, Crawford was probably best remembered as Hero in Sondheim's *A Funny Thing Happened on the Way to the Forum.*) Crawford was on holiday in the West Indies during casting, but after a few urgent telephone calls he flew back to London and got the part.

The title role offered Crawford (who was estimated to earn half a million pounds for his year in the show in London) the part of a lifetime. Musically, the Phantom's themes stalk the opera; physically, the athletic Crawford could dominate the action, command the stage, and even climb to the rafters in pursuit of his *beau ideale.* So pervasive is the Phantom's presence that it comes as a surprise to realize that he is not on stage more; Christine has three times as much music to sing. The third principal role went to Steve Barton, an American who had been working in Austria and West Germany, whom Gillian Lynne, the *Phantom's* choreographer, recommended.* The production musical director was David Caddick, a thirty-year-old Yorkshireman who had studied with Bill Lloyd Webber at the Royal College of Music and had become Andrew's right hand in matters of musical preparation, while the conductor was Mike Reed.

Initially, there had been brave words that *Phantom* was to be a simple show, using only the surviving Victorian stage machinery that was found in Her Majesty's, but it quickly evolved into something as high-tech as *Starlight Express* or *Les Misérables.* In the lake scene, for example, there were more than one hundred candles that arose through the stage floor, each with its own tiny trap door; the boat that ferried the Phantom and Christine was motor-driven and radio-controlled. The production cost was put at two million pounds, raised from large company investments and in two-thousand-five-hundred-pound blocs from individual angels. Nine hundred thousand pounds of the budget went for sets and costumes. The Phantom's latex makeup was designed by Christopher Tucker, who had created the Elephant Man for director David Lynch in the film of the same name. It took three hours (later reduced to two) for Crawford to climb into the Phantom's misshapen skin, and each day the transformation had to be made anew, at a cost of thirty pounds per performance.

Even before the first note had sounded, or the first chandelier had fallen, there was already more than a million pounds' advance in the till. The opening-night performance was rewarded with a ten-minute standing ovation, but the nervous Lloyd Webber wasn't around to hear it; at the interval, he and Mackintosh had nipped out for a jar at the London branch of Maxim's, nearby. "We'd seen every preview, we couldn't take any more so we went round the corner for a quick one," Andrew explained to reporters.

---

*When Crawford missed two weeks of performances in April 1987 due to hospitalization for a hiatal hernia, Barton took over the title role but injured his knee at the first performance and was unable to continue. Understudy Jim Patterson filled in. Brightman, who was contracted for only six of the eight weekly performances during her six-month run in the show, was also hospitalized during the run, for stomach ulcers. Her place was taken by her fine alternate, Claire Moore, who succeeded her in the part.

Oddly, considering the strength of the score and the production's dazzle, there were many bad reviews, some of them nasty. In *The Observer*, Michael Ratcliffe compared the Lloyd Webber *Phantom* unfavorably with the Ken Hill show, complained that it wasn't scary enough, and ridiculed in particular the Phantom's tunes:

> Two themes stand for the Phantom as object of fear and are repeated frequently. Both are absurd. The first is a sequence of descending minor chords of the kind against which Sylvester the Cat used to creep up on the unsuspecting Tweety Pie. The second, sung to the words of the title and the rhythm didum-didum-didum-*tee* is pitched so low on one note until the last that few of the singers can do more than growl their way unfearfully through it until they clutch at the final rising interval like castaways at a raft. This is bogeyman-music and these are tinsel terrors beside those of, say, Sondheim's "Sweeney Todd." Lloyd Webber, who might once have taken a similar path to abrasiveness and the grotesque, has written a romantic lyric spectacle with nothing abrasive about it and all ironies, such as they are, carefully concealed.

In a review headlined "Andrew's trite night at the opera," critic David Shannon of *Today* led:

> Andrew Lloyd Webber's new musical is, he says, "About a man who is hideously ugly who falls hopelessly in love with this girl and is only able to express himself through music."
> Only those of a very cruel frame of mind would suggest the musical was at all autobiographical.

In *The Evening Standard*, Milton Shulman was unimpressed, noting in passing that Brightman "has the appealing waif-like looks that traditionally attract admirers like Dracula, the Hunchback of Notre Dame and the Phantom." John Peter, too, gave it a lukewarm notice at the end of a long theater column in *The Sunday Times*:

> Andrew Lloyd Webber is really playing with fire in his new musical. First, it's about a soprano of pleasant but average talent (Sarah Brightman) who is picked out of the chorus line and turned into a star by a publicity-shunning musical eccentric. Second, several times during the show people sing the line "This is the point of no return"—which raises one's expectations that the end might be near. Then again, the Phantom of the title (Michael Crawford) declares in a disembodied voice that the cast must be sacked because they can neither sing nor act.

Visiting from America, Frank Rich was also heard from. Predictably, he praised Prince—"it's invigorating to see what a crack Broadway director at full throttle can do"—criticized Hart and Stilgoe, and bashed Lloyd Webber. Yet Rich's judgment in *The New York Times* foundered on the perils that inevitably attend amateur music criticism:

> But Mr. Lloyd Webber also undercuts himself. For every sumptuously melodic love song in this score, there is an insufferably smug opera parody that can't match its prototype [Meyerbeer? Salieri?], a thrown-in pop number that slows the action, or a jarring, anachronistic descent into the vulgar synthesizer chords of "Starlight Express." Must a show that is sold out until 1988 . . . sell itself out quite so much?

Rich's review, written several months after the premiere, concluded with a plug for his hero, Sondheim, describing the then-forthcoming London production of *Follies* (designed by Björnson) as "the most eagerly awaited premiere of the London theatrical year."

On the other side of the ledger there was praise, although generally restrained. In *The Financial Times*, Michael Coveney cheered production, performances, and music alike: "The final moments as Christine rips off the mask and the lovers' triangle is resolved in a descent to the lair and an emotional farewell, are almost unbearably moving. You would be well advised to have the Kleenex handy." Michael Billington of *The Guardian* wrote that *Phantom* "is determinedly old-fashioned; but when the new fashion is for boy-meets-laser-beam, it is refreshing to find a musical that pins its faith in people, narrative and traditional illusion." Even a rave from John Barber in *The Daily Telegraph* called the piece "unmitigated tosh. But it is tosh of a high order." It was left to the tabloids—to John Blake in *The Daily Mirror* and Jack Tinker in *The Daily Mail*—to trot out the great-day-for-England panegyrics.

Mackintosh took the reviews in stride; it was clear the show was a hit with the public, and plans could now go ahead for *Phantom*'s conquest of the globe. "The show is going all over the world," he said. "We knew that anyway, but now we are confident about it." Mackintosh, the marketing genius, knew that quotes, which some Broadway theater critics knocked themselves out to provide—the critics nice enough to write their own blurbs—just to see their names blown up on bus cards, were now superfluous. To market *Cats,* all you needed was a pair of yellow eyes; for *Les Misérables,* the little Cosette waif. *Phantom* was even simpler, just a plain white, full-face mask.* If by now Mackintosh–Lloyd Webber shows were critic-proof and cast-proof, they were blurb-proof as well. It didn't matter who was in them or what was said about them, the public still wanted to go and would pay almost any price to get in.

It was with *Cats,* the essentially plotless musical, that Mackintosh first had realized the new realities of marketing. The problem with the classic American musicals was that they were too, well, *American.* In their invincible ignorance, the solipsistic Yanks may have thought that all the earth's peoples were brothers under the skin, but to the rest of the world such a proposition was manifestly not true. "Traditional American musicals really haven't appealed worldwide," Mackintosh told an interviewer, because "musicals that are very slick and have to do with the American way of life just don't appeal as well as *Cats.* The sort of people that inhabit a Sondheim musical on the whole don't inhabit many cities outside America"—surely a classic British understatement. Mackintosh, who was lining his silk purse with the sow's ear of *Les Misérables,* knew whereof he spoke. For most foreigners, it was far easier to identify with the downtrodden and the revolutionary than with the neurotic, the analyst-ridden, and the lawyer-infested. The box office returns were proving it.

To Lloyd Webber, though, the notices were worrying. He wasn't the only one. For many in Britain, Lloyd Webber and the musical theater were synonymous, and any failure on his part might endanger England's hard-won dominance in the field. In *The Sunday Times,* John Whitley noted that "there were signs that his *Phantom of the Opera* might not follow the traditional path of hype-acclaim-sellout. Reviews were what the business calls, in its politest euphemism, mixed":

> None of this might seem to matter to a show which is expected to return its £2m investment in a year. A composer with three shows running simultaneously in the West End can shrug off a bit of heckling from the free seats in the stalls. But to anyone with an interest in the health of the British theatre—a theatre that at present might seem to consist entirely of musicals—whether or not a new Lloyd Webber comes up to scratch is of crucial importance. The innovative musical gifts that created *The Amazing Technicolour* [sic] *Dreamcoat* and *Cats* brought new life and new direction to a stagnant Showbiz UK and provided secure employment for a generation of talented technicians.
>
> Music theatre has now become legitimate: there is no longer a barrier between commercial and subsidised theatre [as *Les Misérables* clearly showed] and the benefits flow both ways. Whether the ticket touts will have to move their pitch as well now depends entirely on Lloyd Webber's ability to rediscover his inspirational touch.

In another sense, though, Lloyd Webber could literally afford to shrug off the reviews. There was no such thing as a "money" review for him any more. His very name now made whatever he did a hit. On October 18 *The Daily Mirror* cattily reported:

> Millionaire gnome Andrew Lloyd Webber has acquired a home in Eaton Square, one of London's most prestigious addresses and the location for the Upstairs Downstairs saga.
>
> His wife, the former Hot Gossip dancer Sarah Brightman, is now at the top of the stairs.
>
> Mr. Lloyd Webber shelled out a seven-figure sum for the penthouse and floor below of Number 73. Mrs. L. W. is now spending some of his £50 million fortune decorating the property to her own taste.

In short order, and at Sarah's urging, he also bought a seaside villa and ten acres on the French Riviera, in the seaside town of Saint-Jean-Cap-Ferrat, and a duplex apartment on the fifty-ninth and sixtieth floors of Trump Tower in Manhattan at a cost of six million dollars. (His neighbor on the floor above was Steven Spielberg.) After two months of renovations, during which all the fixtures were ripped out and replaced, the Lloyd Webbers moved into their New York residence before the end of the year. Among the items removed were eight hundred yards of gold-paneled mirrors installed by the previous owner. In their place came cashmere curtains, "royalty purple" taffeta silk in the master bedroom, and camel's-hair–covered ottomans in the dining room. There was even an opium bed from India and a wooden elephant in the living room that Lloyd Webber promptly dubbed "Trump," after both the eponymous New York builder and an English children's rhyme about an elephant that went "trump, trump, trump."

Lloyd Webber's acquisitions did not stop there. He rented a private jet, a Hawker Siddeley 125, which was kept parked at Luton Airport near London, to ferry him and Sarah between European residences; to get to New York, they took the Concorde. A chauffeur and a new Bentley drove him between Sydmonton and London, and Andrew kept a classic 1939 Bentley in his garage, while Sarah zipped around in a Porsche, which she later traded in for a new Jaguar. When a clutch of jewels from the late Duchess of Windsor's collection came on the auction market,

---

* Not the half-mask the Phantom actually wears in the show.

Andrew bought them for Sarah. Ever since childhood he had been enamored of Pre-Raphaelite art, and his private collection could now rival the greatest in the world.

Lloyd Webber's only regret, and it was a bitter one, was that he had not bought the two thousand four hundred acres of Watership Down, adjacent to Sydmonton. It had come on the market in August, and because at that point even he was feeling strapped, he had let it go to the chief of a computer-leasing company, who got it for five million pounds. At the last minute, Lloyd Webber had topped the bid by seven hundred and fifty thousand pounds, but he was too late.

Financially, he could handle his extravagances. From the royalties of his songs and shows—mostly, the grand rights—Lloyd Webber was now earning twelve million dollars a year; thank you, Bob Kingston. *Vox populi, vox dei: Phantom* was a smash, sold out nearly a year hence. In December the show won Lloyd Webber the "Larry" for Best Musical at the prestigious Laurence Olivier Awards, while Best Actor in a Musical went to Crawford; a month earlier, *Phantom* had been named Best Musical at the *The Evening Standard* Drama Awards as well. (Brightman, however, was snubbed, with the "Larry" for Best Actress in a Musical going to Leslie Mackie, who had impersonated Judy Garland in the show, *Judy.*) The original-cast double album, released in Britain in January 1987, went platinum within ten days; a year later, just before *Phantom* opened on Broadway, it had racked up seven hundred thousand copies in album sales in Britain alone. In April 1987 the Really Useful Group won the Queen's Award for export achievement.

There was only one problem discoloring this otherwise rosy scenario: the refusal of American Actors' Equity to allow Brightman to repeat her role in the United States. This verdict, delivered in June 1987, became a major story on both sides of the ocean. In England, it even took on a melodramatic quality when, at the same time, Brightman underwent surgery for stomach ulcers. Crawford, too, had been initially refused by Equity, but had won his case on appeal, his victory capped by an OBE on the Queen's Birthday Honours' List that month. Since Barton was an American, there was no bother about him.

Lloyd Webber was furious. He had written the piece with Sarah's voice and dancing ability in mind, and who was Equity to tell him whom he could or could not have in his show? Prince, too, was angry. He had provided a great deal of employment for American actors during his many years atop the directorial heap, and only once—once—had he ever appealed an Equity ruling, when he insisted that his all-British cast of *Side by Side by Sondheim* should be imported to offer a different perspective on the show. He had won that one, and he intended to win this one as well. Further, he and Lloyd Webber were discussing plans for a joint operation in the United States to be called Allies, Inc., to seek out and produce new American musicals. Prince wanted a good, continuing working relationship—no more waiting a decade between shows— and he assured Andrew that, come opening night, Sarah Brightman would be singing Christine.*

Prince was aware, though, of a tremendous hostility toward Lloyd Webber and his wife. The composer was invulnerable; take away the Lloyd Webber money machine and Broadway was nearly out of business. But Sarah could be kicked around, and the fact that she was also Andrew's wife made her an especially inviting football. But Prince felt that the composer had an intrinsic right to the cast of his choice, and even if Andrew wanted to write the show for his mother, he had to be defended. Besides, Sarah had auditioned in New York like everybody else, and in Prince's opinion she was better than the ninety-two American actresses who had sung for the part. Backed with an unstated but implicit no-Sarah–no-*Phantom* threat from Lloyd Webber, Prince argued his case and, in the end, won it. In exchange for allowing Brightman to appear in the Broadway *Phantom* for six months, Lloyd Webber agreed to cast an "unknown" American in his next London show.

Arguing his case, Prince had the box office on his side. Travelers returning from Britain had brought back word that *Phantom* was the must-see show of the year; why, Princess Diana had already seen it twice. On the day tickets went on sale in November 1987, buyers snapped up 920,271 dollars' worth of seats—nearly twice as much as *Les Misérables* had taken in on its first day in America. By the time *Phantom* opened at the 1,655-seat Majestic Theatre in New York on January 26, 1988, it had taken in 16 million dollars in advance sales—4 million dollars more than the previous champ, *Les Misérables.* The bidding for *Phantom* among the American producers had been spirited. In December 1986 Mackintosh informed the Shubert Organization that "for technical and artistic reasons" the Majestic was not going to house the show, and *The New York Times* reported that the leading contenders were the 1,200-seat Martin Beck, owned by Jujamcyn, and the 1,621-seat Minskoff, which belonged to the Nederlanders. Eventually, Jacobs and Schoenfeld prevailed.

Which didn't mean that the American critics necessarily were going to like the show any better than their British brethren. The production was nearly identical to the English version, although it had to be compressed to fit a stage that was ten feet narrower.† Although the structural alterations to the Majestic were not as great as those for *Cats* and *Starlight Express,* much work still had to be done; the

---

* Nothing ever came of the Allies idea. After *Phantom* opened on Broadway, it was quietly dropped.

† In Tokyo, where *Phantom* opened on April 13, 1988, it had to squeeze onto a stage at once wider than those in England or America, and shorter. Sung in Japanese, the Tokyo *Phantom* was like watching a Cinerama movie shrunk to fit on television.

proscenium, for example, was raised by six feet, and a false proscenium installed in front of it for the Phantom to scramble on. The basement was excavated and made seven feet deeper to accommodate the machinery needed to realize the Phantom's illusions. Still, the first night went off without a hitch.

The avalanche of pre-opening publicity—cover stories in *Time, The New York Times Magazine,* and *New York* and a major piece in *Newsweek* were the most prominent manifestations—engendered a certain amount of backlash from critics who complained about the "hype," while the fact that New York was now nothing more than an elevated tour stop, a classy bus-and-truck town for productions originating in London, put a few noses out of joint. But in general *Phantom* got a fair shake. Jack Kroll of *Newsweek* wrote, "Lloyd Webber provides the most seductive, romantic score heard on Broadway in a long time. . . .Those lucky enough to see [Brightman and Crawford] will be seeing two reasons why the English musical continues to rule the roost in world theater." Howard Kissel, writing in *The Daily News,* called it "more than just a show about a chandelier. [It] seems a happy sign for Broadway." Now that his opinion didn't matter anymore, Clive Barnes staggered aboard the bandwagon in *The New York Post.* "One word?" he wrote. "Okay, let's try: Phantastic!" Clearly, the years had not withered nor custom staled Barnes's infinite variety of clichés.

The dissent came from Michael Feingold in *The Village Voice,* John Simon in *New York,* and Frank Rich—dubbed "the Butcher of Broadway" by the British press—in *The New York Times.* Feingold, no Lloyd Webber fan, jumped on what he viewed as the score's unapologetic derivativeness and peed on the Phantom's pants leg:

> Yes, yes, I know. The semi-educated middle-class world loves Andrew Lloyd Webber best of all theater composers. . . . Nevertheless, the educated world knows by now that [he] is not a real composer, but a secondhand music peddler, whose pathetic aural imagination was outpaced years ago by his apparently exhaustive memory. I don't accuse him of plagiarism; he never quotes more than 3½ bars of anyone else's work verbatim (does the memory have a radar detector built in?). But instead of developing his *trouvailles* into compositions of his own, he just runs them into each other.

Among other influences, Feingold detected references to Kurt Weill, Leonard Bernstein, Sondheim, and Engelbert Humperdinck (the composer, not the pop singer). "Webber's music isn't that painful to hear," he concluded, "if you don't mind its being so soiled from previous use."

After praising Prince and Björnson, Simon summed up his objections to the show: "The only areas in which *The Phantom of the Opera* is deficient are book, music, and lyrics." Simon, too, seized on what he perceived as Lloyd Webber's lack of originality:

> It's not so much that Lloyd Webber lacks an ear for melody as that he has too much of a one for other people's melodies, especially Puccini's. . . .The thing that Lloyd Webber, with his classical-music background, seems most to lust for is to be taken seriously as a composer, but, on the evidence in thus far, I predict that Gershwin and Rodgers, let alone Puccini and Ravel (another of his magnets), have nothing to fear from him.

Both Feingold and Simon also had harsh words for Brightman. Feingold said her demeanor suggested "a clerk in a smart London shop who has just made a big sale." Simon said her casting "is the triumph of uxoriousness over common sense." Reversing his London judgment, *Time*'s Bill Henry was particularly crude. "Brightman's Maypole figure, long nose and prominent overbite do not aid in explaining why both men adore her," wrote the critic whom *Spy* magazine later characterized as "walrus-shaped." "But these deficiencies might be overcome if she displayed the least hint of star quality, or even stage presence, instead of acting like Minnie Mouse on Quaaludes."

But the last word belonged to Rich. As Prince well knew, the newsweeklies had no influence. It didn't matter what Bill Henry or Jack Kroll said; their audience lived in the boondocks, not in New York City. In the end, Rich's was the only review that would count both to the theater community and to the ticket-buying public. The news was not good. "It may be possible to have a terrible time at *The Phantom of the Opera,* but you'll have to work at it," he began left-handedly. "Only a terminal prig would let the avalanche of pre-opening publicity poison his enjoyment of this show. . . ." Unfortunately for Lloyd Webber, Rich then went on to prove that he was that terminal prig:

> What one finds is a characteristic Lloyd Webber project—long on pop professionalism and melody, impoverished of artistic personality and passion. . . .*The Phantom of the Opera* is as much a victory of dynamic stagecraft over musical kitsch as it is a triumph of merchandising über alles. . . .With the exception of "Music of the Night"—which seems to express from its author's gut a desperate longing for acceptance—Mr. Lloyd Webber has again written a score so generic that most of the songs could be

reordered and redistributed among the characters (indeed, among other Lloyd Webber musicals) without altering the show's story or meaning.

Thus did the country's most influential drama critic prosecute the case of the Broadway Establishment vs. Lloyd Webber. Spray painted with gratuitously inflammatory phrases (in a paper as solicitous of its heavily Jewish readership as *The New York Times,* the Nazi-era locution "über alles" was especially provocative), Rich's review was a good old-fashioned trip to the woodshed. In his peroration, Rich laid out his view of Lloyd Webber as the Demon Composer of Broadway:

> Mr. Lloyd Webber's esthetic has never been more baldly stated than in this show, which favors the decorative trappings of art over the troublesome substance of culture and finds more eroticism in rococo opulence and conspicuous consumption [?] than in love or sex. Mr. Lloyd Webber is a creature, perhaps even a prisoner, of his time; with *The Phantom of the Opera,* he remakes La Belle Epoque in the image of our own Gilded Age. If by any chance this musical doesn't prove Mr. Lloyd Webber's most popular, it won't be his fault, but another sign that times are changing and that our boom era, like the opera house's chandelier, is poised to go bust.

Or was it? As 1988 drew to a close, *The Phantom of the Opera* was playing to full houses in London, New York, Tokyo, and Vienna, where it displaced the long-running *Cats* from the Theater an der Wien and forced it to move to another theater. Rich may have felt that the curtain was coming down on the Reagan era of greed and glitz, but that was his American perspective. In Britain, Mrs. Thatcher and her Tories were still going strong.

Entr'acte Four: NOBODY'S SIDE

"For One Evening Only.... The Bit Players Every Premiere Needs" ran the headline in *The Daily Mail* of October 10, 1986, the day after *The Phantom of the Opera* opened. Accompanying a rave review of the show by Jack Tinker, show-business columnist Baz Bamigboye wrote a set of snappy captions to accompany photographs of the various celebrities who attended the first night. There was a picture of Lucy Crawford, Michael Crawford's daughter (predictably, the cutline was "some daughters do 'ave 'em"); of Steve Harley, the disappointed non-Phantom; of John Gummer, the Tory party chief, and his wife, Penny (who had been a resident of 10 Gledhow Gardens in the Lloyd Webber days); of Melvyn Bragg, the writer and television personality, who was there with his wife ("snapping their D. registration teeth ready for supper"); and, of course, of Andrew and his mother, Jean.

The sixth photograph was of Jane Rice, entering Her Majesty's Theatre with her handbag tucked under her arm and carrying a present clutched in both hands. Baz identified her as the "wife of lyricist Tim, wearing a wait-till-I-see-him look. She was playing pass the parcel but was he playing at Chess?"

The snide double meaning could not have been missed by even the dimmest *Mail* reader. By now the Tim–Jane–Elaine Paige triangle was the stuff of tabloid titillation. Just as Lloyd Webber was routinely referred to as the "millionaire gnome" (or, in America, as the "chipmunk"), so Tim had taken on a public persona. His, though, had nothing to do with fabulous wealth—although Rice was certainly well off—but rather with his love life.

Nearly forty-two years old, Rice was no longer the tall, slender boy with the long blond hair who had conquered America with *Jesus Christ Superstar* and his own quick wit. Now the hair was thinning, and he was more than a couple of stone heavier than in those saladin days of yore. But women still found him attractive, and the image of Tim the lionhearted Lothario maintained a great deal of currency.

On the surface, Rice's relationships with Jane and Elaine defied understanding and probability. Everyone had an opinion about his entanglements. Generally, women said he should leave one for the other, while men marveled at his ability to juggle both relationships—in the press, yet—and somehow manage to keep them going. While Tim certainly did not go out of his way to publicize his infidelity, neither did he try to hide it. His affair with Paige was no secret, darkened-restaurant and rented-flat liaison; on the contrary, the lovers were often seen in public and even lived and traveled together. Nor was Tim bashful about promoting Paige's career: on May 14, 1986, she had opened in Trevor Nunn's production of the Rice–Benny Andersson/Björn Ulvaeus *Chess* at the Prince Edward Theatre, where she had first sprung to fame as Evita.

On September 29, 1986, ten days before *Phantom* bowed, *The Daily Express* ran a piece called "My Love for Tim Rice, by Elaine Paige." The story was actually an interview with Elaine by David Wigg, and it began:

> Elaine Paige has at last openly admitted her love for composer* Tim Rice. Although Elaine has always been reluctant to talk about their relationship, when I asked her this week how she felt about Tim she replied: "I love him. He's a wonderful man and I care for him very much. I can't say much more than that really—that's it. He's very special to me and very important in my life.

---

*As the "composer" designation indicates, the standard of accuracy in the British tabloid press is shockingly low, even about well-known public figures. In 1987, for example, *The Sun* referred to "Andrew Lloyd Webber's smash-hit West End musical Chess."

Wouldn't she then like to share her life with Tim? I asked.

"Well, I do, kind of, really—already," she giggled.

But wouldn't she like it to be more final?

"Nothing's final," she replied. "Anything can happen. That's why I live my life day by day. I think it's the best way to lead it, because you just don't know what's going to happen to you, do you?"

"We have discussed our future and where we are going in our relationship," added Elaine. "I guess it's a question of us all making up our minds. There's more than me involved in this."

Which, of course, was true. There was Jane Rice, and the Rices' two children, Eva and Donald, now eleven and nine years old. By all rights, the tabs should have been in an uproar over Rice's blatant flouting of marital vows and social convention, and Paige should have been pilloried, Brightman-style, as a homewrecker.

In fact, nothing of the sort happened. Rice was so congenial, so one-of-the-lads, that by now this little peccadillo was treated more leeringly than scornfully. As for Paige, she was a very popular singer in Britain—"gutsy" and "feisty" were the descriptive adjectives most often applied to her—and her tough spirit and earthy discourse charmed the watchdogs of Fleet Street, and they tended to let her pass, unscathed.

But it was also true that Elaine was forcing the issue. In the interview, she spoke of the ticking of the biological clock and of her desire to have children. In her late thirties, Paige had been Rice's mistress for seven years, and while she had had considerable popular success as Evita, as Grizabella and, latterly, as Florence (the third given name of Rice's daughter), the heroine of *Chess,* she wanted more. All through the rest of 1986 and 1987, there were rumors that she had given Tim an ultimatum: leave Jane and marry her, or they were through.

The other woman in this unhappy ménage was Jane Rice. Somehow, Jane had managed to survive with her dignity intact. She was Tim Rice's wife, which Elaine Paige was not, and the mother of his children, which Elaine most certainly was not, and she was determined to keep it that way. Jane spent most of her time with the children at their home in Holland Park (Tim lived mostly at Romeyns Court; when in London, he stayed with Paige), and there were the inevitable whispers that Jane kept a lover in London, but if there was one, she was more discreet about it than Tim. When she went out, it was generally either alone or with the kids, although it was not unheard of for her to actually date her husband. They both loved rock and roll, for example, and if a classic band like the Hollies was putting on a show, Tim and Jane might well be there.

As for Tim, his feelings were disguised behind his long-perfected mask of affability. The contrast between Rice and his erstwhile partner was now complete. Andrew, now so powerful that few dared to gainsay him, was an often frightening figure to those outside his very small inner circle, an unapproachable dynamo whose sparks sent others scurrying for cover. Lloyd Webber was not the kind of guy one would spontaneously invite out for a jar (although his fondness for the wine, seemingly the only way he could unwind, was starting to worry his friends), but you would be proud to buy Tim a pint or two and talk some cricket.

Rice was a popular figure in Britain, a fixture on the radio, the host of a pop-music television series. His idea for a book about hit records had come to fruition with the Guinness books of hit singles and hit albums, cowritten with his brother Jo, Paul Gambaccini, and Mike Read. Rice was also the founder and director, along with Colin Webb and Michael Parkinson, of Pavilion Books (which, ironically, was the publisher of *The Complete Phantom of the Opera,* a souvenir book that accompanied and fueled Phantomania; written by George Perry, the book was researched by Jane Rice). Rice was also one of the country's best-known cricket fans (in 1989 he wrote *Treasure's of Lord's,* a nonfiction book about cricket's mecca), and he ran and played for his own gentlemanly club called the Heartaches.

Behind the façade, though, dark forces were at work. Andrew may have had his explosions and then carried on, but Tim nursed grudges, and his anger was fueled by what he himself regarded as his own fatal flaw, excessive complaisance. Rice saw himself as Mr. Nice Guy, a man who let others take advantage, and even a successful career in the theater that spanned two decades had not materially improved Tim's self-image. Just look at what had happened with *Blondel* and *Chess.*

Until *Cricket, Evita* had been the last show Rice had written with Lloyd Webber. The parting had been mutual, but not, strictly speaking, final. Andrew had been angry with Tim ever since Stigwood had replaced Frank Corsaro with Tom O'Horgan while Lloyd Webber was in Vienna on his first honeymoon. "You know that O'Horgan's going to direct *Superstar,*" Tim had said casually to Lloyd Webber upon his return to London, and at that moment Lloyd Webber decided that his relationship with Rice could no longer be the same. Rice had missed that rumble of the volcano; after all, he had no objections to O'Horgan.

The humiliation over "Memory," had made matters worse, and the last straw had been Rice's summary dismissal from the song-cycle project. Rice had naturally envisaged it for Elaine, and they had written a couple of songs, but then Andrew had run off with Don Black, taking most of his tunes with him. Not all of them, though: one of them had come back home to roost in *Cricket* as the song "The Final Stand"

(and would resurface three years later as a principal theme of *Aspects of Love*). Tim had already recycled the original lyric for the Elton John song, "The Legal Boys" on the *Jump Up* album.*

Tim and Andrew worked well together on *Cricket*; it was almost like the old days. The rapprochement had begun early in the year, when Andrew invited Tim onto the board of the Really Useful Group and had given him three thousand and thirty shares. Both men were aware that, in the popular mind, they were still inextricably linked—"Tim Webber," indeed—and that everybody said they still needed each other. As they did: Andrew required Tim's leavening cynical wit to temper his own sentimental romanticism, and Tim needed Andrew's panzer-division force of will to ensure that anything they wrote would get on stage exactly as they wanted it to be.

Contrast the smooth progress of *Cricket* with what had happened with *Blondel* and *Chess*, the two strikingly autobiographical shows Tim had written without Andrew. *Blondel* was the restoration of Tim's idea for a comic musical about the Plantagenets, specifically, Richard the Lionheart, that had once been called *Come Back Richard, Your Country Needs You*. In 1978 Rice had met composer Stephen Oliver at the Sydney International Theatre Arts Forum in Australia and enlisted him in his quest to bring back Richard. Oliver was a prominent figure in the British theater, the composer of the incidental music (and lyrics) to the Royal Shakespeare Company's epic *Nicholas Nickleby* and more than forty other shows. In addition, he had written twenty operas, including *Tom Jones*, staged in 1976 at Sadler's Wells (now the English National Opera), and *The Duchess of Malfi*, presented at the Santa Fe Opera in New Mexico in 1978. Rice saw in Oliver a composer with a strong melodic gift as well as a sense of humor "which, if allowed to remain unleashed upon the outside world for much longer could have caused permanent damage to its owner," as Tim remarked in a liner note to the original-cast album.

Starring Paul Nicholas (the Jesus of the London production of *Superstar*) in the title role, and Sharon Lee Hill (in real life, Trevor Nunn's leading lady) as Fiona, directed by Peter James and produced by Cameron Mackintosh, *Blondel* opened in September 1983 in Bath, where it played for almost three weeks. The production moved to Manchester for about a fortnight before, like *Blondel* searching for Richard, it wandered into London and took up residence at the Old Vic for a limited run of eleven weeks. Finally, it moved on to the Aldwych, where it ran through 1984. Such peripateticism was a guaranteed way to spend money and lose your audience, and the seventy or eighty thousand pounds' profit the show turned at the Old Vic was eaten up by the high costs of moving.

The year 1983 was an especially difficult one for Tim and Jane. The interjection of Elaine Paige into their lives in 1979 had been a terrible shock for Jane. One minute everything was fine and the next minute it wasn't; their son Donald had been only two years old at the time. For four years, Jane had resisted Elaine fiercely. There were rows, ultimatums, reconciliations. Tim was leaving her. No, he wasn't. Yes, he was. Maybe he wasn't. One night, while writing *Blondel*, Tim finished a song and showed it to Jane. "This is yours," he said. "This is how I feel about you." It was the only time he ever did that; most of the time, Tim preferred to let the songs speak for themselves and let the people the songs were about figure the significance out for themselves.

The song was called "The Least of My Troubles." Andrew always said that Tim didn't know how to say, "I love you;" it was always "I love you, but . . . ." Back in *Superstar*, it had been "I Don't Know How to Love Him"—pure Tim. Now Rice said it like this:

The way that I love you is not in the text books,
I know of the trials I bring to your life;
I watch myself hurt you without even trying,
I cut you to ribbons, indiff'rence my knife.
And I'm a fool, Oh, such a fool.

I love to believe that the world is against me,
And sometimes I blame all my failings on you.
But you're my good fortune, the least of my troubles
The one I love most, the one that stays true.
And I'm a fool, Oh, such a fool.

The least of my troubles is right here beside me,
And you deserve more than my dreams will allow.
But when I'm distracted by crazy ambitions
You have to remember the words I say now,
I love you so, I love you so.

---

*As Andrew and Tim had drifted apart, Rice had not remained idle. Starting in 1975, he wrote many songs with other composers, including John Barry, Marvin Hamlisch, Rick Wakeman, Vangelis, Paul McCartney, Francis Lai, and Freddie Mercury.

Of course, there was also an "Elaine" song in *Blondel,* called "Running Back for More." Its words went:

> *From almost ev'ry point of view*
> *I don't need him any longer*
> *Once again I'm going through*
> *All the moves I've made before*
> *Till it comes to leaving,*
> *Till it comes to leaving.*
>
> *Half the world says leave him be*
> *Makes it sound so very easy*
> *They don't know the half of me*
> *How I've tried a thousand times*
> *How my love defeats me,*
> *How my love defeats me.*
>
> *Running back for more*
> *Running back for even more*
> *Hoping things will change, well that's no crime,*
> *Want a second chance just one more time*
> *Running back for more.*
>
> *Running back for more*
> *Running back for something more*
> *Any other road's a long, long climb*
> *Want the love I know and that's why I'm*
> *Running back for more.*

Blondel was a comedy—a human comedy—an underrated work, a brighter *Joseph and the Amazing Technicolor Dreamcoat* that, like *Joseph,* later found a home in the schools. In relating the story of Blondel's quest for the slightly ditzy, imprisoned Lionheart, and of the dastardly doings of slimy King John on the home front, Rice's wit and word play were given free rein in a story that, for some reason, had long obsessed him. There was the familiar use of a narrator, this time a chorus of monks who sang in mock-motet style, and the inevitable homage to rock and roll: the troubadour was a pop singer, backed by an all-girl group called the Blondettes. Oliver's tuneful, well-constructed score had some fine moments, including "The Least of My Troubles" and "Running Back for More," as well as the king's jail-cell lament, "Saladin Days." But the real interest lay in the lyrics, and what they revealed about Tim's life.

Three years later, the same was true of *Chess.* The *Chess* score was even stronger than *Blondel's*—from the standpoint of musical quality, it was not true that Rice's works without Lloyd Webber were not as good, they were just not as popular—and again, the lyrics were startlingly, brutally frank. There had been no role in *Blondel* for Paige, but there certainly was one in *Chess,* and, in Florence's song "Nobody's Side," she gave voice to sentiments that, more than any others, summed up Rice's bleak view of love:

> *What's going on around me*
> *is barely making sense*
> *I need some explanations fast*
> *I see my present partner*
> *in the imperfect tense*
> *And I don't see how we can last*
> *I feel I need a change of cast*
> *Maybe I'm on nobody's side.*

Never make a promise or plan
Take a little love where you can
Nobody's on nobody's side.
Never stay too long in your bed
Never lose your heart use your head
Nobody's on nobody's side.

Never be the first to believe
Never be the last to deceive
Nobody's on nobody's side.

So that was how Tim really felt. Just in case anybody missed the message, later in the show Rice offered a duet for the two women in the Russian chess player's life: his wife, Svetlana, and his mistress, Florence, although it was clear that their names were really Jane and Elaine. The song was "I Know Him So Well":

Svetlana:

No-one in your life is with you constantly
No-one is completely on your side
And though I move my world to be with him
Still the gap between us is too wide
Looking back I could have played it differently

Learned about the man before I fell
But I was ever so much younger then
Now at least I know I know him well

Florence (in counterpoint):

Looking back I could have played things some other way
I was just a little careless maybe
Now at least I know him well

Svetlana: Wasn't it good? (Florence: Oh so good)

Svetlana: Wasn't he fine? (Florence: Oh so fine)
Isn't it madness?

Both:

He won't be mine?
Didn't I know
How it would go?
If I knew from the start
Why am I falling apart?

It doesn't get much more explicit than that, and no one who knew the Rices could miss the significance of those lines, least of all Jane. "My God, I'm married to this man," she thought to herself upon reading them for the first time. Still, she could not leave him. Tim Rice was the great love of Jane McIntosh's life, and by the time of *Chess,* she had come to some accommodation with the unusual circumstances in which she found herself. The experience had made her a stronger, more self-reliant person, and like Tim, she now preferred to let things ride; it was, after all, so much easier to do nothing than to do something.

What Tim saw in Elaine, she thought she knew: he was in love with Paige's voice. Paige certainly could put over a song. Her reputation had never really crossed the Atlantic to America but she was very big in Australia and New Zealand, and connoisseurs of pop singing all over the world admired Paige: "the strongest, smartest voice in today's musical theater," *Time*'s Richard Corliss called her in a rave review of the *Chess* album in 1985. Elaine was something of a belter, but she had learned to control her vibrato so that when she hit a note, she hit it clean. There were many Paige imitators in Britain—Frances Ruffelle, for one, who had been in *Starlight Express* and had created the role of Eponine in *Les Misérables*—but none could sing like the original. She was sexy, too. In life, Elaine was short, shorter even than Jane, but on stage she towered. Back when *Evita* opened, Jane had jokingly warned her husband that he was going to fall in love with his Eva Perón, and now how bitter that joke had turned. Elaine was spunky, and there were times when Jane half thought Tim, who needed a strong woman, might be better off with Paige. But there were more times when she didn't, and so life went on.

None of this, however, clouded Tim's sunny surface. He was trying hard to make a hit of *Chess*, which he had been working on since 1977. He wanted to show Andrew he could do it without him. (Lloyd Webber had been his first choice for the composer, followed by Marvin Hamlisch, both of whom had turned him down.) Like *Superstar* and *Evita*, *Chess* started out in the studio. In a note to the recording, dated September 1984, Rice and "Benny and Björn" (as the two former members of ABBA were dubbed) called *Chess* "a work in progress," and indeed it was. It was, in fact, more "in progress" than comfort allowed. "In chaos" was a more apt description.

Chess had started smoothly enough. The record was finished in 1984, and the show immediately went on a five-city tour to London, Paris, Hamburg, Stockholm, and Amsterdam, and everywhere it was a sensation. The album too, sold very well—in some countries, it outsold *Phantom*; "I Know Him So Well" stayed at the top of the pops for four weeks and another song, "One Night in Bangkok," was an international hit. As thoughts turned to putting *Chess* on stage, a number of prominent directors volunteered their services, including Sir Peter Hall and the ubiquitous Trevor Nunn. But, from America, the Shuberts were pressing hard for their favorite, the choreographer-turned-director Michael Bennett, who had been responsible for both *A Chorus Line* and *Dreamgirls*. Despite the bad "Memory," Rice was leaning toward Nunn—"I can't stand short people, dancers, Jews, and homosexuals," he wisecracked to Andersson, who unfortunately missed the inverted commas around Rice's remark. "Other than that, I've got nothing against Bennett." But Jacobs and Schoenfeld were insistent, and by the spring of 1985, Bennett had been hired.

Tim and the Abbans successfully fought off a Shubert demand that the show open first in New York—there would be no chance for Elaine then—and so the premiere was planned for London. Rice flew to New York for a planning meeting with Bennett and was appalled at the cocaine-and-alcohol atmosphere that surrounded the New York theatrical demimonde. During the summer of 1985, Tim, Benny, and Björn were busy with rewrites and, late that year, they took the revised show on tour in Australia with the stars, Paige, Tommy Körberg and Murray Head, the original Superstar, who was paid four thousand pounds a week for his services. The tour was a mess; the cast was squabbling and there was no evidence of the team spirit necessary to make a show work. Something was very wrong.

Rice, however, felt powerless to do anything about it. What the show needed was a "Hitler," he felt, a tyrant who would kick butts and take names, but he, Rice, was not that man. Andrew, he knew, would have thrown a tantrum and chewed the carpet, scaring the hell out of everybody and getting his way, but Tim was not Andrew. In January 1986 Rice flew to New York to deliver the final script; by now the character of the CIA man, Walter de Courcey (the name was that of a cricketer Tim knew when he was young) had been added, the Russian and the American had both been baptized (Anatoly Sergievsky and Freddie Trumper, respectively), the Hungarian Florence got a last name (Vassy, pronounced "Vashee"), and there were several other important changes. Rice flew back home to England, expecting Bennett's imminent arrival to begin rehearsals, but the director kept putting off his trip until Tim began to suspect that something was amiss.

Something was. Bennett was dying of AIDS, although the excuse given was a heart problem.* At the end of January, Bennett officially withdrew from the show: with the premiere only three and a half months away, with an elaborate set built at a cost of one million pounds, with the cast under contract and the theater booked, the search for a director began anew. To make matters worse, there was a spate of bad press in London; having got the wind up, the curs of Fleet Street were starting to howl.

Nunn had always been the first alternate choice to Bennett, and so, with *Chess* in check and heading rapidly for mate, the director materialized and set to work. Nunn was a Loge-like creature; he could vanish for weeks on end, but when it was showtime, he usually had the magic fire at his fingertips. There was no time to rethink the production; they could do that in New York, Nunn told Rice. Using the set he had inherited from Bennett—a giant chessboard, flanked on either side by banks of television monitors—and retaining some of his staging ideas (he discarded Bennett's notion for a ballet), Nunn got *Chess* up and running successfully; as far as Tim was concerned, Trevor was a hero. Even better, the show was sold out for a year. In the end, the London *Chess* ran for nearly three years.

The dream of Broadway, however, proved to be a nightmare. To begin with, there was a complicated financial arrangement in which, as a quid pro quo, Rice's production company, Three Knights, Ltd., had to invest in the disastrous New York encore production of Nunn's *Nicholas*

---

*Bennett died on July 2, 1987, at the age of forty-four.

Nickleby; the production went a million and a half dollars in the red, of which Three Knights owed seven hundred and fifty thousand dollars, which was to come out of the profits of the Broadway *Chess*. So even before the show opened, Tim, Benny, and Björn were in the hole. Violating the first rule of Broadway, Rice put up an additional three million dollars of his own money to stage *Chess* in New York. The cost of the production was put at more than six million dollars.

Depressed, Rice began to slip into his familiar fatalism, although his hackles rose when Nunn brought in Richard Nelson, an American writer, to rework the plot. *Chess* in London had been entirely sung; in New York, it was like Le Carré with incidental songs. Even little things, like Walter's last name, were changed (goodbye de Courcey, hello Anderson), which infuriated Tim. Robin Wagner's heavy, leaden set was all wrong, too, not to mention horrifyingly complicated. The final insult was Nunn's failure to support Tim's application for Elaine's Equity waiver; when it became clear that Elaine was going to be hung out to dry, Rice withdrew it. It galled him no end: Andrew had gotten Sarah to Broadway for *Phantom,* but he had failed. The part of Florence went to the American actress Judy Kuhn.

Tim was not totally immobilized. He wrote five new lyrics, including one whole new song, the splendid "Someone Else's Story." But his disinterest was palpable, exacerbated by his father's death shortly before the show opened at the Imperial Theatre on April 28, 1988. Rice showed up at the end of the show, because he didn't want the cast to think he didn't care, but he didn't. Naturally, *Chess* was butchered by the Butcher of Broadway, Frank Rich, and the other critics. Although he hated the show in general, mistakenly characterizing the score as rock and roll*—come back, Richard Rodgers, your country needs you!—Rich singled Nunn out for special abuse. Noting the director's obvious pirating of his own ideas in *Nicholas Nickleby* and *Les Misérables,* Rich wrote: "He doesn't seem to be injecting passion into a play, so much as adding a branch store to an international conglomerate."

Now Nunn was not a hero, but a villain. "It's All Nunn's Fault, says Rice" ran the headline on Nigel Dempster's gossip column in *The Daily Mail* on July 7, 1988, twelve days after the show closed. "Whose fault was it?" wondered Rice. "Well, it wasn't Benny's or Björn's . . . and next time I will trust my own judgment. You tell me who's left."

Nor was Rice spared his wrath. Even though *Chess* had been slaughtered, it was still pulling in more than three hundred thousand dollars a week at the box office and was being greeted each night by a standing ovation. It also had a good chunk of its four million dollar advance still in the bank. In London, it could have gone on for years, the object of controversy and disagreement. But in New York, what Rich said, went, and Rich told *Chess* to go. The Shuberts felt that *Chess,* with the bulk of its advance bookings in the autumn, was not going to survive the lean summer months, and so they closed it. "'Chess' is not the sort of show that aging critics—by that I mean in attitude—like," an angry Rice told the press. "But to say that it is three hours of rock and roll, as The New York Times has stated, is an absolute lie. Maybe there is an anti-British thing occurring now on Broadway." Maybe there was. Earlier in June, the Royal Shakespeare Company's seven-million-dollar production of *Carrie* had closed after five performances following a devastating notice in *The New York Times.*

The pusillanimity of the Broadway producers in the face of one man's disapproval had never been more evident. To the critics in other disciplines, it was a wonder that these tough guys could turn out to be such wimps; Donal Henahan, *The New York Times'* chief music critic, couldn't shut down the Metropolitan Opera; Vincent Canby, the movie reviewer, couldn't put Paramount out of business. But let Frank Rich, or whoever was occupying the chief drama critic's chair, so much as frown and the producers went scurrying for cover like a flock of frightened quail.

In the meantime, *Phantom* had gone on to triumph at the Tony Awards, garnering, among other honors, the prize for Best Musical. With *Chess* in ruins, Tim could only fume quietly. The show he had hoped to send up against *Phantom,* with the woman he had hoped to send up against Sarah Brightman, had failed on all counts. *Chess* had received only two Tony nominations, not for itself but for Kuhn and costar David Carroll, and had not won anything. For Rice, nursing his jealousy, there was some small consolation: the prize for Best Score went not to *Phantom* but to *Into the Woods,* Sondheim's latest show. *Woods* was lesser Sondheim, not a patch on *Sweeney Todd*; the Tony voters had delivered a stinging rebuke to Lloyd Webber's pretensions to grandeur. As for Brightman, she had been totally ignored, not even nominated. At the awards ceremony, she sang a duet with Michael Crawford, her head held high; as Andrew took his trophy, he announced bravely, "This one's for Sarah." The question was, would his next show be for Sarah, too?

---

*Rich's error was repeated by many of his colleagues, who were unable to distinguish between rock and pop.

The one hundred and fifty or so invited guests who converged on Sydmonton Court in Hampshire over the weekend of July 8–10 had not come to disport themselves amid the natural beauty of the English countryside. On Friday the weather had turned cold; on Saturday a strong wind began to blow and it rained very hard, while Sunday dawned drizzly and gray. The climate hardly mattered, though, for on Saturday morning everybody was snugly ensconced inside the little chapel on the lawn. Theater professionals, record-company moguls, executives of the Really Useful Group had come from all across England and America to take a seat on the hard wooden pews and hear Lloyd Webber's latest work, *Aspects of Love.*

The history of *Aspects* stretched back nearly a decade, to Rice and Lloyd Webber's abortive search for inspiration at Eugénie-les-Bains in 1980 and through the 1983 Lloyd Webber–Nunn "cabaret" at Sydmonton. Unlike Tim, Andrew was not given to obsessions, but David Garnett's slender, precious 1955 novella about the amorous permutations of a sybaritic English aristocrat named George Dillingham, his French wife, Rose Vibert, his Italian mistress, Giulietta Trapani, his daughter Jenny, and his nephew Alex had gripped him. It seemed an unlikely subject. Lloyd Webber was not a man fired by sex (unlike Rice, who was still trying to deal with its consequences)—or, contrary to widespread belief, by money—but by control. One of the themes of *Superstar* was Jesus' loss of control over his disciples; *Evita* was about the attainment of power, and if there was tragedy in the show, it lay in Evita's forced relinquishing of it. The heroine of "Tell Me on a Sunday" had been helpless; so was the cat Grizabella, and so was the Rusty train until he got a dose of the Starlight Express. And what was *Phantom* about, if not control? Since the day he dropped out of Oxford, everything Lloyd Webber had done was devoted to making himself as impervious as possible to the actions of others. Andrew had been unhappy with his Ross Hannaman songs, so he became his own record producer; he had been unhappy with Land and Stigwood, so he invented the Really Useful Company and became his own manager. When he wanted to raise cash, he took his company public. Very likely, he would take it private again some day if an outside shareholder—the Warburgs, say—got too big. (Lloyd Webber was already chafing at some of the strictures on his latitude that attended a public company.) Nothing was done without thinking two or three moves ahead. Even the great trappings of wealth, such as the multiple residences, had a purpose other than conspicuous consumption: the politically sympathetic Tory government in power notwithstanding, for tax reasons Lloyd Webber had to spend part of each year out of the country.

Where did *Aspects* fit in, then? In the early eighties nothing had come of it because things were falling apart with Tim; the 1983 *Aspects* had not worked because neither music nor lyrics suited the subject. Moreover, a story about sex, or sexual feelings, between a younger man and an older woman, between a younger woman and an older man, between two women, and between a teenage girl and a man in his thirties would seem to have little to do with life as Lloyd Webber led it. Sexually, he was far from adventurous, having contracted his first marriage at an early age and having divorced to marry a woman with whom he had more in common professionally. Lloyd Webber's wealth and position did not seem to bring with it the opportunities for dalliance that many others had experienced; there was no casting-room couch in his theater. Even a troll could get women if he were rich or powerful enough (the plot of Wagner's *Ring* cycle was in part predicated on this fact). Andrew, though, never boasted of a sexual conquest or bird-bonking—not even into his second or third bottle of wine with his buddies, when the tall tales were flying—only of his desire. It still irritated him when the theater queens imputed inversion to his apparently low sex drive, but Lloyd Webber had long ago learned that not even the most ardent heterosexual was immune from those wishful whispers. Maybe what he had once told an interviewer, at the height of the Sarah–Mike Moran gossip, was true: he and Brightman were just too busy for an affair with anyone else. "The morning after *Phantom* opened in London two years ago, I read the reviews, and realized that my wife would be working in it that night and therefore I'd have no one to dine with," he told Sheridan Morley in *The Times*. "So I went to work on the next show."

In the same interview, which took place in late August 1988, Lloyd Webber offered a clue as to what had attracted him about *Aspects*: "Garnett himself was really the old man in the book and also the boy, so you have a sort of double-autobiography about a man obsessed by cats and wine and girls, though I'd rather we didn't explore that analogy in too much more detail." The part about cats was true enough. Cats were not only pets, they were props: if a conversation bored Andrew or made him uncomfortable, he would wander off in search of a cat to address.

The bit about wine was correct, too: Lloyd Webber's wine cellars at Sydmonton were one of England's glories, stocked with the best reds and whites France had to offer. Andrew had become something of a punter as far as wine was concerned and would buy and sell vintages with aplomb, but the cellar's principle destination was the table. For such a volatile personality, Lloyd Webber reacted to professional pressure not by exploding—his famous tantrums were always in reaction to frustration—but by growing colder. His physical resemblance to a cat had been often remarked, not the least by Britain's editorial cartoonists, but it was never more apparent than when he was angry. The object of his wrath would be fixed with a withering stare; the right shoulder would rise like a cat's back and his whole body would go rigid. The words would be spat out, icy and clipped. It was not a pretty sight, and it terrified almost everyone. Somewhat to the concern of Andrew's closest associates, who worried that he was becoming too dependent on the grape, a few glasses of wine tended to keep the tiger in the cage. But when the money was on the table, there was not a clearer or more sober mind in the house. Nothing was worth giving up control.

Despite the implication of his words to Morley, Andrew was not obsessed by women in general. He was obsessed by two women in particular, the two he had married. "The young wife," he called Brightman, and it was hard to tell which he loved more, Sarah's physical beauty or her singing. Like Tim with Elaine Paige, Andrew had fallen in love first with the voice and then with the woman, and, like Tim, Andrew wanted her for everything he wrote. Still, the happier he seemed with Brightman, the more wistful he would grow when discussing the first Sarah. After an initial period of hurt and hostility, they had been seeing more of each other, and he had bought her the house in Oxfordshire. Once they went off with the children to see a road production of *Evita*, and suddenly all the old memories came flooding back; it was all Andrew could do to prevent himself from reproposing to her on the spot, even though by this time Sarah had remarried, to a man named Jeremy Norris. Could you love two people at once? In *Aspects of Love*, Garnett had said you could: "You can have two emotions at the same time," the character Alex says. "One makes the other even more acute and then cures it." What the cure was, however, Andrew had no idea.

Sarah Norris had been an exemplary wife, of that there was no doubt. Very few women could have handled the demands of sudden fame and wealth—not to mention the demands of Andrew—as well as she had. Sarah was the kind of woman whom a husband could telephone at three in the afternoon, inform that he was inviting a dozen people home for dinner, and by eight o'clock she would have a party for fourteen on the table. Sarah Brightman was not like that; what she offered Andrew was glamour, a presence, and a voice.

That was why the pounding that Brightman had taken in *Phantom* had hurt him so much. He had warned her it might be like this, that his enemies would use her to get at him, and that she was in for a few rough years as Mrs. Lloyd Webber before she would be able to step out again as Ms. Brightman. Sarah's experience in *Phantom*, he knew, was actually three different experiences. In Britain, she had been a natural target for the leerers: "Wrote a piece for the missus, did he? (wink, wink, nudge, nudge)." Then came the Equity mess, in which American national pride could only be satisfied by Andrew's taking a few lumps before he got his way. And then there were the New York reviews . . . Minnie Mouse on Quaaludes, indeed.*

The truth was, however, that Brightman was a very good singer, and she projected exactly the air of vulnerability and innocence that the role of Christine demanded. "The Equity row over Sarah's admission was unfortunate," Lloyd Webber told Morley, "but we knew that we really hadn't got a show without her, because that kind of European vulnerability just doesn't seem to exist on Broadway." Now there was British understatement for you, as anyone who had ever attended an open call in New York—or seen *A Chorus Line*—could testify. Brightman had not begun studying voice seriously until she was almost twenty and still had a long way to go, but she was improving each year, slowly shedding the nasality of her upper register while maintaining its purity and gradually discovering a chest voice that she never knew she had.

---

*Contrast this gaucherie with David Richards's estimation in *The Washington Post*: "Sarah Brightman's luminous eyes and cherubic features are those of the eternal, and eternally enchanting, ingenue," although Richards also remarked that Brightman "tends to play the languishing victim better than the exalted prima donna."

(Andrew had her record "English Girls" from *Song and Dance* and was delighted with the new, throaty Brightman.) How quickly everybody forgot, if they had ever noticed, that when she opened in *Phantom,* Brightman had been only twenty-six years old. Any other singer would have been hailed as a dazzling new discovery—a real-life Christine Daaé.

And yet, despite all this, *Phantom* had been a hit. What was it that Frank Rich had said? "If by chance this musical doesn't prove Mr. Lloyd Webber's most popular. . . ." (You had to love the gentility of *The New York Times*; even when it was kicking you in the teeth the paper still called you Mister.) Well, there was no chance. In April 1989 *Variety* had trumpeted the news that, after sixty straight sellout weeks, *Phantom* had recouped on Broadway. The show was earning one hundred and fify thousand dollars' profit a week on grosses of five hundred fifty thousand dollars—and it still had an advance sale of more than twenty million dollars. And that was just New York. In Los Angeles, where the show opened on May 31, there was already sixteen million dollars in the till. In Toronto, where *Phantom* opened on September 20 with Colm Wilkinson, Sydmonton's original Opera Ghost, in the title role, there was twelve million Canadian dollars more. (On the day tickets went on sale in Toronto, there had been an advance order of over one million Canadian dollars, besting the previous single-day record five times over.) In addition, there was a *Phantom* in Tokyo and a *Phantom* in Vienna, and *Phantom*s planned for Sweden and West Germany.

Cats may have been "the pension fund," but *Phantom* was proving no slouch, either: Lloyd Webber, Richard Stilgoe, and Charles Hart, along with the original London production as licensor, were splitting an aggregate weekly royalty of 9.35 percent of the gross, about fifty thousand dollars a week, while Prince, with a 2.55-percent royalty, was pulling down roughly fourteen thousand dollars a week. Cameron Mackintosh and the Really Useful Group were splitting the producer's 1.7-percent weekly royalty of more than nine thousand dollars. When *The Beggar's Opera* had swept London two hundred years ago, the witticism was that the show had made "Rich [John Rich, the producer] gay and Gay [John Gay, the librettist] rich." Things were no different now. Take that, Rich (Frank, the critic).

But what made a show a hit? The obvious answer was money, and *Phantom* certainly had plenty of that. Strictly speaking, the obvious answer was also true. Everybody, and not just Lloyd Webber, defined hit shows by their success at the box office. Sharply divided critical opinion about the worth of a score was nothing new in either musical or theatrical history, and a bad review did not disprove a piece's quality. Nicholas Slonimsky, the brilliant Russian-born composer, conductor, and musicologist, had collected the nasty things critics had said about great men and great music into an amusing and instructive little volume called *The Lexicon of Musical Invective* (it was Derek Jewell's idea, effected a couple of decades earlier). It was easy, and fun, to read the lexicon and have a good laugh over Eduard Hanslick's remark that the finale of the Tchaikovsky Violin Concerto was music that "stinks to the ear." God knows, Tchaikovsky didn't laugh about it at the time, though, and that was why it never got easier for Lloyd Webber to face the mornings after. There was always a Frank Rich to read.

Not that he wasn't getting some respect in the United States: in the spring of 1988 Lloyd Webber was honored by both ASCAP and the National Institute for Music Theater for his achievements. ASCAP gave him its first "Triple Play" award in recognition of Andrew's twice having had three shows playing simultaneously in London and New York, while the NIMT, whose focus tended to be operatic, celebrated him at the Kennedy Center at its eleventh annual National Music Theater Awards. John Rockwell, in a *New York Times Magazine* cover story, had speculated that Lloyd Webber's works might "lead to a new synthesis of artistic seriousness and popular appeal." Sure enough, the Cologne Opera in West Germany was making noises about wanting to stage *Phantom,* and the English National Opera was after *Aspects of Love.*

The simmering animosity between Lloyd Webber and Rich, however, was developing into a composer–critic feud on the order of the Wagner–Hanslick conflict of the late nineteenth century, with Stephen Sondheim, Rich's favorite, cast in the role of Brahms. It was a small irony that Sondheim, eighteen years Andrew's senior, and Lloyd Webber shared the same birthday, March 22—and a greater one that they should ever be pitted against each other, since the future of Broadway depended on both men retaining a high degree of creativity. To critics looking for a club with which to beat Lloyd Webber, Sondheim came in handy, laden as he was with the "complex" tag that attended his music. To the untrained ear, Sondheim's often studious avoidance of chart busters meant one of two things: either he couldn't write a melody, or his tunes were incredibly sophisticated. In his 1974 biography *Sondheim & Co.,* Craig Zadan quoted Sondheim's friend, the actor Keith Baxter: "It seems to me, that when Steve composes a song, whenever he hears a melody creeping in, he slams his foot down and stomps on it!"

That was a joke, of course, although it was true that given a choice between Sondheim the lyricist (*West Side Story, Gypsy*) and Sondheim the melodist (*Company, Follies*), most people would opt for the former. "A Hart in search of a Rodgers," said Clive Barnes. "Or even a Boito in search of a Verdi." But Sondheim could write popular melodies when he chose to—"Send in the Clowns" from *A Little Night Music,* for example—and in *Sweeney Todd* (arranged and orchestrated by the magnificent Jonathan Tunick), he had written a masterpiece. It was true that Sondheim's words-and-music shows had a low batting average. *Follies* was a critical sensation in some quarters, but a public dud; *Sweeney Todd* didn't run as long as it should have; and *Merrily We Roll Along* failed on both counts.* The fairy-tale *Into the Woods* was a hit, in large part because of the subject matter (although even here, the characters had been transformed into stereotypical New York neurotics, more grim than Grimm) and in part because Bernadette Peters had been in the original cast as the witch. But by mid-April 1989 it was falling off, playing to three-quarters' capacity, and half-price seats were readily available at the Times Square TKTS booth. That week, the only musicals not on discount were *Phantom* and *Les Misérables,* and it was a sign of Lloyd Webber's total dominance of Broadway that, in America, *Les Misérables* was often mistaken for another of his shows. The point was that Sondheim and Lloyd Webber were not mutually exclusive (neither were Wagner and Brahms). If anyone had a right to an opinion about the works of both, that man was Hal Prince, and he let his professional activity speak for him: champion of Sondheim, champion of Lloyd Webber.

Why then, Lloyd Webber's low critical repute in some publications? "It's just jealousy, and isn't that too damn bad," said Prince. Civilians, too, rose to Lloyd Webber's defense. "When will the critical bashing of this musical [*Phantom*] and its composer ever end?" wondered a reader of *The Washington Post* in the letters column of February 6, 1988. "Let the experts complain all they want of repeated musical themes, fully aware that Puccini's *La Bohème* and Wagner's *Ring* have more. They may even recall the weak story lines of Verdi's *Il Trovatore* and Mozart's *Magic Flute.* The rest of us lesser mortals will continue to enjoy the pleasant memory of wonderfully old-fashioned romantic music, state-of-the-art special effects and the once-in-a-lifetime performance by Michael Crawford in *The Phantom of the Opera.*"

Rich, of course, didn't see it that way. His legit stage savvy was great and his knowledge of the minutiae of the musical theater wide — he had written a book on the theater art of Boris Aronson, the designer of such Sondheim shows as *Company, Follies, A Little Night Music,* and *Pacific Overtures* — but like most of his drama-desk colleagues he had to write around music, not about it. In Rich's articles, Lloyd Webber was emblematic of all that was wrong with the contemporary music theater, and he rarely failed to drag the composer into a discussion of its ills; for Rich, Lloyd Webber was the ultimate invidious comparison.† For his part, Andrew tried to restrain himself whenever Rich's name came up. He knew that artists were not supposed to take criticism personally (although how could they not?), but occasionally he would lose his temper and start to rant, sometimes publicly. At the lavish opening-night party for *Phantom* in New York, held in the Beacon Theatre at Broadway and Seventy-fourth Street (which had been transformed into a Belle Époque space at a cost of a quarter of a million dollars), Lloyd Webber had insisted that Fred Nathan, the press agent, show him the reviews, including Rich's. Nathan resisted, because he was aware that the table was surrounded by Fleet Street reporters, and because he knew that Lloyd Webber's reaction — the more intemperate the better — would be printed in the English newspapers the next day. The Lloyd Webber boil quickly turned into an eruption. "This is a man who knows nothing about love," shouted Andrew, citing as proof Rich's impending divorce, and in private he could be even ruder. Now the feud really had turned personal.

Still, the critics, even Rich, made him think; ever since Meirion Bowen's negative review of *Joseph,* Andrew had respected not their expertise, which was arguable, but their clout. Critics, he knew, in part created the word of mouth about a show, the buzz, and one simply had to react to what they said; if you ignored it, then you had lost touch with the pulse of the public.

Just as the *Requiem* and *The Phantom of the Opera* had been envisaged with Sarah in mind, there seems little doubt that Lloyd Webber's first intention was to make *Aspects* a vehicle for her as well. There it was: that is what he saw in *Aspects of Love.* Rice, for one, thought so too, which had only served to dampen further any desire he had to work on the show. That and the fact that, since Andrew wanted every word sung, there would have to be lines like "Please pass the salt," which didn't allow a lyricist much imaginative scope.

After Sarah's hostile reception in *Phantom,* however, Lloyd Webber was determined not to expose her to that kind of flak again. Isolated songs, maybe;‡ her own albums, certainly, among them a collection of songs from failed shows that included "Half a Moment" from *Jeeves:* and even a television film about the life of Jessie Matthews, the popular entertainer. But no shows. Besides, he had a deal with Equity: one of the stars of his next show had to be an "unknown" American.

It was a veteran London theater cast that took the chapel's tiny stage, accompanied by two pianos and a small chorus, for the first complete performance of *Aspects of Love* on Saturday, July 9. Welsh tenor Michael Ball, who had made a name for himself as Marius in *Les Misérables*

---

*Reviewing *Merrily* in *New York* magazine, John Simon trashed the composer, librettist George Furth, and director Hal Prince. "There are plot, staging, design, music, and dance concepts from just about all their previous shows cluttering up the stage: rehashed, warmed-over, or half-baked. Thus we get the interweaving of two song numbers, progression by alternating fits and starts in book and score, present and former selves interacting (*Follies*), movable platforms on different levels (*Company*), closely packed human blocs dancing as a viscous mass (from Prince's *Evita,* likewise choreographed by Larry Fuller), and reams of music and lyric writing that broken-wingedly take off from, or are takeoffs on, former Sondheim songs. No wonder audiences applaud bits of the overture as they ordinarily do only at revivals: They are welcoming back old Sondheim melodies even if they sound older and leaner after a long absence of invention." Change the names and it could almost be a Frank Rich review of a Lloyd Webber show.

†At a New York dinner party shortly before *Aspects of Love* opened in London, Arthur Gelb, managing editor of *The New York Times,* asked one of Lloyd Webber's associates if the new show was something Rich would like. Before the man could reply, Gelb's wife, Barbara, interjected, "Oh, Arthur, you know Frank never likes anything Andrew writes."

‡One of Brightman's hit singles, "Him," was a Lloyd Webber updating of Hubert Parry's anthem "Dear Lord and Father" — a musical pun that Bill would have appreciated.

and was then appearing as Raoul in the London *Phantom,* was Alex; Susannah Fellows, who had been Elaine Paige's understudy and alternate in *Evita,* was Rose; Grainne Renihan, who was singing Florence in *Chess,* was Giulietta; Mary Millar, the first Madame Giry in *Phantom,* was the housekeeper and the circus chanteuse; Dinsdale Landen was George Dillingham, and Zoe Hart and Diana Morrison played Jenny at ages twelve and fourteen. The performance—the most fully realized presentation of any Lloyd Webber work ever done at Sydmonton—was directed by Trevor Nunn.

To anyone outside the theater, Lloyd Webber's selection of Nunn as the director of his new show must have seemed incomprehensible. Andrew had publicly disowned Nunn's work on *Starlight Express,* humiliated him over the first version of *Aspects,* and fallen out with him in the planning stages of *Phantom.* Furthermore, the director Lloyd Webber really wanted was a young Englishman named Nicholas Hytner; at Andrew's fortieth birthday party, held in his apartment in the Trump Tower in New York (among the guests were Bernadette Peters, Mandy Patinkin, and composer Charles Strouse), he had confided that Hytner, a rising star on the British opera scene, was the man for the job. But, plead as Lloyd Webber might, Hytner had a previous commitment, which he would not cancel, so Andrew once more turned to Nunn, who came running back for more.*

The truth was that personal feelings didn't matter. Lloyd Webber had his stable—Prince and Nunn as directors, Lynne and Phillips as choreographers, Martin Levan as the sound designer, and the Davids Caddick and Cullen as the music director and the orchestrator—and he didn't want to break it up. True, he didn't need Mackintosh any more; Biddy Hayward was doing such a great job producing that he no longer felt the need for Mackintosh's expertise, and he had no desire to share the profits of *Aspects* with him. He also had a splendid new personal assistant, a pretty young woman named Jane Fann who was another Hayward-in-the-making: crisp of accent, cool of manner, and very reliable. Andrew felt a certain degree of loyalty to his team, he liked their work and, in any case, one did not argue with success. Audiences had certain expectations about a Lloyd Webber show and one frustrated them at one's peril: since *Aspects of Love* was intended to be a departure from the megamusical tradition of *Cats, Starlight,* and *Phantom,* Lloyd Webber didn't want to disturb the public any more than necessary.

Despite his experience with *Aspects* so far, Nunn was happy to take on the job. He had already devoted a lot of time and study to the novel, and even when Andrew had been on his shopping spree for a lyricist—for a while, around the time of *Song and Dance* in America, Richard Maltby had a leg up, but then he and Andrew seemed to have had a dispute—Nunn had stayed interested and available until the call came: Andrew was thinking about *Aspects* again and would Trevor like to think with him? Not as the lyricist this time, but as the director? At the time, Nunn was living in the south of France, working on a book about his experiences with subsidized theater in the wake of his controversial departure from the Royal Shakespeare Company, but it didn't take him very long to say yes.

Meanwhile, Lloyd Webber had found his lyricist—or, rather, had found two of them. Charles Hart, his *Phantom* protégé, would collaborate with Don Black, of "Tell Me on a Sunday." The unusual arrangement was necessitated by Lloyd Webber's clear-headed assessment of each man's strengths. Hart, the tyro who affected the languorous ennui of an Evelyn Waugh character, had a flair for romantic imagery, as *Phantom* had shown, but his youthful reliance on cliché and shopworn British figures of speech hampered his effectiveness; Black, the veteran professional with a good sense of humor, would be a much-needed counterweight. (In the end, Black wrote most of the lines, while Hart's job was to maintain the project's "literary" tone, according to the structure and plot dictated by Lloyd Webber, the uncredited "book" writer.) In the summer, Lloyd Webber, Nunn, Black, and Hart gathered at Andrew's place at Cap Ferrat. By the end of 1987, Act One was finished, with Act Two completed during the first couple of months of 1988.

Following his preferred method of working, Lloyd Webber wrote the music first. The speed with which *Aspects* had to be composed meant that it could not all be written to order. From the 1983 cabaret came the Pyreenean folk song—itself Andrew's recollection of one of the tunes from his juvenile *Toy Theatre* Suite—and, more noticeably, a song that Julie Covington (the original Evita on disc) had recorded in 1984 under the title "Remember Why We Fell in Love," which became the theme of a television show called "Executive Stress."

To Tim Rice's extreme annoyance, *Cricket* also was raided in Lloyd Webber's quest for serviceable tunes. As far as Rice was concerned, Andrew's contention (in a program note for the *Aspects* premiere) that, aside from the folk song, the Covington tune and another theme, "all of the principal melodies and the great body of the work were written, therefore, during the course of my collaboration with Don and Charlie" was untrue. Upon hearing a tape of the Sydmonton performance, he counted four or five *Cricket* tunes in *Aspects,* among them a song called "The Final Stand" that turned up prominently in *Aspects* as a playful theme for George and Jenny.† Whatever hopes Rice had of someday

*Hytner was promptly grabbed by Cameron Mackintosh to direct the follow-up to *Les Misérables* by Boublil and Schoenberg, *Miss Saigon,* which opened in London in the fall of 1989.
†This song, in turn, had been originally conceived for the song cycle that Andrew and Tim were writing for Elaine Paige, which eventually became the Lloyd Webber–Black "Tell Me on a Sunday" for Marti Webb.

staging an expanded *Cricket* were destroyed; gone too was any likelihood that any of the *Cricket* songs, with Rice's original lyrics, would be covered by other singers on records. *Cricket* was a total loss, and Rice felt hurt and betrayed. Nothing Andrew did surprised him any more, but this time he really had thought things were going to be different. The teamwork on *Cricket,* the seat on the board of the Really Useful Group—Tim could have sworn that this time it was going to work out. But no. A gentleman to the end, Rice was asked about the future of *Cricket* during an interview in the April 8, 1989, issue of *The Daily Telegraph.* "I believe some of the tunes have been reused in 'Aspects of Love,'" Tim replied. "You know what composers are like. . . ."

In directing *Aspects,* Nunn's challenge was to flesh out what Garnett had first intended to be no more than a short story, to give the characters more background and motivation and to set up the relationships better. The ending of the novel, when Alex and Giulietta finally meet, make love, and go off together, was particularly unsatisfactory, and after the Sydmonton performance Nunn decided the action had to be "framed," to introduce Giulietta earlier. Lloyd Webber's professed intention all along had been to open the show without a conventional overture, with just a boy, a piano, and a three-chord song called "Love Changes Everything," but Nunn insisted that Giulietta must be on stage at the beginning, too, even if she was silent.

Nunn had identified the salient problem of *Aspects of Love,* but he didn't know what to do about it. For Rice had been right: the story was thin, and it got thinner every time one looked at it objectively. Andrew, however, was adamant about wanting his *Aspects* to be as close to the original as possible. From the way he talked about Garnett—a minor Bloomsbury Group figure who passed up a chance to have an affair with Lytton Strachey to marry Angelica Bell, the daughter of painter Duncan Grant and Vanessa Bell, Virginia Woolf's sister—one would have thought he was speaking of Shakespeare, or at least T. S. Eliot. During the festival, Melvyn Bragg had introduced, and then shown, a tape of an interview with Garnett he had conducted at the author's home in France in 1979 (Garnett died in 1981 at the age of eighty-nine), which was greeted with great reverence by all, as was a talk by Garnett's son, Richard, who played the Martin Sullivan–P. G. Woodhouse–Valerie Eliot role as the imprimatur of the project.*

Reaction to the Sydmonton *Aspects* was generally positive. Although there were some who were puzzled by its seriousness, *Aspects* seemed to many Andrew's best score. It didn't matter where the tunes had come from; Lloyd Webber had welded them together almost seamlessly. In sound and feel, *Aspects* reminded listeners of Puccini's underrated operetta, *La Rondine.* There was the same wistful quality about *Aspects,* of love won and lost, of the pain that inevitably attends romance. Still, the subject made some of the visiting Americans uncomfortable. The British, for whom the south of France had a special emotional resonance, could accept a story about a randy aristocrat like George Dillingham; in any case, George's license seemed more philosophical ("Life goes on, love goes free," was George's motto) than physical. But sex, especially when presented as an end in itself—as A Good Thing without a lot of attendant chatter about Caring, Sharing, and Meaningful Relationships—made Americans very nervous. The sexual revolution in the United States had been something of a fraud to begin with (all a European had to do was look at the repressed and censored American television programming to see that), but now, with the spector of AIDS, the story seemed terribly dated and even a little offensive. There might have to be some changes for New York.†

Lloyd Webber had talked of opening *Aspects of Love* first on Broadway, but the American reservations—and the prospect of letting Frank Rich have the first say—discouraged him. By the end of the summer of 1988, plans called for an April 1989 premiere in London, and Lloyd Webber busied himself with all aspects of *Aspects.* His desire for complete control, backed with the indisputable evidence of his successes, had left him in position to have the final say on everything: casting, design, marketing, advertising. Lloyd Webber spent a good deal of time, for example, on the show's distinctive, heart-shaped logo of a man and a woman wrapped in a passionate embrace, rejecting two variations prepared by the designer, Dewynters, before settling on the third.‡

A far greater test of his control came in the fall when, in a coup stage-managed from the wings by Lloyd Webber, the fifty-three-year-old Brian Brolly was forced out as managing director of the Really Useful Group. To eyes in the City and on Wall Street, Brolly's stewardship had been a success: in 1987, only its second year as a public company, earnings were up 33 percent after a 59-percent increase the year before. Brolly, who had known Andrew since the MCA *Superstar* days, was a fierce defender of copyright; "If the Tierra del Fuego Operatic Society

---

*Following Sydmonton tradition, the other principal events were the Saturday evening dinner, followed by the annual Sydmonton Debate. That year the topic was "Sydmonton Believes the Welsh Sing No Better than Anyone Else." Among those arguing for the house was the Conservative politician John Selwyn Gummer, while the Welsh held up their end with the entertainer Max Boyce and boy soprano Aled Jones. For a change, the host won, only the second victory for the home side in fourteen years. Due to the weather, a ballooning exhibition had to be canceled, as did the Sunday afternoon croquet match.

†The subsequent success of *Aspects of Love* in Britain, however, proved an unexpected windfall for the Garnett family, which received profit participation in the show. The novel, long out of print, was reissued in Britain by Hogarth Press, and the American rights were auctioned for one hundred thousand dollars; German, Dutch, and Swedish editions also were announced.

‡Dewynters' fortunes climbed along with Lloyd Webber's. In 1979 it was a one-man operation; a decade later, the company occupied two floors of prime Leicester Square office space.

produced *Evita* without permission," noted *The Evening Standard,* "Brolly would have a writ-server in the front row on opening night." Aware that the company could not stay viable very long without Lloyd Webber's continued good health and musical fecundity, Brolly had diversified the group, establishing the Really Useful Record Company, the Really Useful Picture Company, which made television commercials and corporate films, acquiring the book publishing house of Aurum Press, and buying a 44-percent stake in Interactive Information Systems, a firm that created software programs for industrial management training. There was even talk of buying a London classical radio station.

For a time, Lloyd Webber seemed enthusiastic about the turn his company was taking. Besides, he would sway, shrugging his shoulders, as a nonexecutive member of the board of directors, there was nothing he could do about it; it was all up to Brolly and Biddy Hayward. Except, of course, that it wasn't; Lloyd Webber may have been a nonexecutive director, but he was an eight-hundred-pound gorilla of a nonexecutive director. When in October 1988 the company's share price slipped to five pounds twenty-seven pence, from a high of six pounds ten pence, and revenues and profits dropped as well, both Lloyd Webber and Lord Gowrie, the company's chairman, became alarmed.

On October 26 Brolly, who was earning an annual salary of one hundred and thirty thousand pounds, lost a vote of confidence over the direction the company was taking, and he resigned. Brolly's "golden parachute" included an eight-hundred-thousand pound buyout (nearly one and a half million dollars) — a two-hundred-thousand-pound lump sum and six hundred thousand pounds in lieu of pension — as well as a retention of one and a half million shares in the Really Useful Group. "This was a board decision," said Lloyd Webber in his public statement. "Obviously Brian has contributed a great deal to the company since we started and I wish him every success." The next day, the stock dropped seventeen pence, to just over five pounds a share.

Two days later, Brolly's departure from the board of the Really Useful Group was followed by Tim Rice's. For Tim, who owned three thousand and thirty shares of the company, the *Cricket–Aspects* transformation had been the last straw, and his resignation grew more out of his animosity toward his former partner than out of any feelings of loyalty to Brolly. Rice's departure was explained by the classic euphemism that he had left "in order to devote his time to pursuing other interests." In the reshuffle that followed, Lloyd Webber (who still owned four million two hundred thousand shares) once again became a managing director. Now the tune was different. Brolly was taking the company into areas beyond its expertise; it was better to stick close to the business of producing theater shows; and just what was an interactive video, anyway?

Andrew was too busy to shed many tears for either Brolly or Rice. On October 29 he hosted Biddy Hayward for a Saturday lunch at Sydmonton. On Monday he was at the Playhouse Theatre in London, where auditions for *Aspects* were being held; at three o'clock that afternoon he had a meeting with RUG legal affairs director Keith Turner about the board meeting the following morning. The rest of the week was occupied mainly with *Aspects* auditions and rehearsals for Sarah Brightman's showcase concert of Lloyd Webber's music performed that week in Nottingham and Brighton by Sarah, Ball, two other solo singers, the twelve-voice Stephen Hills Singers, and the seventy-piece London Concert Orchestra conducted by Mike Reed.

The next week found Lloyd Webber in Washington, D.C., where he attended the last state dinner given by President Ronald Reagan for Mrs. Thatcher. Lloyd Webber had more than a passing acquaintance with the American president, having dined with him previously at Walter Annenberg's estate in Palm Springs; in June Andrew had also been a guest of the Reagans at Spaso House, the residence of the American ambassador in Moscow, where he found himself mingling with pianist Dave Brubeck, arms negotiator Max Kampelman, Yuri Dubinin, the Soviet ambassador to the United States, and, of course, Soviet premier Mikhail Gorbachev.

As the City speculated on possible retrenchment, Hayward assured investors that related industries, such as the publishing house of Aurum Press, would remain untouched. "The group's continuing policy is to diversify—we don't see it as a Lloyd Webber cottage industry—and Aurum Press is very much a part of that policy," she said. Hayward and Turner were named as interim executive directors until Brolly could be replaced. On February 23, 1989, John Whitney, director-general of the Independent Broadcasting Authority since 1982, was named RUG managing director, at a salary of one hundred fifty thousand pounds. As far back as October 28, 1988, two days after Brolly's resignation, Lloyd Webber had his eye on Whitney, the former chief of Capital Radio whose duties with the IBA included overseeing Britain's independent television stations. Whitney had run into political difficulties with the Tory government over programming, especially on the enterprising Channel Four, and so was kindly disposed when RUG came calling. His February resignation from the IBA came eighteen months before his contract was due to expire. As for Brolly, he used part of his payoff to establish a company with songwriters Eric Woolfson and Alan Parsons (collectively known as the Alan Parsons Project) called Freudiana holdings, whose purpose was to develop a four-million-pound musical on the life of Sigmund Freud.

There were, however, some things that remained beyond even Lloyd Webber's reach. One was the BBC, whose Radio One station was not playing "Love Changes Everything," which the twenty-six-year-old Ball had recorded and released, complete with a high B-flat on the song's final note, in February 1989 as a kind of calling-card for the new show. (The "B" side was called "Aspects of Aspects," a full-orchestra fantasy on three of the opera's themes: "Seeing Is Believing," "Hand Me the Wine and the Dice," and "Love Changes Everything.") The song had risen to number two on the charts, but the rock station said it did not fit its play list, and it never got any higher. "By my reckoning that's four of my last five songs that haven't got airplay," Lloyd Webber told the press. "I'm not saying it's a vendetta, but it's bizarre."

Another was his own commercial instincts. No matter how often Lloyd Webber might say that he wanted *Aspects* to be simple—"Mozartean" was a word he had used to describe it—it seemed inevitable that, when the curtain went up, *Aspects* would in some way approximate a typical Lloyd Webber–Nunn spectacle; from his experience with the New York *Chess,* Rice could testify to that. Still there was hope that *Aspects of Love* might be somewhat restrained, for Lloyd Webber had a perfect chance to tap the zeitgeist again. Everybody was sick of spectacle, and were *Aspects* to prove the small-bore chamber piece he claimed it was, Andrew stood a good chance of being congratulated for bucking his own trend and establishing intimacy as the new norm. "Intimate, intimate," he said to Mark Steyn in *The Independent,* "It's got to be intimate." With typically felicitous timing, *Aspects* was scheduled to open the month after a show called *Metropolis,* whose principal claim to fame was the dazzling set of Ralph Koltai, which sought to recreate the look and feel of Fritz Lang's classic movie. Starring Judy Kuhn, late of *Chess,* the show's music, lyrics, and book were by songwriter Joe Brooks; the cost of the production was two and a half million pounds. Opening March 8, 1989, it was panned by the critics, who were enchanted by the set but not much else.

The failure of *Metropolis* once again set London's pundits to worrying about the future of the West End musical. In January revivals of *Sugar Babies* and *Can-Can* closed, as did a new musical called *Budgie,* which had music by Mort Shuman and lyrics by Don Black; across the Atlantic, there was the epic disaster of Peter Allen's *Legs.* Somehow, Elton John's announcement that he planned a musical based on Anne Rice's vampire novels did not inspire confidence. Only Lloyd Webber, it seemed, could not lose.

Or could he? In January, after considering actors such as Albert Finney (the early favorite) and Christopher Plummer for the role of George, Andrew cast Roger Moore, best known as the longest-lived of Sean Connery's successors in the James Bond movies. As the publicity machine swung into action, the papers were filled with stories headlined, "Why I'm Singing for My Supper—by 007" and "Licensed to sing!" along with photo opportunities for Moore and Diana Morrison, who had been cast as Jenny. "I've never done a musical in my life," Moore told the press. "It's a tremendous challenge—and it could be an even bigger one for the audience."* There were reports that Moore would take a bubble bath on stage. Lloyd Webber defended the star casting by noting that George Dillingham had to be suave and plausibly irresistible to women—the late David Niven was the type he had in mind—and Moore filled that bill handsomely. "Andrew has promised that *Aspects* will either make me a great stage star," Moore told *The Times,* "or finish my career once and for all."

The truth turned out to be closer to the latter. The problem was that Moore couldn't sing, and in a show that was entirely through-composed this handicap proved to be an insurmountable problem. On March 13, 1989, a month before the opening, RUG released a statement that quoted Moore: "After many hours of rehearsal and much soul searching, I have decided to withdraw from the cast of *Aspects.*" "Roger and Out," cracked *The Star.* Lloyd Webber knew this possibility lurked when he cast Moore, and he had understudy Kevin Colson (who had created the role of Walter de Courcey in *Chess*) standing by to take over; after a decent interval, Colson's hiring was announced.

Although its performers would not have to dance or roller-skate or impersonate various biblical personages, *Aspects* was still difficult to cast. Even more than *Phantom, Aspects* was operatic in both the real and popular senses of the word, and it needed genuine singers. Andrew's audition notes, taken in a small, crabbed hand, were short, pithy, and to the point. "Hasn't got that chesty French quality," he wrote of one girl in early October; "Too British," he wrote of another, "but also notes not there." British actress Gemma Craven he dismissed with the comment, "[Voice] v. tiny—never be able to sing Giulietta." Referring to Mackintosh's rival show, Lloyd Webber wrote of one boy: "Send him to *Saigon*"; of another, "Too tall & odd looking." In the margins of the casting sheets, he scribbled a wish list: Moore's name appeared frequently, while for the parts of Rose and Giulietta, he coveted Natasha Richardson, Julie Covington, and Linda Ronstadt.

In the end, much of the cast came from the Sydmonton performance, including Ball (the finest British tenor since Stuart Burrows) and the two girls, Hart and Morrison; another Sydmonton holdover was Paul Bentley, cast as Marcel, the actor-manager. The conductor was Mike Reed. To fulfill his part of the Equity quid pro quo, Lloyd Webber chose not one but two "unknown" Americans for the parts of Rose and Giulietta. As the French actress he cast Ann Crumb; she had been bumping around in minor roles (the Factory Girl in the Broadway *Les Misérables,* for example) and as an understudy (*Chess* in New York). The part of Giulietta went to Kathleen Rowe McAllen, a soap-opera actress who had played Cinderella in the Los Angeles production of Sondheim's *Into the Woods* and had sung Fantine in *Les Misérables* in the West End.

Moore's resignation was all the scent the hounds of Fleet Street needed to sniff trouble, or at least a story. Stories began to appear that

---

*Although Really Useful Group claimed in a press release that his appearance as George would be Moore's West End debut, an enterprising historian unearthed evidence of Moore's minor role at the Aldwych Theatre in a 1954 play called *I Capture the Castle* by Dodie Smith.

Aspects of Love was in dire straits, that it was shaping up as a disaster. When the premiere was postponed five days, from April 12 to April 17, the tabs went wild. "New show shock as Lloyd Webber calls off his opening night," wrote *The Daily Mail,* misleadingly; "Aspects of failure," said *The Star*; "Aspects of Chaos," cracked *Today.* There were reports that the preview audiences were responding tepidly, that Lloyd Webber was frantically composing a new song, that the stagehands were balking at the complicated scene changes Nunn's staging and Maria Björnson's sets entailed. A couple of newspapers even broke the opening-night embargo and reviewed the show in advance—"in the spirit of genuine inquiry." The news was bad.

One look at Lloyd Webber, however, spoke otherwise. Usually he was a wreck before opening night, but even with the Moore departure he seemed remarkably sunny to his colleagues. He was cross about the breach of journalistic etiquette, though, and a few discreet phone calls to editors quickly resulted in a retraction. Reversing the verdict of its own "Bizarre" column, *The Sun* ate crow:

What a Love-Ly Show!

> *BIZARRE exclusively reviewed* Aspects of Love *last week and said it was more of a slushy slow-burner than a sizzling blockbuster.*
> The Sun'*s Editor saw a preview this week and disagreed. Here is his verdict:*
> Only one word does justice to *Aspects of Love*: BRILLIANT.
> Lloyd Webber proves he hasn't lost his golden touch with this sparkling romantic musical.

And so on, ever more fulsomely.

Naturally, Lloyd Webber's mien darkened as the opening approached, and on the weekend before the show bowed, he was muttering darkly of his absolute certainty that there was a plot among the stagehands to sabotage the premiere. Contrary to reports, he was not writing a new song—although he, Nunn, Black, and Hart were tinkering with the ending, trying to get it right—but in general his mood was good. It could afford to be. With a five-million-pound advance, *Aspects* had recouped even before it opened and was effectively sold out for a year. Before the first official review had been written, *Aspects of Love* was a hit.

Aspects of Love is at once Lloyd Webber's best work and his most problematic. The score is radiant, even more adept than *Phantom* and without reliance on pastiche. From first note to last—with the exception of the dramatically irrelevant circus scene—it displays Lloyd Webber's familiar melodic gifts, this time wedded to a solid technical foundation to produce moments of penetrating psychological insight and great emotional power. Unlike any of his other works, even *Phantom,* there are few distinct "numbers"; instead, the score flows from one scene to the next, hardly stopping for breath (or applause). The penultimate scene, in which Rose begs Alex not to leave her, is the composer's finest dramatic creation, surpassing even the ending of *Phantom.*

Yet as staged by Nunn in London, the show had great problems as well. Nunn had wanted to skip a theater incarnation altogether and go directly to film, and his busy staging—the twirling pillars of the Broadway *Chess* were back, spinning, spinning—was almost cinematic in its quick-cutting images. But *Aspects* didn't need quick-cutting; it was never better than on the bare stage at Sydmonton, where the human drama was not overwhelmed by busyness. Then, too, as right as Björnson's dark vision had been for *Phantom,* so it was wrong for *Aspects.* Most of the action takes place at George's villa in Pau, a lovely town on the edge of the Pyrenees, yet Björnson's setting was an extended brown study. The villa looked like a jail; the predominant colors were brown, russet, and gray; the vines were burnt-out and the mountains looked cold and forbidding. There is a good deal that is autumnal about *Aspects of Love,* but the story is primarily about love and not death.

The opera opens with Alex, who sings "Love Changes Everything." The simple but affecting tune is based on three chords, A major, D major, and E major and, later (in the key of B-flat), B-flat major, E-flat major and F major. "I always wanted to write a three-chord song," Lloyd Webber told Steyn a few weeks before the show opened. An admirer of the rock band Creedence Clearwater Revival, Andrew once found himself on a plane with the band's leader, John Fogerty. "You're the greatest three-chord band in the world," he gushed, to which Fogerty replied: "Andrew, we're a *two-chord* band":

> *Love,*
> *love changes everything:*
> *hands and faces,*
> *earth and sky.*

Love,
love changes everything:
how you live and
how you die.

Love
can make the summer fly
or a night
seem like a lifetime.

Yes, love,
love changes everything.
Now I tremble
at your name.
Nothing in the world
will ever
be the same.*

The scene flashes back to Montpellier in 1947, where Rose Vibert is performing *The Master Builder* on its last night before a sparse provincial audience. Starstruck, the seventeen-year-old Alex has been in the theater each night, and, ushered backstage by Marcel, he arrives to meet the object of his affections. Rose and Alex repair to a café, where the show's only pastiche, a little chanson called "Parlez-vous Français?" is playing on the radio. Impulsively, Alex asks Rose to travel with him to Pau, where, he says, he has a villa; just as impulsively — she has two weeks before her next engagement and nothing better to do — Rose accepts.

On the train, they sing the luminous duet, "Seeing is Believing," whose pliant melody is one of *Aspects'* fundamental thematic building blocks:

Seeing is believing
and in my arms I see her:
she's here,
really here,
really mine now —
she seems at home here . . .

Seeing is believing,
I dreamt that it would be her:
at last
life is full now,
life is fine now . . .

Whatever happens,
one thing is certain:
each time I see
a train go by,
I'll think of us,
You and I, the night, the sky,
forever.

Upon arrival in Pau, the truth comes out when Alex has to break into the villa. All right, he tells Rose, it really belongs to my uncle, George, who is in Paris. A quick cut to Paris reveals George, an art forger (in the novel he is Sir George, a poet) with his mistress, the sculptress

---

* In the Sydmonton version, the song began in G major and modulated up a half step to A-flat. When Andrew discovered Ball's ringing top note, he transposed the song up a whole step.

Giulietta. "Damn the boy!" exclaims George, who has been informed of the goings-on by a telegram from his gardener. In a parlando sequence, he decides to head south immediately, and the agreeable Giulietta lets him go with a wave: "Don't look so sad, George! What times we've had, George!" His exit line is his motto: "Life goes on, love goes free."

Back in Pau, Rose rhapsodizes about the beauty of the mountains ("this is what I ought to feel on stage"), and the orchestra intones the "Chanson d'enfance" motive derived from Lloyd Webber's childhood melody, a stepwise descending scale whose first four notes are the same as "Seeing is Believing." Another important motive is also heard at this point, a chordal sequence in 6/8 that is perhaps this poignant score's most poignant moment. When it is heard in full form a few moments later, its progression is G minor, B-flat major, D minor, E-flat minor, B-flat major, E-flat major, B-flat major, which underpins the ineffably wistful melody—constructed, as so many of the best Lloyd Webber tunes are, from the interval of a sixth.

George arrives and, sure enough, love does change everything. When Rose dons the dress of George's deceased wife, Delia, he is thunderstruck and falls in love with her on the spot. She desires him, too, and the idyll is ended: Rose, pleading an urgent message from Marcel, tells Alex she must go to Lyon, but in reality heads back to Paris and George. Alex is devastated by her departure.

Two years pass. Alex is in the army, and in a scene at a fairground ("Everybody Loves a Hero"), he wins a stuffed donkey for his marksmanship. Arriving at George's Paris flat, he is astounded when Rose emerges to greet him; he had thought Giulietta was George's mistress. "I should have known where you were hiding!" he sings. "You like the good life, George likes trinkets! God, what a fool I was to love you! What was all that searching for? It's never hard to find a whore!" Rose replies (to the music of George's motto): "Well, if it makes you happy, think it. The truth is we're a perfect pair. Shout and scream, I don't care." George, she says, has made her a "better, fuller, stronger person." Even so, she can't resist Alex and leads him by the hand into the bedroom.

The next morning, Rose, feeling guilty, asks Alex to leave. The young lover is furious, and he pulls his service revolver. There is a tussle and the gun goes off, wounding Rose. At this moment, George comes in and his first impulse is to worry about his art collection ("My only genuine Matisse! Thank God, no damage done"). The two men sing a duet, "She'd Be Far Better off with You," which, under the circumstances, seems inappropriately comic. The whole scene, in fact, rings false, mirroring the character of George, the bogus artist. Rose, bleeding in the corner, sends Alex packing.

The scene changes to Venice, where George is regaling Giulietta with a phony tale of how he heroically disarmed his nephew, while Giulietta attempts to sculpt a bust of him ("Stop. Wait. Please."); the music of this episode was recycled from *Aspects'* 1983 cabaret version— the tune that underlines George's words, "Darling, it's over, so don't be so cynical," for example, is the "Executive Stress" theme song. Unexpectedly, the wounded Rose arrives, preceded by Marcel and a host of creditors. Like Mimi or Violetta, she collapses melodramatically on a divan and passes out.

Again, the scene borders on the risible. Rose's actions, and Marcel's hand-wringing account of them, are never explained. Did George simply abandon her in the Paris flat? His attitude and his actions positively scream that he is a phony, yet Lloyd Webber, Hart, and Black clearly meant him to be sympathetic and implicitly endorse his hedonistic, carpe diem philosophy.

Two weeks pass, during which Rose recuperates at Giulietta's. The two women have gotten to know and like each other—Nunn's staging at this point implied a lesbian relationship. But Rose is really in love with George. (Or is she? By this time, having seen her involved with Alex, Giulietta, and George, the audience has no clue as to her real feelings.) In a 6/8 tune that will return in the second act, she proposes to George: "Take a deep breath and prepare yourself. My mind is in such a mess, but really, George, all that I wanted to ask was this: would you be willing to marry me?" George replies: "I've already told you, yes." And he was going to leave her just five minutes before! At the wedding, Rose and Giulietta exchange a passionate kiss, and George, the old roué, exclaims, "Bravo!" In a military encampment in Malaya, Alex gets the news, to the tune of "Love Changes Everything."

Act Two begins thirteen years later. Rose is now a famous stage and screen star, and she and George have had a daughter, Jenny. (Rose also has a lover, Hugo, to George's evident approval.) There is a brief exchange between father and daughter, to the tune of "The Final Stand" from *Cricket,* and then, in one of the score's best songs, the F-major ballad "Other Pleasures," George marvels at the miracle that is his daughter:

> *Other pleasures*
> *and I've known many,*
> *afternoons in warm Venetian squares,*
> *brief encounters*
> *long siestas*

pleasures old and new
can't compare with you

In Paris, meanwhile, Rose is triumphing as Natalia Petrovna in Turgenev's *A Month in the Country*; George's forgeries have been found out, and she is now the family's breadwinner. Backstage is none other than Alex, resplendent in uniform and sporting a mustache. This time, it is she who invites him down to Pau ("Hugo, your trip is canceled"), and he accepts. He attempts to embrace her, but she rebuffs him: "Oh, come on, Alex, those days are over. We had our moment and it passed us by."

In Pau, Alex is introduced to Jenny, and the young girl quickly develops a crush on her cousin. Giulietta was supposed to have spent the weekend, but she writes from Venice to say she can't make it; "Looks like I'll never meet your friend," remarks Alex. George, now nearly eighty, announces that it's time for his nap, to a melodic line that will return prominently in "Anything but Lonely," and heads off to bed. Left alone with Alex, Jenny sings the "Mermaid Song," whose 6/8, B-flat minor melody is identical to the music Rose sang when she asked George to marry her.* In it, she asks Alex, "If you were a sailor and heard my song, would you be lured by me?" Alex's reply: "I wouldn't be foolish enough to go near your rock."

Released from the service, Alex spends more and more time in Pau. Two years pass, and Jenny is now on the cusp of womanhood. To George's evident displeasure, she and Alex are obviously attracted to one another. Rose, too, is annoyed; when Alex tells her that Jenny needs a Paris education, the suddenly-bourgeois Rose assumes it is a plot to break up their happy home life. (What happy home life?) They argue. Out on the terrace, George reflects on his present estate. "What could be sweeter," he wonders. "Nothing is sweeter." Thinking ahead on his approaching death, he reprises "Other pleasures." It is one of the few times in the show that one can sympathize with, or feel any affection for, the old faker.

Jenny appears, wearing Delia's dress. Rose and Alex are fearful of its effect on George, but the old man is delighted. He sings "The Very First," a gentle foxtrot in E-flat:

I want to be
the first man you remember.
I want to be
the last man you forget.
I want to be
the one you always turn to,
I want to be
the one you won't forget.

By now, it is clear to everyone that Jenny is in love with Alex. On a trip into the mountains, she tells her cousin that she loves him, to the strains of "Love Changes Everything." Yes, Alex tells her, "Love changes everything, but not always for the best. Love can sometimes be a most unwelcome guest."

Later, we see George making out his will: beluga caviar, the best champagne, his ashes to be spread among the vines, his funeral oration to be written and delivered by Giulietta. He discusses the Jenny-Alex relationship with Rose, and waxes wroth. George's anger comes to a head at a Paris circus, where the family is celebrating Jenny's birthday. The music ("The Journey of a Lifetime") is an expanded version of the fairground melody, made worse by expansion and repetition; in Nunn's staging, the scene degenerated into a shabby spectacle replete with a knife thrower, chubby circus girls, and a chanteuse. There is a row between George and Alex, and the latter stomps off in a huff, much to Jenny's distress.

At this point, Lloyd Webber interpolated a quartet ("Falling") for Rose, Alex, Jenny, and George that was not in the Sydmonton version. A brief, bleak meditation on their tangled lives—four separate soliloquies, in fact—the highly chromatic ensemble contains some of the composer's most striking and adventurous writing. The action moves to Jenny's bedroom, where Alex is tucking his cousin into bed. The mood turns sexual, and, fully clothed, he climbs in to hold her. Outside the door, George is listening. "I should have stopped this long ago," he sings. "Selfish little cradle snatcher, twisted little heartless monster, filthy little callous bastard." Suddenly, George collapses. It is a heart attack, and he dies on the spot.

---

*This song is distinctly reminiscent, in feel, of the "Castle on a Cloud" number in *Les Misérables*. Although Lloyd Webber did not like that show, its notion of a fanciful ballad for a young girl obviously found favor.

At the funeral, Giulietta leads the mourners in a fierce, Prokofievian bacchanal ("Hand Me the Wine and the Dice") that celebrates George's love of life:

> Hand me the wine and the dice
> I want my carnival now
> While I have thirst and lust for living!
> You gather all you can reap
> Before you're under the plough
> The hand of death is unforgiving!

The song is in 4/4, but the tempo switches to 7/8 as Alex and Giulietta finally meet during the wild dance. "Tell me, are you still shooting women?" she asks him. "Do you dance with women of your *own* age?" Bewitched, they run off together to a nearby barn to consummate their animal passion. "You have put the fun in funeral!" sings Alex in the show's most inelegant line. "Never thought a wake could be so thrilling!" Unseen by either of them, Jenny follows and watches them couple.

Now in love with Giulietta, however implausibly, Alex determines to break the news to Jenny and, by extension, to Rose. "What we feel is wrong, unnatural," Alex says to Jenny. "Our bodies must not rule our minds"—strange sentiments indeed from this crew. Undissuaded, Jenny proposes to Alex, but before he can answer, Rose appears and sings her big aria, "Anything but Lonely." The song, whose melody is borrowed from *Cricket*'s "All I Ask of Life," is a stand-and-deliver torch song in B-flat major that rings out with passion and pathos:

> Anything but lonely,
> Anything but empty rooms.
> There's so much in life to share
> What's the sense when no one else is there?
>
> Anything but lonely,
> Anything but only me.
> Quiet years in too much space,
> That's the thing that's hard to face and
>
> You have a right to go
> But you should also know
> That I won't be alone for long.
> Long days with nothing said
> Are not what lie ahead
> I'm sorry but I'm not that strong.

With a wrench, the song ratchets up a notch to B major, as Rose's cry becomes even more intense. Echoing the circumstances of her proposal to George, Rose asks Alex to promise her one thing, but to say yes in advance. "Alright, what is it?" he says. "Don't ask me questions, you must promise me first." Alex says he can't without knowing what it is. *"Don't leave me!"* she sings, and the "Seeing Is Believing" motive that first characterized their love rings out in the orchestra. It is a moment worthy of Puccini.

The final scene, which gave Lloyd Webber and his lyricists such trouble, is unsatisfactory in any form. "We are a fortunate pair," says Giulietta. "Thank God we met when we did. We are each other's only solution. You see when George was alive I couldn't love other men, but now that he's gone I'm free to love you." In Lloyd Webber's original conception of the ending, *Aspects of Love* then closed with Giulietta singing, "Hand me the wine and the dice; perish the thought of tomorrow," ending on a stark C-major chord.

Ever the showman, Andrew threw out this dramatically inapposite but musically correct finale and replaced it with another reprise of "Love Changes Everything," offering Ball the opportunity to display his high B-flat and send the audience home humming. (Contrary to Lloyd Webber's professed intention of beginning the show with this number unadorned, he nevertheless wrote a conventional overture to precede it.) If it seemed a shameless song-plugging, it was, and it was no solution. A better course would have been to discard the final Alex–Giulietta scene altogether and conclude *Aspects* after its most powerful moment, Rose's impassioned and desperate plea. There is no need, and no motivation, for Alex to take up with Giulietta; he hardly knows her, and no one in the audience believes for a moment that theirs is the love affair toward which the whole show has been building.

Aspects of Love, in fact, is nearly brought down by its book—both the novel and the libretto as it finally evolved, and it is only the transforming power of Lloyd Webber's music that makes the listener suspend disbelief as long as he or she does. The unfortunate decision to make George a forger sends a signal to the listener that the man is a fake and, by extension, that his emotions are false, too. The excessive reliance on Garnett's plot also results in wild mood swings. In the first half hour alone, Alex meets Rose and invites her to Pau, turns petulant when she is a little late arriving at the railway station, and sings of his love for her on the train; Rose, meanwhile, becomes cross when they have to break into the house and then turns affectionate again once inside. By this time the audience is thoroughly confused as to which aspects of love these characters are feeling for each other.

Lloyd Webber's position all along was that was the way Garnett had written it; the Hart-Black adaptation, in fact, was faithful to even small details, such as the (unexplained and never referred to again) apparition of a woman's slipper outside the villa on the first night Alex and Rose spend there. A stronger librettist would have chopped, discarded, and rewritten as necessary, for in the musical theater there are no extra points given for textual fidelity. Boito's libretto for Verdi's *Otello,* for example, hacked away much of Shakespeare's play and, in so doing, improved on it; closer to the West End, Lerner altered Shaw's *Pygmalion* to create the masterpiece of *My Fair Lady.* For all the brilliance of Lloyd Webber's score, the London *Aspects* was crippled by its reliance on the novel that was its source.

After all the talk that Lloyd Webber might this time fall on his face, the press response was generally enthusiastic. In a front-page article in *The Daily Telegraph* on April 18, the paper's arts correspondent led: "Andrew Lloyd Webber confounded the skeptics and West End rumour-mongers last night when *Aspects of Love,* his new £2 million musical, was given a rapturous first-night reception at London's Prince of Wales Theatre." The applause, said Nigel Reynolds, proved that Andrew "had not lost his golden touch despite less than enthusiastic advance notices and a run of misfortunes."

In *The Financial Times,* Michael Coveney agreed:

> *Aspects of Love* is a remarkably daring piece of work that captures with some wit and fidelity the sybaritic insouciance of David Garnett's 1955 novella and, in Trevor Nunn's very fine production, is a rare example of theatrical intimacy succeeding the large-scale circumstances. . . . You will want to see this show not because of its showbiz hype, but because there are new creative forces at work here which may yet define the lyric theatre of the future.

In *The Independent,* Mark Steyn rejected this viewpoint. Not for Steyn were the techniques of operatic construction; he wanted an old-fashioned "number" show and he misunderstood Lloyd Webber's intention. While Steyn expressed sympathy for Black and Hart ("a marvelous job in unenviable circumstances"), he found the composer's score both parsimonious and repetitive. In a review headlined "An Evening of Encores," Steyn wrote:

> *Aspects of Love* resembles one of those snow-scene knick-knacks with a built-in music box: every few minutes, it's shaken furiously and the scenery rearranges itself, but, after the dust settles, the same tune re-emerges . . . with each lyrical variation, the melody is further diluted: would the young Lloyd Webber have been as impressed by "Some Enchanted Evening" if it had popped up 10 minutes later as "Would You Like a Biscuit?"

> As for the merits of through-sung chamber opera, I'm still open to persuasion, but on the evidence of this score Lloyd Webber's power as a producer is not yet matched by his inventiveness as a composer. Those few people who have any influence over him should urge him to rethink drastically Act One, if not for London, then for Broadway. At the moment, 15 minutes in, you've heard all Act One's best shots and, as that realisation dawns, many theatregoers could feel short-changed. Andrew Lloyd Webber may be critic-proof, but is he audience-proof?

Echoing its front page, the headline in *The Daily Telegraph* was "Lloyd Webber's best so far," but critic Charles Osborne's rapture was considerably modified. The score, he wrote, was Lloyd Webber's "least eclectic to date, for it is reminiscent only of Claude-Michel Schoenberg, composer of 'Les Misérables.'" That hurt. So did Osborne's comments about the two American actresses. "Both these leading female roles suffer a certain loss of verisimilitude by being played, as it were, mid-Atlantic," he wrote, reflecting a typically British bit of solipsistic snobbery. After all, no one had complained when *Les Misérables* was turned into The Glums by transforming the French-in-name-only characters into cockneys and English aristocrats.

In *The Times,* Irving Wardle's bland and curiously nonjudgmental review congratulated the creative team for transforming Garnett's novel "into a well-crafted show which is technically streets ahead of the book while faithfully preserving its essence," while, at the other end of the respectability spectrum, *The Sun*'s Maureen Paton took note of the risqué subject matter, but assured readers that there was "nothing that would frighten the horses, unless you count the sight of the passionate Mr. Ball in his boxer shorts."

Searchlights stabbed the night sky as the guests congregated at the Waldorf Hotel for the cast party. The photographers snapped furiously when Lloyd Webber, with Sarah Brightman on his arm, sat down at the head table and joined Sarah Jane Tudor Hugill Lloyd Webber Norris, and their two children, Nicholas and Imogen (Jeremy Norris was there, too, but opted out of the one-big-happy-family photo session), and the next day pictures of Andrew and his extended family were in nearly every tabloid. *The Sun* ran a piece called "How Love Changes Everything For Me, by Andrew Lloyd Webber," which was really by one Ingrid Millar:

> I come from a small, but very close family. And no matter what happens in life to hurt you, if there is love around, you survive.
>
> I've had some tremendous knocks. People have said some cruel things about me. That I'm unattractive, impossible to work with, that I write pap. But I never get bitter or angry about it. After all, we're only here for a few years, so why waste time looking on the black side?

Why indeed? The objective viewer, looking at Lloyd Webber's life from the outside, could see nothing black about it. He was rich and famous. He had his own company to look after his business affairs. He had the admiration, if not the love, of his colleagues in the theater. His commanding position allowed him to do almost anything he wished, and with his wealth he could afford to do almost anything. There was nothing standing in the way of the realization of his vision, nothing at all: no director he couldn't hire or fire, no producer he couldn't dominate, no cast he couldn't handpick; just put his name on the poster and watch the paying customers line up. His mother and father, Westminster, Oxford, David Land, Robert Stigwood, Tim Rice, Stephen Sondheim, Frank Rich, even Cameron Mackintosh—he had outlasted, or would outlast, them all.

The only thing he couldn't do was fail.

Finale: GOOD NIGHT AND THANK YOU

This book ends in the spring of 1989, just after the opening of *Aspects of Love* in London, when Andrew Lloyd Webber was forty-one years old—the same age, practically to the day, that Stephen Sondheim was when *Follies* premiered in 1971. Like Sondheim, who was hammered by some prominent critics for early works such as *Anyone Can Whistle, Company,* and *Follies,* Lloyd Webber has survived his beatings and prospered, handsomely. Obviously, though, Andrew's story is not over; he and his works likely will remain the subject of fierce debate for years to come. "It is a symptom of the way our theatre has been debauched by the values of Broadway that a new Lloyd Webber show is preceded by weeks of ballyhoo and that, on the first night, one can hardly get in or out of the theatre without being waylaid by broadcasters all wanting a 'sound-bite' and a snap verdict," wrote Michael Billington of *Aspects of Love.* "It is, in the end, only a musical. . . . What I question is its elevation by the press and television (not Mr. Lloyd Webber's fault) into an event of breathtaking cultural magnitude."

That his works are treated in precisely that way is a tribute to the effect Lloyd Webber has had on the musical theater. Billington's parenthetical remark is a nice, diplomatic equivocation, for even while decrying the "values of Broadway" that Lloyd Webber has done so much to inject into the British theatrical scene, the writer specifically exculpates the composer. Yet one cannot have it both ways if an extreme position is to be adopted: Lloyd Webber is either the savior of the British musical theater or its ruination, the man who restored its glamour or dragged it down to the muddied, trivial American level at which everything—sports, entertainment, even politics—is transformed into showbiz: "infotainment," in current parlance.

In Britain, of course, there is the added element of national pride to complicate Lloyd Webber's reputation—"He's all British!" as the tabloids keep proclaiming—along with England's civilized recognition of the favorable balance of trade that attends successful endeavor in the arts and entertainment. The British monarchy has long bestowed the favor of knighthood upon industrialists, business tycoons, and artists, especially those who bring hard currency into the United Kingdom, and no one doubts but that, on a coming Honours List, the plumber's grandson will be dubbed Sir Andrew Lloyd Webber. The American dream is not only to be lived in America.

It is always risky to forecast what Lloyd Webber will do in the future, no matter what he says will be his next project: *The Phantom of the Opera* was, after all, practically an afterthought to the first version of *Aspects.* Lloyd Webber has bruited subjects as disparate as Waugh's black comedy, *The Loved One,* the Norwegian film *Little Ida* (about a young girl whose mother is accused of collaborating with the Nazis), and American television game shows. The last is a particular fascination: at Sydmonton and in his office at the Palace Theatre, Lloyd Webber keeps several sets of a computerized push-button game-show game on display, whose central figure is a caricature of a braying, asinine American TV host. Still, the best bet is that it will be none of the above. The Rum Tum Tugger will do as he do do.

What is certain is that the film version of *Evita* is finally underway, in Argentina (where in 1976 importers of the original double album were arrested), with Oliver Stone directing Meryl Streep in the title role. No doubt the tiresome debate over whether Rice and Lloyd Webber have "glamorized" Evita will begin all over again, especially in the American media, which never tires of debating the morality of events that occurred thirty, forty, and fifty years ago while ignoring the implications of what is going on today. The rights to the show belong to Robert Stigwood, not to Lloyd Webber, although Andrew and Tim Rice have had veto power over Streep's casting. Lloyd Webber approved Streep after hearing her audition tape, which included creditable versions of "Don't Cry for Me, Argentina" and "Buenos Aires," but it was clear she will never be a singer in Elaine Paige's league.

A ten-year battle has been waged over who would direct the film and who would play Evita: would-be directors have included Ken Russell, Herbert Ross, Michael Cimino, Sir Richard Attenborough, Alan J. Pakula, Hector Babenco, and Francis Ford Coppola, while prospective Evitas have counted among their number Barbra Streisand (who in 1979 wanted three million dollars to grace the movie with her presence), Liza Minnelli (Russell's choice but no one else's), British rock singer Kim Wilde, Paige (Rice's favorite), Patti LuPone (who refused a screen test), Bette Midler (!), Derin Altay (a fine road-company star, but no name), and Madonna (a prima donna who self-destructed). There is also supposed to be a film version of *Phantom,* directed by Steven Spielberg and starring Sarah Brightman as Christine—and, according to which rumor one chooses to believe, Marlon Brando, Sammy Davis, Jr., or Michael Jackson as the Phantom, among other unlikely choices. *Cats,* too, has been mentioned as a candidate for celluloid.

The composer has said that his next work may not be a musical at all, but a book about Victorian architecture, and by watching him dive into his well-stocked Sydmonton library on the subject or thumb through an old guide book heavily annotated in his own hand, the visitor can credit both his enthusiasm and his determination. One need only look at the Palace Theatre, whose terra-cotta exterior has been handsomely restored by the architect John Muir at a cost of one million six hundred thousand pounds—three hundred sixty-eight thousand pounds of it provided by the London division of English Heritage, which engendered widespread criticism, as did Muir's use of a cheaper terra-cotta substitute called "cold cast terra cotta"—to see Lloyd Webber's passion realized in bricks and mortar. The next step is to refurbish the Palace's frayed and cramped interior, but work cannot begin until—a long "until"—*Les Misérables* finally closes.

Another important activity for Lloyd Webber will be attending to the Really Useful Group in his encore capacity as an executive director. In February 1989 the company reported a decline in pretax profit of one hundred thousand pounds, to two million eight hundred thousand pounds for the six months' period ending in December 1988; the company blamed the results on falling income from *Cats* and delays in getting *Phantom* productions put on around the world, as well as on poor fiscal performances by subsidiary businesses. Few investors felt, however, that RUG shares had become a risk, and the price rose on the same day by five pence to six pounds twelve pence.

Indeed, Lloyd Webber's nose for business, and his appetite for control, has never been keener. On April 21, 1989, he (through the Really Useful Group) bought back the remaining rights to *Joseph and the Amazing Technicolor Dreamcoat* from Novello, for a sum of one million pounds. This purchase of the famous 20 percent of the grand rights that Desmond Elliott had let slip by—made without Rice's advice or consent, much to the lyricist's fury—effectively gave Lloyd Webber control of the property, since he thus owned 60 percent of *Joseph,* to Tim's 40 percent. Under threat of legal action from Tim, however, Lloyd Webber sold back 10 percent to Rice, and they are equal partners once more—for *Joseph,* at least. (In April 1988 Novello itself had been sold by Granada Group for four million seven hundred thousand pounds to Filmtrax, a rival music and magazine publisher.) Filially, Lloyd Webber also bought from Novello the rights to his father's church music.

At home in South Kensington, Jean Lloyd Webber has survived a bout with cancer and was at her son's side at the opening of *Aspects of Love,* still wearing her cloth coat; earlier that same day, she had bicycled over to the London College of Music, where she works as an outside examiner. Success may have changed him, but not her. Since Bill's death, Andrew and his mother have drawn closer, and she has accompanied him on several foreign trips, including one to East Germany. In April the divorce of Julian and Celia Lloyd Webber came before the courts—the couple had been living apart for two years, their marriage a victim of Julian's peripatetic concert-artist existence—and Julian was escorting Zohra Ghazi, a twenty-five-year-old exiled Afghan princess. An impending marriage was widely speculated.

As for Rice, he put Romeyns Court on the market for more than a million pounds when it was announced that a new town of six thousand homes, to be called Stone Bassett, was to be built a mile away. More than one bid has fallen through, however, and Rice's plans to buy a house in Hambleden, near Henley-on-Thames, for Jane have evaporated. At last report, there was a new bid on Romeyns Court, but what will happen to the Rices' marriage if and when the splendid country house is sold remains to be seen. Meanwhile, Tim's relationship with Paige continues apace: on July 4 she opened at the Prince Edward Theatre as Reno Sweeney in Cole Porter's *Anything Goes,* an importation of the popular Lincoln Center Theater production at the Vivian Beaumont in Manhattan. To capitalize the show at one and a half million pounds, Rice formed Anything Goes Productions Limited, whose majority shareholders were the producers, Robert Fox Limited and Anchorage Productions Limited, jointly owned by Tim and Elaine. For Paige, who signed a two-hundred-and-fifty-thousand-pound contract for her year in the show, it was her third consecutive starring role at the Prince Edward: *Evita, Chess,* and *Anything Goes.* The film stardom that she seeks, however, still eludes her. Meanwhile, Julie Covington, who turned down *Evita* in 1978, took the part in a stage production in Australia—where, as it happened, Jim Sharman was restaging Rice's *Chess* as well.

In the pages of *The Independent,* Mark Steyn visited New York, stopped in to see Richard Greenberg's play *Eastern Standard,* an AIDS-era drama, and found it wanting: "After the show, I found myself, like several other theatre-goers, lingering on the sidewalk, reading in disbelief the reprint of Frank Rich's rave in *The New York Times,* the only reason this show is on Broadway at all. Apparently, he first saw it out of town, liked it, but made a few suggestions. The producers obligingly bunged them all in, effectively hoisting Rich by his own petard. A lesson for every critic there."

Meanwhile, the Mark Hellinger Theatre, where Tom O'Horgan assaulted *Jesus Christ Superstar* in 1971, was leased in February to the nondenominational, fundamentalist Times Square Church for five years at an annual rent of one million dollars. The deal followed in the aftermath of *Legs*. "There's no shows being produced," explained James M. Nederlander, chairman of the Nederlander Organization, which owns the theater. "We have to keep the theaters filled." His apologia was immediately rejected by James B. Freydberg, an independent producer, who said: "It's not really looking into the future. If 'Cats' is to continue to play and 'Les Misérables' and 'The Phantom of the Opera,' and with 'Aspects of Love' and 'Miss Saigon' coming, there are going to be fewer large musical theaters available. And if one of the larger and better houses is going to be locked away for five years, it shows very little insight into the future of the theater." To which Nederlander retorted, "In show business, you have to take the first booking." After all the talk about what was killing Broadway, the answer was simple: suicide.

That was one crime no one could lay at Lloyd Webber's door. With *Aspects* open, he muttered about taking a holiday, but instead turned almost immediately to recording the original-cast album and revising the score for London. He wasn't going to wait for New York: in went a new, warmer Act Two aria for Giulietta and out went the show's problematic final scene, to be replaced by a brief denouement after the emotional climax of "Anything But Lonely"; additionally, Rose's character in the second act was softened and there were smaller changes elsewhere. Maybe Garnett wasn't sacred after all. Lloyd Webber was fond of quoting what was supposed to have been the show's final line, were art, not commerce, in theatrical ascendancy: *Pone merum et talos. Pereat qui crastina curat* — "Set down the wine and the dice and perish the thought of tomorrow." But nobody really believed he would, or could.

INDEX

PHOTOGRAPH CREDITS

TEXT CREDITS

During the course of Andrew Lloyd Webber's musicals, the lyrics are often changed, sometimes considerably, as a show is revised, reworked, and exported. The excerpts quoted in this book may therefore vary from production to production — Michael Walsh.